THE VOLUNTEER

THE VOLUNTEER

One Man, an Underground
Army, and the Secret Mission
to Destroy Auschwitz

JACK FAIRWEATHER

WH
ALLEN

1 3 5 7 9 10 8 6 4 2

WH Allen, an imprint of Ebury Publishing,
20 Vauxhall Bridge Road,
London SW1V 2SA

WH Allen is part of the Penguin Random House group of companies whose ad-
dresses can be found at global.penguinrandomhouse.com

Penguin
Random House
UK

First published in the United States by Custom House in 2019
First published in the United Kingdom by WH Allen in 2019

www.penguin.co.uk

A CIP catalogue record for this book is available from the British Library

Hardback ISBN 9780753545164
Trade Paperback ISBN 9780753545171

Printed and bound in Great Britain by Clays Ltd, Elcograf S.p.A.

Penguin Random House is committed to a sustainable future for our business,
our readers and our planet. This book is made from Forest Stewardship
Council® certified paper.

To Philip and Lynn Asquith for their support,
and to my grandparents Stella and Frank Ford

Whoever loves much, does much. Whoever does a thing well does much. And he does well who serves the common community before his own interests.

—Thomas à Kempis

CONTENTS

PART III 223

PART IV 295

INTRODUCTION

Witold Pilecki volunteered to be imprisoned in Auschwitz. This barest out-line of a story sent me on a five-year quest to retrace his footsteps from gentleman farmer to cavalry officer facing the Blitzkrieg to under-ground operative in Warsaw and then human chattel in a camp-bound cattle car. I've come to know Witold well. Yet I find myself returning to that simple sentence and the moment he sat waiting for the Ger-mans to burst into his apartment as I reflect on what his story promises to tell us of our own time.

I first heard about Witold's story from my friend Matt McAllester at a dinner in Long Island in the fall of 2011. Matt and I had reported together on the wars in the Middle East, and were struggling to make sense of what we'd witnessed. In typically bravura fashion Matt had traveled to Auschwitz to confront history's greatest evil and learned of Witold's band of resistance fighters inside the camp. The idea of a few souls standing up to the Nazis comforted us both that night. But I was equally struck by how little was known about Witold's mission to warn the West of the Nazis' crimes and create an underground army to destroy the camp.

Some of the pictures were filled in a year later when Witold's lon-gest report about the camp was translated into English. The story of the report's emergence was remarkable in itself. A Polish historian named Józef Garliński gained access to the document in the 1960s, only to discover that Witold had written all the names in code. Gar-liński managed to decipher large portions of it through guesswork and interviews with survivors to publish the first history of the resistance movement inside the camp. Then in 1991, Adam Cyra, a scholar at the Auschwitz-Birkenau State Museum, discovered Witold's unpublished memoir, a second report, and other fragmentary writings that had been locked away in Poland's archives since 1948. This material came with Witold's key to identifying his coconspirators.

The report I read in 2012 showed Witold to be an exacting chronicler of his experience in Auschwitz who wrote in raw and urgent prose. But it was only a fragmentary and sometimes distorted account. He didn't record critical episodes for fear of exposing his colleagues to arrest, hid devastating observations, and carefully framed events to suit his military audience. Many questions remained, none more critical and elusive than this: What became of the intelligence he risked his life to gather in Auschwitz? Did he provide the British and Americans with information about the Holocaust long before they publicly recognized the camp's role? Was his reporting suppressed? How many lives could have been saved had his warnings been heeded?

Students of the Holocaust quickly learn that it is a story not only of millions of innocent Europeans being murdered but of a collective failure to recognize and act on its horror. Allied officials struggled to discern the truth, and when confronted with the reality they stopped short of the moral leap necessary for action. But this wasn't only a political failure. The prisoners of Auschwitz also struggled to imagine the scope of the Holocaust as the Germans transformed the camp from a brutal prison to a death factory. They too succumbed to the human impulse to ignore or rationalize or dismiss the mass murders as separate from their own struggle. Yet Witold did not. Instead he staked his life on bringing the camp's horror to light.

I have tried in this book to understand what qualities set him apart. But as I uncovered more of his writings and met those who knew him and, in a few cases, fought beside him, I realized that perhaps the most remarkable fact about Witold Pilecki—this farmer and father of two in his late thirties with no great record of service or piety—is that he was not so different from you and me. This recognition brought a new question into focus: How did this average man expand his moral capacity to piece together, name, and act on the Nazis' greatest crimes when others looked away?

I offer his story here as a provocative new chapter in the history of the mass murder of the Jews and as an account of why someone might risk everything to help his fellow man.

Charlotte, 2019

NOTE ON TEXT

This is a work of nonfiction. Each quotation and detail has been taken from a primary source, testimony, memoir, or interview. The majority of the two-thousand-plus primary sources this book is based on are in Polish and German. All translations were carried out by my brilliant researchers, Marta Goljan, Katarzyna Chiżyńska, Luiza Walczuk, and Ingrid Pufahl, unless otherwise stated.

There are two established sources for understanding Witold's life in the camp: the report he compiled in Warsaw between October 1943 and June 1944, and a memoir written in Italy in the summer and fall of 1945.[1] Remarkably few mistakes crept into his accounts given the circumstances under which he wrote, on the run and without access to notes. But Witold is not a perfect narrator. Wherever possible I have tried to corroborate his writings, correct errors, and fill in the blanks. The Auschwitz-Birkenau State Museum has 3,727 prisoner accounts, including two dozen that describe Witold's activities and hundreds more recording events he witnessed. Other archives with important details and context include Archiwum Akt Nowych, Archiwum Naro-dowe w Krakowie, Centralne Archiwum Wojskowe, Instytut Pamięci Narodowej, the Ossolineum, the British Library, the Polish Institute and Sikorski Museum, the Polish Underground Movement Study Trust, the Chronicle of Terror Archives at the Witold Pilecki Institute, the National Archives in Kew, the Wiener Library, the Imperial War Museum, the National Archives in Washington, D.C., the United

States Holocaust Memorial Museum, the FDR Presidential Library, the Hoover Institution, the Yad Vashem Archives, the Central Zionist Archives, the German Federal Archives in Koblenz and Berlin, the Swiss Federal Archives, the Archivum Helveto-Polonicum Foundation, and the International Committee of the Red Cross Archives.

Over the course of research, I have also had access to the Pilecki family papers, and unearthed letters and memoirs kept by the families of his close collaborators that shed light on his decisions. Incredibly, several of those whom Witold fought alongside were alive when I began research and offered their reflections.[2]

I have been guided in writing by Witold's own rule for describing the camp: "Nothing should be 'overdone'; even the smallest fib would profane the memory of those fine people who lost their lives there." It has not always been possible to find multiple sources for some scenes, which is reflected in the endnotes. At other times, I have included camp details that it's clear Witold would have witnessed but does not mention in his reports. I cite sources in the endnotes in the order in which they appear in each paragraph. When quoting conversations, I note the source of each speaker once. In the case of conflicting accounts, I have given Witold's writings primacy unless otherwise stated.

Polish names are wonderful and sometimes daunting for an English speaker to read. I have used first names or diminutives for Witold and his inner circle, which also reflects how they spoke to one another. I have also tried to cut down on the use of acronyms, and hence refer, for example, to the main resistance group in Warsaw as the underground. For place-names I have retained prewar usage. I use the name Oświęcim for the town, and Auschwitz for the camp.

LIST OF MAPS

CHAPTER 1

INVASION

KRUPA, EASTERN POLAND
AUGUST 26, 1939

Witold stood on the manor house steps and watched the car kick up a trail of dust as it drove down the lime tree avenue toward the yard and came to a stop in a white cloud beside the gnarled chestnut. The summer had been so dry that the peasants talked about pouring water on the grave of a drowned man, or harnessing a maiden to the plow to make it rain—such were the customs of the Kresy, Poland's eastern borderlands. A vast electrical storm had finally come only to flatten what was left of the harvest and lift the storks' nests off their posts. But that August Witold wasn't worrying about grain for the winter.[1]

The radio waves crackled with news of German troops massing on the border and Adolf Hitler's threat to reclaim territory ceded to Poland at the end of World War I. Hitler believed the German people were locked in a brutal contest for resources with other races. It was only by the "annihilation of Poland and its vital forces," he had told officers at his mountain retreat in Obersalzburg on August 22, that the German race could expand. The next day Hitler signed a secret nonaggression pact with Josef Stalin that granted Eastern Europe to the Soviet Union and most of Poland to Germany. If the Germans succeeded in their plans, Witold's home and his land would be taken and Poland reduced to a vassal state or destroyed entirely.[2]

A soldier stepped out of the dusty car with orders for Witold to gather his men. Poland had ordered a mass mobilization of half a million reservists. Witold, a second lieutenant in the cavalry reserves and member of the local gentry, had forty-eight hours to deliver his unit to the barracks in the nearby town of Lida for loading onto troop transports bound west. He had done his best to train ninety volunteers through the summer, but most of his men were peasants who had never seen action or fired a gun in anger. Several didn't own horses and planned to fight the Germans on bicycle. At least Witold had been able to arm them with Lebel 8 mm bolt-action carbines.[3]

Witold hurried into his uniform and riding boots and grabbed his Vis handgun from a pail in the old smoke room, where he'd hidden it after catching his eight-year-old son, Andrzej, waving it at his little sister earlier in the summer. His wife, Maria, had taken the children to visit her mother near Warsaw. He'd need to summon them home. They'd be safer in the east away from Hitler's line of attack.[4]

Witold heard the stable boy readying his favorite horse, Bajka, in the yard and took a moment to adjust his khaki uniform in one of the mirrors that hung in the hallway beside the faded prints depicting the glorious but doomed uprisings his ancestors had fought in. He was thirty-eight years old, of medium build and handsome in an understated way, with pale blue eyes, dark blond hair brushed back from his high forehead, and a set to his lips that gave him a constant half smile. Noting his reserve and capacity to listen, people sometimes mistook him for a priest or a well-meaning bureaucrat. He could be warm and effusive, but more often gave the impression of holding something

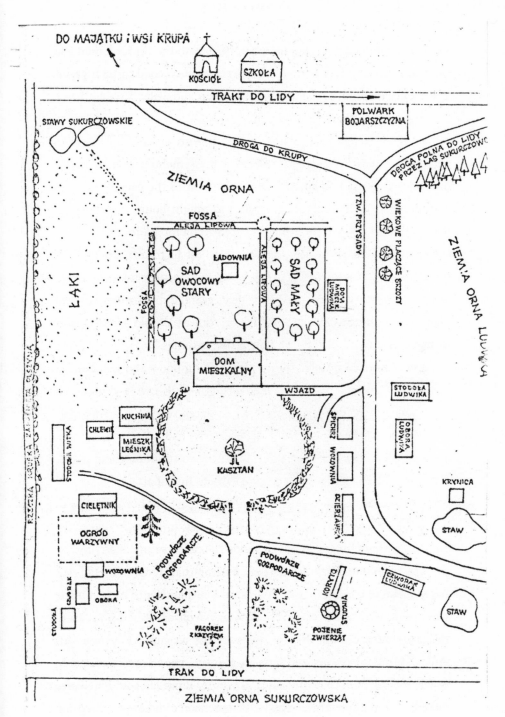

Map of Sukurcze from Witold's sister's memoir.

Courtesy of PMA–B.

back. He held exacting standards for himself and could be demanding of others, but he never pushed too far. He trusted people, and his quiet confidence inspired others to place their trust in him.[5]

Witold Pilecki and a friend in Sukurcze, c. 1930.
Courtesy of the Pilecki family.

As a young man he'd wanted to be an artist and had studied painting at university in the city of Wilno, only to abandon his schooling in the tumultuous years after World War I. Poland declared independence in 1918 out of the wreckage of the Russian, German, and Austro-Hungarian empires but was almost immediately invaded by Soviet Russia. Witold skirmished against the Bolsheviks with his scout troop and fought on the streets of Wilno. In the heady days that followed victory, Witold didn't feel like picking up his paintbrushes. He clerked for a while at a military supply depot and a farmers' union. Then in 1924 his father fell ill and he was honor bound to take on his family's dilapidated estate, Sukurcze, with its crumbling manor house, overgrown orchards, and 550 acres of rolling wheat fields.[6]

Suddenly, Witold found himself the steward of the local community. Peasants from the local village of Krupa worked his fields and sought his advice on how to develop their own land. He set up a dairy cooperative to earn them better prices, and, after spending a large chunk of his inheritance on his prized Arabian mare, founded the local reserve unit. He met his wife, Maria, in 1927 while painting scenery for a play in Krupa's new schoolhouse and courted her with bunches of lilac flowers delivered through her bedroom window. They married in 1931, and within a year their son, Andrzej, was born, followed twelve months later by Zofia, their daughter. Fatherhood brought out Witold's

Witold and Maria shortly after their wedding, c. 1931.

Courtesy of the Pilecki family.

caring side. He tended to the children when Maria was bedridden after Zofia's birth and taught them to ride and to swim in the pond beside the house. In the evenings, they staged little plays for Maria when she came home from work.[7]

But his quiet home life was not cut off from the political currents sweeping the country in the 1930s, and Witold worried. Poland had been one of the most pluralistic and tolerant societies in Europe for much of its thousand-year history. However, the country that had re-emerged in 1918 after 123 years of partition had struggled to forge an identity. Nationalists and church leaders called for an increasingly narrow definition of Polishness based on ethnicity and Catholicism.

Witold, Maria, Andrzej, and Zofia, c. 1935.
Courtesy of the Pilecki family.

Groups advocating greater rights for Ukrainian and Belarusian minorities were broken up and suppressed, while Jews—who comprised around a tenth of Poland's prewar population—were labeled economic competitors, discriminated against in education and business, and pressured to emigrate. Some nationalists took matters into their own hands, enforced boycotts of Jewish shops, and attacked synagogues. Thugs in Witold's hometown, Lida, had smashed up a Jewish confectionary and a lawyer's office. The main square was filled with shuttered shops belonging to Jews who had fled the country.[8]

Witold disliked politics and the way politicians exploited differences. His family stood for the old order, when Poland had been independent and a beacon of culture. That said, he was a man of his time and social class. He likely held a paternal view toward the local Polish and Belarusian peasants and shared in some of the prevailing anti-Semitic views. But ultimately his sense of patriotism extended to any group or ethnicity that took up Poland's cause. They would all need to unite now to repel the Nazi threat.[9]

*

Once mounted on his horse, it took Witold a breathless prayer to get to Krupa a mile away, where he likely called Maria from one of the few houses to have a telephone. Next he rode to the training ground beside the manor to assemble his men and gather supplies. Witold received ammunition and emergency rations from the regimental headquarters in Lida but had to arrange the remaining provisions from the community: bread, groats, sausages, lard, potatoes, onions, canned coffee, flour, dried herbs, vinegar, and salt. The horses needed the best part of 30 kilograms of oats a week. Not everyone in the village was happy to contribute, hardly having enough for themselves, and it was a long day in the sweltering heat to load the wagons in the manor courtyard.[10]

Witold had offered up the manor as a billet for officers and may have been camping with his men. At any rate, he wasn't at home when Maria and the children finally arrived the following evening, hot and bedraggled, to find soldiers dozing in their beds. She was annoyed, to put it mildly. It had been a long journey. The train was so packed that infants had been passed into the carriages through the windows, and they had stopped constantly to make way for military traffic. Witold was promptly summoned from the field and had to ask the men to leave.[11]

Maria was still upset when she woke up to the news that some peasants had broken into one of the baggage trains and stolen some supplies. But she put on one of Witold's favorite dresses for the send-off in Krupa, and she made sure Andrzej and Zofia were in their Sunday best. The children of the village gathered outside the school, and Krupa's single street was packed with well-wishers waving flags or handkerchiefs. A cheer went up as Witold led his column of horsemen down the street. He was dressed in a khaki uniform, with his pistol and saber strapped to his waist.[12]

Witold passed his family without looking down, but as soon as the column rode by and the crowd started to disperse he came galloping back, his face flushed, and stopped before them. He was leaving Maria with only his sister and old Józefa, the chain-smoking housekeeper, for protection. The Germans had been notorious in the last war for carrying out atrocities against civilians. He hugged and kissed the children. Maria, her unruly brown hair done up and lipstick on, was trying not to cry.[13]

"I will be back in two weeks," he told them. He could hardly say that in riding off on horseback to confront the most powerful military machine in Europe, he would be lucky to survive the next few days. Hitler commanded an army of 3.7 million men, almost twice the number of Poland's, with two thousand more tanks and almost ten times

Witold on his horse Bajka on parade, c. 1930s.

Courtesy of the Pilecki family.

the number of fighter planes and bombers. Furthermore, no natural features separated the two countries along their shared border that ran for a thousand miles, from the Tatra Mountains in the south to the Baltic coast in the north. Poland's best hope lay in holding out long enough for its allies, the British and French, to attack from the west and expose Germany to a war on two fronts.[14]

Witold next visited his parents' grave near the house. His father had died years earlier, but he had buried his mother only a few months before. Witold tied his horse to a tree, took off his saber, and struck a salute. Then he was off, wondering whether he would see those lime tree avenues again.[15]

Witold caught up with his men as they reached the barracks in Lida. They formed up on the parade ground with the other units, and a priest walked the ranks sprinkling holy water. Witold could see the transport train waiting on the sidings through the crowds of people who'd gathered to see them off. His men were excited for the most part, carried away by the thought of riding to war. Even Witold, who had experienced real fighting, felt stirred. The commanding officer of the regiment gave a rousing speech and the regimental orchestra played, but by the time Witold's unit had loaded their horses and supplies and found spots on the straw in the freight cars, the musicians had long finished and the townsfolk had gone home.[16]

Their train finally lurched forward in darkness. Progress was stop-and-go during the 240-mile journey to Warsaw. They arrived near midnight, August 30. From his carriage, Witold caught glimpses of the city: cafés and bars had blacked out windows in anticipation of German air raids; people with gas masks over their shoulders filled the streets, too hot and anxious to sleep. They waved at the troop transports as they passed.[17]

The million-strong capital was one of the fastest-growing cities in Europe. The baroque palaces and pastel-colored Old Town overlooking the Vistula River evoked Warsaw's past; the cranes and scaffolding and half-finished streets ending in fields spoke to its half-imagined future. The city was also the richest center of Jewish life outside New York, home to a vibrant music and theater scene that had swollen with escapees from Nazi Germany, Yiddish and Hebrew presses, and a multitude of political and religious movements, from secular Zionists who dreamed of Israel to Hasids who spoke of miracles in Poland.[18]

Warsaw's main station was packed with soldiers jostling to board trains or slumped against their packs across the floor, trying to sleep. The sheer logistics of moving over a million Polish soldiers to rallying

Poland, 1939

SWEDEN

Baltic Sea

ESTONIA

LATVIA

LITHUANIA

• Wilno

Free City
of Danzig

GERMANY
East Prussia

Krupa •• Lida

⊙ Berlin

Vistula

Ostrów
Mazowiecka •

Sochaczew • ⊙ Warsaw
• Łuków

G
E
R
M
A
N
Y

Breslau
•

Piotrków
• Trybunalski

• Włodawa

P O L A N D

Kłobuck •

• Prague

(Annexed by
Germany 1939)

Oświęcim • • Krakow

*Tatra
Mountains*

• Lwów

SOVIET
UNION

C Z E C H O S L O V A K I A

(Annexed by
Hungary 1939)

AUSTRIA
(Annexed by
Germany 1938)

HUNGARY

ROMANIA

N
W   E
S

0   50   100   150 miles

0   100   200 km

John Gilkes

points along the German border had overwhelmed the railway system. Witold and his men finally reached their disembarkation point in
Sochaczew, another thirty miles west, three days after leaving Lida.
They still had over a hundred miles more to march to reach their
positions near the small city of Piotrków Trybunalski, guarding the
main road to Warsaw. The long procession of several thousand was
constantly held up by broken wagons. Witold's unit skipped across the
fields on horseback, but the rest were forced to march all day and into
the night without reaching their destination. "We look with envy at
the cavalry—how they gallop as if in some parade, sit erect in their
saddles, with perky faces," noted one of the soldiers forced to trudge.[19]

The next morning, September 1, Witold saw the first waves of
German Heinkel, Dornier, and Junker bombers appear on the hori-
zon, their fuselages glinting in the morning light. Most of the planes
stayed high, bound for Warsaw, but one took a pass over the road and
drew fire. A lucky shot sent it crashing into a nearby field with a muffled roar, briefly raising spirits. But come evening the men were still
marching, and the next day too. They were starting to look as bedraggled as the refugees they passed on the road. They finally rested on the
evening of September 4—more than a week since mobilization—in
woods near Piotrków Trybunalski. There was little solid news of the
front, but plenty of rumors abounded that the Germans were advancing rapidly. The ground vibrated with the tremor of distant artillery.[20]

Witold's commanding officer, Major Mieczysław Gawryłkiewicz,
showed up the next morning in his open-top Fiat jeep to order the
troops into position south of the town. Gawryłkiewicz told Witold to
stick to marching on the roads, instead of the woods. They'd be open
targets, Witold realized, but he followed orders. They'd hardly set off
when a German fighter buzzed over them, only to return a few minutes
later with half a dozen bombers that proceeded to attack the column.

Witold's unit scrambled off the road, and pulled their horses down into the ditch as the bombs fell. The aircraft returned to strafe them with machine guns, then soared away. No one was hurt, but they had tasted what was to come.[21]

*

Witold watched the inferno consuming the center of Piotrków Try-bunalski as he passed by with his men that evening. He set up camp a few miles away on a low rise facing west toward Germany and then took eight of his troopers on a scouting patrol. From the woods, he caught his first glimpse of the Germans: an armored reconnaissance unit deployed in a village across a narrow stream. He rode back, set a guard, and then watched the flames of the burning city light the sky. The fighting would begin tomorrow. His men, knowing this might be their final night, talked of families or loved ones at home. One by one they settled down to rest.[22]

What Witold couldn't know was that his detachment had been po-sitioned directly in the front of the main thrust of the German First and Fourth Panzer divisions toward Warsaw. The force had already punched through Polish lines on the border at Kłobuck and advanced more than sixty miles in the first few days of fighting. The Poles had no means of countering the Germans' new Blitzkrieg tactic of massive tank concentrations with Stuka dive bombers flying in close support. Barreling toward the men from Lida were more than six hundred Pan-zers moving faster than their horses could gallop.[23]

At first light orders came for Witold to fall back to the woods near Proszenie, a tiny hamlet about six miles northeast of Piotrków Trybu-nalski where the division had set up its headquarters and baggage train. A short while later the German attack began. Artillery hit them in the forest, shattering the trees and blasting spears of wood into men and horses. The bombing was worse to the east, where a single regiment had been left to guard the approach to the city. They hunkered down as best they could, but then word spread that the Panzers had broken through, and the headquarters began an urgent retreat along the main road to Warsaw. Witold brought up the rear with the baggage train as it retreated. They had gone only a few miles when they got stuck in traffic trying to cross a narrow bridge in the small town of Wolbórz. At least with the darkness, the bombers had lain off.[24]

Just after 8 p.m. they heard the sudden rumble of tank tracks, and before they had time to react, the Panzers barreled into them with such force that those at the back were thrown from their mounts, and the rest were quickly mowed down in a hail of cannon fire. Witold's horse, Bajka, crumpled beneath him, riddled with bullets. He pulled himself free and rolled into a ditch, lying beside the still-shuddering horse as the tanks' 7.92 mm guns tore through bodies and strafed the cottages along the road.[25]

His instincts told him to lie perfectly still but it was an agony to listen to the shrieks and groans of his men being massacred. Eventually the guns fell quiet and he slipped away from the carnage and found a dozen survivors and horses in the dark fields beyond the town. The assault had lasted only a few minutes, but he'd lost most of his men; dead or injured or captured, he didn't know. He hoped the Polish line had held more resolutely elsewhere. Witold made for Warsaw with the other survivors, knowing that all would be lost if they couldn't hold the capital.[26]

At first they seemed to be behind the front line. Following Hitler's edict to destroy the Poles, the German military bombed and strafed fleeing civilians, and corpses littered the roadside beside carts piled high with luggage and furniture. But as they neared Warsaw the following day the roads started to fill with the living, and Witold realized he'd overtaken the Germans. The crowds of men shouldering bundles or herding live-stock and women dragging children looked nervously to the sky.[27]

*

Witold rode into Warsaw on the evening of September 6. He had no radio and no way of knowing the scale of the disaster that had unfolded elsewhere: the Germans had broken through Polish lines at multiple points and were moving rapidly to encircle Warsaw. Advance units were expected at any moment. Britain and France had declared war on Germany, but there was no sign of action. The Polish government had already fled, and the British delegation in the city was preparing to.[28]

"Inside the Embassy, cases of the Ambassador's wine lay abandoned in the hall, his butler was in tears and the steps were littered with all sorts of personal kit, including an immaculate pair of polo boots," recalled Peter Wilkinson, one of the delegation members, who made sure the embassy's excellent wine cellar got loaded onto their five-ton truck before departure.[29]

The only defenses Witold saw, riding toward the city center, were a couple of overturned tram cars that served as a barricade. Residents ran past layered in what looked like their entire wardrobe or kitted out as if for the ski slopes in garish pants and bandanas. Soldiers straight from the front were slumped on the pavements. Just the look of them, weary and disinterested, was enough to know what had happened. Even the air raid sirens had ceased to sound. Stopping to ask one man in a hunting cap and smoking a cigar for directions, Witold was answered in German with a smirk. He was a member of the country's sizable ethnic German population that the Nazi leadership was urging to turn on its Polish neighbors. Incensed, Witold struck him across his face with the flat of his saber and rode off.[30]

Witold finally located Warsaw's military headquarters on Krakowskie Przedmieście Street near the royal castle, where he learned that there was a plan to defend the city and enlist the help of civilians in building barricades and preparing for a siege. Witold was given oats and hay for his horse, but he had no clear instructions on which unit to join or what to do. He decided that they'd be better off falling back and joining whatever Polish forces were regrouping in the east to launch a counterstrike. On September 9, with the Germans' encircle-ment almost complete, Witold and his men slipped away to the city of Łuków, fifty miles southeast of Warsaw, where he was told he could find the Polish military's overall command. By the time Witold ar-rived, the small city had been bombed and reduced to smoking ruins. A peasant woman lay beside one crater, her skirts blown over her head to expose her pale white thighs, a mangled horse beside her.[31]

In Łuków, he was told that the commanders had retreated to the next town, but when he got there it was the same story. And so it went in place after place, bombed and abandoned. The German strategy was to strike towns and infrastructure far in advance of its ground troops to prevent the Poles from regrouping. Even the train station in Witold's distant hometown, Lida, was attacked. The roads were jammed with civilians and soldiers pursued and harried by dive bombers as they moved east. "We are now no longer an army, a detachment, or a bat-tery," recalled one soldier, "but individuals wandering collectively to-wards some wholly indefinite goal."[32]

The truth was unavoidable: Witold knew that Poland had lost its independence once again, and that the question facing him—every Pole—was whether to surrender or to fight on knowing that to do so was futile. Witold could never accept the first option. On September 13, German bombers caught them again in the town of Włodawa, 150 miles east of Warsaw, but at least there Witold found an officer he'd known from the Bolshevik campaign—Major Jan Włodarkiewicz—

who was preparing to take a stand. The major, a short, powerfully built man who carried himself like a boxer, had received orders to gather at the Hungarian border. Like Witold, he'd been picking up stragglers, and together they had a company. But then on their way to the border they bumped into Major Gawryłkiewicz, still chauffeured, and other command staff in their own cars. The officers looked surprisingly un-ruffled and explained that they planned to rally outside the country to continue the fight. For Witold that was tantamount to desertion and he protested, but they just shrugged and drove away.[33]

That left Witold and Jan to come up with their own plan. There was no sense in continuing toward the border, which was sure to attract German attention sooner or later. So they made for the woods, where they could stage hit-and-run attacks and maybe find enough like-minded souls to plan a bigger operation. Over the following days they attacked several German convoys and even a small airstrip, blowing up a plane, but Witold knew such attacks didn't achieve much. German checkpoints were springing up everywhere, forcing them to keep to the thickets and marshes and scrounge for food in the woods or from isolated peasants. To make matters worse, it rained constantly. Water coursed down their backs in rivulets and mud sucked at their feet.[34]

At the end of September, they learned that Soviet forces had en-tered Poland from the east. Stalin claimed it was for the protection of Poland's minorities, but his intention was clear to most Poles; the Soviet dictator had decided to seize his share of the spoils. Any hope that Witold harbored of rallying enough men to stage a rally promptly evaporated. He had other worries to contend with now: given his fam-ily's reputation for resisting the Russians, Maria and the children were almost certainly in danger.[35]

On September 28 Warsaw surrendered, and a few days after that the first snow fell. The city had held out for another fortnight after he'd left, much to the fury of Hitler, who had instructed his generals to darken the skies over Warsaw with falling bombs and drown the people in blood. The resulting aerial and artillery bombardment had left forty thousand dead and destroyed or severely damaged a fifth of the city's buildings. Schools, hospitals, and churches had been bombed indiscriminately. The Old Town was a ruin, and the city's new opera house, the largest in Europe, reduced to a few colonnades. Tens of thousands, newly homeless, squatted amid the debris.[36]

Witold only heard rumors of the city's devastation. Huddled with Jan in some woods near the town of Lubartów, dirty and unshaven, Witold realized that the fight to reclaim the country wouldn't start there, but in Warsaw, where power resided. They ordered the men to dig holes and bury their weapons, and then they exchanged their uniforms for civilian clothes from the locals. Witold received an old sheepskin jacket.[37]

As they headed west again, the men peeled off one or two at a time for home. Before reaching Warsaw, Witold decided to make a detour to Ostrów Mazowiecka, the town sixty miles to the north of the capital where Maria's mother, Franciszka, lived, hoping to find Maria and the children. He and Jan clasped hands and agreed to meet at his mother's flat in Warsaw in a couple of weeks' time. "We will finish what we have started," promised Jan.[38]

*

Witold set off through the fields and picked his way through the brush for several days to reach the Bug River near Ostrów Mazowiecka. The swiftly flowing waterway had recently become the new border between German and Soviet forces. Russian troops patroled Witold's side of the bank. He hid until darkness fell and then persuaded a local fisherman to ferry him across the water in his skiff during a gap in the patrols. The vessel bobbed and weaved in the currents, but they made the far bank, where the Germans had strung lines of barbed wire. Witold found a way through and hurried on to Ostrów Mazowiecka, a few miles farther.[39]

He found the place eerily quiet. Half of the town's seventeen thousand residents were Jewish, and most had fled to Soviet-occupied territory. Their shops and homes had been looted and in some cases occupied by Polish families. Franciszka lived in a farmhouse on the outskirts of town. As Witold arrived he saw German vehicles parked in the yard of the brewery opposite the house, which had become the headquarters of the German secret police, or Gestapo. He made sure to enter the farmhouse from the rear. Franciszka was there—alive and safe—but she had no word on Maria. Witold went to sleep on the sofa in the living room while Franciszka poured herself a stiff drink.[40]

Over the following days he learned about the brutal new racial order the Nazis had imposed on the town. The Germans had rounded up

The Ostrowski family house.

several hundred townsfolk, locked them in the school gymnasium, and divided the group into ethnic Poles and Jews. Most of the Catholics were quickly released, but the Jews were selected for work gangs. The Germans encouraged the ethnic Poles to abuse and beat the Jews and point out their shops for looting. As Jewish families were evicted from their homes, some of their Catholic neighbors jeered at them. Most residents, though, refused to follow the German lead. The town's mayor hid a family in his basement. Maria's parents did what little they felt they could, letting Jews fleeing through the town take apples from the orchard.[41]

Witold doesn't say much about his time in Ostrów Mazowiecka. He likely felt dismayed by exhibitions of anti-Semitism among the locals, which clearly played into the Germans' hands. Each morning he woke up praying for Maria to come walking through the door with the children, and each night he went to bed fearing the worst.[42]

Eventually, he must have surmised that Maria had remained in Krupa, perhaps hiding among friends, and he had to choose between waiting for his family and resuming the struggle against the Germans. He knew that the chance of finding her and the children if they were traveling was perilously small given the numbers of refugees streaming across the border. Either way, the decision was clear: country before family. On the morning of November 1, he borrowed a bicycle and set off for the long ride to Warsaw to meet Jan. It was All Saints' Day, when graveyards blossomed with candles and the living prayed for the dead, but Witold had no time for that: he was heading to Warsaw to fight.[43]

CHAPTER 2

OCCUPATION

WARSAW

NOVEMBER 1, 1939

Witold approached the city on his clattering bicycle unsure what he would find or what form his resistance would take. The main road to Warsaw was dotted with German checkpoints, so Witold stuck to country lanes, picking up snatches of news. There was no word of any attack from the British or French, but he assumed one was coming. The best chance of driving out the Germans lay in planning an uprising to coincide with an Allied offensive. Witold knew there would be others who felt like he did and that he needed to start building a network.[1]

Witold merged with the crowds crossing the single bridge still standing over the Vistula. The sight of Warsaw's broken skyline on the far bank must have startled him. The city center had born the brunt of the German bombardment. Collapsed buildings blocked the streets and people had made trails through the banks of rubble. Hundreds paused at the intersection of Marszałkowska Street and Jerozolimskie Avenue to light candles before a giant mound of bricks and masonry that marked the city's largest mass grave. Glass from broken windows screeched underfoot. Reich propaganda chief Joseph Goebbels, visiting the city around then, concluded, "This is hell. A city reduced to ruins. Our bombs and shells have done a thorough job." Even in those bits of Warsaw left untouched, a change had taken place. "At first sight everything looked as it had before, but it was somehow different, submerged in the strange atmosphere of a city in mourning," recalled one witness.[2]

Witold made his way to a friend's apartment in the south of the city. His shock and dismay at the devastation were tempered by the practical need to understand the Nazis' plans and decide what form his resistance would take. Hitler's terrifying racial vision for the country had come into focus. In September, he had ordered Western Poland annexed to the Reich and over five million Catholic Poles and Jews expelled to make way for German settlers. The remaining territory, which included Warsaw and Krakow, was to become a German colony. Hitler had made his former lawyer, Hans Frank, administrator for the "General Government for the Occupied Polish Territories" and had given him orders to exploit it ruthlessly and impose a brutal racial hierarchy.[3]

The Germans in this rubric were the master race, along with any Poles who could prove German ancestry and agreed to sign a special "Volksliste" registry. They were given jobs in the administration, property seized from Jews, and exclusive use of parks, public phones, and taxis. Public transport and cinemas were also segregated and notices appeared on shops declaring "no Poles or Jews."[4]

Ethnic Poles, as members of the weaker Slavic race, were to serve as laborers. Hitler considered them to be Aryans with some Germanic blood that had been diluted by mixing with other races. Tens of thousands of Poles were pressed into work in the Reich that autumn. Killing squads known as the Einsatzgruppen preempted resistance by round-

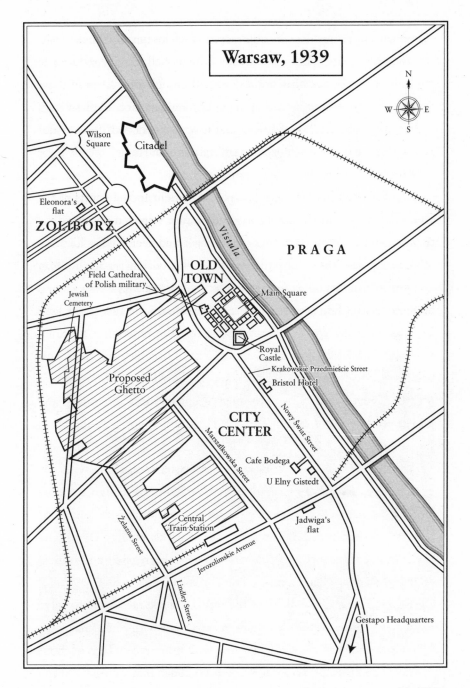

Warsaw, 1939

N
W E
S

Wilson Square

Citadel

Eleonora's flat

ZOLIBORZ

Vistula

PRAGA

Field Cathedral of Polish military

Jewish Cemetery

OLD TOWN

Main Square

Royal Castle

Krakowskie Przedmieście Street

Bristol Hotel

Proposed Ghetto

CITY CENTER

Nowy Świat Street

Marszałkowska Street

Cafe Bodega

U Elny Gistedt

Żelazna Street

Central Train Station

Jadwiga's flat

Jerozolimskie Avenue

Lindley Street

Gestapo Headquarters

John Gilkes

ing up and shooting some 20,000 members of the Polish educated and professional classes—lawyers, teachers, doctors, journalists, or simply anyone who looked intellectual—and buried their bodies in mass graves. Newspapers were censored, radios banned, and high schools and universities closed on the basis that Poles only needed "educational possibilities that demonstrate to them their ethnic fate."[5]

At the bottom were Jews, whom Hitler didn't consider to be a race at all, but rather a parasitic subspecies of human bent on destroying the German people. Hitler had threatened Europe's Jews with annihilation in the event that "international Jewish financiers" provoked another world war. But in the autumn of 1939, the Nazi leadership was still formulating its plans toward them. The occupation of Poland had brought two million Jews—ten times more than lived in Germany—

Polish women on their way to be shot, 1939.

Courtesy of Narodowe Archiwum Cyfrowe.

under Nazi control. The deputy head of the SS, Reinhard Heydrich, advised units in September that the Jewish problem would have to be dealt with incrementally. He issued orders for Jews to be concentrated in cities ready for their deportation to a reservation along the new border with the Soviet Union. In the meantime, Jews were required to wear a Star of David on their sleeve or chest, mark their shops and businesses accordingly, and were subjected to continual harassment. "A pleasure, finally . . . to be able to tackle the Jewish race physically," Frank declared in a speech that November. "The more that die, so much the better."[6]

Witold almost certainly noticed Frank's official decrees plastered on lampposts around the city and understood that the Germans meant to destroy Poland by tearing apart its social fabric and pitting ethnic groups against one another. But he also saw encouraging signs of resistance: stickers declaring, "We don't give a damn" (a direct translation of the Polish idiom is: "We have you deep in our ass") and a giant poster of Hitler in the city center that had sprouted curly whiskers and long ears. On November 9, Witold contacted his coconspirator Jan Włodarkiewicz and arranged a meeting of potential recruits at his sister-in-law's flat in the northern suburb of Żoliborz. Witold hurried through the rainy streets trying to beat the 7 P.M. curfew.[7]

His sister-in-law, Eleonora Ostrowska, lived in a two-room apartment on the third floor. Żoliborz was relatively untouched by the bombs, although the windows of most apartments were blown out and the electricity wasn't working, so Witold had to wait for someone to enter in order to get in. Eleonora showed him inside with her two-year-old son, Marek, at her feet. The two had met only briefly before. She was a charming, tough thirty-year-old, her dark blond hair pulled back into a bun, with thin lips and pale blue eyes. Her husband, Edward, Maria's brother, was a cavalry officer who'd been missing since

Entrance to 40 Wojska Polskie Avenue.

Courtesy of PMA-B.

the start of the war, leaving her to take care of Marek and hold down
a job at the agricultural ministry, one of the few government depart-
ments that the Nazis hadn't abolished.[8]

Jan was one of the next to arrive, wheezing and shuffling up the
steps. He'd taken a bullet through the chest on his way to Warsaw that
somehow missed his vitals, and had been laid up at his mother's. Half
a dozen more followed, mostly officers and student activists selected by
Jan. Eleonora had put brown paper over the windows, but it was cold
and they kept their coats on. They gathered around the living room
table where Eleonora had lit a candle.[9]

Jan had reached some stark conclusions about their situation: Poland had lost because its leaders had failed to create a Catholic nation
or use the country's wellspring of faith against the invaders. Jan be-

Eleonora Ostrowska, 1944.
Courtesy of Marek Ostrowski.

lieved they needed to see in Poland's defeat an opportunity to rebuild a country around Christian beliefs and awaken the religious fervor of the younger generation. He harbored ambitions to appeal to right-wing groups, but for now he fashioned a broad rallying cry of resistance to the country's double occupation.[10]

Witold certainly shared Jan's anger at the Polish government, a common sentiment in Warsaw, but he rarely sought to share his faith with others and feared that an avowedly religious mission would alienate potential allies. For the moment, he was probably more focused on assessing the viability of building a secret and effective resistance.[11]

They talked strategy late into the night before getting to the subject of their roles. Jan would lead; Witold would serve as chief recruiter. They would call themselves Tajna Armia Polska, the Secret Polish Army. At dawn they stole out of the apartment to the Field Cathedral of the Polish Military, a Baroque church on the edge of the Old Town. They knew a priest there and asked him to witness their oath. Getting down on their knees at the dimly lit altar, they swore to serve God, the Polish nation, and each other. They received a blessing in return, before emerging, bleary-eyed but elated.[12]

*

Winter came early that year as Witold started to recruit. The snow fell in flurries, the Vistula froze solid, and a hundred resistance cells sprang up across the city. There were other officer-led groups like his, as well as Communist agitators, trade unionists, artist collectives, even a group of chemists planning biological warfare. The Germans had commandeered popular meeting spots like the Bristol and Adria hotels, but new places sprang up that became known as underground haunts. At U Elny Gistedt's—a restaurant named after the Swedish operetta singer who'd set the place up to employ her out-of-work artist friends—groups of conspirators sat hunched over their tables in fur coats. The conspirators mostly knew each other, and shared the latest news from around the city or scraps gleaned from illegal radio sets about the Allied counter-offensive expected in the spring.[13]

At the same time, a black market flourished near the central railway station trading in clothes and food, dollars, diamonds, and forged papers. Peasants from the countryside smuggled goods in the hems of their clothing, hidden pouches, and bras.[14]

"Never before have I seen such oversized busts as in Poland at this time," recalled Stefan Korboński, an underground member. One enterprising smuggler brought butchered pigs into the city hidden in coffins.

The Germans, busy setting up their administration, offered only cursory inspections, and even when someone was discovered they might get off with a bribe or, on rare occasions, a little wit, as was the case with the smuggler who tried to disguise a trotter as a peasant woman. "When discovered by gendarmes, even they, bereft though they were of all sense of humor, nearly died of laughter," wrote Korboński.[15]

Witold avoided public gatherings and sought recruits who shared his natural reserve and reticence. He grasped a fundamental truth of resistance work. Nationality, language, culture were important bonds in any group, but ultimately his network relied on a more basic quality: trust. The act of recruitment meant placing his life in the hands of his recruits, and vice versa. At times, those whom Witold selected appeared surprised by his confidence in them.[16]

"Why do you trust me?" asked one man.[17]

"Dear boy, you have to trust people," Witold answered.[18]

He was not always successful in judging temperament and constantly worried that an overeager member of his team would expose them. That winter, Tajna Armia Polska compiled a handbook of advice for new recruits that warned how "people had gone mad with resistance activity and were getting caught far too easily . . . If we want to have our revenge on the Germans, we have to survive long enough to get it."[19]

Witold did his best to nurture his young army, which by December numbered nearly a hundred, mostly young men. "He was very sensitive," recalled Eleonora. "Other people's troubles had an effect on him." One soldier he recruited joked appreciatively that he was the group's very own "Nanny."[20]

Witold knew there was little his group could do to directly oppose the occupation, but he recognized they could serve as an effective intelligence-gathering operation. Tajna Armia Polska's intelligence chief, Jerzy Skoczyński, had contacts among the Polish police. The Germans had retained the force to perform basic law-and-order duties, but were frequently informed of major operations in advance.[21]

Witold and his colleagues were able to use their tips to warn German targets. But they struggled to comprehend the disorienting pace with which the Nazis were carrying out their plans. That winter the SS began mass deportations of Poles from the recently annexed provinces of western Poland as the weather touched negative Fahrenheit. Cattle trucks stuffed with half-frozen families arrived daily at the main train station in Warsaw, and when the doors were peeled back, stiff corpses toppled to the ground like statues. The survivors had to sleep in the ruins or else pack into the already crowded homes of friends and families. By January 1940, more than 150,000 Poles—Catholics and Jews alike—had been deported to make way for German settlers, and there were plans to expel hundreds of thousands more.[22]

The Germans made no preparations for the influx of refugees to the city. Governor Frank announced countrywide food rationing: around six hundred calories a day for so-called Aryan Poles and five hundred calories a day for Jewish ones, barely a third of what was needed to survive (Germans in Poland were entitled to 2,600). Ration cards were issued that could be used only at designated stores, and there were few items available: bread that was mixed with sawdust "flour," marmalade made from beets, bitter acorn coffee, and potatoes, the one constant in everyone's diet. The black market met some of the shortfall, but many went hungry. Crowds of malnourished refugees appeared on street corners to beg.[23]

The city's cramped, dirty conditions soon led to an outbreak of typhus. Few diseases terrified Germans more. The liceborne fever had ravaged the eastern front during World War I and killed around three million people. Nazi officials considered Jews to be prone to infection

and accelerated their plans to restrict them to a sealed ghetto in Warsaw to help contain the disease.[24]

Frank was aware that the brutality of his policies was stirring resistance and vowed to swiftly stamp it out. That spring saw a marked
escalation in the execution of the Nazis' real or imagined enemies. Several underground groups were broken up and murdered en masse in the
Palmiry woods north of Warsaw, along with lawyers, dentists, even the
country's top chess player. Yet such reprisals did little to quell the resistance and actually served to winnow out careless outfits and encourage
the growth of more competent groups. The dominant force to emerge
from these arrests was the Związek Walki Zbrojnej, or the Union for
Armed Struggle, which had gained the backing of a Polish exile government established in France the previous fall. Although some in Tajna Armia Polska saw the Union as rivals, Witold thought they would
need to join forces, in some capacity, to oust the Nazis when the time
came for an uprising.[25]

In the meantime, the intelligence chief Jerzy was keen to crack
down on Poles who had started to collaborate with the occupiers,
mostly drawn from the country's million-strong ethnic German community. The Nazis relied on such informers to enforce the racial order. Despite the claims of Nazi scientists that they could distinguish
anatomically between races, the truth was most Germans struggled
to tell Poland's ethnic groups apart and needed informants to reveal
the complex fabric of Polish society. Informants took full advantage
of their power to exact petty revenge. "In every community there are
people who had no scruples about ridding themselves of trouble or denouncing an unwanted husband, wife or mistress," observed one underground member. Whatever their motivation, snitches posed a real
threat to the underground and had to be eliminated.[26]

The informants often congregated at a basement nightclub located off Nowy Świat Street named Café Bodega. The premises were owned by the Polish wife of the Italian ambassador, which gave the location protection for its singular attraction: jazz. Hitler's distaste for "Negermusik" was well known, but it wasn't officially banned, and the Gestapo tolerated Bodega because they found its dark, noisy auditorium the perfect place to meet informers at the bar or at one of the reserved tables beside the bandstand.[27]

Jerzy set up a small observation post above a printshop opposite the club's entrance, from which he took note of attendees and snapped pictures of likely informers when the flickering streetlights permitted. He had also started working with the staff to listen in on conversations, and occasionally sent in men to pose as informants to denounce actual collaborators to the Gestapo for some made-up crime. It was a common enough sight at Bodega to see a phalanx of Gestapo men dragging away

George Scott with his band, c. 1941.

Courtesy of Narodowe Archiwum Cyfrowe.

some protesting snitch. George Scott, the bandleader and drummer, whose African American father had met his Polish mother working in a circus, never stopped his medley of beats.[28]

*

That spring, Witold finally received word that Maria and the children had arrived at her mother's farmhouse in Ostrów Mazowiecka. He hurried to them, taking a rickety bus line that the Germans rarely inspected. Maria's account of their flight and the conditions in the Soviet-occupied east was harrowing.

The Soviet secret police were deporting Poles to the gulags of Siberia or for resettlement in central Asia. Maria had been tipped off before Christmas that they were soon to be arrested and only had time to pack up some clothes and escape in a cart, leaving behind the family dog, Nero. For most of the winter, they'd hidden with family friends in Krupa. When the cold had eased, they took the train to the new border between the Soviet Union and the Reich in the hope of reaching her mother's home. They were stopped by the Russian police in the small town of Wołkowysk, twenty miles from the frontier, where Maria was led off for interrogation in an underground bunker near the train station while the children had to wait overnight in the town hall nearby. When she was finally released the following morning, minus her money and wedding ring, eight-year-old Andrzej was catatonic with fear and cold.[29]

They made it to a cousin's house in a neighboring town, where they rested a week and tried again. This time they hired a guide to sneak them across the border at night. It was subzero, and a full moon lit the wind-scourged no-man's-land. Halfway across Andrzej had stumbled and fallen against a roll of barbed wire that snagged his sheepskin jacket. At that moment a German searchlight had swept the area and caught them as they struggled to free the jacket. They were quickly rounded up but were lucky: the border guards who collected them showed little interest in their case and let them pass.[30]

They had arrived in Ostrów Mazowiecka to find it devastated by the unfolding German racial project. Maria was told that on November 11, the Germans had marched 364 Jewish men, women, and children to woods outside the town and shot them, one of the first such massacres of its kind. The execution site was only a mile or so from her mother's house, and adjoined the family orchard where Andrzej liked to play (despite being told not to go there, Andrzej did, and found a little boy's sodden cap among the trees).[31]

Witold did what he could to make sure his family was properly settled and then returned to Warsaw with a new urgency, only to discover Jan flirting with anti-Semitic views. Witold knew Jan wanted to produce a newsletter on behalf of the group for some time. The underground was awash with publications of different political hues—eighty-four titles were published in 1940—but Jan wanted a newsletter that would focus on the moral underpinnings of the resistance. At least that was how he pitched it to the likes of Witold and Jadwiga Tereszczenko, a friend of Jan's who'd agreed to be the editor.[32]

Witold wasn't opposed to the idea, and in fact helped arrange one of the distribution points at a grocery shop on Żelazna Street near where he was staying. But in the first issues of *Znak*, or "The Sign," he read articles that seemed lifted straight from the manifestos of prewar right-wing groups: strident talk of a Polish nation for the Poles, and creating a true Christian country, views that were disturbingly close to those of the ultranationalists who saw the Nazi occupation as a means of getting rid of the Jews for good.[33]

Witold explained as tactfully as he could to Jan that Poles must rally together in the face of mounting German repression. Jadwiga also raised the issue of anti-Semitism among Poles with other editors during late-night writing sessions in her flat, but they dismissed her concerns: the Jews didn't know whose side they were on and were better off gone. Meanwhile, the walls were going up around the ghetto and Jewish families were being forced to relocate, including Jadwiga's next-door neighbor. Rather than helping them, ethnic Poles in her block were taking whatever was left behind. There did need to be a moral awakening among Poles, Jadwiga believed, starting with the edict to "love thy neighbor."[34]

Yet Jan was unrepentant and started work on a right-wing manifesto for the organization that he appeared to want to turn into a po-

Witold and Jan, c. 1940.
Courtesy of the Pilecki family.

litical movement. He also began talks with nationalist groups about a possible union, including one whose members had sounded out the Germans about forming a Nazi puppet administration. Jan was clearly losing his way, and Witold felt compelled to go behind his friend's back to stop him.[35]

At some point that spring, Witold sought out the head of the rival Związek Walki Zbrojnej, Colonel Stefan Rowecki, to discuss joining forces. The forty-five-year-old had supported the creation of an underground civilian administration that answered directly to the Polish exile government in France, and which regularly issued calls for a "truly democratic" country with equal rights for Poland's Jews. Rowecki, a self-professed Sherlock Holmes fan who deployed a variety of disguises, rarely expressed his own views but was an astute observer of the national mood. He had already written to Polish leadership in France of his concerns that the Nazis were deliberately stoking racial hatred to divert Poles from anti-German activity. There had been a significant escalation in attacks by ethnic Poles on Jews, Rowecki reported, and he was concerned that a right-wing politician might emerge as a German stooge who would use the persecution of the Jews to justify their position.[36]

Like Witold, Rowecki had few illusions about what the underground could achieve against the might of the occupiers. But he felt that their resistance served a deeper purpose of rallying morale as they slowly built capacity. In the meantime, he wanted the underground to start documenting Nazi crimes to inform the West and pressure the Allies to act.[37]

Rowecki had established a network of couriers who traveled in secret over remote mountain passes of the Tatras and on to France. So far, his reports had yet to stir the imagination of Western leaders, although the Germans were embarrassed by some of the revelations, and had even released one group of academics they'd detained after an international outcry. Rowecki believed that the accumulating details would help stiffen British and French resolve.[38]

Witold came away impressed by the caliber of the quiet, secretive man and convinced of the need to submit to his authority. But Jan immediately dismissed a merger at their next meeting, pointing out that he had sent his own courier to the Polish exile government for endorsement. He then announced the manifesto he'd prepared was to be jointly signed by several fringe groups.[39]

Stefan Rowecki, prewar.

Courtesy of the Polska Agencja Prasowa.

"Such a declaration would destroy all our work!" Witold exclaimed. "Let us focus on the armed struggle. We can worry about constitutional matters later."[40]

Jan looked taken aback. He'd been counting on Witold to fall into line. Instead, several others agreed with Witold, including the group's new chief of staff, a doughty colonel named Władysław Surmacki. Jan capitulated and agreed to meet with Rowecki, a victory of sorts for Witold.[41]

But Jan pressed ahead with his declaration, which was just as divisive as Witold had feared. There was no reference to Jews or other minorities in the article, but the subtext appeared clear. "Poland has to

Władysław Surmacki, c. 1930.

Courtesy of PMA-B.

be Christian," the declaration announced, "and Poland has to be based around our national identity." Those opposed to such ideas should be "removed from our lands." Witold knew that their partnership was ruined. "On the surface we agreed to keep on running the organization," Witold recalled, but there was no hiding the "deeper resentment."[42]

*

On May 10, Hitler's forces swept into Luxemburg and the Low Countries on their way to France. This was the moment the underground had waited for when the combined might of the Allies would take on the Germans, and either defeat or else distract them enough to make an uprising in Poland worthwhile. Jan's mother had set up an illegal radio in her flat. They gathered to listen, eagerly at first, and then with increasing grimness as the BBC reported that German forces had routed the British at Dunkirk and swept into Paris. It soon became apparent that Germany was about to inflict a cataclysmic defeat on the French, and that the war was going to stretch on indefinitely.[43]

Governor Frank, believing he no longer had to worry about negative coverage in the foreign media, ordered mass roundups of military-age men. On June 20, 358 people were shot in the Palmiry woods. Thousands more were deported to concentration camps in Germany. On one occasion, Witold was nearly caught when the SS raided Eleonora's flat. He heard trucks outside and just had time to hide documents under the floorboards and slip out the door before the police barged in and rifled through the apartment. He moved from safe house to safe house and started using the identity papers of one Tomasz Serafiński, which he'd picked up at one apartment.[44]

The intensified crackdown damaged Witold's network. A Gestapo raid on the Bodega saw most of the waiters arrested. Their places were filled by new recruits, but this time the Gestapo managed to plant a spy among them. She was a flighty young Pole who had fallen for an SS officer, and she supplied him with several names, including one of Witold's colleagues who also happened to be her uncle, a gynecologist named Władysław Dering. On July 3, 1940, shortly before dawn, the SS dragged Dering and his wife from their flat.[45]

The underground wasn't sure what happened to Dering, but reports were emerging that the SS had opened a concentration camp in a former Polish army barracks outside the small town of Oświęcim in June. The Germans called the place Auschwitz. Such camps had been a common feature of political life in Germany since Hitler's rise to power. Under emergency decree, Hitler had approved the indefinite detention or "protective custody" of any citizen the SS judged to be an enemy of the state. By the start of the war, the Nazis had detained thousands of politicians, left-wing activists, Jews, homosexuals, and other so-called social deviants in half a dozen camps across Germany.[46]

The Nazis hadn't pioneered the concept of locking up their opponents, but Auschwitz was different because it was the first German camp to target a group according to its nationality, in this case Poles. At that point, the Germans did not distinguish between the ethnic backgrounds of the Poles they sent to the camp: Catholics predominated, but there were Jews and ethnic Germans among the first prisoners. Auschwitz's aim was to crush the resistance of men like Witold.[47]

The underground knew little about the place but heard that the Germans were dispatching more and more prisoners to the camp. By August of that year, more than a thousand people were held there. Letters from prisoners in the camp revealed little. But the violence of Auschwitz was suggested by the number of death notices the SS sent to the families of deceased inmates and their occasionally blood-splattered personal effects.[48]

A few weeks later in August, Tajna Armia Polska's chief of staff,

Władysław Surmacki, was arrested, and Jan convened an emergency meeting at Jadwiga's. The heat was stifling, and cigarette smoke hung in the air. Jan called the room to order. He began by announcing the group's merger with the mainstream underground, just as Witold had urged.[49]

Then Jan turned to Witold. The tension between the two men was palpable.

"A great honor has befallen you," said Jan.[50]

The camp had come up in his discussions with Rowecki, he explained. Rowecki believed that so long as the place remained shrouded in secrecy, the Germans could get away with anything there. He needed someone to infiltrate the camp, gain intelligence, and, if possible, raise a resistance cell and stage a breakout.[51]

"I've mentioned your name to Rowecki as the only officer capable of doing this," said Jan.[52]

Witold struggled to hide his shock. He knew that he was being punished for his refusal to back Jan's ideology, but he wasn't going to give him the satisfaction of a reaction. Jan continued: a police informant had alerted him that the Germans planned a mass roundup in a few days. The SS wanted to send anyone with an education or who appeared to be an intellectual to Auschwitz. Those suspected of resistance work were likely to be shot immediately. Here was a means to get sent to the camp.

But given the risks, Jan couldn't order Witold to take the mission. He needed him to volunteer.[53]

Witold's mind raced. Walking into a German roundup was madness. Even if the Germans didn't shoot him at once, he might still be interrogated and exposed. And what if he made it to Auschwitz? If the camp was as violent as the underground feared, his prospects of forging a resistance group and staging an uprising seemed dim. And if it was just another internment facility, then he might spend months or longer languishing in captivity when the center of action was in Warsaw. He weighed those risks against the fact that he had pushed Jan to accept Rowecki's leadership. How would it look if he balked at the very first request Rowecki gave? He was trapped.[54]

Witold told Jan he needed time to think it over. The days passed as he contemplated the decision. In his later writings Witold makes no mention of fear for his own safety, but he must have worried about his family. Maria had accepted his work for the underground in Warsaw, which allowed him to make occasional visits to Ostrów Mazowiecka and be on hand in case of an emergency. Going to Auschwitz meant abandoning her and potentially exposing the family to German reprisals if discovered.[55]

The roundup began on August 12 as Witold equivocated. SS men and police set up roadblocks on the main roads around the city center and started hauling military-age men off the streets. "Naturally, the action was not conducted particularly gently," noted the diarist Ludwik Landau. "Trams were stopped at bayonet point, with threats to use them if anyone tried to escape; apparently, two people were killed attempting to slip away, one bayoneted, the second shot." More than 1,500 men were arrested over the course of an afternoon. Witold kept his thoughts to himself. "He would sit silently brooding on the subject, and I knew not to ask him about it," recalled Eleonora.[56]

Jan met Witold a few days later with news. Dering and Surmacki were confirmed in Auschwitz. "Oh, you missed a fine opportunity," Jan needled him.[57]

Witold's response is not recorded, but knowing his colleagues were in the camp might have been the decisive factor persuading him to set aside his concerns and accept the mission. He'd been friends with Dering since the Bolshevik campaign, and Surmacki was a neighbor of his from the Lida area.[58]

He was ready to volunteer, he told Jan. A second roundup was scheduled to take place in Żoliborz in a few weeks' time when he planned to be taken. Having made his decision, he now embraced the practicalities of preparing for his impending arrest, handing the management of his men and recruitment role to others. He made a final trip to see Maria and the children, but decided against telling her about his mission. It was better that she be able to claim ignorance if the Gestapo came calling. Maria knew only that he had been selected for an important mission and that Witold had once again chosen his country over his family.[59]

Witold and Marek, c. 1940.

Courtesy of the Pilecki family.

*

On September 18, Witold packed his possessions into a knapsack and headed to Eleonora's apartment. The Germans were likely to raid the block during their sweep of the area the following morning. There was the air of a last supper as he dined with her and his little nephew, Marek. Witold appeared calm as the boy was put to bed in the next room, and he and Eleonora double-checked the apartment to ensure there weren't any incriminating documents on hand.[60]

He went over the plan again with Eleonora. If he made it to the camp, she would be his point of contact with Jan, who would pass

Witold and Eleonora working together, c. 1940.

Courtesy of Marek Ostrowski.

on any intelligence he gathered to the underground leadership. Given the censorship of prisoners' letters, Witold would have to find another means of smuggling her reports. Eleonora would be the first person the Gestapo came calling for if his efforts were discovered. But she knew the risks; if anything, she was even more unflappable than Witold, which must have been reassuring to him as he settled down to sleep on the living room couch. He hoped that the Tomasz Serafiński alias he planned to use would keep his family safe.[61]

Witold woke and dressed before dawn the following morning, September 19. He didn't have to wait long to hear the rumble of the trucks approaching. A few moments later there was a rap at the door. Eleonora, also dressed, opened it. The building caretaker Jan Kiliański stood in the hallway, tense and fearful.[62]

"The Germans are here," he announced. He recognized Witold but wasn't aware of his scheme. "Hide in the basement if you want, or get out through the gardens at the back."[63]

"Thank you, Jan," said Witold. He retreated to the bedroom Eleonora shared with Marek. The boy was standing up in his crib, wide-eyed. They could hear bangs and crashes and the barking of German orders outside now. Marek's favorite teddy bear had fallen to the floor, and Witold stooped to pick it up and hand it to him. The boy was scared, but knew he shouldn't cry. The door to their apartment building crashed open and footsteps rang up the concrete steps, followed by shouts and screams.[64]

Kiliański appeared at the door again. "They're in the building. It's your last chance."

"Thank you, Jan," said Witold again, and the caretaker was gone.

Then there was a thudding at the door and a soldier barged in, brandishing his weapon. "Up, up!" he shouted, but Witold already had his jacket on, and instead of making a run for it, he calmly walked toward the man. Under his breath he whispered to Eleonora: "Report back that the order is done."

Soldiers and plainclothes police crowded the stairwell. They escorted him and other men from the building down to the street. Dawn was breaking, and Witold recognized his gangly neighbor Sławek Szpakowski among the prisoners. There must have been a hundred or more of them by then, some with bags and coats, as if on a business trip, others barefoot and still in their pajamas.[65]

After finishing their searches, the Germans marched them to Wilson Square, half a mile away, where a line of soldiers checked their papers, released those deemed essential workers, factory hands, railway workers, and the like, and ordered the rest into the covered rear of the trucks. Witold joined the others in scrambling aboard as the vehicles' engines rumbled into life.[66]

CHAPTER 3

ARRIVAL

AUSCHWITZ
SEPTEMBER 21, 1940

The trucks stopped outside a horse barracks where Witold was registered in a riding hall, relieved of his valuables, and then ordered to lie
on the hard-packed dirt with a thousand prisoners. Guards held them
in that position for two days, during which time a few were released
or selected for labor in Germany. Then, early on September 21, they
were loaded back onto the trucks and taken to a train station, where
a line of freight cars waited. Witold pressed into one of the carriages
with sixty others. The Germans gave them no food or water, and only a
single slop bucket to relieve themselves in, which soon overflowed onto
the lime-covered floor. The prisoners around Witold shared a vacant
look, and the slow rocking of the train and warm, fetid air sent many
to sleep, slumped against each other on the floor. A few kept watch at
the chinks in the carriage walls, peering through them for a clue as to
their destination.[1]

The train stopped after dark. Somewhere up the track, a freight car
door crashed open and was followed by shouts, screams, and yelping

dogs. Witold felt the crowd shift inside the carriage. The door ripped open and a light stunned the crowd. To shouts of "Out! Out! Out!" the prisoners surged toward the entrance and tumbled forward. Witold struggled to keep his footing in the press of bodies. For a moment he was caught in the doorway by the spotlights, glimpsed the night sky and drizzling rain, and dropped into the crowd. He hit the gravel siding and stumbled as a club whistled past his head. Men with sticks were laying into those who fell and dragging stragglers from the train. Hands clutched at him. He tore himself free and joined the others, half running, half stumbling across a muddy field.[2]

On either side of their ragged column, SS guards smoked and laughed among themselves. They ordered a prisoner to run over to a fence post beside the path. The man, confused, staggered off only for the guards to gun him down. The column came to a halt, and the guards dragged out ten more men from the crowd and shot them, too. Collective responsibility for the "escape," one of the Germans announced. The march resumed; the bodies of the executed men were dragged at the rear of the column by other prisoners as guard dogs snapped at their heels.[3]

Witold was so absorbed by the chaos of the scene that he barely noticed the barbed wire fence looming out of the dark, the gateway, and the iron trellis that crowned the threshold with the words ARBEIT MACHT FREI. *Work Sets You Free.* Beyond the gate were rows of brick barracks, the windows unbarred and dark. They flanked a brightly lit parade ground, where a line of men in striped denims carrying clubs were waiting. They wore blazers with the word KAPO on their arms, and with their rimless hats they looked like sailors. They ordered the prisoners into ranks of ten, relieving them of their watches, rings, and other valuables as they did so.[4]

In front of Witold, a kapo asked one of the prisoners for his profession. A judge, the man replied. The kapo gave a cry of triumph and struck him to the ground with his club. Other striped thugs joined in striking at the man's head, his body, his crotch, until all that was left of the prisoner was a bloody pulp on the floor. The kapo, his uniform splattered in blood, turned to the crowd and declared, "This is Auschwitz Concentration Camp, my dear sirs."[5]

The kapos began singling out doctors, lawyers, professors, and any Jews for beatings. It took a while for Witold to realize they were targeting the educated, but once he did, it made sense given the Germans' stated aim of reducing Poles to mere chattel.[6]

The fallen were dragged to the end of each row, and by the time a strip of metal was beaten to signal roll call, several piles had accrued. SS-Obersturmführer Fritz Seidler, a thirty-three-year-old former builder from outside Leipzig, addressed the newcomers from atop a low wall beside the yard. "Let none of you imagine that he will ever leave this place alive," he declared. "The rations have been calculated so that you will only survive six weeks. Anyone who lives longer must be stealing, and anyone stealing will be sent to the penal company, where you won't live very long."[7]

The speech was followed by more blows as groups of a hundred men were led off to one of the single-story buildings beside the yard. There they stripped, deposited their belongings in sacks beside the entrance, and tossed any food in a wheelbarrow before entering the building one at a time. When Witold's turn came, he found a scrap of bread in his pocket and mindlessly threw it away.[8]

Inside the building, he entered a small, whitewashed room, where naked men queued at a desk to receive their prisoner identification numbers on a small card. Witold's was 4859. In the next room a gang of barbers was bent over a line of low benches shaving the heads, armpits, and genitals of prisoners with blunt blades. Raw patches were hastily swabbed with disinfectant. The washroom followed, where Witold took a blow to the face from a kapo's club because, the man said, he wasn't holding his ID card between his teeth. Witold spat out two molars and a gobful of blood, and continued forward. Jewish prisoners, recognized by their circumcisions, were set upon with a special fury, punched and pummeled into heaps on the slick floor. In the last room, Witold received his blue-and-white prison denim stripes—a jacket that buttoned up to the neck, pants, and a pair of ill-fitting wooden clogs. Some of the prisoners also got a round cap without a bill.[9]

By the time he emerged from the building, the sky had lightened a little to reveal the parade ground, sloping from one side of the barracks to the other, where a giant gray puddle stood in the corner. The buildings along the square were clipped-gabled and mostly plastered in white, although some were stripped to expose the ochre-red bricks beneath. Two sides of the square were open, one to the field over which they must have stumbled, and the other toward a road and a line of trees along what looked like a riverbank. A single strip of barbed wire formed the enclosure, with wooden guard posts every few hundred feet.[10]

The prisoners were lined up once again and assigned a block, which denoted a single floor of each barrack. They were still bullied by the kapos, though in the pale predawn the wild men looked smaller than before. The prisoners hardly recognized one another, stripped and shorn as they were, and dressed in ill-fitting prison stripes or old army uniforms.[11]

Witold's block was 17a on the second floor of a barrack on the square, where they were packed a hundred to each room of three hundred square feet. The block's bare walls, dated tiles, and old-fashioned lights gave it the air of a Victorian reformatory. Witold and the others sewed their numbers onto their shirts, along with a red triangle indicating their status as political prisoners. Exhausted, they finally laid thin jute mattresses on the floor to rest in what was left of the night. Witold shared his with two other men; they spooned each other, using their clogs and striped uniforms for pillows. The window was closed, and the walls were wet with condensation. Men groaned, snored, and cursed at one another as they tried to shift position. Witold's shock had given way to a dull torpor. He had succeeded in getting into the camp. Now his work would have to begin.[12]

*

Witold had barely closed his eyes when a gong sounded, and Alois Staller, the German kapo who ran the block, charged in and laid into anyone not already on their feet. The prisoners hurriedly stacked their mattresses, collected soup tins, and pushed into the corridor while Staller emptied the other rooms. He then rushed them down the stairs, their wooden clogs clattering, to dress outside.[13]

Fog had rolled in from the river, turning the camp into a milky bowl. Witold followed the dark shapes of the others as they scurried around the back of the building to the latrine, an open trench over

The entrance to Witold's block, renumbered as 25a in 1941.

which a beam had been set lengthwise. A queue had already formed, and a kapo counted twenty men onto the post and gave each batch three seconds. Washing was obligatory but the inmates had access to only one cistern on the yard, around which a scrum of men jostled and pushed. Witold struggled to catch a little brackish water in his tin before some unseen signal scattered the crowd like startled birds.[14]

Breakfast was served back in the rooms. One of Staller's helpers dispensed ladles of a bitter-tasting liquid referred to as coffee into their tins from a metal vat. The men gulped it down, stacked their cups, and returned outside, where prisoners from earlier transports, thinner and grayer, clustered around the arrivals for news from the outside. The newcomers asked them about the camp. You'll need to have eyes in the backs of your heads, was all they offered.[15]

In the Night, by Jerzy Potrzebowski, postwar.

Courtesy of PMA-B.

Washing by the Pump, by Jerzy Potrzebowski, postwar.
Courtesy of PMA-B.

Staller swaggered out of the building. He was a former construction worker and Communist from the Rhineland, thirty-five years old, with a long, thin nose and ears that jutted out at odd angles. He had been arrested in 1934 for putting up anti-Nazi posters in his hometown and detained indefinitely in the concentration camp system. "The prisoner's defective character means he must be considered an enemy of the state," the prison director had concluded in a report advising against parole.[16]

Whatever spark of resistance Staller had once shown was gone, and he'd been rewarded for his willingness to serve with a kapo position at Auschwitz. His brother, a soldier, had been killed during the invasion of Poland. He hated Poles with a passion, and blamed them for starting the war. To his face, they were expected to call him "Herr Kapo," doff their caps, and stand to attention, but in the camp he was nicknamed "Bloody Alois."[17]

The daily running of the camp was carried out by kapos like Staller, who received extra food and were excused from hard labor provided they kept the other prisoners in line. The kapo system had been well established in other concentration camps, but Hitler's stated desire to destroy racial enemies had added a murderous intensity to the hard labor and military drills the Auschwitz kapos forced the prisoners to perform. Priests and Jews, a small minority in the camp, were subjected to extra-harsh treatment in a penal company.[18]

The kapos were pressured to constantly prove their ruthlessness. "As soon as we are no longer satisfied with him, he is no longer a kapo and returns to the other inmates," SS chief Heinrich Himmler later explained. "He knows that they will beat him to death his first night back." In Auschwitz, the kapos were German prisoners who had learned the system at the Sachsenhausen concentration camp outside Berlin. They in turn appointed helpers on their blocks, usually Poles from the local area who could speak German.[19]

That first morning, Staller ordered the prisoners into ranks of ten with the tallest men at the end of each row. The older inmates knew the drill and guided newcomers. The prisoners had to call out their position in the rank in German or be beaten.[20]

Staller singled out Witold and a couple of other German speakers and led them inside to the second-floor corridor. They lined up facing the wall, and Staller instructed them to bend over to receive what he called "five of the best." The kapo struck them hard with his cudgel, and Witold had to grit his teeth to avoid crying out. The prisoners apparently met Staller's approval, because he told them they were to be room supervisors and have their own clubs. The beating was "just so

Alois Staller, c. 1941.

Courtesy of PMA-B.

you know what it tastes like and just so you use your clubs like that, ensuring cleanliness and discipline on the block."[21]

Witold rejoined the inmates in the square for the roll call. Prisoners from the other blocks had gathered in rows. The metal strip hanging from a post in the yard was struck, and the first SS men appeared in green field uniforms and calf-high leather boots. The numbers on each block were checked twice and then tallied by a baby-faced German who doubled as the camp executioner, SS-Hauptscharführer Gerhard Palitzsch. Five thousand souls, judging by Witold's registration number, plus the overnight dead who had been stacked at the end of each row. Witold and the others had to stand at attention until the count was done, and then at the command "caps off" remove their berets if they had them and slap them against their thighs. Those without had to mimic the action with their hands. Few managed the drill neatly, and it was repeated until the deputy commandant, SS-Hauptsturmführer Karl Fritzsch, signaled he was content. With a rasping voice he addressed the prisoners.[22]

"Your Poland is dead forever, and now you are going to pay for your crimes through work," he declared. "Look there, at the chimney. Look!" He pointed toward a building hidden by the row of barracks.[23] "This is the crematory. Three thousand degrees of heat. The chimney is your only way to freedom."[24]

After the speech, a group of kapos dragged a prisoner from the crowd and pummeled him until he was bloody and motionless as the tower guards watched with machine guns. "They wanted to break us," recalled a prisoner, Władysław Bartoszewski, "and they achieved their goal because we began to fear."[25]

Drawing of Karl Fritzsch by Wincenty Gawron, c. 1942.

Courtesy of PMA-B.

The gong sounded again, and the prisoners were dismissed. It was a Sunday, a rest day, when prisoners were confined to their blocks in the morning to clean and shave. The new arrivals, however, were kept in the yard in order to practice military drills. Witold, as a room supervisor, was allowed back onto the block, but he surely caught glimpses from the upstairs windows of what transpired outside. Staller, club in hand, was instructing the newcomers how to stand to attention and remove their caps in unison, and he meted out group "sport" for infractions: push-ups, squats, jumps, and any other grueling exercises he could imagine. Kapos from the other blocks did the same with their charges. Soon, the yard was crisscrossed with dozens of prisoners running, hopping, tumbling, and swirling their arms like ballerinas. The kapos chased after flagging prisoners, much to the delight of the SS guards.[26]

Witold felt he had slipped into a waking dream. The world looked the same, but the people in it seemed strange, ghoulish even. He finished tidying the room and explored the block, which consisted of half a dozen rooms off the corridor and Staller's private quarters at the top of the stairs. The prisoners in the other rooms paid him no heed. They were too caught up in their own affairs, squabbling over a couple of needles to repair their dirty clothes or else slumped against the wall. In one room, the block barber was shaving heads and bodies. He charged a scrap of bread in return for using a sharper blade.[27]

Most inmates underwent a personality change upon arriving in Auschwitz. The camp's unremitting violence broke down the bonds between prisoners, forcing them to turn inward for survival. They became "cantankerous, mistrustful and in extreme cases even treacherous," recalled one prisoner. "Since the great majority of the inmates adopt these characteristics, even a placid person must assume an aggressive stance." Some inmates tried to secure protection by organiz-

SS guards in Auschwitz.

Courtesy of Mirosław Ganobis.

ing themselves into small gangs, but that only seemed to escalate the violence. Prisoners frequently denounced each other to the kapos over petty gossip in the hope of a little more food. Most Jews who escaped initial identification in the showers were shopped to the kapos and sent to the penal company.[28]

The camp list of official regulations—and potential violations—was incomprehensibly long, and with the particular prurience that was the hallmark of National Socialism, it covered the most intimate of details. Offenses included: talking at work, smoking, sluggishness, putting one's hand in one's pocket, walking too slowly, running without appropriate athletic pose, standing around, leaning on a freshly painted wall, wearing dirty clothes, imprecisely saluting an SS man, an impudent look, a sloppily made bunk, relieving oneself at the improper time and place. The list went on.[29]

ARRIVAL · 61

The SS punished these offenses with floggings and beatings, which were meant to be cleared up the chain of command and formally administered in the roll call square. But in practice, kapos dealt with infractions on the spot, according to their whim. The sheer volume of potential transgressions meant that at almost any time prisoners were in violation of the rules.[30]

Yet survival of a sort was possible if you kept your head down, which was the only law that truly mattered: don't expose yourself, don't be the first in or the last out, don't be too fast or too slow. Avoid contact with the kapos, but when impossible, be submissive, helpful, nice to them. "Don't ever let them see what you know, because you know that they are shit," one prisoner wrote after the war. "And if you're in for a beating, always fall down on the first punch."[31]

There was only one rule between inmates—don't steal another man's food. But that didn't stop prisoners from devising a thousand schemes to winkle a little more sustenance from their fellow inmates. Food was the coin of the camp: a spare button, a sliver of soap, a needle and thread, paper for writing, a packet of cigarettes were worth a portion of bread or more. New arrivals were exploited before they were hungry enough to understand the value of a meal.[32]

The first few days were the hardest for newcomers, before they got their "camp skin." Inmates who couldn't accept the camp's subverted moral order were quickly finished off, like the prisoner who complained to an SS man about the violence of the kapos and was promptly beaten to death. Others lost the will to live and were preyed on by others. Some became twisted like the kapos. Most adapted as best they could by narrowing their focus to the pursuit of food, safety, and shelter.[33]

Witold picked up the rules and wondered how he was going to connect with prisoners or inspire them to join a resistance cell in such a desperate environment. He already felt a few pangs of hunger and was regretting tossing away his crust of bread when the gong for lunch sounded. As a room supervisor, his task was to fetch and distribute soup, which came in fifty-liter kettles from the open-air kitchen on the other side of the square. He hurried across the parade ground with the other supervisors. One of them, Karol Świętorzecki, came from the same part of the Kresy as Witold, and they exchanged a few details before catching themselves.[34]

Witold and Karol struggled back to the room with the pots as the prisoners assembled for a noon roll call, which was over quickly. The thin barley and potato soup was served in the rooms, although the prisoners were required to eat outside. The old-timers, so lethargic in the morning, jostled around the kettle as they tried to be served first. Supervisors frequently had to use their wooden ladles to smack hands and heads.[35]

The newcomers, sweaty and covered in dust from five hours in the square, looked disbelievingly at their paltry tinfuls. Old hands finished their portions quickly and got back in line again to beg and cajole for more. Witold recognized his power as he doled out portions and every eye was turned on him.[36]

*

As it was Sunday, prisoners were allowed to leave their blocks in the afternoon and wander where they liked. Many stayed out of trouble in their rooms or went to check on friends in other buildings; others gathered around dark entranceways or in the center of the square, knowing that to approach the fence was to risk being shot. This was Witold's chance to look for Dering and Surmacki, who, he was coming to realize, might already be dead.

The fog had dispersed and the parade ground shone in the thin autumn light. Around its edges, a track for training horses was still visible. The entire camp was no more than two acres, and a short walk in any direction led to the barbed wire fence. The camp's twenty buildings were arranged along streets that led off the main square. A single-story block opposite the barracks where they'd been shaved the night before contained the camp hospital, which was little more than a few rooms set aside to house prisoners too sick to work. There was no medicine for treatment, but the SS needed to keep an appearance of adequate prisoner care. German internment facilities for foreign nationals were meant to be open for inspections by the International Red Cross, and though the SS rarely gave outsiders access to its camps, it liked to maintain the fiction that all was aboveboard.[37]

Witold had a hunch he'd find Dering at the hospital but didn't know how to gain admittance, so he scoped out the rest of the camp. In the far corner of the camp was the block reserved for the penal unit of priests and Jews. In the opposite corner beside the small open-air kitchen was a small shed that belonged to a carpentry unit. The camp's registration office containing prisoner records stood next to the main gate and the guardhouse.[38]

To one side of a throng of internees, Witold spotted a handsome man sitting on a pile of stones. He wore his own dirty dress shoes—the SS had run out of clogs—as if he'd been nabbed at a dinner party. His striped shirt was rolled up his back, and another inmate was examining his bruises.

"Those bloody kapos know nothing about military drill," the man on the rock complained bitterly. "If they'd only let me take charge, I could have the whole block marching like it was on parade—and without hitting anyone!"[39]

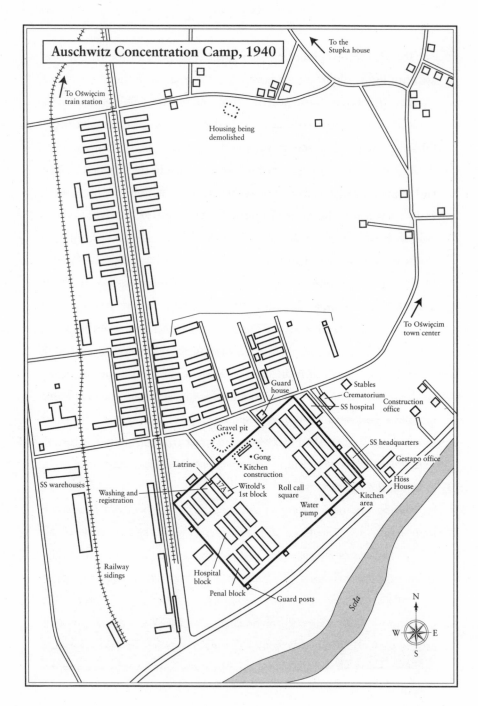

Auschwitz Concentration Camp, 1940

To the
Stupka house

To Oświęcim
train station

Housing being
demolished

To Oświęcim
town center

Stables
Crematorium
SS hospital
Construction
office

Guard
house

Gravel pit

SS headquarters
Gestapo office

Gong
Kitchen
construction

Höss
House

Latrine

Witold's
1st block

Roll call
square

Kitchen
area

SS warehouses

Washing and
registration

Water
pump

Hospital
block

Penal block

Guard posts

Railway
sidings

Soła

N
W E
S

John Gilkes

The idea was so preposterous that his colleague, a thin, scrawny lad with an impish look, couldn't restrain himself. "Where do you think you are? In the military academy drilling cadets? Look at yourself—you look more like a bum or a convict than an officer. We must forget what we were and do the best with what is left of us."[40]

Witold approached and asked if they were officers. The impish one introduced himself as Konstanty Piekarski and he went by Kon or Kot, Polish for "cat." The bruised man was Mieczysław Lebisz, and they were lieutenants in the horse artillery who'd arrived with Witold the night before. Mieczysław had received some of his bruising from a beating in the washroom after objecting to the kapos about the treatment of a Jewish prisoner.

The three of them exchanged details. Kon did most of the talking, even sharing his triumphs over the cavalry at horse jumping, which made Witold smile. Witold was about to break away when the kapo who ran Kon's block, a heavyset German, lumbered into view. He wanted volunteers, and when none were forthcoming, he pointed at ten men, Kon and Witold included, to follow him into his block to

Kon Piekarski, c. 1941.

Courtesy of PMA-B.

stuff mattresses with wood chippings. It was an easy enough task, and certainly an improvement on afternoon drill for Kon. From the square they could hear the sounds of beatings, and then, for a time, desultory singing.[41]

As they worked, Witold gently questioned the younger man about his career. "He spoke very softly, without authority," recalled Kon, "a man who preferred to listen rather than express opinions." He didn't realize that Witold was testing him out as a potential recruit.[42]

There was a final roll call before supper, where sick prisoners seeking to gain admission to the hospital were obliged to strip naked and parade before Deputy Commandant Fritzsch. Most were dispatched back to the ranks with a blow or two; only those with broken limbs or severe exhaustion were sent to the hospital. Witold thought again of Dering and must have wondered how to get inside the building without subjecting himself to an examination. The day's dead were stacked, counted, and carried to the crematorium.[43]

After roll call, the prisoners returned to their rooms for supper. Each block had a small quota of loaves that came from a bakery outside the camp. Witold's job was to divide the dark, heavy bread into half-pound portions, which he served with a strip of pork fat and a cup of the bilge-water coffee. The older prisoners advised newcomers to save some of their bread for breakfast, but most were too hungry to resist.[44]

After supper, Staller's assistant, Kazik, instructed them in the camp song, the jaunty strains of which Witold had heard that afternoon. The kapo was very musical, Kazik explained, and would be disappointed with a lackluster performance. In a reedy, plaintive voice that would have been ridiculous in other circumstances, Kazik launched into the opening line, adapted from a military song: "I am in the Auschwitz camp, for a day, a month, a year / But I'm happy and I gladly think about my loved ones far away." For the rest of the evening they practiced, with Staller occasionally looming in the doorway, leaning forward to listen with his hands clasped behind his back, as if enjoying himself.[45]

At last the lights-out gong sounded, the mattresses were placed on the floor, and each prisoner lay down so that Witold could count them and report to Staller. The kapo then walked the line of men, occasionally ordering an inmate to show him a foot to check if it was clean. Offenders were given a few blows on the buttocks, until at last Staller, breath rasping, turned the lights out. After a day in the camp, Witold was beginning to realize that the idea of staging a breakout was naïve. He needed to alert Warsaw to conditions in the camp and felt instinctively that others would react with the same horror he had. If Rowecki informed the British, he was sure they would retaliate. But whom could he trust to help him get a message beyond the camp walls? He hoped Dering would have some answers—if he could just find him.[46]

CHAPTER 4

SURVIVORS

AUSCHWITZ

SEPTEMBER 23, 1940

The next morning after roll call, Witold made his way to the hospital block to look for Dering. The kapos were calling out for the prisoners to form squads for work outside the camp. The newcomers milled around in confusion at the gate as a foreman screamed at them that he'd have them all flogged. Witold was surprised to see the man, a Pole, turn away from the SS guards and give the prisoners a knowing wink.[1]

Witold joined a line of stricken prisoners outside the single-story hospital barrack waiting to be inspected. The morning procedure was different from the evening one; there was no ritual in front of the other prisoners, but those rejected were deemed to be dodging work and sent to the square for sport. Dozens still queued each morning. The German kapo Hans Bock, who oversaw admissions, stood on the hospital steps in a white gown with a wooden stethoscope in hand. He had no medical training and was known to offer young inmates hospital jobs in return for sexual favors.[2]

Witold managed an excuse to get past Bock and enter the building to discover a long corridor where prisoners stood naked for further inspection. Others were being doused with icy water in a washroom. Most of the remaining rooms were wards where the sick lay in tightly packed rows on the floor. The block reeked of rot and excrement.[3]

Witold found Dering on one of the wards. He was pasty and gaunt—scarcely recognizable—and seemed to have difficulty standing on his oddly swollen legs. They likely retreated to a nurses' room at the back of the block to talk. Dering had been initially assigned to the road-building squad, one of the most brutal assignments available. After a few days he was dragged semiconscious and feverish to the hospital. Bock had rejected him at first, but Dering had been lucky. A Warsaw colleague, Marian Dipont, who already worked in the hospital, spotted Dering doing punishment drills in the square and persuaded Bock to change his mind. Dering had recovered and eventually gained a job on the wards as a nurse.[4]

Dering agreed with Witold's assessment that a breakout was inconceivable. Only a single prisoner had succeeded in escaping by making a dash under the barbed wire. The SS had responded with a brutal twenty-hour roll call. Dering also warned Witold that he'd yet to experience the camp's real killer. The kapos' clubs were one thing. They could be avoided with sense and a little luck. The real danger, he explained, was hunger. SS-Obersturmführer Seidler, who had addressed them that first night, had been only slightly exaggerating when he'd told them they had six weeks to live. Prisoners were assigned a daily ration of around 1,800 calories, two-thirds what a man performing hard labor needed. Given the fact that the kapos pilfered supplies and inmates stole from one another, most inmates were on a rapid starvation diet of less than a thousand calories (the SS later came up with a sim-

ple formula for calculating survival time: Life expectancy in months =
5,000/Deficit of Calories).[5]

The camp had already developed nicknames for those on the edge
of starvation: cripples, derelicts, jewels, but the most common was
"Muselmänner," or "Muslims," seemingly in reference to how they
rocked back and forth in their weakness as if in prayer. Witold had
probably already seen some around the camp. The fat from their cheeks
had been consumed, giving their skulls a bulbous appearance, far too
large for their scrawny frames and distended limbs. They usually loi-
tered around the kitchens looking for scraps to eat, and were easy prey
for the kapos, who singled them out for abuse.[6]

Hunger, in Dering's telling, was more than a mortal threat: it
formed the corrosive underpinnings of the kapo system. Prisoners
would shop their fellows to the SS for a scrap of bread. The camp had a
small Gestapo office—officially known as the Political Department—
beside the camp entrance, where a line of inmates queued most mornings and evenings. The rest of the prisoners avoided these informers,
but there was no telling who might reach their breaking point. Somehow, Witold realized he had to forge an underground capable of with-
standing the crushing pressure of starvation.[7]

One way was to ensure food was more evenly distributed. Witold
thought he could persuade some of the room supervisors to do so by
appealing to their faith and patriotism, but that wouldn't be enough to
sway most. To compete with the kapos, Witold needed to offer food and
safety. Dering informed him that procuring extra provisions might be
possible. Their colleague from Warsaw, Władysław Surmacki, was still
alive and worked in the SS construction office with a team of inmate
surveyors on building projects around the camp. Surmacki had made
contact with a local family near the train station who gave him supplies

Evening Market, by Jerzy Potrzebowski, postwar.

Courtesy of PMA-B.

to bring into the camp under his stripes. It was a first contact with the outside that opened up the possibility of not only extra food but of sending intelligence to Rowecki in Warsaw.[8]

Witold parted from Dering and slipped back to his block. That evening the newcomers assembled early for roll call—they were getting better at following orders—and watched as the other work squads returned. Columns of broken men dragged the fallen between them or pushed the dead in wheelbarrows, their limbs knocking against the sides, to be dumped in the square and counted.[9]

Witold's block was lined up opposite the priests and Jews of the penal company who did the hardest work of all in the gravel pits. The Jews were distinguished by a yellow star on their dusty uniforms. Their

Ernst Krankemann, c. 1941.

Courtesy of PMA-B.

kapo was an obese former barber from Berlin called Ernst Krankemann, who had been committed to a mental asylum before the war
and earmarked for the Nazi sterilization program only to wind up in
Auschwitz. Even the other kapos were scared of him. "He was a repulsive, horrible toad," one prisoner wrote later. "A giant chunk of meat
and fat, endowed with unusual strength."[10]

Krankemann was carrying a knife up his sleeve, and Witold watched
him move down a row stabbing those he determined to be out of line.
He singled out one man and pummeled him to death. Witold had already witnessed a dozen murders by then, but this one seemed to jolt
him out of his ongoing torpor. Looking down the line of inmates, he
was sure they felt it too, a white-hot rage that cut through their collective fear and apathy. For the first time since arriving, Witold thought
he might succeed in rallying a force capable of fighting back against the
kapos. If he could get enough men, he could start leaning on the other
prisoners to stop denouncing one another and aid the weakest.[11]

*

The euphoria was brief. Witold's attempts over the next few days to bring a spirit of collectivity to his room did not find favor with Staller. The kapo seemed to instinctively understand that Witold's ability to keep his room orderly without brute force was a challenge to the camp's ethos. He warned Witold to use more violent methods, and then one morning the German finally exploded and kicked him off the block for three days to find work in the camp.

"Just so you see what it tastes like," said Staller, "and get to appreciate better the comfort and peace you have here on the block."[12]

The old hands knew how to land a good squad in the melee after roll call, but Witold hadn't learned the trick and was assigned to the gravel pits. The camp sat on an old riverbed, so there was plenty of loose stone, and a pit near the main gate. One group of inmates shoveled the wheelbarrows high with gravel, while another pushed them up a gangplank to a well-beaten track along the camp fence. There were kapos every dozen yards toting clubs.[13]

Witold was assigned to the second group. The laden barrow was heavy, and Witold struggled to keep his balance as the dark sky began to drizzle. He and the others had to run with their loads, and the track along the camp fence was muddy and treacherous. Rounding the corner, he finally saw what the stones were for: thrusting out of the ground was the single dark column of the crematorium, wreathed in smoke like a shroud. Witold had glimpsed it before beyond the gate, but this was the first time he'd been so close, and the smoke clung to his nostrils with the horrifyingly sweet smell of cooked meat.[14]

The facility had been in service for only a month, but already the camp administration was worried about whether it could meet their needs "even at a rather good time of year." The low building beside the chimney contained a double-muffle, coke-fired oven capable of incin-

Crematorium oven.

Courtesy of PMA-B.

erating seventy corpses in twenty-four hours. The SS had put in an order for another oven, and also wanted to increase the burn rate of the existing furnace by insulating the building's wall with a sloping rampart that Witold was now helping to construct.[15]

After an hour or two running with stacked barrows, Witold was shattered. He stole breaks when he could, but the kapos beat those they spotted dawdling. Longer breaks came when the kapos decided to finish someone off for dropping or overturning their loads. At that point, the column halted and Witold drew in gulps of air and tried to slow his racing heart. After a while, he inadvertently started picking out those most likely to fail next—"some lawyer with a tummy . . . a teacher with glasses . . . an older gentleman"—to predict how long it would be for his next break.[16]

By the end of the day he could hardly walk. Evening roll call was interminable in the rain, and it took all his willpower to save some bread for the morning. He awoke hungry and aching and put on his sodden clothes. By the third day, he was weakening rapidly, and he knew it wouldn't be long before the kapos set upon him.[17]

That lunchtime, Staller announced he could come back onto the block.

"Now you know what work in the camp means," Staller told him. "Take care with your work on the block, or I'll kick you back out into the camp for good."[18]

But Witold wasn't about to make a show for the German. One morning after roll call, he went to report to Staller that there were three sick men on the block who couldn't go to work. Staller flew into one of his rages. He clearly thought Witold should have given the men a thrashing.

"A sick man on my block?! . . . I don't have sick men! . . . Everyone works . . . you too! Enough!" Staller shouted.[19]

He charged into the room. Two of the men were lying along the wall, panting heavily. A third was kneeling in the corner.

The kapo pointed at him. "What's he doing?"

"He's praying," replied Witold.

"He's praying?" said Staller incredulously. "Who taught him to do that?"[20]

Staller started screaming that the man was an idiot, there was no God, that it was he, not God, who gave him bread. But he didn't touch him. Instead he saved his rage for the other two, beating them until they managed to drag themselves to their feet.

"See!" cried Staller. "I told you they weren't sick! They walk, they can work! Get out! Off to work! And you too!"[21]

And with that, he cast Witold off the block for good. He had put his mission in danger, but how could he expect to lead others in the camp if he allowed himself to be compromised? The squads had already left for the day, so Witold joined the rejected invalids from the hospital for punishment drills in the square. They stood at attention and waited for the kapos to appear. After two days of rain, it was cold. Some of the prisoners didn't have caps, or socks, or even shoes, and they could feel the damp of the river through their denims. They stood and shivered, and their hands and lips turned blue, but they didn't move. Staller appeared at one point. He had, apparently, taken the praying inmate to the hospital for treatment—he was a strange man, this kapo. When Staller saw Witold he stopped and guffawed.[22]

"Life's just seeping away," he said, and he held out his hand and twinkled his fingers, imitating rainfall.[23]

After a few hours, the sun shone through the mist, and a pack of functionaries arrived to start the training. A kapo named Leo Wietschorek usually ran the sessions, a pasty forty-year-old with pencil-thin eyebrows and languid brown eyes. Wietschorek liked to play the mouth organ on the steps of his block after a particularly murderous session. He ordered the prisoners to form a circle and issued the first

Leo Wietschorek, c. 1941.

Courtesy of PMA-B.

order: hop, hop, hop like a frog. Witold immediately discovered that was impossible with his ill-fitting clogs. The alternative was to hold his shoes in his hands, which exposed his undersoles to the rough gravel of the square, but he did it anyway. His feet were soon lacerated and bleeding, and each hop tore them further. The only moment of rest came when someone fell and Wietschorek or one of the other kapos finished him off. The kapos usually joked as they beat a man to death, and mocked the sounds of his death rattle.[24]

Witold was suddenly cast back to a scene from his childhood in Sukurcze. A group of farmhands was torturing some animal they'd caught. It was dying and screaming in fear, but they were laughing. He'd been terrified by the cruelty but had dismissed the incident and

The Regular Roadroller Squad, by Jan Komski, postwar.
Courtesy of PMA-B.

grown up believing in people's intrinsic goodness. Only now he remembered that dead animal and realized how naïve he'd been. His childhood self had seen man for what he really was, carnal and vicious.[25]

In the afternoon, the penal company joined Witold and the others. The camp had a giant roller used for road construction that was meant to be pulled by four pairs of horses. Fifty Jewish prisoners had been harnessed to the draw bar. A second, smaller roller was pulled by twenty priests. Riding triumphantly atop the former was the quivering mass of Krankemann. He held his club aloft like a scepter and then intermittently brought it crashing down on some inmate's head. Back and forth he rode across the square, and if someone fell from his blows or exhaustion, he insisted on continuing over them. The savage exercise didn't stop until evening roll call, when Krankemann dismounted to inspect the flattened bodies and the day's survivors were dismissed.[26]

*

By the third morning of sport, Witold thought he wouldn't survive the day. He was standing with the others in the circle, his back to the gate.

Otto Küsel, c. 1941.

Courtesy of PMA-B.

The squads were marching off to work; Deputy Commandant Fritzsch was checking off numbers; the punishment was about to begin. Some instinct made Witold look over his shoulder to see the kapo in charge of squad assignments running toward them. His name was Otto Küsel, a thirty-one-year-old drifter and petty thief from Berlin. Witold was so desperate he stepped forward to meet him.[27]

"You're not by any chance a stove fitter?" Otto asked.[28]

"Yes, sir. I'm a stove fitter," Witold lied.[29]

"But are you a good one?"

"Of course I'm a good one."

Otto told him to pick four others and follow him.

He dashed off to a work shed near the gate. Grabbing the nearest men, Witold chased after him to receive buckets, trowels, brick hammers, and lime. Otto must have forgotten to form a work squad—hence his haste and readiness to believe Witold. The team lined up at the gate in time to be presented to Fritzsch and assigned two guards.[30]

Scarcely believing his luck, Witold found himself marching through open country toward the train station. Mist still clung to the scattered farmhouses and untilled fields beside the road. The SS had claimed the territory around the camp for their own purposes and were clearing out the locals: the better homes near the station and along the river were appropriated for the families of SS officers; the rest were demolished and the raw materials used for other building projects.[31]

The old town of Oświęcim occupied a low bluff on the opposite bank of the Soła about a mile from the camp. Its skyline was dominated by a fourteenth-century castle used by the Haberfeld family, a major vodka and liqueur producer, to store their renowned schnapps and flavored spirits. While the surrounding countryside was mostly Polish, half the town was Jewish. On the so-called Jews' Street, there were half a dozen synagogues, cheders, and yeshivas. The river itself became a mikvah, or ritual bath, on summer evenings, when hundreds of Jewish men in black gabardines and white stockings would converge on its sandy bank. Unsurprisingly, the Germans were disgusted by these residents and the conditions of the town, which gave "an impression of extreme filth and squalor." The SS had already burned down the Great Synagogue, one of the town's largest buildings, and had plans to deport the Jewish population to a nearby ghetto.[32]

Witold's detail was brought to a townhouse and introduced to an SS officer. His wife was coming, the officer explained, and he wanted to renovate the kitchen. Could they move the ceramic tiles to a different wall, and the stove to a different room? The officer was civil, almost normal. He didn't need five workers for the task, he said, as if embarrassed, but he didn't mind if some of them just tidied the attic, provided the work was done well. And with that, he left.[33]

Postcard of Oświęcim, c. 1930s.

Courtesy of Mirosław Ganobis.

As the two guards stayed outside, the prisoners were left to their own devices. Witold turned to the others to check whether any of them knew a thing about stoves, which, of course, they didn't, so he set them to work removing the tiles while he focused on dismantling the range and the flues. How hard could it be? His life might depend on the work, but at least there was no immediate threat of a beating. From one of the windows he could see backyards and lines of laundry. He heard children playing nearby and church bells ringing.[34]

Suddenly, he felt he might cry at the sharp reminder that life continued, indifferent to their suffering. Knowing that he'd left his own family in relative safety in Ostrów Mazowiecka was no comfort now that he knew this abhorrent world existed and that at any moment Maria might be caught in some roundup and brought to Auschwitz or a place like it. Then he thought of the SS man whose flat they were renovating, how he talked excitedly about his wife's arrival, no doubt imagining her joy when she saw the new kitchen. Outside the camp this SS officer appeared to be a respectable man, but once he crossed its threshold he was a sadistic murderer. The fact that he could inhabit both worlds at once seemed most monstrous of all.[35]

The rage that coursed through Witold now was a desire for revenge. It was time to start recruiting.

CHAPTER 5

RESISTANCE

AUSCHWITZ
OCTOBER 1940

Witold worked on the stove for several days, figuring things out as he went, painstakingly removing each valve and duct and memorizing its position. He knew that if he made a mistake his lie would swiftly be revealed, but in his weakened state he couldn't be sure he'd gotten it right. The evening before the stove was due to be tested, Witold turned in desperation to the winking foreman at the gate for help. His instincts proved correct. The foreman was a Polish army captain named Michał Romanowicz, who offered to slip him into another work detail. Witold decided right then to trust Michał with his true mission, and the foreman agreed without hesitation to swear an oath to serve Poland and the underground. The next morning, instead of reporting to the stove fitters, Witold marched out the gate with another squad. He heard the kapos calling his number and searching for him among the melee of prisoners, but he didn't look back.[1]

His new squad was laying out a garden for a villa near the crematorium, which Witold soon learned belonged to the camp commandant,

Rudolf Höss. The Nazi leadership had started to develop plans for the ultimate colonization of the rest of Eastern Europe, which called for the enslavement or expulsion of its Slavic population, and Auschwitz was a test case for future colonial rule. Like many senior Nazis, Höss saw himself as a farmer reluctantly called to duty and was devising a plan that autumn to turn Auschwitz into a vast agricultural estate powered by inmate labor. "The possibilities which existed here had never been possible in Germany itself," he wrote from a Polish prison cell after the war. "Certainly there were enough workers available. Every necessary agricultural experiment was to be tried out there."[2]

Witold's squad worked to level the land and raise beds according to the commandant's design. It rained hard that day, and the next. At one point, a passing kapo ordered them to work without shirts; when the rain eased they "steamed like horses after a run," recalled Witold. The men worked to keep warm, hauling earth for the beds and crushed brick for the paths in between. There was no chance to dry off, and it rained through evening roll call, so the whole camp went to bed with wet clothes.[3]

At the end of a second day in the garden, Michał again came to his rescue. When they met in the square after roll call, Michał explained that his performances at the gate had earned him a promotion. He would now be taking charge of a twenty-man detail to unload trains bearing supplies to the camp's warehouses. He could handpick the squad himself. It was a prime opportunity to convene and assess underground recruits. Michał had some names in mind; Witold suggested his mattress-mate, Sławek, with whom he'd been arrested in Warsaw.[4]

The warehouses had a reputation for finishing off prisoners, but Michał had no intention of actually working there. The next morning, he marched his squad over to the warehouses and simply informed the kapos at the site that his detail had orders to demolish one of the farmhouses in the fields opposite. It sounded plausible enough given the SS clearance operation around the camp, and he was waved away.[5]

The farmhouse he selected was on the grounds of a manor that had already been reduced to a shell, its gardens churned to mud by the feet of inmates as they dragged out the building's innards—furniture, door frames, and windowsills—and tossed them onto a bonfire in the fore-court. Others loaded rubble from already demolished walls into wheel-barrows they pushed through the mud to a road being constructed nearby. Where the manor's orchard had once stood was a tangle of broken limbs, mottled-gray apple trees, and a shattered pear tree that flashed its brilliant orange heartwood.[6]

Michał set a watch and made sure two stretchers were loaded with debris, ready to be carried outside if a kapo approached. The team worked on the house as slowly as they could, just enough to stay warm, and making sure to keep the roof intact until the inside was gutted. Witold and Michał had time to discuss the creation of the first cell. Witold knew he would have to weigh carefully who to trust. He had come to realize that a decent operative in Warsaw or a decorated officer might become a Gestapo informant as readily as anyone else. The camp had a way of stripping away pretensions to reveal a man's true per-sonality. "Some—slithered into a moral swamp," Witold wrote later. "Others—chiseled themselves a character of finest crystal."[7]

Witold would need to home in on little signs of altruistic behav-ior among the more reserved and quiet prisoners—the sharing of a piece of bread or the nursing of a sick friend—and then proceed to gently probe their motivations. He would explain to those selected that they'd been chosen for their selflessness. His recruits were not to ask for seconds "even if [their] guts were screaming," Witold insisted, while room supervisors had a duty to divide food evenly and give to the weakest first. Such exacting standards weren't always kept, but to break the power of the kapos they needed to prove that goodness could endure.[8]

He also drew some harsh conclusions: not everyone could be saved, either physically or spiritually. Some prisoners seemed to embrace the camp's hierarchy and competed with one another to earn the kapos' admiration; others gave up almost at once and refused to be rallied. Then there were those like the priests and Jews kept apart in the penal block, and thus unreachable.[9]

Witold began by tracking down two more of his former War-saw colleagues, Jerzy de Virion and Roman Zagner, whom he knew he could trust. At Dering's suggestion, he also vetted an exuberant twenty-year-old named Eugeniusz Obojski—Gienek for short—who worked in the hospital morgue. Together with Dering and Władysław Surmacki, they formed what Witold called a "five." Using the same underground principles he'd employed in Warsaw, the men would know each other but no one in the subsequent cells that Witold created. Dering would be in charge of the hospital; Surmacki, outside relations; while Witold was recruiter in chief.[10]

He tried to select men in each work squad to broaden the reach of the organization. The evenings between roll call and the curfew were the best time to operate. The SS guards withdrew to the guard tow-ers, leaving the kapos in charge, and the prisoners were free to move around the camp. Some liked to visit friends in neighboring blocks, to gossip or swap stories, but it was dangerous to linger in the blocks and risk running into a kapo or being overheard.[11]

Witold preferred to walk the strip between the barracks and the fence closest to the river, which had become the camp's unofficial promenade. The water wasn't visible from behind the fence and con-crete wall, but he could see the old willows along its banks. The main road to town also ran past that side, and though the traffic was mostly military, it seemed to connect them to life beyond. On clear, warmer nights the strip was crowded. A black market usually sprang up at one end, where prisoners bartered; a stick of margarine stolen from the kitchen bought a cigarette and a loaf of bread could get almost anything, although prisoners had to be careful it hadn't been hollowed out and filled with sawdust.[12]

Witold would lead a potential recruit out of earshot of the gaggle of prisoners and quietly tell him he'd been selected for the resistance. Most accepted immediately, but a few were reticent, like Kon, his acquaintance from the first day. He'd lost his pluckiness and was covered in welts and bruises after two weeks spent unloading freight trains at the warehouses. There the head kapo was a one-armed predator called Siegruth, who claimed he was a baron from a German area of Latvia

Area used for prisoner promenade.

Courtesy of PMA-B.

who had been convicted of silk smuggling, although the story kept changing. He liked to fell prisoners with a single blow of his good arm, and then stamp and kick them.[13]

Witold took Kon to one side. "What I have to say to you, Kon, is in great confidence," he told him. "You must swear on your officer's honor that you won't mention it to anyone without my consent."[14]

"If it is such an important secret you have my word," said Kon cautiously.[15]

He explained his real name was Witold Pilecki.

"If that's your secret," Kon said, laughing, "then perhaps I should tell you I'm really twenty-four, one year older than the Germans think I am. I've given my new birthday a date I won't forget—the third of May, Polish Constitution Day. What's more, I'm an engineering student who's supposedly never been in the army."

"Don't interrupt," said Witold sternly. He then explained how he'd voluntarily come to Auschwitz.

"You must be nuts!" cried the younger man, but he was clearly impressed. "Who in his right mind would do such a thing? How did you do it? Don't tell me you asked the Gestapo if they'd be so kind as to send you to Auschwitz for a couple of years?"

"Please don't joke," Witold replied. He explained that the underground considered Auschwitz to be the center of the German effort to crush the resistance and that the camp would continue to expand. It was vital for an underground cell to function there.[16]

"If what you say is true," Kon replied, "you're either the greatest hero or the biggest fool."

Kon looked like he thought the second option more likely. He told Witold bitterly that he'd been caught because of the stupidity of a senior officer in the Warsaw underground, who'd been arrested with a list of names on him. He doubted Witold's ability to rally an underground force and wasn't sold on what a camp underground could achieve given the risks that surrounded them.

Witold explained that they were starting small. "The first and most immediate purpose is to help the weaker among us survive the camp," he explained.

Kon looked startled at the suggestion that anyone might survive. He had accepted the German promise that his death was inevitable. Now, suddenly, he wasn't so sure.

At last he said: "I may be as nutty as you are, but let's give it a try."

Witold hugged him impulsively. "We'll call on you," he said.

*

The first snow of 1940 fell in fat, wet flakes that lingered on the skin as the men stripped the roof from the farmhouse that October. Witold worked with his back to the icy gusts that came howling off the Tatra Mountains in the distance. His thoughts turned to the question of how to send a report to Warsaw that would provoke an international outcry.[17]

The family that Surmacki had befriended, the Stupkas, lived near the railway station, and whenever the surveyors approached, the mother, Helena, a vivacious forty-two-year-old with a boyish bob and bright red lipstick, hailed the guards with vodka and food. While they drank in her upstairs apartment, the surveyors visited the ground-floor toilet where Helena usually stashed some food or medicine. She also passed on news of the war. Witold was relieved to learn that England still stood and made sure his recruits spread the word to boost morale after roll call. But when it came to sending a report to Warsaw, Helena couldn't help: she had no links to the capital or any fake papers that would allow her to travel.[18]

Witold sent two coded messages to his sister-in-law Eleonora via the camp mail office. The authorities insisted prisoners write home twice a month in German that they were fine and doing well. Mail room censors ensured compliance. "Auntie feels good, she is healthy and she greets everybody." And then a short while later, "Auntie plants trees that grow really well." Even that level of contact with Eleonora felt dangerous, so he resolved that these would be his only letters. Witold needed to identify an alternative method of reaching Warsaw.[19]

In the meantime, the camp was expanding fast, with transports bringing in hundreds of prisoners each week. The rooms were packed, and work had begun adding stories to existing blocks and digging foundations in one corner of the roll call square for new barracks. It was painful to watch the arrivals being broken in. "Remember, do not

Helena Stupka and her husband, Jan, c. 1935.

Courtesy of the Stupka family.

try to comfort them," the old hands advised. "For then they will die. Our task is to try and help them adapt." Others were less forgiving. "It was easy to forget that a newcomer had not yet developed . . . a protective skin," another prisoner recalled. "Such a person's bewilderment, emotional outbursts, and dismay frequently inspired mockery and contempt."[20]

The newcomers also reminded veterans like Witold of what they were becoming. As Dering had predicted, the prisoners who'd arrived with Witold had started to starve, and fear hung over every block. The crowds of so-called Muselmänner lingering outside the kitchen after work had grown to hundreds. Witold felt his own body changing. In the mornings, he woke to gnawing pangs of hunger and odd chills in his feet. His joints ached and his skin scaled off in yellow flakes. He shivered incessantly and found it increasingly hard to focus on resistance matters. He and Sławek talked compulsively about food instead, savoring the words as if they had flavor. Witold's favorite treat in Sukurcze had been young cucumbers from the garden dipped in the amber honey from his clover fields. Sławek dreamed of a plate piled high with potato blinis, fried in butter until toasted at the edges and topped in pungent sour cream, which he promised to cook for Witold when they got out. In the meantime, they scavenged for a few rock-hard mangel-wurzels that the farmer had grown for the animals. They gnawed on them raw, but the roots did nothing to satisfy their hunger.[21]

They finished demolishing the farmhouse around mid-October, hacking into the frozen earth to remove its foundations until only a broken field remained. Someone had saved a gold-framed picture of the Madonna from the wreckage of the farmhouse and hung it on a nearby bush. In the cold weather, the moisture on the glass pane had frozen into a delicate filigree across the face that obscured everything

Queuing at the Barrel for Food, by Jan Komski, postwar.

Courtesy of PMA-B.

but the eyes. Those eyes reminded Witold of his wife, Maria, a fact he registered without emotion; all he felt was a vast emptiness.[22]

*

Michał announced that he had figured out how to send a report to Warsaw as they started work tearing down the next house. The camp authorities occasionally set prisoners free, after families paid a hefty bribe or pulled the right strings in Warsaw. The Germans swore them to complete secrecy about what they had witnessed in Auschwitz on pain of return. In most cases, that was enough to ensure compliance.[23]

But Michał knew a young officer, Aleksander Wielopolski, who was due to be released and might carry a message. The thirty-year-old Aleksander, a chemist by training, had fought in the underground with a quixotic group of noblemen known as the Musketeers, who had concocted several schemes to attack the Germans with biological weapons. The SS remained sensitive to the charge that they were abusing prisoners, so Aleksander had been placed in a quarantine block, exempted from work, and was generally well fed. Michał knew the kapo of the block and was confident he could get into the building to deliver a report. It was too dangerous for Aleksander to carry a written document, so instead they'd need to prepare an oral message for him to memorize.[24]

The prospect of contacting his underground colleagues in Warsaw gave Witold a jolt of energy. He'd compiled a mental list of the crimes he witnessed, although the details still seemed inadequate to describe the enormity of the Nazis' brutality. He needed facts, but the crucial statistic—the death toll—was a closely guarded secret. Then one day at work it suddenly dawned on him: the Nazis had encoded this data in the numbers sewn onto their shirts. Every prisoner who registered in the camp was given a number in the order in which they arrived—the latest arrivals in October 1940 were in the six thousands. Yet the number of prisoners at roll call was only around five thousand. In other words, a thousand men had perished, nearly a dozen a day since the weather had turned cold.[25]

The grim figures clarified for Witold the hopelessness of their situation. One day while scratching in the frozen earth for roots he'd had the grim thought that they'd be better off if the British simply bombed the camp and brought an end to their suffering. The moment of despair passed, but over the following days he gave the idea more thought. Perhaps it wasn't as crazy as it seemed. The camp was around eight hundred miles from Great Britain, at the very limit of how far a plane could fly and safely return. But theoretically a squadron of a dozen Wellington bombers using auxiliary fuel tanks could reach Auschwitz carrying a load of one thousand pounds of explosives each—more than enough to destroy or severely damage the camp. He'd learned from Kon that the SS had unloaded weapons and ammunition at the warehouses. If the bombers could hit the buildings they could trigger an explosion. Witold recognized that many prisoners would surely perish in the attack, but at least their "monstrous torture" (as he later phrased it in the report he prepared for Aleksander) would be over, and in the chaos of an air raid some might get away. No one would die in vain if Auschwitz were to be obliterated, he believed.[26]

Michał briefed Aleksander in person and ensured he memorized the points. The decision to bomb the camp was "the urgent and well-thought request sent on behalf of comrades by the witness of their torment," he instructed Aleksander to say. Given the fact that British planes had no onboard radar and so relied on navigating by landmarks on the ground, Witold also included some instruction for finding the camp by following the Vistula.[27]

Aleksander was due to be released at the end of October after a final medical inspection. But just before he left on October 28 the camp was subjected to a new torment. At noon roll call that Monday, the prisoner count didn't tally. This in itself was not unusual: the SS men often stumbled over their arithmetic, but this time a prisoner really was missing. The camp siren wailed, and a furious Fritzsch announced that no one would leave the square until the escapee had been found. The pots of soup at the kitchen went untouched.[28]

The morning drizzle turned to sleet, and the wind picked up from the northwest, driving sheets of ice against the men standing in the front row. The prisoners were forbidden from moving, so Witold vainly tensed and released his muscles to keep warm. Soaked through and ankle deep in slush, the men swayed and shook. As darkness fell and the blizzard set in, they began dropping one by one.[29]

In the hospital, the kapo Bock had the nurses on standby. Dering was posted at the entrance as the penal company, working as stretcher bearers, started bringing in stricken inmates. "It was terrible to see these men," recalled Dering after the war. "Comatose, half-conscious, crawling, reeling like drunks, babbling incoherently and with difficulty, covered with spittle and foaming at the mouth, dying, gasping out their last breath."[30]

The afflicted were stripped in the washroom and sprinkled with water, per the regulation to rinse every admission. They were then

Evening Roll Call, by Jan Komski, postwar.

Courtesy of PMA-B.

laid out on the floor in one of the wards with thin blankets. When the room filled up, they were lined up in the corridor, and yet still more came. The only thing the nurses had to give them was acorn coffee.[31]

It wasn't until the evening that the "escaped" prisoner was finally found, dead, behind a pile of logs in a work yard. The men were still kept on the square until 9:00 P.M., when Fritzsch released them. The whole shivering mass of prisoners descended on the hospital. The orderlies had to hold the door shut as the sick tried to force their way in. Bock, enraged, ran to get his club and flung the door open to charge the mob, which rapidly dispersed back to the blocks. By the morning eighty-six had perished of pneumonia. The body of the so-called escapee was put on display at the gate.[32]

Witold had endured the previous day's cold well enough, but Michał had developed a cough. Insisting he was fine, he took up his usual lookout position beside the building they were knocking down. The storm had cleared and the late-autumn sun shone fitfully, and whatever gloom Witold felt from the roll call was lifted the following day with the news that Aleksander had been released. Warsaw would soon know the truth. Something surely would be done.[33]

It should have been a moment to savor, but Michał's cough continued to get worse. He was racked with dry spasms and had started spitting blood. He put on his usual show of shouting and swearing in front of the other kapos, and for the next few days insisted on standing watch. But by the evening he was drained, and after a week he was so unsteady on his feet that he had to lie down in the cottage most of the day, coughing and shuddering on the floor.[34]

Witold took him after roll call to see Dering, who diagnosed pneumonia, and made sure he was quickly admitted to the hospital. Dering had entirely recovered from his earlier ordeal and made himself so useful

around the wards that Bock had given him the job of inspecting prisoners. Choosing who would live or die each day was a hellish job, but it gave
Dering real power to aid prisoners. Under normal circumstances, Michał
would take a course of antibiotics and likely recover in a few weeks, but
Dering had nothing to give. Michał died a few days later. Witold only
touched on his death in his later writings, but he did have this to say: "So
we watched a comrade's slow death and one died, as it were, with him . . .
and if one dies like that, let us say if only ninety times, then, no way for
it, one becomes someone else."[35]

His corpse was laid out on the parade square to be counted with
the others. An SS man drove a spike through each chest to make sure
they were dead before the bodies were tossed onto a wagon. There were
too many dead at the end of each day to carry them in coffins to the
crematorium.[36]

*

Without Michał's protection, Witold and the rest of the squad went
to work at the warehouses, unloading trains under the kapos' glare.
His early recruit, Kon, had already warned him about the one-armed
Siegruth, but equally murderous were two kapos both named August,
nicknamed "black" and "white" to distinguish them. Then there was
the kapos' gang of teenage helpers, mostly Poles from the border region
who'd rediscovered their Germanness and took delight in harassing
inmates as they staggered from the trains with their heavy loads. One
of the teens was eventually found hanged in the barracks, but that did
little to dissuade the others from their hazing.[37]

Staller also took over a work squad digging ditches nearby. Due to
the influx of prisoners, his barracks had been converted to additional
storerooms, and Witold and the other prisoners had been assigned to
different quarters. Staller, with no block to run, was forced outside.

There was a certain irony for Witold in seeing the man who had kicked him off the block now standing pinched and cold in the rain. He'd lost some of his passion for beating prisoners and spent most of his time inside a little shack he'd had built that contained a woodstove.[38]

Witold did his best to avoid Staller, although Kon worked in his squad and was forced to deal with him. At one stage, Staller had asked for carpenters to build a table for his cabin, and Kon, desperate for some indoor work, had volunteered, despite his lack of skills. He gamely tried to fashion a table by hammering together several boards to make the top, but there were nails sticking out everywhere.

"What is this?" exclaimed Staller upon inspection. "A bed for some Indian Fakir? I will roll you on those nails until you're so punctured the stink leaks out of you!"[39]

"Those nails are obviously too long," Kon replied hurriedly. "That's why they're sticking out. We used them temporarily until you could get us some shorter ones."

Staller seemed uncertain whether this was a proper carpenter's argument but agreed to bring shorter nails. Kon hastily set the surface on four legs, banged in some more nails, set the teetering edifice against the wall, and fled just in time to find another work squad. He later saw Staller roaming around the fields brandishing one of his table legs, looking for him.

Kon's stories of outwitting Staller provided Witold with brief respite from the gloom. Trains arrived at the railway sidings daily bearing iron bars, bricks, piping, tiles, and hundred-pound sacks of cement. Everything had to be unloaded on the double. Witold had been conserving his strength for weeks but now he was burning through his last reserves.[40]

By this time, he was a Muselmann in all but spirit. Even resting, his body ached. His skin was shiny and translucent and sensitive to the

touch; his fingers, ears, and nose had turned blue from poor circulation. A telltale sign of his emaciation was the swelling in his legs and
feet caused by the fact that it took longer for the water content of the
body to reduce than the fats and muscle tissue. It was almost impossible to get his trousers and clogs on in the morning. He could stick his
thumb into his legs as if they were made of dough.[41]

His thoughts were jumbled and incoherent, and he sometimes
lost consciousness walking back to the camp in the evenings, but
he somehow managed to keep marching. Then his brain would re-
engage, slowly at first, before with a jolt he realized how close he'd
come to stumbling, and he commanded himself, "You are not to give
up for anything!" He'd see the crematorium then, its smoking chimney lined against the sky, and finally understood the true meaning
of those iron letters over the camp gate: *Work sets you free*; that is, it
set "the soul free of the body . . . sending that body . . . to the crematorium."[42]

And then his thoughts would drift off again. He only knew that
he'd made it back to his bunk because he awoke the next morning to
start again. Hours seemed to last for weeks, yet whole weeks passed
by in a flash. The only constants were his hunger and the cold. It was
still November, but there were already drifts of snow in the roll call
square and his eyebrows were rimed with frost. In the blocks at night,
he clung to his mattress-mates for warmth. Some of the prisoners received caps and jackets in a consignment from another concentration
camp, but the new clothes only brought a new torture: lice, which
quickly infested the camp. Soon the prisoners had developed a new
evening ritual of picking the bugs from their underwear and blankets,
yet however many Witold and the others killed, they could still feel
greasy little legs crawling over them when they lay down on their
mattresses, and sleep was impossible.[43]

Marching to work.

Courtesy of PMA-B.

At times like those, hungry, cold, and eaten alive, Witold found he could detach his mind from his body's suffering. His spirit would soar, and he looked down on his body with a kind of pity, as he would a beggar on the street. "While the body underwent torments, at times mentally one felt splendid," he recalled.[45]

Dering was increasingly alarmed by Witold's condition. In late November, he arranged to meet Witold at the hospital but he could hardly pick him out from the crowd of bone-thin, stinking wretches pressing against the door to get in. The SS were converting three additional barracks to hospital blocks in recognition of the fact that almost a quarter of the camp was either sick or injured, but even then there wasn't enough space.[46]

Casting his expert eye over his friend, Dering asked how he was bearing up and offered to admit him to the hospital and perhaps even arrange a job.

Witold insisted he was fine. Those who entered the hospital as patients rarely left alive. Besides, most of his recruits were in worse shape than he was. "How would it have looked if just once I had complained that I felt bad . . . or that I was weak . . . and that I was so overwhelmed with work that I was looking for anything to save myself?" he wrote later. "It was obvious that then I would be unable to inspire anyone else or require anything of them." He subsequently arranged a hospital job for Kon, who was on his last legs.[47]

*

Finally, Witold had to save himself. One of his recruits, Ferdynand Trojnicki, was employed in a carpentry workshop located in the barracks next to the main gate. The kapo was an ethnic German from Poland named Wilhelm Westrych, who wasn't as violent as the others. Ferdynand said he could arrange an interview with him, but Witold would have to impress the man with something other than carpentry. Witold decided to take the bold step of saying he was in the camp under an alias and was in fact one of the wealthiest aristocrats in Poland, a gentleman who would surely reward Westrych for a good deed. Ferdynand primed Westrych well, because when he and Witold met, the kapo seemed to buy the story. Westrych was due to be released shortly and perhaps he saw an opportunity to gain a favor. At any rate, Witold landed the carpentry job and found a spot in the workshop for Sławek shortly afterward.[48]

After the warehouses, Witold spent his first few days with the carpenters in a state of delayed shock. The workshop was clean. There was a tile stove in the corner. There were no beatings. He was issued a coat, cap, and socks. Of course, he and the others did have to do some woodworking, but Westrych shielded them from the scrutiny of the other kapos.[49]

With his newfound comfort Witold could appreciate the news that electrified the camp a few day later. The latest arrivals informed the other prisoners that word of Auschwitz had reached Warsaw in November. The underground had published a full report in its main newspaper and people were talking about the camp's horrors. Witold must have thought that it couldn't be long before London was informed and took action.[50]

As Christmas approached, the camp's sudden notoriety appeared to force one change. On learning of the inmates' plight, Poland's archbishop, Adam Sapieha, wrote to Commandant Höss asking if the church could organize relief and a Christmas mass. Höss agreed to a one-off food package weighing no more than two pounds for each prisoner, but not to the mass; his clemency stretched only so far, and he had his own ideas for how to observe the occasion.[51]

Carpentry workshop.

Courtesy of PMA-B.

That bitter season, the prisoners spent their evenings on the blocks rehearsing the German version of "Silent Night." At one point, Witold heard the sound of music emanating from the room next to his in the carpenters' workshop (when he looked he saw a motley collection of kapos wheezing and puffing over their instruments). Then on Christmas Eve, the prisoners returned from work early to find a massive Christmas tree installed beside the kitchen. The tree was easily as big as one of the guard towers, thick with needles and festooned in colored lights that seemed to dance as the branches shifted in the wind. For a joke, the SS had stacked as presents under the tree the bodies of prisoners who had died that day in the penal company, mostly Jews.[52]

A small podium had been constructed beside the tree, and after roll call SS-Hauptscharführer Palitzsch climbed up on it alongside one of the kapos with an accordion, another with a guitar, and a third to lead the singing. They struck the opening chords of "Silent Night," and en masse, the assembled ranks of prisoners joined in. They returned to their blocks without a word.[53]

*

The weather was still cold when the prisoners went back to work a few days later. The snow between the blocks had crusted over to form sheets of ice and the roll call square was a frozen sea of ruts and troughs. Witold was glad of his job indoors, but it brought other problems. Westrych had found him and a colleague jobs as handymen in one of the hospital blocks reserved for so-called convalescents. The patients were packed into five small wards, a hundred in each room. Most were little more than skeletons with grotesquely swollen legs. Others had open abscesses the size of dinner plates or broken limbs splayed at

Christmas Eve, 1940, by Władysław Siwek, postwar.

Courtesy of Anna Komorowska.

awkward angles that had been left unset. They moaned and whimpered beneath their soiled rags. Lice crawled over their bodies. The stench of excrement and filth was so overwhelming the windows were kept open despite the freezing temperatures.[54]

The hospital kapo set them to work constructing a wooden aisleway in each room. It wasn't long before the other carpenter started to complain about feeling unwell. The next day he was coughing and unsteady on his feet, and was laid out in one of the wards with pneumonia. The following morning he was dead. Witold, who had yet to catch a sniffle, felt the sickness touch him and then slowly settle inside. At first it was a warm, lugubrious sensation, like he'd slipped into a tepid bath that dulled his senses. He felt an overpowering urge to rest, to close his eyes, to forget, but knew he had to avoid lying down on one of those dirty mattresses at all costs. Then the chills began and he started to shake violently, his joints ached, and the light strained his eyes. He staggered off to find Dering, who diagnosed a lung infection and fever but had no medicine to give him.[55]

He made it through the next few roll calls without collapsing. He thought he might recover, but then the SS announced a campwide delousing that evening. Every prisoner was to take a shower and have their clothes disinfected. Witold's block was ordered to the storehouse and told to strip for washing. The shower didn't last long, but it took hours for their clothes to be returned and they had to stand while they waited. One of the rooms in the block had been converted into a primitive delousing facility by sealing the door and window with strips of paper and installing a fan. The Germans used a cyanide-based disinfestation agent known by its trade name, Zyklon B, the blue pellets of which turned to gas on contact with air. It was extremely toxic, so inmates wore gas masks to scatter the pellets around the stacks of clothes and then aired the room before collecting the garments.[56]

The day was breaking by the time their clothes finally arrived, tinged with blue and smelling of bitter almonds. Witold took a dozen

Tin of Zyklon B.

Courtesy of PMA-B.

steps across the street from the storeroom block and collapsed. The
night of standing had finally broken him. Nurses dragged him to the
hospital, and he was stripped down again, doused in yet more cold
water, and his number written on his chest in indelible ink. Then he
was given a soiled hospital gown and underpants and taken to the
very room where he'd been working and tossed onto the festering
matting. He was too exhausted to move yet unable to sleep, because
no sooner did he stretch out than lice swarmed over him. Looking
down his blanket he was horrified to see the folds heaving with lice
like glinting fish scales. They came in different shapes and sizes:
striped ones, scaly ones, white, gray, and bright red ones that had
already gorged on blood.[57]

He killed them by the handful until his hands were bloody, but it
was futile. The invalid to his right was motionless, his face covered in a
crust of lice that had burrowed into his skin. The inmate to his left was
already dead. Witold doubted he had the strength to fight, or whether
he even wanted to. He asked for a paper and pencil from one of the
nurses to write a short note for Dering.[58]

"If you don't get me out of here at once," he managed to scribble,
"then I will use up all my reserves of strength fighting lice. In my
present condition I am rapidly approaching the crematorium chimney."[59]

He added his location and asked the nurse to take it at once. A couple of hours later, Dering and another nurse appeared, chaperoned by
Bock. Dering pretended to be carrying out some sort of inspection; despite his increasing influence in the hospital, he still had to be cautious.

"What's wrong with this fellow?" he said, stopping beside Witold.
"Can you look him over?" he said to the other nurse. Dering then diagnosed Witold and said he would take him for tests at the dispensary.

They helped him to his feet and half-carried him over to the other block, where one of the upstairs rooms had been fitted with beds and new mattresses that had yet to be infested with lice. Witold had a bed to himself. He stretched out and fell into a deep and boundless sleep, all thoughts of resistance gone.[60]

CHAPTER 6

BOMBER COMMAND

WARSAW

OCTOBER 1940

The messenger Aleksander Wielopolski boarded the first train to Warsaw after his release from the camp at the end of October. Poles were
restricted to unheated third-class carriages at the back of the train, but
at least there were no Germans. His shaven head drew stares, and he
longed to rest at his family's home in the country, but he was determined to keep his promise to Witold.[1]

Aleksander took a rickshaw through the rainy gray streets of Warsaw to the apartment of his cousin Stefan Dembiński, a fellow Muske-
teer. Stefan ushered Aleksander inside and offered him what food he
had. Much had changed in Warsaw in the six weeks that Aleksander
had been interned. The brick and barbed-wire wall of the ghetto was
almost complete, and Jewish families had been forcibly evicted from
the "Aryan quarter" of the city. Poles went in the opposite direction,
taking over Jewish homes that the Germans hadn't appropriated. The
sealing of the ghetto was expected any day, and posters on street cor-

ners warned that Jews found outside its walls would be shot. Everywhere food was short and disease rampant, especially typhus.[2]

It took Aleksander a day or two to arrange a meeting with the head of the Musketeers, Stefan Witkowski, and a deputy of the underground leader, Stefan Rowecki. Since Witold's internment, Rowecki had subsumed most of the city's resistance groups into the main underground except for a few like the Musketeers. Witkowski, a flamboyant aircraft engineer who built rockets in his spare time, valued his autonomy too much to take orders from Rowecki, but the two men had reached an agreement over intelligence gathering, a core activity that provided valuable leverage with the British, the only country in Europe capable of coming to Poland's aid.[3]

Aleksander's description of the camp was the evidence Rowecki had been seeking of German crimes against the prisoners that contravened international law. The 1907 Hague Convention safeguarded the rights of prisoners of war and offered some protection to civilians from arbitrary arrest and maltreatment. Perhaps the Nazis claimed that Polish citizens were now subject to the same indefinite detention as Germans. But Witold's report would almost certainly create an international response. Even more valuable, Witold's plea to bomb the camp proposed an opportunity for Allied action against the Germans.[4]

Rowecki had Witold's report written up and attached it to a broader summary of conditions in Poland. The report described the camp's appalling treatment of prisoners, location, and its warehouses containing food, clothing, and possible weapons and ammunition.

"The prisoners beg the Polish Government, for the love of God, to bombard these warehouses" and end their torment, went the report. The bombing would create panic and give the prisoners a chance to escape. "Should they [the prisoners] die in the attack, it would be a relief given the conditions," the report stated and concluded with Witold's words that it was the prisoners' "urgent and well-thought request" by the "witness of their torment."[5]

The question for Rowecki was how to get the report to London, where the Polish exile government had established itself after the fall of France, under the leadership of Władysław Sikorski, a moderate general and former prime minister. Rowecki had a radio transmitter that could send only short messages and had to be used sparingly to avoid detection. Couriers also brought risks. Germans had infiltrated his Tatra Mountain network that autumn, so a new route needed to be found. Witkowski suggested a noblewoman he knew named Julia Lubomirska, who was planning to flee for neutral Switzerland with her half sister. The thirty-five-year-old princess's parents had been murdered by the Russian secret police, and she was eager to help her country.[6]

In early November, Julia boarded a train bound for Switzerland with the report and instructions. The thousand-mile journey to Geneva took more than twenty-four hours, but the trains ran smoothly and she was able to deliver the report to Stanisław Radziwiłł, the chargé d'affaires of Poland at the League of Nations.[7]

The next leg took several weeks to prepare. The legation lined up Stefan Dembiński's brother, Stanisław, who was in Geneva at the time and agreed to courier the material through the unoccupied region of southern France and over the Pyrenees to Madrid. He reached the Spanish capital around December 10 and passed on the report, along with a short note, to the local Polish station chief. From there it found its way into a diplomatic pouch bound for Sikorski in London.[8]

*

Bombing Request Report, 1940

SWEDEN

North Sea

DENMARK

Baltic Sea

GREAT BRITAIN

NETHERLANDS

London •

BELGIUM

• Berlin

Aleksander Wielopolski

Warsaw •

GREATER GERMAN REICH

Paris •

OCCUPIED FRANCE

Julia Lubomirska

Katowice
Oświęcim • • Krakow

Vienna •

HUNGARY

Bern
SWITZ.
Alps

Vichy •   Geneva •

Stanisław Dembiński

ITALY

YUGOSLAVIA

Adriatic Sea

Pyrenees

• Madrid
SPAIN

• Rome

ALBANIA

Mediterranean Sea

N
W — E
S

0   100   200   300 miles
0   200   400 km

John Gilkes

So far, Sikorski had struggled to develop an effective relationship with his British hosts, who knew little of Poland beyond the usual stereotypes of peculiar, unruly foreigners with hard-to-pronounce names. "Sozzle-Something," Winston Churchill is reported to have called the senior Polish commander Kazimierz Sosnkowski. The foreign minister, August Zaleski, was "notoriously lazy," according to one British government report, while the finance minister, Adam Koc, was described as "friendly but not a 'flier.'" As for Sikorski himself, the British thought he might well be the worst of the bunch.[9]

"[His] vanity is so colossal and unfortunately he is encouraged to display it in certain circles here," observed the British ambassador to the Polish exile government, Sir Howard Kennard. "Something should be done to make him realize that he is not the only pebble on the beach."[10]

In fact, Sikorski was well aware of the constant intriguing of his rivals and equally frustrated with his British hosts, who he believed had ignored his warnings about the German Blitzkrieg, and often seemed to treat Polish forces with disregard despite their demonstrated effectiveness during the Battle of Britain, when the Polish 303 Squadron had shot down more German planes than any other unit.[11]

More troubling, the British had failed to take his early reports of German war crimes seriously. At that point, the name of Auschwitz was largely unknown to British officials, although they understood the role of the German concentration camp system in crushing opposition to the Nazis. Indeed, the British government had published a white paper in 1939 describing the brutal treatment of prisoners in the Dachau and Buchenwald camps. However, the British were cautious about publicizing stories about Nazi wrongdoings in case they were accused of propaganda. The government's use of fabricated atrocity stories during World War I—such as the claim that the Germans used

Władysław Sikorski, c. 1941.
Courtesy of Narodowe Archiwum Cyfrowe.

corpses to manufacture soap—had created widespread public distrust. British officials were likewise skeptical of what other governments told them. Frank Roberts, the acting first secretary in the Central Department of the Foreign Office, went so far as to doubt the accuracy of Polish reporting altogether. So far, the British had limited themselves to a general statement against the Germans' "brutal attacks on the civilian population in defiance of the accepted principles of international law."[12]

Sikorski also faced the challenge of making atrocities in Poland stand out when Britain itself was under devastating attack. In September, Hitler had ordered the Blitz offensive against London and other cities to cripple British infrastructure and break the people's will. The capital had been hit almost every night through the fall; 27,500 bombs had hit the city, killing 18,000 people, mainly around the East End and docks, and rendering hundreds of thousands homeless. The Germans mixed incendiary bombs with their payloads, so most nights a raging inferno engulfed one part of the city or another.[13]

When the sirens sounded, indicating the bombers were twelve minutes out, residents dashed to basements or prefabricated structures in gardens. As public shelters quickly filled, people took to church crypts, railway bridges, and the London Underground. Commuters working late passed platform after platform packed with "tubeites," as they became known, makeshift communities numbering in the thousands. The authorities initially disapproved of the use of stations as shelters, but eventually agreed to distribute tea and buns at some and carry out health checks for lice and scabies.[14]

Some shell-shocked residents simply stayed underground for days at a time rather than risk losing their spots. A few complained about the state of shelters in poorer areas and believed that privileged groups like the Jews had it better than them—a reflection of widespread anti-Semitism rather than reality. Most adjusted to the dire circumstances and found camaraderie among their fellow sufferers. Churchill, who had taken over from the ineffectual Chamberlain in May, made a point of visiting bomb sites and speaking to survivors. At night he sat out on the roof of his secure accommodation overlooking St. James Park and watched the city's destruction. British morale had not been broken, but the prognosis was otherwise grim: the British were on the back foot against Italian forces in Africa, the only active front, while German U-boats were threatening to strangle the transatlantic supply of food and equipment from America, which remained on the sidelines. The onslaught left little time to consider the fate of those trapped on the continent.[15]

Sikorski had agreed to collaborate that autumn with a new clandestine organization known as the Special Operations Executive, or SOE, in the hope of improving relations with the British. The SOE's purpose was to carry out sabotage and subversion attacks in Nazi-occupied Europe. But the organization had gotten off to a poor start. It was led by an Eton-educated socialist named Hugh Dalton, who also served as minister of economic warfare. His hectoring manner had not endeared him to other officials in Whitehall, and an early decision to staff the SOE with civilians rather than soldiers to appeal to left-wing groups on the continent had also backfired. The accountants, lawyers, and

Hugh Dalton, 1945.

National Portrait Gallery, London.

bankers he hired had a variety of plans for causing mayhem, but little idea how to carry them out. The fact that Dalton had brought on most of the partners working for the legal firm Slaughter and May led one office wit to observe: "We seemed to be all 'may' and no 'slaughter.'" Indeed, the SOE might have failed completely that winter but for Dalton's partnership with the Poles, which allowed him to claim some of the Polish underground's success as his own.[16]

Sikorski was with Dalton visiting Polish troops billeted in Scotland that Christmas in an effort to cement their relationship when Witold's report arrived at the Polish headquarters in the Rubens hotel in London. Dalton, who'd had a few run-ins with Whitehall, understood the obstacles Sikorski would face in getting Witold's request to bomb the camp implemented. A direct approach to Churchill might take weeks to arrange given his schedule. The Foreign Office could also be ruled out for its earlier reluctance to engage with the issue of German crimes. The best option was therefore to take Witold's request directly to the Royal Air Force.[17]

On January 4, 1941, Sikorski's aide de camp, Stefan Zamoyski, composed a single-page version of the report that focused on the bombing mission. He passed this on to the head of Bomber Command, Richard Peirse, at his headquarters in the little village of Walters Ash, near High Wycombe in Buckinghamshire, safely away from London. The lull in bombing the capital had ended on December 29, when, shortly after 6 P.M., on a cold clear night with a "bomber's moon," the sirens had wailed, and the bombardment recommenced; twenty-two thousand bombs fell on the capital in just three hours, many of them incendiary devices, in what became known as the second Great Fire of London.[18]

Witold's request crossed Peirse's desk during a moment of introspection for the RAF. Despite the fact that Churchill had made a strategic bombing campaign of Germany his top priority, the RAF was struggling to keep its small fleet of bombers airborne, let alone hit anything in Germany. In October the RAF had 290 serviceable aircraft but had lost almost a third by the end of November, the vast majority to accidents that were the result of rushing newly trained crews into the air with poor equipment. The lack of radar meant that in heavy cloud cover, the best game plan was simply to open the bomb doors after they'd flown for the right amount of time. As a result, the majority of bombs fell nowhere near their targets, and frequently left the Germans unsure what the objective of any particular raid had been. One crew hit a magnetic storm and got turned around without realizing it. Peering in the dark for a landmark, they finally spotted a river they took to be the Rhine, and their target airfield. It was only on their return journey that they realized they'd been flying over Britain the whole time and had dropped their bombs on an RAF station in Bassingbourn, in Cambridgeshire.[19]

"Deplorable," Churchill called the RAF's performance, and he insisted they do better. He was in favor of retaliation against German cities, which seemed to at least carry some chance of success, and had ordered the first such raid against Mannheim in December. But Peirse and his boss, Charles Portal, the chief of the Air Staff, worried about the morality of attacking civilians and stuck to their belief that the only way to knock Germany out of the war was to hit at its war production, which meant targeted bombing of industrial facilities. Indeed, using the grossly inflated reporting of aircrews, Peirse seemed to think their strategy was succeeding, and was in the midst of planning a major bombing offensive of German synthetic fuel production when Witold's request landed on his desk.[20]

The idea of bombing Auschwitz intrigued Peirse. He recognized that bombing the camp held no strategic value, and the decision to attack the camp was therefore a political one if they could pull it off. The 1,700-mile round trip from the Stradishall air base in Suffolk to Auschwitz was longer than any mission the RAF had yet undertaken. The mission would require the aircraft to carry extra fuel and a reduced load. The Poles had supplied directions for finding the camp, but even if RAF bombers located Auschwitz, Peirse knew that the limited number of bombs they carried reduced their chances of hitting Auschwitz.[21]

On January 8, Peirse sent the request to Portal at the Air Ministry in London, saying that while the mission was possible, it required ministerial approval, given Bomber Command's upcoming offensive and the challenges of the operation. Peirse made no mention of the prisoners' plight, which was hardly surprising. Over the course of its transmission to London, the idea of the bombing raid had commanded everyone's attention, while the description of the camp's horrors had been reduced to a single line. Shorn of its context, Witold's request had lost its moral imperative.[22]

Portal's response a few days later was curt and to the point:

"I think you will agree that, apart from any political considerations, an attack on the Polish concentration camp at Oświęcim is an undesirable diversion and unlikely to achieve its purpose. The weight of bombs that could be carried to a target at this distance with the limited force available would be very unlikely to cause enough damage to enable prisoners to escape."[23]

Portal's assessment was accurate, and if anything he underplayed the extreme difficulty of hitting the camp. But he failed to appreciate that an attack on Auschwitz in 1940 would have alerted the world to

Charles Portal.

Yousuf Karsh.

the camp, and that by declining to bomb the facility he was spurning an opportunity for the British to make a political declaration against Nazi atrocities, thus setting a precedent for nonintervention.

As it was, Peirse did not protest the decision and was left to break the news to Sikorski. In a letter of January 15 he was careful to stress to Sikorski the practical difficulties of the mission. "Air bombardment of this nature would need to be extremely accurate if serious casualties were not to be caused amongst the prisoners themselves," he wrote, adding that "such accuracy cannot be guaranteed."[24]

Sikorski's response is not recorded, but it appears that Dalton gave him some assurance that he should keep trying. Meanwhile, the SOE launched a program in the western highlands of Scotland to train Polish exiles as agents. Dalton planned to parachute these men into Poland with radio equipment and orders to establish contact with Warsaw and smuggle intelligence back to Britain. For Sikorski, it was an endorsement of the material his network had provided so far, and an invitation from the British to supply more.[25]

The first three jumpers arrived at Stradishall air base in Suffolk on the evening of February 15. The night was still, with only a thin band of cloud overhead. Clear skies were forecast for Poland. The men wore long overalls and elbow-length gloves for the five-hour journey. Rucksacks contained civilian clothes, carefully tailored in the Polish style, several packs of German cigarettes and razors, and for each man a cyanide tablet hidden in a button in case of capture. A further eight hundred pounds' worth of equipment—four radio transmitters and plenty of dynamite—was stored in specially designed containers that could survive impact without exploding. Before departing, Sikorski had told them, "You are the vanguard to Poland. You have to show the world that even now, even in these current circumstances, it is possible to land in Poland."[26]

The plane, a Whitley MK1, then lurched down the runway and climbed steadily over the North Sea. Once over the continent a cold wind started blowing through the craft's ventilators, and the men leaned against each other for warmth. It was too cold to sleep, and it was hard to talk over the roaring engines. Anti-aircraft fire targeted them as they passed the Dutch coast and enemy searchlights caught them over Dusseldorf, but German air defenses were minimal, and most of the cities did not operate blackouts. Around midnight they spotted the lights of Berlin, and then clouds started to thicken near the Polish border. The pilot, Flight Lieutenant Francis Keast, perhaps betraying his unfamiliarity with the journey, veered off course and only realized he'd overshot his mark when he spotted the Tatra Mountains.[27]

There was no time or fuel to adjust course; the men would have to jump where they were, which turned out to be almost directly over Auschwitz. One of the crewmen hurriedly opened the Whitley's specially fitted side door. The jumpers took one look at the full moon glinting on the snowy mountainsides and then leaped into the dark in rapid succession. Keast made another pass to drop the equipment before banking away from the mountains and climbing back to cruising altitude.[28]

Given the stillness of the night, the prisoners below would have heard the low rumble of the Whitley's Medium Tiger IX engines without guessing what they signified. The jumpers landed, and the plane returned safely. There was to be no help for them this time, but the mission proved to Sikorski that the British could reach Auschwitz.

CHAPTER 7

RADIO

AUSCHWITZ

JANUARY 1941

Witold fevered in bed for ten days, dreams looping with waking thoughts, only certain of the passage of light to dark and back again. Occasionally he felt the window open, or a rough sponge against his body and hot soup pressed to his lips. Other patients arrived, moaning and whimpering or else suddenly quiet at the sound of a gunshot or nearby beating. The musicians from Christmas were now practicing a Bavarian waltz for the deputy commandant Fritzsch, the strains of which drifted into the room in the evenings.[1]

By the tenth day, the fever passed and Witold slowly regained his strength. The nurses kept feeding him, and he started to hobble around the ward, until Dering judged him well enough to transfer to the convalescents' block. The fact that Dering had sheltered Witold for so long indicated the hospital's importance to the underground. Dering had worked his way into the trust of SS-Hauptsturmführer Max Popiersch, the doctor who oversaw the hospital. Popiersch was anxious to prove that National Socialism was compatible with a doctor's ethics. So long as Dering paid lip service to the Nazi racial order and demonstrated toughness with prisoners, he was allowed to perform his medical duties to save lives.[2]

Witold helped the nurses where he could and soon fell into the rhythm of the block. Every patient had to wash at dawn. They were bundled or carried from the recently installed three-tiered bunks to the washroom to be stripped of soiled underwear and paper bandages. The convalescents were then drenched under cold showers. One nurse recalled how the mass of shivering bodies resembled "one mortally wounded beast watching its thousand links in the throes of death." The patients were returned to their beds and the floors

Hospital block.

Courtesy of PMA-B.

Josef Klehr, 1962.
Courtesy of PMA-B.

scrubbed with chlorine, mess buckets emptied, and windows opened to clear the air.[3]

Surgery began at nine in a downstairs room and lasted for most of the day. Popiersch was around for only the first hour or so, leaving the running of the hospital to SS-Unterscharführer Josef Klehr, a former cabinetmaker from Austria who liked to think of himself as a doctor. He arrived at the hospital on his motorcycle and expected one nurse to buff the paintwork and another to remove his boots and wash his feet at his desk. A third administered a manicure as Klehr puffed on his pipe "like a pasha," as one prisoner recalled.[4]

Fortunately, Klehr was so preoccupied with arranging the illicit sale of the hospital's tiny supply of morphine to SS men and the kapos that the nurses were able to care for patients. That February, the temperature hit minus 22 degrees Fahrenheit. The inmates had been issued coats that were little more than knee-length cotton shirts. A few prisoners like Witold had received parcels of underclothes from family, but most were forced to secretly fashion extra layers from cement sacks or any other material they could find, at the risk of severe punishment. During the coldest periods, the SS kept prisoners inside, but roll call was always in the square, and dozens showed up at the hospital with hands and feet frozen hard white, which soon turned black with rot.[5]

One bitter evening, with the wind driving against the windows, an SS guard brought twelve Jews from the penal company to the hospital with severely frostbitten feet. Some of the nurses had gathered to pick over a copy of a German newspaper the doctors had left behind when Dering suddenly shouted for assistance. It was unusual for Jews from the penal company to be treated, and the Polish doctor wanted the job done quickly. The suffering men removed their clogs to reveal feet that had been stripped of flesh to expose the bone. The bone itself was brown in color, probably frozen as well.[6]

"Just sprinkle the bones with disinfecting powder and apply some bandages," Dering ordered and walked away. Kon, one of the nurses summoned to help, set to work wrapping the men's feet in cloth bandages to try to ease the chafing, but Dering, monitoring from a distance, barked: "Paper bandages!"[7]

Kon went over to Dering and said quietly, "When they walk out into the snow, those bandages will last less than five minutes."[8]

"Yes," he replied. "And how long do you think they are going to survive after they leave this place? More than five minutes? One hour? Maybe two? We have only a few cotton bandages and we need them where they'll be useful."

Kon understood that some of Dering's demonstrations of ruthlessness were intended to impress the SS and gain their trust, but he also knew that Dering kept a stash of bandages and medicine for the kapos' exclusive use. He didn't broach the incident with Witold, recognizing that Dering was simply too important to risk alienating.[9]

*

Władysław Dering, c. 1941.

Courtesy of PMA-B.

Dering showed his worth a few weeks later when one evening he led Witold into Popiersch's office in the main hospital block. A radio sat on the desk, probably one of the Telefunken models that were popular among the SS: a varnished wooden chassis with Art Deco curves and two knobs for dialing in the frequency on either side of the speaker's grill. Dering explained that he'd arranged for it to be stolen from the camp's electrical workshop and then prepared a hiding place for it under the floorboards beneath the sink. He'd suggested to Popiersch that he install a phone line between his office and one of the new hospital blocks and arranged with the inmate electrician who installed the line to bundle in a radio wire. Popiersch was delighted with the results, as was Dering, although for very different reasons.[10]

Dering flipped the switch and waited for the radio's tubes to warm up and the speaker to hum. He turned the dial, the signal whined and crackled, and then the two men were overwhelmed by sounds from the forgotten world: songs, jingles, and voices that spoke in German, Italian, Slovak, and Greek; the main commercial and state-run stations used shortwave frequencies, as did military units and aircraft pilots and fishermen at sea.[11]

Dering searched for the BBC, which, unlike the tightly controlled German broadcasts, was largely accurate (the British government had calculated that reporting the news, even when it was bad for the Allies, made it more credible and thus more listened to). Despite Nazi efforts to jam the signal, the BBC's German-language service was increasingly popular within the Reich, and could be picked up by the mass-produced Volksempfänger radio, nicknamed the "Goebbels snout." The propaganda chief had resorted to mass arrests, and labels on the tuning knobs warned that listening to foreign radio stations was a crime against the German people, but such measures met with only partial success.[12]

Dering and Witold tuned the knobs until they caught four drumbeats—Morse code for victory—signaling a BBC news bulletin. Then the electrifying greeting: "Here is England . . . Here is England . . ." They didn't dare listen long. But they were back again the next night, and the night after. The news was bad. Britain had seen off the immediate threat of invasion, but the Germans continued to bombard British cities. In March, the German general Erwin Rommel had landed in Libya to bolster a flagging Italian offensive, and immediately took the initiative against the British. The Germans seemed poised to capture Egypt and the Suez Canal. Crucially, America remained on the sidelines.[13]

Witold could surmise from events that the British were probably too pinned down to attack Auschwitz, but he was sure the camp's accumulating horror would eventually compel the Allies into action. In the meantime, he used Karol Świętorzecki to distribute what little nuggets of good news there were among the other prisoners (he wasn't sure whether the camp's fragile morale could take the unvarnished truth) and was gratified over the following evenings to see excited gaggles of prisoners in the square discussing a U-boat sunk in the mid-Atlantic, or an Italian trouncing in the highlands of Ethiopia. "People were living on this," recalled one prisoner. "From this news we took fresh energy."[14]

Witold had nearly recovered by the end of February, and after obtaining a set of prisoner stripes to replace his patient gown, and grabbing his old toolbox for cover, he was able to move around the camp on underground work while still officially a hospital patient. Such a ruse would have been impossible to contemplate a short while ago, but after six months in the camp he'd learned the kapos' daily routines and which bits of the camp to avoid. The underground had grown in size to more than a hundred men stretched across most work details. Their impact was felt on the blocks as they exhorted prisoners to work together and leaned on men they judged at risk of turning to the Germans. Witold also encouraged his recruits to moderate the behavior of kapos with small bribes—a stolen stick of margarine from the kitchen or a loaf of bread the surveyors smuggled into the camp—and to seek positions of power within their squads.[15]

As the camp grew, there were constant openings for kapos and foremen and not enough German prisoners to fill them. Otto Küsel, who ran the camp's labor office, seemed to genuinely want to help fellow prisoners, had learned a little Polish, and never asked for payment for arranging transfers for Witold's men. One recruit landed the kapo job on a new block; another ran the stables. They were able to shelter others, secure a little extra food, and exert a measure of control over the camp.[16]

Witold visited his old block mate Karol most days in the stables where he worked to give him the latest radio news and was greeted in return with a special treat: a mess tin of wheat bran mixed with water

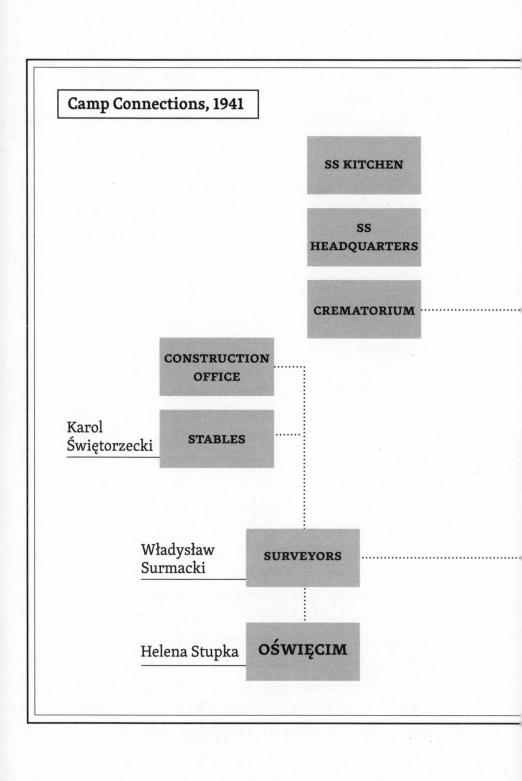

Camp Connections, 1941

SS KITCHEN

SS HEADQUARTERS

CREMATORIUM

CONSTRUCTION OFFICE

Karol Świętorzecki — STABLES

Władysław Surmacki — SURVEYORS

Helena Stupka — OŚWIĘCIM

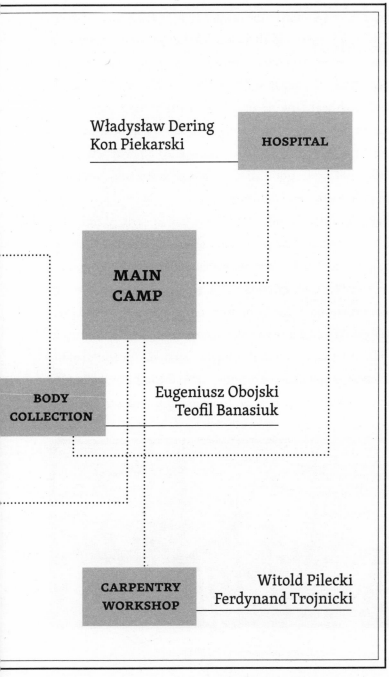

Władysław Dering
Kon Piekarski

HOSPITAL

MAIN CAMP

BODY COLLECTION

Eugeniusz Obojski
Teofil Banasiuk

CARPENTRY WORKSHOP

Witold Pilecki
Ferdynand Trojnicki

John Gilkes and Beata Dejnarowicz

and, the rarest of treats, sugar. The camp had received a train carriage of the stuff for the horses, and though it had been contaminated with salt and charcoal, Karol had discovered that if he added water, the salt dissolved faster than the sugar and could be poured off (the charcoal was good for diarrhea). The resulting blend made the "finest cake," recalled Witold. They washed it down with a glass of milk after Karol had persuaded the SS that their prize stud needed a bucket every day (of course the stud never got a drop, although Karol was careful to daub a little milk foam around its mouth).[17]

Karol had his own news for Witold one day in early March. The camp had been put on lockdown for the visit of an unknown German official. The entourage had visited the stables, where Karol recognized SS-Reichsführer Heinrich Himmler. The security chief had come to order a major expansion of the camp from ten to thirty thousand prisoners, which would make it one of the biggest concentration camps in the Reich. Himmler was eager to develop the economic potential of his camps and was accompanied by executives from the industrial giant IG Farben. He hoped to persuade them to invest in a synthetic fuel and

Karol Świętorzecki, c. 1941.

Courtesy of PMA-B.

rubber factory nearby that would be built by inmates for a small fee per prisoner.[18]

Witold gleaned some of Himmler's intentions over the following days from Władysław Surmacki in the SS construction office. Władysław had established several contacts among the inmates that the SS employed to draft architectural drawings for the expansion. They informed him of plans to build over the roll call square with twelve new blocks and add additional floors to existing buildings to vastly increase the camp's capacity. Transports of Polish prisoners began arriving daily that spring, and the blocks overflowed with disoriented newcomers hauled off the streets or detained for real or alleged resistance work.[19]

Witold took advantage of the influx by stepping up recruitment. By March his force had grown to several hundred men, influential enough

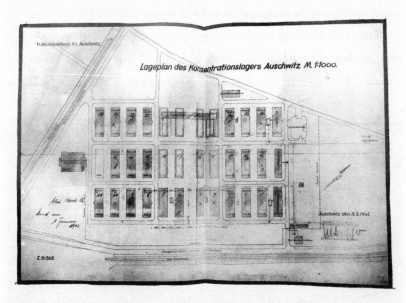

Expansion plans for camp, March 1941
(twelve central blocks under construction).

Courtesy of PMA-B.

to finally provide a modicum of security for its members and anticipate German plans, but of a size that made secrecy increasingly difficult to sustain. Indeed, the camp authorities suspected the underground's existence. But the SS had not pieced together the scale of Witold's organization or the fact that it was affiliated with the resistance movement in Warsaw. Instead it assumed that the prisoners had segregated themselves into gangs, as was common in other camps.[20]

Witold, for his part, made sure that he was the only person who knew everyone in the underground, and kept his profile low by issuing orders and information through confidants like Karol. But there was no doubt he was becoming known around the camp.[21]

Occasionally the Gestapo would sift through their files in search of prisoners with a prior record of underground work. At morning roll call, they would summon a half dozen or so for execution in the gravel pits later. Witold lost several recruits that way.

Then one evening after work, he and Karol were walking through the crowds, checking out new arrivals, when suddenly someone shouted Witold's name—his real one—and he turned to see a friend from Warsaw rushing toward him.[22]

Witold, c. March 1941.

Courtesy of PMA-B.

"Ah, so there you are!" he exclaimed. "The Warsaw Gestapo chopped my arse into little pieces asking what had happened to Witold."[23]

Witold did his best to nonchalantly lead the man away and swear him to secrecy. Still, several prisoners had noticed the reunion.[24]

Around this time, in early March 1941, the SS set up a darkroom in the clothing block and found several inmates with camera experience to take mug shots of the prisoners. Witold had to queue with men from his transport, more than a quarter of whom he quickly calculated were already dead. When his turn came, he sat on a revolving stool with a metal rod positioned behind his head to keep his face in line with the lens. "No smiling, no crying . . ." said the operator, the first injunction so absurd as to almost warrant a grin. Witold kept his eyes flat but pressed his chin into his neck to distort his features, in case the Gestapo found a picture of him.[25]

But he'd almost been too clever. A few days later, he was summoned to the storeroom block. The SS had a small records office in the building where they stored registration material, including camp photos. An SS officer sat at a desk thumbing through paperwork. He looked irritated. After Witold saluted and reported his number, the man took out a couple of photos of prisoners and asked him to identify them. Witold didn't know either, though he could see from their numbers they had registered in the camp at the same time as him. It was highly suspicious, said the German, that he didn't recognize those he had traveled with. Then he looked at Witold's photograph and then back at him.

"It looks nothing like you," the SS officer exclaimed.[26]

Witold explained his puffy appearance as a symptom of kidney trouble. The SS man gave him a long look, then waved him away. It was nothing, Witold told himself. But a few hours later, back at the hospital, Dering was tipped off that Witold was to be summoned the next day. Witold immediately suspected he'd been identified. The only prisoner outside the organization who knew he was in the camp under an alias was the carpentry kapo Wilhelm Westrych, but he had been released two weeks before. Had someone else betrayed him?[27]

His only chance was to come up with a plausible explanation for the confusion; denial would lead to torture. Dering coached him on how to fake meningitis symptoms, which might get him released back to the hospital so that he could rally his strength or, though Dering didn't say it, take a dose of cyanide.

The next morning, Witold's number was read out at roll call, along with twenty or so others. The gong sounded, and they marched to the records block and lined up in the corridor as their numbers were checked. Witold was singled out and led to the mail room.

Several SS men poring over prisoner letters for suspicious content looked up from their desks. One of the Germans beckoned him over.

"Ah! My dear boy," he said. "Why are you not writing letters?"[28]

Witold suddenly realized why he'd been summoned and almost laughed out loud. It was true he hadn't been writing letters, for fear of drawing attention to Eleonora, but he'd anticipated this might alert the SS and had stashed a bundle of letters marked "rejected" by the censorship office in the block.[29]

"I do write," he told the man. "I can prove it."

"Well, I never! He has proof!" the German declared.[30]

A guard escorted Witold back to his block to get the letters. He was in the clear. But any satisfaction was tempered by the sound of shots as the other prisoners who'd been called out with him that morning were executed in one of the gravel pits.[31]

*

Spring made the prisoners restless. The kapos had started staging boxing matches on Sundays behind the kitchen, where they were partially
hidden from view from the guard towers. They fought among themselves, or occasionally pummeled some desperate prisoner. One Sunday
afternoon in March, Witold and some other inmates were in the yard,
likely picking lice from their clothes, a compulsory weekend chore,
when they all heard the yells of a match. A prisoner ran over, flushed
with excitement. The kapo from the camp's abattoir, Walter Dunning,
was offering to fight anyone who dared.

"I've heard that some of you can box," he said. Bread was on offer.[32]

Everyone looked at Tadeusz Pietrzykowski, shirt off atop a pile of

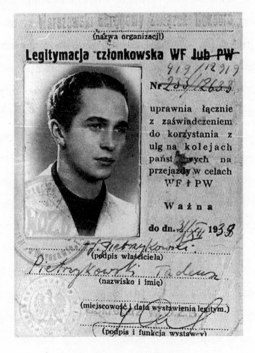

Teddy Pietrzykowski, 1939.

Courtesy of PMA-B.

bricks beside one of the pits. Teddy, as he was known, was a recent re-cruit who had trained as a bantamweight in Warsaw, although he was hardly in fighting shape.[33]

Teddy's room supervisor warned him that it was crazy; Dunning was known for breaking jaws. Teddy just shrugged and jogged through the puddles in the square toward the kitchen, where a crowd of ka-pos and their followers jostled for a view. The muscled, two-hundred-pound Dunning stood shirtless in the center of a makeshift ring. He was a former middleweight champion from Munich who got as much food as he wanted on the job. At the sight of little Teddy, the crowd chanted: "He's gonna kill you, he's gonna eat you."[34]

Teddy's hunger overcame his fear. He entered the ring, and some-one gave him a pair of workman's gloves as Dunning looked on. Teddy held out his gloves for a tap, Dunning raised a single nonchalant fist in return, and then Bruno Brodniewicz, the head kapo and referee, shouted: "Fight."[35]

The German came in fast, trying to finish Teddy off, and didn't bother keeping his fists up. Teddy was able to land a left jab before ducking out of the way. Dunning came at him again, still swinging wildly, so Teddy skipped inside and landed another blow. The pattern repeated, until the roll call gong was sounded for the end of round one. "Beat the German!" came the cries of a few emboldened Poles in the crowd.[36]

Teddy quickly held up his glove for them to stop, but once the next round started and Teddy landed a left hook that bloodied the German's nose, the prisoners started chanting again. This time Bruno grabbed his stick and started laying into the noisiest section of in-mates, quickly joined by Dunning, blood dripping down his chest. The prisoners scattered, except for Teddy, who still stood in the ring, fearing the worst. Dunning marched over and threw down his gloves.

Then he shook Teddy by the hand and led the young Pole over to his block.

"When did you eat?" he asked on the way.[37]

"Yesterday," said Teddy.[38]

Dunning gave him half a loaf of bread and a piece of meat. "Very good, young man, very good," was all he said. Teddy ran back to his block to share the rewards, and landed a prized job in the stables after that.

The camp buzzed with stories of the fight for the rest of the day, and they grew with each retelling. In the square, Witold started to hear talk of uprisings and breakouts coming from a group of colonels who had arrived in the camp with the new influx of prisoners. Most evenings they could be found marching up and down the riverside promenade as if on parade. The walkway had recently been planted with an avenue of silver birches and given a street name, "Birkenallee." A wooden signpost had been carved to show two men sitting on a bench, while a third sat to one side with an oversized ear turned in their direction. From what Witold gathered, the colonels' plan was for one of their number to attack the main gate and escape to rally what forces he could in a nearby town. Another colonel would hold the camp until backup arrived.

Witold thought the plan ill-conceived and premature given the fact that each colonel had recruited only a few men. He held back from contacting them, concerned about their indiscretion and that they might try to pull rank on him. But he needed to keep an eye on them in case they launched into an attack that might lead to a German crackdown. His own thinking about a breakout remained unchanged: the bulk of prisoners were too weak to make it far, and the SS would surely exact a terrible revenge on the hundreds if not thousands left behind.[39]

He wanted guidance from Warsaw for how to handle the colonels and around April started work on a report. Karol was getting released after his family had pulled the right strings in Warsaw. Witold was happy for him, although it meant losing an important lieutenant. They took stock of the underground's achievements over another sugar cake: the continued expansion of the organization and its ability to sustain lives, the smuggling network, and Dering's radio listening post. Those successes were measured against the mounting death toll. More than fifteen thousand prisoners had entered Auschwitz since its opening, but less than a year later only around 8,500 were still alive. Security had also tightened; the single line of barbed wire around the perimeter had been replaced with a double row of electrified fences, and Comman-dant Höss had instigated a grim new form of collective punishment for escapes: ten prisoners were chosen at random from the escapee's block to starve to death in retribution. (The first time this happened, Marian Batko, a forty-year-old physics teacher from Krakow, had volunteered to take the place of a teenager who'd been selected, to the amazement of those who witnessed this self-sacrifice.)[40]

Witold included these sorts of details in the oral report he asked Karol to memorize. He also struggled with a more personal dilemma. The number of prisoners being released from the camp—over three hundred since the camp's opening—raised the prospect that Maria would try to secure his freedom. And the truth was, he didn't want to leave the camp, not with his work just beginning. Contrary to his fears of being removed from the action of Warsaw, he had come to see Auschwitz as the heart of the Nazis' quest for domination and that he was standing at the point of opposition. It felt strange to admit, but he'd almost started to feel happy. It's probable that Karol carried a message for his family that under no circumstances were they to try to free him.[41]

Witold found an opportunity to be near the gate to see his friend off. The weather had turned balmy. Karol was in the same dress suit he'd been arrested in, complete with cuff links. The Warsaw actor Stefan Jaracz was being released at the same time. He had tuberculosis, and had suffered from frostbite so deep his finger bones had been exposed. Both men had been layered in powder to hide their wounds from the medical inspection and their cheeks had been touched up with beetroot juice, so they looked as if they were off for a final turn on the stage.[42]

As Karol was about to leave, he looked over at Witold and saw him lost in thought for a moment. Then Witold looked up and winked.[43]

A few days later, Commandant Höss showed up at the stables for one of his customary horse rides around the fields to survey his domain. Teddy the boxer had taken note of that fact, and on this occasion had placed a button under the horse's saddle. No sooner had Höss swung his leg over than the horse took off at a gallop, and the commandant had to cling on for dear life. Teddy watched with delight as the horse skidded to a halt and then sprang away in another direction. A few moments later, the horse came trotting back without its master. Höss was carried to the hospital on a stretcher with a badly twisted leg. Teddy and the others had a good laugh about that afterward. It wasn't an uprising—yet—but at least one Nazi had been overthrown.[44]

CHAPTER 8

EXPERIMENTS

AUSCHWITZ

JUNE 1941

As he waited on Warsaw's response, Witold listened to the BBC for mention of the camp. But there was nothing. The Germans had seized the Balkans and routed the British in Crete. In Libya, Rommel's men bore down on Cairo. The camp orchestra, a daily fixture at the gate, played military marches for prisoners as they departed to and returned from work. Inmates caught occasional glimpses of off-duty SS men sunbathing in their gardens in the evening or playing with their children down by the Soła River.[1]

The prisoners found comfort in the warm weather, but it also delivered the camp's first outbreak of typhus. The disease was spread by lice, which were endemic in the camp's filthy, overcrowded blocks. Prisoners were infected by scratching the insect's typhus-laden feces into the skin after a bite. The illness began with flu-like symptoms and red spots on the torso and arms, resembling little jewels embedded in the skin, and rapidly progressed to feverish hallucinations, narcosis, and a

Camp Orchestra, 1941.

Courtesy of PMA-B.

catastrophic immune response as the bacteria colonized the linings of
the blood vessels and major organs.[2]

"A ward full of typhus patients in the second week of the disease bears more resemblance to an acute mental ward in an asylum
than to a hospital ward," one doctor wrote. Patients often had to be
strapped down so they could not attack staff or throw themselves
out windows or down flights of stairs. The camp's four hospital
blocks were packed with delirious patients whose cries kept the
camp on edge. There was no cure and survival rates were low, but
those who pulled through were subsequently immunized against
reinfection.[3]

The easiest method to contain the disease was to alleviate the un-
hygienic conditions, but the SS resorted to more ineffectual methods
like camp-wide delousings that involved dunking prisoners in vats

Delirious Dreams, by Stanisław Jaster, c. 1942.

Courtesy of the Sławiński family.

of chlorine solution. Dering and the other nurses also heard dark
mutterings among the SS doctors about the need to clear out the
wards. "What is the point of keeping so many sick prisoners in the
hospital?" declared one newly arrived doctor, SS-Sturmbannführer
Siegfried Schwela. Some of the SS medical staff started to experiment by injecting patients with various substances—hydrogen per-
oxide, gasoline, evipan, gasoline perhydrol, ether—in an attempt to
euthanize the sick.[4]

Dering and the other nurses came under increasing pressure to
take part in the killings. The SS had discovered that a shot of phenol
administered by syringe straight to the heart acted quickest, and rou-
tinely disposed of a dozen patients per day. The SS physicians justified
these murders as acts of mercy. "A doctor's duty is to heal patients, but

only those who can be cured. Others we should prevent from suffering," declared Schwela.[5]

One day, Dering was working on a sedated prisoner laid out on the table when a German doctor brought his attention to a syringe on a side table filled with a yellowish-pink fluid. It's a glucose shot, said the man. His eyes betrayed a flicker of excitement. Dering picked up the syringe, knowing it was phenol.[6]

"I'm sorry, I cannot do it," he said softly and returned the needle to the table. The German appeared more disappointed than angry. He ordered Dering confined to the block for two weeks and then instructed someone else, probably Klehr, to inject the man. The patient shuddered and died, a pink spot blossoming on his chest. But Dering, who would later face charges of war crimes for experimental surgeries, otherwise followed German orders, preferring to believe that he could save more lives that way.[7]

Then at roll call on the morning of June 22, Witold picked up on a strange new mood in the camp. The guards seemed quiet, downcast, almost fearful. The kapos didn't beat the prisoners as much as usual. Word spread quickly: Germany had invaded the Soviet Union. Witold sought out Dering to confirm the news on the radio. Hitler's hatred of Communism was well known, but the idea that the Germans would open a second front seemed incredible. Yet the BBC confirmed that in the early hours of the morning Germany had attacked the Soviet Union with the largest army ever assembled: four million men drawn from the Axis powers with six hundred thousand tanks and motorized vehicles spread across a thousand-mile front. The SS Einsatzgruppen and militarized police units known as the Orpo followed in their wake on "cleansing" operations directed at Communist agents and military-age Jewish men who were accused of being sympathizers. Hitler had not yet conceptualized the Final Solution. But he believed Communism to be a Jewish invention intended to subjugate the Aryan race and that the Jews encountered in the Soviet Union were therefore enemy combatants. The hour had arrived, Hitler announced, to take action against "this conspiracy of the Jewish-Anglo-Saxon warmongers and Jewish power-holders of the Bolshevik Center in Moscow." Within weeks the SS were also shooting Jewish women and children.[8]

Witold knew little of events farther east and likely considered Hitler's focus on the Jewish dimension of the invasion to be the Nazi leader's usual ranting. He saw the invasion from a military perspective, and it filled him with hope. Hitler might deliver Stalin a fearsome blow, but the Germans would struggle to fight on two fronts and surely would be defeated. Soon Poland could reclaim its independence. His confidence was shared by the other men. That evening he saw a jubilant crowd gather around one of the new colonels in the camp, Aleksander Stawarz, as he sketched out Germany's downfall in the gravel of the square.[9]

But within days came reports of swift German advances through the Soviet-occupied eastern provinces of Poland. Brześć Litewski fell, then Białystok, Lwów, Tarnopol, Pińsk. The Red Army collapsed so quickly that the BBC reports started to sound like Nazi propaganda. Hundreds of thousands of Soviet soldiers were captured each week and held in vast pens with little food or water. Stalin's regime seemed on the brink of collapse, and the Nazi leadership drew up plans for the long-term occupation of Soviet territory. In July, a few weeks after the invasion began, several hundred Soviet prisoners of war arrived in Auschwitz and were brutally beaten to death in the gravel pits by kapos armed with shovels and picks.[10]

Edward Ciesielski, c. 1941.

Courtesy of PMA-B.

Despair swept through the camp as the German victories mounted that summer of 1941. Most days began with a prisoner rushing at the electric fence to die from the 220-volt charge or a hail of bullets; "going to the wires," the prisoners called it. The SS left the bodies strung out like broken scarecrows until evening roll call.[11]

Witold's youngest men were particularly shaken. "I can see that you surrender to bad moods," Witold said gently to Edward Ciesielski, nicknamed "Edek," a nineteen-year-old with a dimpled chin and baby cheeks in the carpentry workshop where they worked.[12]

"Remember, we are not allowed to break down mentally in any circumstances. The victories of the Germans only postpone their final defeat. But it must happen, sooner or later."

"I count only on you, sir," said Edek, using a bandaged hand to wipe away his tears.[13]

At night, Witold calmed his latest mattress-mate—Wincenty Gawron, a thirty-three-year-old artist from the Tatra highlands south of Krakow—with stories of his escapades during the Bolshevik campaign. The younger man was usually asleep by the time he got to the scene where he charged the Russians' positions on horseback. Privately, though, Witold had his doubts. What if Germany prevailed? Maybe it was better to rise up and die fighting.[14]

*

A few weeks later, Commandant Höss made a curious announcement at morning roll call. He was a slight man, with pursed lips and dark eyes, and the massed ranks of prisoners strained to hear him.

"All ill or crippled can report themselves for a visit to a sanatorium," he said. "Everyone will be cured there. Please report to the clothing block."[15]

Witold watched with concern as a motley crowd staggered to the storeroom block to put their names down. Then he sought out Dering, who told him that the hospital staff had been ordered to draw up a list of "incurables." Dering promised to find out more. He'd gained new influence by convincing the Germans to elevate him to head surgeon and establish an operating theater complete with a table, ether, and a set of scalpels, scissors, saws, and clamps. The SS intended to employ Dering and the facility to practice their surgical skills on inmates. But Dering saw this development differently. His new position gave him authority to accept patients and determine their stay in the recovery ward—the power, in other words, to turn it into a shelter for the underground. Dering asked Bock if the SS meant to treat the so-called incurables and was assured that the German offer was sincere.[16]

Dering submitted a list of sick inmates to the SS in early July. A few weeks later, on July 28, a medical commission arrived at the hospital for a further selection. The weather was warm, so the SS doctor

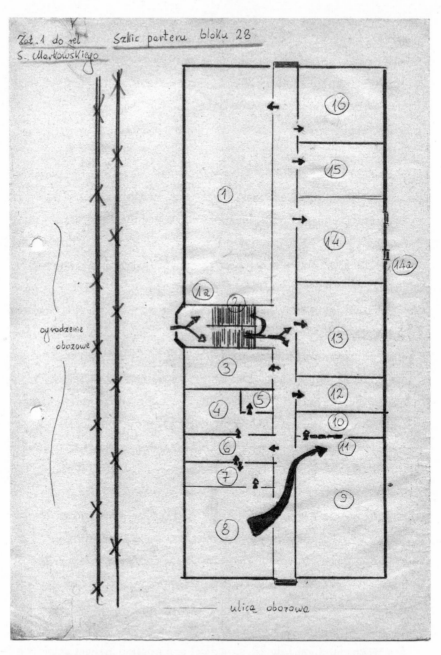

Plan of hospital block with new surgery, by Stefan Markowski, postwar.
1. Orderlies' room. 2. Staircase. 3–7. Doctors' rooms. 8. Admissions.
9. Examination room. 10–11. Block clerk. 12. Toilets. 13. Washing room.
14. Diet kitchen. 15–16. Wards.

Courtesy of PMA-B.

Popiersch set up in the street. SS-Sturmbannführer Horst Schumann, the neatly coifed director of the professed sanatorium, took a seat at a table as the first inmates hobbled forward. Klehr took the medical cards of the sickest and sent those selected to the clothing block to be deloused and given fresh stripes and blankets.[17]

"Lucky guys," the other prisoners dubbed them. Over the course of several hours, patients went to increasingly desperate lengths to get on the list, faking coughs and limps and bribing the nurses with bread. "Take me, take me," cried one inmate, Aleksander Kołodziejczak, raising his hand to show a missing thumb from an old injury. Schumann nodded kindly and added his name to the list, which grew to 575 patients, around a fifth of the hospital.[18]

The sick were already on the way to the waiting train when one of the SS doctors let slip to Dering the truth. Those selected weren't going to a spa. They were heading to a secretive medical center in Sonnenstein outside Dresden and were almost certainly doomed. What he didn't know was that the facility was part of a Nazi program to eliminate German citizens deemed mentally ill or disabled. The so-called T4 program had been established in 1939 and served as a laboratory of sorts for developing methods to kill large groups of people. Its doctors pioneered mass gassing by crowding people into enclosed rooms and flooding them with carbon monoxide. The program was meant to be secret. But it spilled into public view as tens of thousands, many of them children, were killed over the next two years. Public disquiet forced the Nazi leadership to suspend the program.[19]

Himmler, though, saw it as a possible model for clearing "nonproductive elements" from his concentration camps, which had seen a huge increase in the number of sick inmates over the winter of 1940. He had reached an agreement with the T4 killing experts to select sick prisoners for gassing that spring.[20]

Dering watched powerlessly as the inmates traipsed through the camp toward the waiting train. The SS had fitted the carriages with mattresses, pillows, and pots of coffee to maintain the illusion of a holiday. The sight of the patients eagerly boarding and getting settled down was too much for the kapo Krankemann.[21]

"You're all going to be gassed, you idiots," he blurted out, according to one account. In the ensuing panic, Deputy Commandant Fritzsch drew his pistol and ordered Krankemann hung by his own belt from the carriage rafters. Another kapo, the one-armed Siegruth, was ordered onto the transport as well.[22]

The dead prisoners' belongings and clothes were returned to the camp a few days later. One of the SS doctors confirmed to Dering that they'd been gassed with carbon monoxide, except for Siegruth, who'd been murdered on the train by the prisoners. Dering had been keeping his fears to himself, perhaps hoping it wasn't true, but there was no point now. The news stunned the nurses. The idea of mass extermination was a fresh horror. "From now on we realized that the SS might do anything," recalled one orderly.

*

A few weeks after the Sonnenstein transport, Schwela demanded a second list of incurables, and rumors spread that another train was being organized. Witold started a campaign to warn prisoners not to volunteer. Dering helped to release any patients capable of walking. That thinned the numbers but hundreds remained trapped on the wards. Dering gave Schwela a list of a dozen of the sickest prisoners in the hopes that would satisfy him.[23]

Toward the end of August, the SS ordered the blocks to be more thoroughly cleaned than usual and warned the prisoners that the next selection could begin any day. Dering redoubled his efforts to empty the wards and prepare those who would be staying on what to say to minimize their illnesses when the Germans began their culling. To his frustration, some prisoners didn't want to believe him, preferring to trust in Schwela's promise of a spa visit.[24]

He and Witold assumed that the SS would send another transport of prisoners to Dresden. But there were signs that the Germans had a new plan in mind. The penal company block in one corner of the camp was emptied, and the half-sunken windows of the basement levels filled in with concrete. Some prisoners thought that the Germans were building an air raid shelter for an impending Allied offensive. Others were not so sure. A camp lockdown, confining prisoners to their room, was twice announced, but each time the men were released without incident.[25]

But the SS planned to carry out the next round of selections and executions inside the camp now that it had established the logic and efficacy of gassing prisoners en masse. What's more, they planned to expand the program to contend with an anticipated influx of Soviet POWs. Himmler had reached an agreement with the German military to transport 100,000 Soviets to Auschwitz. He hoped to put most to work as forced labor, while uncovering and eliminating communist agents and Jews in their ranks.[26]

Then one morning in early September, Schwela and two other doctors swept into the hospital to announce that the selection was beginning. The sky was gray and flat, and the air heavy with moisture. The chlorine in the blocks stung the nostrils but did little to hide the stench. Schwela, a "small, bulbous, gingerish-blond with a good-natured face," according to Dering, set up at a desk and instructed the prisoners to come forward. He smoked and smiled benignly, pointing out candidates and promising relief, his cigarette ash gathering on the floor beneath him as Klehr ticked off the numbers. Dering was able to make the case for a few, but Schwela was looking to fill a quota. Practically the whole block of tubercular patients was selected, and there were no reprieves for infectious diseases.[27]

Schwela added nearly two hundred and fifty prisoners to his list and pronounced himself satisfied at midday. He sent their cards to the main hospital building, and the nurses started transporting the sick to the basement of the penal block to wait for the supposed train. Many were unable to walk the hundred yards, and the nurses carried them out on stretchers as far as the basement steps, at which point they had to be brought to the cells below on piggyback.[28]

One nurse, Jan Wolny, recalled how the man on his back gripped him around the neck so hard he couldn't breathe, and he wouldn't let go once they reached the airless, dimly lit rooms. It was only when an SS man beat them both to the floor that Jan could extricate himself. He looked back and saw the light from the stairwell catch the stricken man's face for a moment. Then he hurried away.[29]

"You could see from their terrified faces that they were guessing they were going to die," recalled Konrad Szweda, another of the bearers. He was a priest and whispered absolutions to those he carried down. Comatose patients were stacked one on top of the other, as if already dead.[30]

The rest of the prisoners were ordered to stay on their blocks, tense and nervous. No one could sleep, but neither did they feel like talking.

*

Witold sat in the gathering dark, waiting. Then he heard the sound of heavy diesel engines. Those who dared peek out of their windows called out that they saw a procession of trucks bearing a new transport of prisoners. The men wore soiled uniforms and *ushanka* caps. Soviets, perhaps six hundred in all. SS men escorted them into the closed court of the penal block.[31]

The trucks pulled away, leaving the camp in wakeful silence. Just after midnight, Witold heard a scream from the penal block. It wasn't a single voice, but many, roiling up and down the octaves. There were words amid the cries, but they drowned each other out. On and on it went, the same anguished sound, then silence.[32]

The next day, a Saturday, the camp was filled with rumors, and the next: one prisoner had seen SS men in gas masks, another had heard a German complaining that the Soviets had got what was coming to them. On Monday, after evening roll call, there was another block lockdown and further activity at the penal block. The following morning a nurse named Tadeusz Słowiaczek tracked down Witold with a message from Dering. Tadeusz was shaking and wild-eyed as he spoke. The screaming from the other night, he gasped, was the sound of eight hundred and fifty men being gassed. The patients they'd brought there and the Soviets who came afterward were all dead. Tadeusz and the other nurses had spent most of the night carrying out their bodies. His account was terrifying. Commandant Höss had summoned the medical workers into the street and sworn them to secrecy. Then he'd led them over to the basement of the penal block, donned a gas mask, and descended the steps. He emerged a few moments later, then signaled the nurses to follow him inside.[33]

The cell doors were wide open, and in the dim light of a single bulb they could see the contents of each room. The dead were so tightly pressed into each space that they still stood, limbs locked together, eyes bulging, mouths gaping, and teeth bared in silent screams. Their clothes were shredded in places where they must have torn at one another, and several had bite marks. Wherever the flesh was exposed, the skin had a dark bluish hue. Every doorway framed the same scene. Farther down the corridor were the hospital patients who'd been placed in less crowded cells. They seemed to have guessed what was coming, some having stuffed rags in their mouths and nostrils. Scattered on the floor were little blue pellets of what some of the nurses recognized as the delousing agent Zyklon B. The place already stank of decomposing flesh.[34]

Several of the orderlies retched on the floor, but Gienek, the hospital morgue worker, remained calm and directed the others to start with the bodies of the patients, who seemed to be less tangled than the Soviets. They carried them up to the washroom to be stripped, one corpse held between two men, until they found it was quicker to simply drag the dead bodies over the slick floor. The patients were naked, but the Soviets were dressed. Clothes, cigarettes, keepsakes were gathered in a pile. Occasionally an SS man would slip some bauble into his pocket when he thought no one was looking.[35]

Teofil, the other morgue worker, remained outside to oversee the corpses being loaded onto wagons, where the dead had the final indignity of having mouths pried open and any gold fillings and dentures removed with pliers. The bodies were then carted off to the crematorium. The nurses worked all night, but they barely got through half the rooms.

Tadeusz was almost incoherent by the time he finished recounting his story to Witold. Don't you see, he said, this is just the beginning. What's to stop the Germans from gassing us all, now that they realize how easy it is to kill?[36]

The nurses returned that night to finish loading the corpses onto the wagons. The bodies had started to bloat and were slippery from the light rain that was falling. They used their belts to wrap around arms and legs for added purchase as they slung the bodies on board. Gienek oversaw one wagonload stacked with eighty bodies as it teetered and swayed and then toppled over, burying a nurse under a pile of corpses that slithered onto the floor like wet fish. The others rushed to pull the half-choked man free. The SS guards laughed and fetched additional nurses, including Dering, to carry the bodies on their backs to the crematorium. The morgue was already full, so they laid the corpses out by the door.[37]

Witold couldn't grasp the Nazis' intentions. The earlier gassing of incurables outside Dresden had at least conformed to the logic of eliminating those who couldn't work. It made no sense for the SS to kill off the Soviets without extracting their labor. What he did know was that the experiment represented an unprecedented new evil that might shock the Allies into understanding the importance of the camp. On September 14, one of the nurses, Marian Dipont, was released from the camp, and likely carried a first eyewitness account of the gassing to Warsaw and an oral report. Witold tried to unearth more information over the next few days, but the experiment in the penal block was not repeated.[38]

A week later, Witold's block was selected for use as an additional delousing facility, and he was moved to a barracks along the perimeter facing the crematorium. The weather had turned cold, and a sharp wind whipped down the streets. Roll call was about to begin, and Witold was hurrying out of the building when he saw SS guards using their rifle butts to herd a long column of naked men arranged in ranks of five into the crematorium. Witold guessed they must be Soviets who had arrived the night before in the camp and that they were being issued with underwear and clothes, though he wondered at the use of the crematorium for that purpose.

That night he learned that the SS had emptied tins of Zyklon B onto the screaming men through specially drilled holes in the flat roof.

Witold likely recognized the sinister logic of murdering the Soviets in the crematorium. Gassing victims beside the ovens avoided the challenge of hauling corpses through the camp. The morgue's ventilation system also meant the Zyklon B residue could be quickly cleared. But he didn't understand that he had witnessed the creation of the camp's first gas chamber with the power to kill on an industrial scale.[39] Nor could be conceive of an ideology of mass muder. He surmised that the Soviets had been killed because no accommodation was ready for them. His conclusion was reinforced a few days later when several blocks in the camp were cordoned off with a barbed wire fence and designated the "Soviet POW camp."[40]

In October, the first of a dozen freight trains carrying thousands of Soviet POWs arrived. The men were forced to strip and jump into a vat of foul-smelling disinfectant before being chased into the camp, where a cry went up: "They're coming." The kapos shooed the other prisoners into their blocks. It was bright and cold, and the first frost had come, lining the block windows with ice, but Witold could catch glimpses of the Soviets, crouching outside their blocks, naked and shivering. Some of the SS men had cameras and were taking photos. They left the Soviets in the yard overnight, and they howled in the cold.[41]

The next morning the camp woke to see the wretches, still crouching but gray and motionless. Dark clouds had rolled in on a freezing northern wind. Witold's friend Michał from the carpentry shop went to check on them. "They're going to finish these people off," he reported upon returning. "The kapo says they will be outside until the evening." He took out a cigarette and fumbled with the matches. The Soviets hadn't been fed, either.[42]

"Who kills prisoners of war can never win the war," observed one inmate. "When the other party finds out about it, it will be a fight to death."[43]

The crematorium morgue of the main camp.
Courtesy of Jarosław Fiedor.

Further transports of Soviet POWs arrived every few days. Witold recognized that the German atrocities against the soldiers needed to be reported on. This required him to cross an emotional barrier, given the Soviet Union's role in the destruction and occupation of his country. Indeed, his tone in describing the Soviets' predicament is notably restrained. He briefly considered forging an alliance, but the Polish nurses appointed to care for Soviet POWs in a rudimentary hospital block reported back that the men were too broken and demoralized for Witold to risk confiding in them. Instead, Witold turned his attention to reporting on their plight. He prepared a second oral report on the gassing experiments and the sudden influx of Soviet POWs, likely carried out of the camp on October 22 by another released prisoner, named Czesław Wąsowski.[44]

By early November, the Soviet contingent stood at ten thousand—almost equaling the number of Poles in the camp. They were put to work building a new camp for the expected one hundred thousand POWs two miles away in an area of marshes and silver birch copses that gave the place its name: Brzezinka, or Birkenau in German. The Soviets were demolishing the small Polish village near the site to salvage supplies for the new barracks. The SS planned for 174 brick barracks over eighty-one hectares of water-logged terrain.[45]

Witold could only guess at the completed camp's role: its sheer size meant the Nazis must be planning to make it a central collection point for Soviet prisoners. Witold likely surmised that they would be worked to death. The Soviet contingent limped home from work each day, pulling harvest carts stacked with their deceased comrades or those no longer capable of moving. The existing crematorium couldn't cope with the load, and so the SS switched to burying the bodies in Birkenau's woods and then, after the ground froze solid, they kept them in one of the Soviet blocks in the main camp, filling up the basement first, and then the next two floors as the dead replaced the living.[46]

Witold was determined to get a handle on the numbers dying and placed a recruit in the camp's records office, where prisoners worked as clerks. According to his source, 3,150 Soviet POWs had died in roughly a month—more than all the Poles that had perished in the camp's first year of existence. Witold could not discern the direction of the camp—the Nazi leadership itself had yet to decide—but he saw that the horrors were mounting and that he needed to provoke an Allied response. His next messenger, the carpenter Ferdynand Trojnicki, was released in mid-November with news of Birkenau and the latest figures. The camp surveyor Władysław Surmacki left a few weeks later

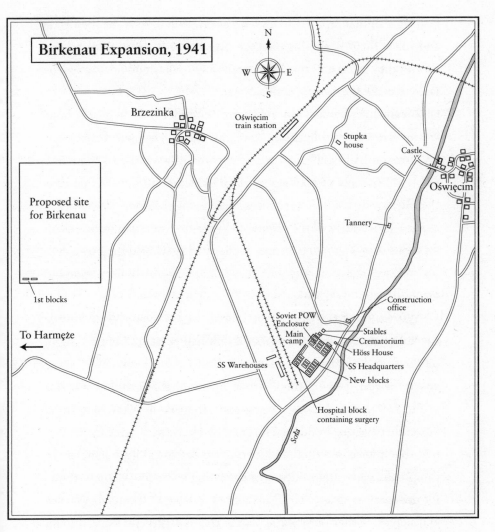

Birkenau Expansion, 1941

N
W E
S

Brzezinka

Oświęcim
train station

Stupka
house

Castle

Oświęcim

Proposed site
for Birkenau

Tannery

1st blocks

Construction
office

To Harmęże

Soviet POW
Enclosure

Main
camp

Stables

Crematorium

Höss House

SS Headquarters

SS Warehouses

New blocks

Hospital block
containing surgery

Soła

John Gilkes

bearing a similar report. On each occasion, Witold took the men aside and made them repeat his message over and over again until he was certain they had memorized the details and understood how to use the facts to make the case for action.[47]

Meanwhile, he began to reluctantly consider that their only hope was to stage a camp uprising. The odds hadn't changed. In fact, the SS garrison had doubled in recent months to around two thousand. Many if not most of his men would be killed in a fight. But perhaps their lives were the necessary cost of destroying the camp. To stand any chance, he would need the colonels. Witold had been monitoring them for months with growing respect as they had developed their own cells and avoided detection. Together they might number almost a thousand men—enough to do some damage.[48]

Witold knew that military etiquette would require him to cede control of a combined underground. He had come to admire a slight officer from Bydgoszcz in western Poland named Kazimierz Rawicz above the rest. During the German invasion, Rawicz's unit was one of the few that had fought to the end. The two men met one frigid November evening beside the hospital block. Rawicz agreed with Witold that a force of a thousand men could destroy at least some of the camp and nearby train lines, while creating a window of opportunity for prisoners to escape. He also claimed to have a channel to Warsaw and suggested they present the plan to the underground leadership for approval.[49]

Witold knew the uprising could take months to plan, and that organizing an army of that size was fraught with danger, but he went to work over the following days with a renewed sense of purpose. He had found a position at an old tannery complex outside the camp where the SS employed several hundred skilled workers. The assembled leather workers, locksmiths, blacksmiths, and tailors had their own workshops and were meant to produce camp staples, but the kapos had created a little business offering up the prisoners' services to SS men. The constant comings and goings of the Germans brought him tantalizingly close to his tormentors. Höss swung by to order a model airplane for his eldest son; Fritzsch came next wanting candlesticks engraved with Snow White and the seven dwarfs. Then Fritz Seidler, who'd threatened Witold with imminent death on his first night in the camp, stalked right up to his desk in the carving workshop, where his friend Wincenty was working on a portrait of Hitler for their kapo. Seidler eyed them and the painting. They all tensed awaiting his verdict.[50]

"It looks good," he said at last. "When it's finished I will take it and hang it at home."[51]

"An honor, sir," the kapo interjected. "It's a great honor."[52]

Marching back from work with the others, Witold longed to strike. He stole moments whenever he could to plan with the others. One of his recruits among the tanners had fashioned a hideaway in the main hall of the tannery complex. The room contained a dozen deep pits for

Kazimierz Rawicz, c. 1941.

Courtesy of PMA-B.

holding chemical solutions. The tanners had kept one of the pits dry and draped logs strung with strips of drying leather to cover the opening. The pit was the perfect place to discuss underground matters. The tanners often served cow and pig ears roasted in the stove of the drying room. They had another treat on offer: a bath in the large tank of warm water for soaking skins. "I took a bath and felt as I had once felt as a free man," Witold recalled. "It was inconceivable."[53]

Such moments couldn't last, nor would he want them to, with the uprising approaching and death all around him. On November 11, Armistice Day and the anniversary of Polish independence, the SS called out the names of 151 prisoners at roll call and marched them off to an enclosed courtyard that had recently been constructed beside the penal block. The men were shot one at a time with a pneumatic bolt-action gun of the kind used to kill cattle. There was so much blood, it ran down the gutter and oozed under the gate to the courtyard and into the street.[54]

Witold was still at work when he heard the news. He sat in stony silence. One of the carvers burst into tears. Otto, the friendly German kapo, staggered in.

"There is no God!" he declared, his hands shaking as he thumbed out a cigarette. "They cannot get away with it. They must lose the war over this wickedness."[55]

"You think so?" asked one of the carvers, with a slight edge to his voice.[56]

"I do what I can," Otto said.[57]

"I know that, I know," replied the carver. "But try not to think about anything else, until we stop those bastards."

A few days later, Witold noted to Wincenty that the number of SS men guarding the tannery had been reduced to twenty. Then one day in December there were barely a dozen. Perhaps a stomach bug was doing the rounds; it didn't matter.[58]

"Do you see?" Witold whispered to Wincenty when they got to the workshop. "We could easily overpower them, dress in their uniforms, and surprise the camp."[59]

Wincenty wanted to laugh, but Witold had a look in his eye and his voice sounded different.

"It's doable in theory," the younger man ventured.[60]

The next stage had begun.

———

CHAPTER 9

SHIFTS

WARSAW
NOVEMBER 1941

The underground leader Stefan Rowecki received Witold's reports on the gassing of Soviet POWs that autumn. He, like Witold, was unsure what to make of this development. It certainly contravened international law. But Rowecki didn't connect the Nazis' capacity to kill to their brutal project in Warsaw. By contrast, the policy toward Jews was murderous. The Germans had packed the city's four-hundred-thousand-strong Jewish community into the cramped streets of the ghetto, where thousands died each month due to shortages of food and medical care. What's more, Rowecki's men were reporting that Germans—and some Polish collaborators—were committing mass shootings of Jews in what was now German-occupied Poland. But Rowecki saw these incidents as isolated Nazi pogroms and not as the start of a campaign of mass murder.[1]

The gassing in Auschwitz seemed to be a one-off, and Rowecki's colleagues theorized that the gas was a new weapon being tested for

use at the front. The news that the camp was to become a major holding facility for Soviet POWs suggested that the Nazis wanted to use
the Soviets as slave labor like the Poles.[2]

Rowecki had Witold's reports written up and gave them to his
best courier, Sven Norrman, a staid fifty-four-year-old Swede who ran
the Polish branch of a Swedish electrical engineering firm in Warsaw. Norrman despised what the Nazis were doing to his adopted city
and believed that as an outsider he had a duty to share what he saw.
Sweden's neutrality in the war meant he could travel between Poland
and Stockholm, making him the ideal courier. Rowecki regularly met
Norrman at U Elny Gistedt in the city center, where they could be
assured of the hostess's discretion, a decent meal of black market fare,
and beer served secretly in paper cups.[3]

Norrman left for Berlin in mid-November carrying a report that
contained the news of the gassings on a roll of 16 mm or 35 mm microfilm hidden in a false-bottomed suitcase. Microfilm had been developed before the war to preserve newspapers. A single roll, produced
using a camera fitted with a microscopic lens, could contain 2,400
pages of reports and had the virtue of being unreadable to the naked
eye, buying time in the event of capture.[4]

Norrman loudly professed his admiration for National Socialism
to his companions on the train and passed through Berlin's Tempelhof
airport without problems to board a Douglas plane to Stockholm. Despite German pressure, the Poles had kept open their legation in the
Swedish capital. Norrman probably handed over the microfilm there
so that it could be sent on the clandestine mail run that the British
operated around the northern tip of Norway to the Leuchars air base,
near St. Andrews on the Scottish coast. From there, the report was
delivered to London for vetting by the British authorities before finally

reaching the Polish leader, Władysław Sikorski, at his Rubens hotel headquarters at the end of November.[5]

＊

The report reached London as British officials were developing their own understanding of German atrocities in the Soviet Union. The immediate threat of an invasion of Britain had abated, and though the Luftwaffe continued to strike at British cities, the Blitz was less intense. Londoners talked quietly about the passing of the storm, but Churchill knew the war hung in the balance.

"Every week [Hitler's] firing parties are busy in a dozen lands," Churchill had told radio listeners on May 3, 1941. "Mondays he shoots Dutchmen. Tuesdays, Norwegians. Wednesday, French or Belgians stand against the wall. Thursdays it is Czechs who must suffer, and now there are the Serbs and the Greeks to fill his repulsive bill of executions. But always, all the days, there are the Poles."[6]

Such public statements by Churchill fit within the established narrative of German brutality and were mainly intended to remind British listeners of the need to keep fighting Hitler. But Churchill also knew that the start of the German offensive against the Soviet Union in June 1941 marked a disturbing shift in the nature of Nazi atrocities. British cryptographers at Bletchley Park had been listening in on some of the signals the Germans sent via so-called Enigma machines, a device that used rotors to mechanically scramble letters. The Germans were so confident that the Enigma could not be cracked that they rarely changed their codes, but Polish intelligence had made a secret replica of an early version of the machine and had passed it on to the British in 1939. In late June 1941, the cryptographers started picking up intercepted radio messages sent by the Orpo militarized police units to Ber-

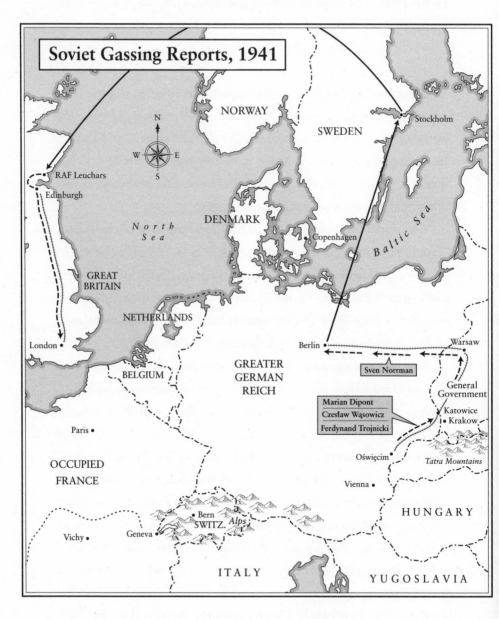

Soviet Gassing Reports, 1941

NORWAY

SWEDEN

Stockholm

RAF Leuchars

Edinburgh

DENMARK

North
Sea

Copenhagen

Baltic Sea

GREAT
BRITAIN

NETHERLANDS

London

Berlin

Warsaw

Sven Norrman

BELGIUM

GREATER
GERMAN
REICH

General
Government

Marian Dipont
Czesław Wąsowicz
Ferdynand Trojnicki

Katowice
Krakow

Paris

OCCUPIED
FRANCE

Oświęcim

Tatra Mountains

Vienna

Vichy

Bern

SWITZ. Alps

Geneva

HUNGARY

ITALY

YUGOSLAVIA

John Gilkes

lin listing the huge numbers of Jews they had shot alongside so-called partisans and Communist sympathizers.[7]

The numbers were so shockingly high that at first, British analysts puzzled over the decoded lists.

"Whether all those executed as 'Jews' are indeed such is of course doubtful," wrote one analyst. "Many no doubt were not Jews; but the fact that this heading invariably produces the biggest figures shows that this is the ground for killing most acceptable to the Higher Authorities."[8]

By the end of August 1941, Churchill understood that the Nazi campaign against the Jews was murderous and unprecedented in scale. But like Rowecki in Warsaw, he too failed to identify it as genocidal. He knew of prewar Nazi policy targeting German Jews and that Hitler had threatened to make all Jews pay for the war, but he doesn't appear to have connected Nazi dogma with the details emerging from Russia. On August 25, he told listeners of the BBC that "scores of thousands—literally scores of thousands—of executions in cold blood were being perpetrated by the German police-troops on the Russian patriots who defend their native soil . . . we are in the presence of a crime without a name."[9]

The speech drew headlines but also underscored the challenges of calling attention to the killings. Churchill's failure to mention that many of those killed were Jews was possibly intended to disguise the origin of the material. But the omission also reflected the reasoning of some officials that focusing on the plight of the Jews would stir anti-Semitism at home, an argument that mostly reflected their own genteel racism.[10]

Victor Cavendish-Bentinck, the chairman of the Joint Intelligence Committee, remained skeptical of the facts, despite being one of the few officials with access to the German order police intercepts. When he learned from Soviet sources about the massacre of thirty-three thousand Jews in the Babi Yar ravine outside Kiev at the end of September, he called the report "the product of Slav imaginations" and cited the fact that Britain itself had "put out rumors of atrocities and horrors for various purposes" during the previous war. He concluded, "I have no doubt that this game is widely played." He thought Nazi atrocities, if there were any, were a subject best left to be dealt with after the war.[11]

Anti-Semitism probably played a role in the collective failure of the British government to grapple with the evidence. But so too did the sheer magnitude and historical novelty of the crime. As the Dutch theologian Willem Visser 't Hooft wrote after the war, "People could find no place in their consciousness for such an unimaginable horror, and . . . did not have the imagination, together with the courage, to face it." It was possible, Hooft concluded, to live in the "twilight between knowing and not knowing." Put another way, until British officials accepted the reality of the mass murders, either through the weight of evidence or a sudden leap of empathy, there was no chance of the twilight lifting.[12]

*

In the meantime, the Polish leader Sikorski represented the best hope to focus British attention on the mounting atrocities, including Auschwitz. Over the summer of 1941, the Polish exile government had released the first English-language account of the camp in a government fortnightly newspaper, largely based on Witold's first report. The British government was content to allow the Poles to disseminate such material, but it refrained from endorsing their findings and advised newspaper editors against taking up the theme. "Sheer 'horror' stuff such as the concentration camp torture stories . . . repel the normal mind," ran a British Ministry of Interior memo in July 1941. "A certain amount of horror is needed but it must be used very sparingly and must deal always with the treatment of indisputably innocent people. Not with violent political opponents. And not with Jews." British newspapers had yet to publish details about the camp, and the public continued to treat stories of German brutality with skepticism.[13]

Sikorski tried to persuade the British to issue a broad declaration condemning Nazi atrocities in the hopes of building momentum toward bombing raids against German targets in Poland. However, the Foreign Office was reluctant to endorse Sikorski's proposal, which it viewed as a distraction from the main war effort. But just as Sikorski's case appeared to be lost, the U.S. president Franklin Roosevelt delivered a speech threatening "fearful retribution" for German war crimes in France.[14]

Roosevelt's comments were widely read as a signal that America was gearing up for war. Churchill, eager to court the Americans, issued his own statement that the prosecution of war crimes was now a major aim of the war. Foreign Secretary Anthony Eden hastily agreed to host a war crimes conference in January at which a joint Polish and Czech statement would be presented.[15]

Sikorski made the most of the opening. He commissioned a compendium of German crimes called *The Black Book of Poland* in preparation for the conference. Material from Witold's first report once again featured prominently in the book's discussion of the concentration camp. The book's authors were mostly focused on Nazi crimes against Poles. The treatment of Polish Jews in the ghetto was briefly described but not the mass murders of Jews in Soviet-controlled territory, which might have required a discussion of the role of Poles in some of the killings. Nor did it mention the gas experiments against Soviet POWs in Auschwitz. Nonetheless, Sikorski was confident the book would galvanize support for his proposed bombing campaign.[16]

That hope became more of a viable possibility when America entered the war after the Japanese attack on the U.S. Pacific Fleet at Pearl Harbor on December 7. The British were no longer alone and Churchill could start to think concretely about a joint invasion of the continent perhaps as soon as the following year. The St. James Conference in Westminster, as it became known, represented the first full gathering of the Allied powers. Eden, the U.S. ambassador Anthony Drexel Biddle, and his Russian counterpart, along with a host of officials from other exile governments, listened to Sikorski's opening address on January 11, in which he sought to rally the Allies around the issue of German crimes and establish the principle of retribution.[17]

"Let this be a warning to everybody who is harming civilians in our countries that they will be punished," Sikorski told the gathering. "It should also be a spark of hope to those millions of people who are doing their job in occupied countries. They will know now that there's a punishment for aggressors."[18]

No consensus was reached about what form retribution should take. But Sikorski knew that gathering more evidence of Nazi atrocities was essential. He had been pushing Dalton to arrange more parachute jumps for Polish SOE operatives. Cloudy skies and Britain's preoccupation with supporting the Soviet war effort meant that only three airdrops had been completed to date. Sikorski knew they needed to do more to make the case for action.[19]

CHAPTER 10

PARADISE

AUSCHWITZ

DECEMBER 1941

Witold's men were energized by the plan for the uprising. But it worried Witold that he had received no word from Warsaw since he had arrived in the camp. Were his messages getting through? Had he failed to convey the staggering nature of the crimes he had witnessed? The BBC was reporting that Churchill and Roosevelt were preparing for a major offensive against the Germans. Somehow Witold needed to make them see that Auschwitz represented the heart of the Nazis' evil. So as Rawicz finalized plans for the revolt, Witold turned his attention to German plans for the rapidly expanding camp.[1]

He was intrigued to learn from his men that they had bumped up against another resistance cell running its own intelligence-gathering operation. Its leader was a well-known, left-leaning activist and parliamentarian named Stanisław Dubois, who'd been jailed before the war for his opposition to the government's right-wing and anti-Semitic policies. He had arrived in Auschwitz on the same transport as Witold under a false name, but the Gestapo had summoned him back to

Warsaw for further questioning. He had returned to the camp in the summer of 1941 and formed a socialist cell.[2]

Witold had kept his distance at first, perhaps fearing he was still under Gestapo observation, but the Germans seemed to be leaving him alone. Stanisław—Stasiek to his friends—could be found most nights outside his block defiantly puffing on a cigarette. He wasn't physically imposing, recalled one friend. "He was a bit pale but he had these sparkling eyes. He was determined and somehow impertinent." Witold reached out to Stasiek after discovering that they'd both planted recruits in the SS headquarters, and the two men agreed to coordinate efforts.[3]

They met again with other resistance leaders on Christmas Eve, a day off for the camp. It was minus 13 degrees Fahrenheit that night, snow was coming down in crystal shards, and the SS guards at roll call were eager to retreat inside. The prisoners returned to the barracks for soup and bread, and the kapos left them in peace. Wincenty had smuggled a small fir tree into one of the rooms and decorated it with angels, stars, and an eagle carved from root vegetables. Professor Roman

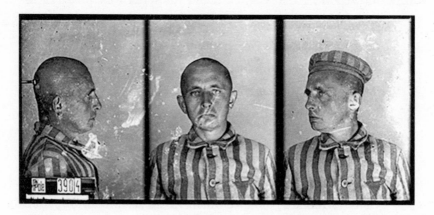

Stanisław Dubois, c. 1941.

Courtesy of PMA-B.

Drawing of an eagle wearing a crown, Poland's national emblem,
that adorned the Christmas tree in 1941, by Wincenty Gawron, postwar.

Courtesy of Ewa Biały and Zofia Wiśniewska.

Rybarski, a right-wing politician, gave a speech and handed out smuggled Christmas wafers. He then embraced Stasiek, a former political adversary, much to Witold's quiet satisfaction. "One had to show Poles daily a mountain of Polish corpses in order for them to reconcile," he later observed.[4]

The best speech that night was the simplest, given by the block's clerk. "Dear friends!" he declared. "Support one another, be kind to one another, so the chimney is smoking as little as possible."[5]

As they returned to their blocks that night, they could hear a German guard in one of the watchtowers whistling "Silent Night."

The SS records office presented Witold and Stasiek with a trove of data. The office contained a ledger known as the Stärkebuch, or daily count book, which noted new arrivals, transfers, releases, and every death. Here was the evidence the underground needed to fully document Nazi crimes. Until then, Witold had forbidden keeping written records over safety concerns, but he realized that the full extent of the atrocities could only be accurately preserved on paper and agreed to a change in policy.[6]

In January 1942, Witold's and Stasiek's recruits in the record office started making a copy of the Stärkebuch. There was no chance of doing this during the day, but when multiple transports arrived at once, the clerks sometimes had to work through the night with little or no supervision. The copied papers were then brought over to the storage block, where another underground member collated the information and hid the documents. Stasiek later prepared written reports for the surveyors to take out of the camp. By March 1942,

Kazimierz Jarzębowski, by Jan Komski, postwar.
Courtesy of PMA-B.

he calculated that 30,000 Poles had been registered in the camp, of which 11,132 were still alive. The figure included around 2,000 Polish Jews brought to the camp, of whom most were dead. Of the 12,000 Soviet POWs who had arrived in the camp, only around a hundred were alive.[7]

Leadership of the smuggling operation had fallen to a placid-looking engineer named Kazimierz Jarzębowski, who was in charge of the inmate surveyors. He hid the documents in map cylinders or the hollowed-out components of their measuring tools, then left the material at various pickup points in the fields around the camp to be collected by Helena Stupka and others.[8]

Helena had started using her six-year-old son, Jacek, to deliver and collect messages, since the family had been forcibly evicted from their

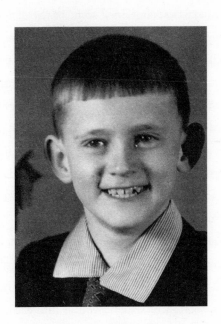

Jacek Stupka, during the war.
Courtesy of the Stupka family.

house near the camp to the other side of the river. Jacek would wait by the bridge for the surveyors to march past and knew to approach them if they were singing a certain tune, which meant the SS men had been bribed. One time he mistook the tune, and a guard picked him up by his ears and carried him back over the bridge, tearing his lobes in the process, but a lucky escape all the same.[9]

While the underground prepared its reports for smuggling, Witold found a more direct method for contacting the outside world. By February 1942, there was one area of the camp that the resistance had been unable to penetrate: the SS headquarters' radio room, where camp authorities conversed with Berlin. Auschwitz, like other concentration camps, had a so-called Enigma machine for encoding messages and a telephone switchboard for internal communication. Unbeknownst to the Germans, the British had started to intercept radio traffic from Auschwitz in January that contained some of the data that Witold and Stasiek were copying and smuggling out of the camp. The intercepts confirmed Auschwitz's particular harshness but failed to capture the increasingly systematic way in which prisoners were being killed—exactly the sort of context contained in Witold's report.[10]

Inmates were forbidden from approaching the radio room, but one of Witold's recruits, an engineering student named Zbigniew Ruszczyński, worked in the construction office, which had a storeroom for spare radio parts. Zbigniew believed it housed everything that they needed to construct their own transmitter.[11]

The radio would be a simple device, capable of relaying only Morse code. All Zbigniew needed was a battery with a switch to create a current, a couple of valves to boost the frequency, and several meters of copper wire, a section of which, wound into a coil, conducted the signal to the antenna. The valves contained vacuum cylinders that were the most delicate piece of any radio, and thus the hardest to smuggle

Zbigniew Ruszczyński, c. 1941.

Courtesy of PMA-B.

into the camp. If Zbigniew was right, their creation would be heard in Warsaw and beyond.[12]

First, though, they would have to steal the equipment and move it into the camp for assembly. Witold volunteered himself for the mission and tapped Kon to join him. The young recruit had established a reputation as one of the most brazen thieves or "organizers" in the camp, assisted by a small repertoire of magic tricks he'd picked up at the university. Kon had landed a job in the SS kitchen preparing food for the guards after impressing the German kapo who ran the squad with a trick for palming cigarettes. The kapo, nicknamed Mamma, saw the value of having someone with thieving skills on his team, and soon roped Kon into stealing sausages and smuggling them into the camp under his shirt. Mamma paid off the guards with a portion, took his own cut, and left Kon a little to share around.[13]

Witold had witnessed Kon's skills standing in the square one evening a few weeks before. He had heard a commotion at the gate and saw the guards beating a man they'd caught stealing a piece of salami. They ordered him to run between the electric fence posts and then shot him for trying to escape. Kon had been next in line and passed the inspection without incident.

"We were afraid you might be carrying some food tonight," Witold had exclaimed when they met. "Thank God you weren't."[14]

"I don't know how I got through," Kon had replied. He pulled out the two sausages that he'd hidden in the front of his waistband.

Witold had grinned and declared he made a better thief than an officer.

A day before the radio operation was to begin, Witold led Kon out of the block to talk.

"When you two get all the steaks from the secret steakhouse, don't forget about your friends!" a colleague shouted after them.[15]

It was bitter outside, the snow piled in drifts around the buildings. Kon was impatient and pointed out that they were the only ones in the square.

"You're right, we cannot walk here," admitted Witold. "Let's pretend I am sick and you are taking me to the hospital."[16]

He leaned on Kon and feigned a limp.

"I have to ask you to make a big sacrifice for the organization," Witold began. He explained the mission. Kon seemed unfazed by the task but was unhappy about leaving his job in the kitchen. Witold assured him that he could switch back again after the task was complete. Besides, he'd already asked Mamma to let him go for a week, and Otto in the labor office had approved the switch.

"It appears I have no choice," said Kon.[17]

The next day, Witold and Kon joined a dozen inmates in the construction office to find the camp's chief architect, SS-Hauptsturmführer Karl Bischoff, scrambling to modify the plans for Birkenau. The slow pace of construction had already obliged Bishoff to switch from building brick barracks to using prefabricated horse stables for rapid assembly. Now he had orders to construct a large new crematorium. The Nazis had envisioned that Auschwitz would house an influx of Soviet POWs captured in the wake of victory in the east. But a new purpose was coming into focus as Germany faced a war of attrition against the combined might of Britain, America, and the Soviet Union. The Jews were coming.

Hitler had long threatened to resolve the so-called Jewish problem in the event that the fighting grew into a global conflict, and historians once believed that he delivered a single order to kill Europe's Jews. But in fact the program of extermination that we have come to call the Holocaust came into being in the winter of 1941 through the acceleration of murderous processes already occurring at all levels of the Nazi state. The T4 euthanasia program pioneered in 1939 represented an early strand. The SS experiments in the concentration camps to eliminate sick prisoners and POWs further consolidated techniques and moral logic. The mass shootings of Jewish men, women, and children by Einsatzgruppen and Orpo police units in the Soviet Union marked the beginning of genocide and focused attention on finding more industrial killing methods. The T4 program had already developed special gassing trucks that pumped carbon monoxide into their cargo bays for killing patients who lived too far away from a gas chamber. In November 1941 Himmler approved the deployment of the trucks to occupied Russia to spare his men the trauma of shooting civilians. Similar vehicles were deployed to a camp outside the village of Chełmno in territory annexed from western Poland, which became the first of four regional gassing facilities intended to kill Eastern European Jews. Then, in January 1942, senior Nazis and state officials met in the Berlin suburb of Wannsee to discuss plans to deport Jews from the rest of Europe to the occupied East either to be murdered immediately or worked to death in labor gangs. They called this secretive program the Final Solution.[19]

Himmler was responsible for putting into motion the policies that would eventually make Auschwitz the epicenter of the Holocaust. But his initial thinking about the camp reflected the often ad hoc nature of Nazi policy-making. The lack of Soviet POWs for Birkenau meant he had an empty camp. So shortly after the Wannsee conference he met Hitler for lunch and proposed that he fill it with Jews. A note for his office diary that day reads: "Jews into KL [Concentration Camp]." A few weeks later, in early February 1942, Himmler told the Auschwitz hierarchy to expect transports of Jews from Slovakia and France.[20]

Witold had no knowledge of the Nazis' emerging plans for the exploitation and mass murder of Jews. It's possible he overheard the SS architects discuss the incoming Jewish workers. But the news would have fitted in his mind with the existing Nazi practice of exploiting Polish

Construction office staff.

Courtesy of PMA-B.

and Soviet labor. Indeed, Witold would have been intrigued by the lack
of Soviet POWs, an indication of German failure on the eastern front.

Witold gleaned what information he could and found a moment to
leave his desk and scope the building. It was a single-story construction
with several rooms off a central corridor. The radio room was at one
end and strictly out of bounds, but through the door it was possible to
see a bank of radio equipment. After a week of careful pilfering, Witold
had assembled the pieces he needed to construct a transmitter. One afternoon Witold approached Kon's desk with a flushed face. All the radio
parts were in a box in the bathroom stall, he told Kon. They had to be
moved immediately.[21]

"Let me look at it," Kon replied.[22]

A few minutes later Witold heard a crash in the corridor, and then
Kon shouting: "Where do you think you're going? Out you go, you
swine dogs."

Kon reappeared in the room, looking nonchalant. The kapo asked
what the shouting was about.

"Oh, it was nothing," said Kon. "A couple of dirty Muselmänner
wanted to hide in our washroom and I just chased them back to work."

He cast a quick glance Witold's way.

"What did you really do there?" asked Witold, when they were finally left alone.[23]

Kon explained he'd almost been discovered by a couple of prisoners
as he stashed the box in a supply cupboard in the corridor. Luckily
they'd run away once he shouted at them.

The new hiding place was an improvement on the bathroom but also
temporary. The conspirators discussed solutions that evening outside
the blocks. The only way to bring the box back to the camp without detection would be to employ one of the roll wagon teams. They decided
that Gienek's morgue cart was the most likely to escape inspection at

the gate. Gienek readily agreed to pick up the box if they could place it in a garbage pit around the back of the building. But that still left the problem of how to get the box to the pit, two hundred yards from the building in a wasteland beside the main road. Witold said they should sleep on it, but the next day they were no closer to an answer.

He spent the morning worrying that someone would find the box. It wasn't until the evening approached that Witold struck upon a plan. The kapo informed them that they would be working late to finish maps, meaning soup would be served in the office. When they had finished eating, Witold leaned over to Kon and whispered, "I'll test the SS guard to see how thorough he is."[24]

He asked to go to the toilet.

"Go," the guard replied, "but don't try anything stupid or I'll fill you full of holes."[25]

The guard opened the door to the corridor and stood at the doorway.

Witold came back shortly. He'd noticed that the bathroom's window had no bars and faced the garbage dump. One of them might be able to climb through, deposit the box, and rush back again.

"How can you take that huge radio from the cupboard in full view of the SS guard?" asked Kon.[26]

"I'll pretend that I have diarrhea and will go to the toilet every fifteen to twenty minutes," said Witold. "During one of these trips you will start performing your magic tricks for everybody. Get the guard sufficiently involved to keep him away from the door. When you think there's enough time for me to get the radio out, say loudly: 'Now, watch very carefully!' That's my signal."

Kon smiled. "All right," he said.

Witold began to groan, holding his stomach, while Kon tried to get his neighbor's attention by making a coin dance over his knuckles. The kapo wasn't impressed.

"No funny business there!" he shouted. "Get back to work!"[27]

Witold was allowed to go to the toilet, but was only gone a minute when the guard grew suspicious and came to check on him. Luckily he was in the correct position, but the guard lingered. Witold returned. There was no chance of making a move.

The kitchen cart arrived with acorn coffee. During the break, Kon started up his tricks again, this time quite openly. One of the German guards had a deck of cards in his pocket, and he challenged Kon to show what he could do.

Kon picked a couple of cards from the deck. "Watch very carefully!" he said, and then started a simple monte trick where one card transformed into another. He performed the trick over and over, until the SS guards were demanding to know how it was done. Witold requested the toilet, and this time the guards waved him away. In the corridor, he forced the supply cupboard's doors open, eased the box off the shelf, and shuffled to the bathroom, where he stacked the box on the window shelf.[28]

Kon went to the toilet next. Witold waited nervously. After a few minutes, he heard a crash outside, and the sound of guards shouting. The SS men in the room looked up. He had to do something. "Toilet!" he shouted, and rushed into the hallway and started banging on the door.[29]

"Get out of there!" he yelled. "Don't you see that I'm going to do it in my pants?"

It was the only way he could think to hide the commotion outside. He heard someone scrambling back through the window.

"How can you just sit there and let me suffer?" Witold continued to shout.

Kon instantly got the ruse and shouted back, "You've camped here already for half the night! You'll get your turn soon enough!"[30]

Kon emerged a moment later and gave Witold a thumbs-up before returning to the room. On the march back to the camp, Kon revealed that he had stumbled into the garbage dump, and the commotion had alerted some nearby SS men. Fortunately, he'd managed to make it back to the building before they could spot him. Gienek picked up the box a few days later.

Witold arranged for the transmitter to be set up in the basement of the convalescent block, where few SS men went for fear of catching a disease. Alfred Stössel, an orderly known as Fred and one of the few Poles of ethnic German origin to be part of the underground, was assigned responsibility for guarding the device, while Zbigniew assembled it. A few days later, he sheepishly admitted to Witold that one or two more parts were needed, but he knew where to get them.[31]

Portrait of Witold, drawn by Stanisław Gutkiewicz, c. early 1942.

Courtesy of PMA-B.

*

Spring came early that year. The sun warmed the leafless trees and the first swallows appeared. In early March, the last surviving Soviets were transferred to the newly completed barracks in Birkenau. The inmates referred ironically to Birkenau as "paradise" because being sent there meant death. The Soviets' fenced-off blocks in the main camp weren't empty for long. Witold had returned to work in the tannery, where one of the kapos talked of women arriving in the camp. The other prisoners dismissed the rumors. But then, on the afternoon of March 19, a shout went up.[32]

"They are coming!"[33]

It wasn't the Jews that Himmler had ordered sent to the camp but a batch of Polish female political prisoners. Everyone rushed to the windows to catch a glimpse of five SS trucks carrying the women.[34]

A carpenter named Kluska rushed in a short while later to confirm their arrival at the main gate and that, incredibly, his own fiancée, Zosia, was among them, wrapped in her favorite brown fur. Their eyes had locked.[35]

"From now on, from this moment, I've a purpose in life," Kluska told them. "I will take care of her. I will give her my food, I will feed her."[36]

They will be treated like the men, Witold told Wincenty quietly.[37]

That evening they were marching back to the camp when an SS man headed off their column before they reached the crematorium and spoke to the kapo, who turned suddenly pale, and sounded almost panicked as he ordered the prisoners to run and keep eyes left, away from the building. "Whoever doesn't listen will be shot!" he yelled.[38]

They broke into a trot, but Wincenty stole a glance at the crematorium. The gate that split the high wooden fence recently built around the entrance was open, revealing stacked bodies of women and girls. The crematorium workers were stripping the dead. One of the corpses was still wearing a fur coat.[39]

Jewish women from Slovakia arrived later that month. They were stripped, shaved, and given the dirty bloodstained uniforms of the dead Soviets, and then assigned to some of the same blocks. The next day they were formed into work squads. The only concession to their femininity was permission to wrap their bald, torn scalps in scarves or scraps of cloth. Wincenty recalled how he and his other block mates would crowd around their window to stare at the female marchers. His friend had fallen for one: "Rózia, there goes my Rózia. Look at her, what a figure. With what fashion she has tied that scarf on her head!"[40]

Such yearning didn't last long as the women's health deteriorated. "Initially holding up well," noted Witold, "the girls quickly lost the sparkle in their eyes, their smiles and the spring in their step."[41]

The arrival of the women heralded other changes. There were ru-

Female Jewish prisoners, 1944.

Courtesy of Yad Vashem.

Henryk Porębski, c. 1941.
Courtesy of PMA-B.

mors that Jewish men had started arriving in Birkenau. The first solid information reached the underground in early April. Inmate electricians from the main camp were powering the fence around the new camp, among them one of Stasiek's men, Henryk Porębski. He was in position to report that transports of around a thousand Jewish men were arriving daily from Slovakia and that one had come from France. The newcomers were dumped at a railway siding and then marched a mile to the camp, where they occupied the horse stables that were in the process of being thrown up in the vast muddy enclosure. The Jews were assigned the same murderous tasks as the Soviets, digging ditches and laying roads.[42]

Witold confirmed the information with a few French Jews brought to the main camp in April. From those discussions he caught a glimpse of the European-wide scope of the Nazis' actions against the Jews, although he still had no inkling of their extermination plans. The men had come from the Drancy internment camp in the Paris suburbs and from another facility outside the town of Compiègne; by early 1942 around ten thousand Jews had been detained in areas across occupied France.

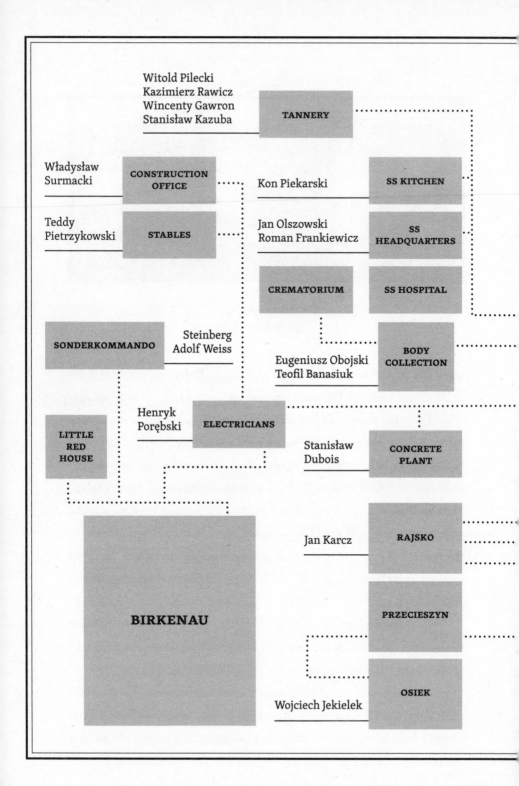

Witold Pilecki
Kazimierz Rawicz
Wincenty Gawron
Stanisław Kazuba

TANNERY

Władysław
Surmacki

CONSTRUCTION
OFFICE

Kon Piekarski

SS KITCHEN

Teddy
Pietrzykowski

STABLES

Jan Olszowski
Roman Frankiewicz

SS
HEADQUARTERS

CREMATORIUM

SS HOSPITAL

SONDERKOMMANDO

Steinberg
Adolf Weiss

Eugeniusz Obojski
Teofil Banasiuk

BODY
COLLECTION

LITTLE
RED
HOUSE

Henryk
Porębski

ELECTRICIANS

Stanisław
Dubois

CONCRETE
PLANT

BIRKENAU

Jan Karcz

RAJSKO

PRZECIESZYN

Wojciech Jekielek

OSIEK

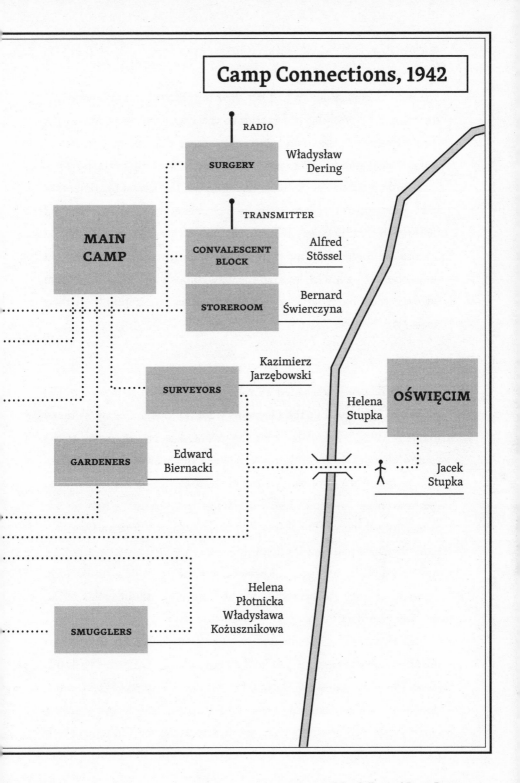

Camp Connections, 1942

RADIO

SURGERY — Władysław Dering

TRANSMITTER

MAIN CAMP

CONVALESCENT BLOCK — Alfred Stössel

STOREROOM — Bernard Świerczyna

SURVEYORS — Kazimierz Jarzębowski

GARDENERS — Edward Biernacki

OŚWIĘCIM

Helena Stupka

Jacek Stupka

SMUGGLERS — Helena Płotnicka Władysława Kożusznikowa

John Gilkes and Beata Dejnarowicz

The men Witold spoke to had left their families behind and been told they would be working in factories in the East. The SS were treating Jews registered in the main camp well compared to the Jews in Birkenau, and had asked them to write letters home attesting to the fact.[43]

Witold guessed the SS were trying to use the letters to trick other Jews into boarding transports in France. He appears to have warned the French that they were being used, but was ignored; at least Witold later called the Jews he interacted with "foolishly stubborn" and went on to note how a Jewish kapo in the penal block quickly finished them off once their letter-writing task was complete by stepping on their necks with a spade.[44]

*

The rush of news persuaded Witold that he needed to send another courier to Warsaw, but the Germans were no longer freeing as many inmates. Witold speculated that they wanted to prevent news of the camp's changes from leaking. Whatever the reason, it forced him to consider other options. Around then, a recruit of his in the local Gestapo office informed him that Berlin had ordered a halt to collective punishments for escapes. Wehrmacht high command was apparently concerned that German prisoners in Allied custody might be similarly punished. Witold understood at once the cable's significance: he could arrange for breakouts for his couriers without endangering the lives of others.[45]

The risks were still inordinately high. There had been around two dozen escape attempts in 1941, and all but a couple had ended in death. Most involved impulsive dashes for freedom by prisoners on work details outside the camp and ended in a hail of bullets, but even the better-organized attempts required luck to avoid the German search parties that combed the area with dogs. Those who did manage to get away were still in danger of being picked up by other police units once their details had been shared with regional security offices.[46]

Witold had identified a promising escape point from a nearby farming estate known as Harmęże, where the SS were using inmate labor to expand the fish ponds and breed Angora rabbits for wool. The prisoners stayed on-site in a mansion and the guard was reportedly lax, plus anyone escaping was already several miles away from the camp.[47]

Witold's handpicked leader, Rawicz, vehemently opposed the idea of an escape. He probably didn't trust that there would be no reprisals, and feared what would happen if the messenger was caught and compelled under torture to reveal the network's secrets. Witold tried to reassure him about the route and the courier he'd selected, Stefan Bielecki, whom he knew and trusted from the underground in Warsaw. But Rawicz remained unconvinced.[48]

Witold decided to go ahead anyway; the information he wanted to send about the massive influx of Jews to Birkenau was too important to wait. Furthermore, Stefan was marked as a likely saboteur in his Gestapo files, having been arrested in Warsaw in possession of a firearm. The SS might execute him at any time in one of their periodic culls.[49]

*

Using his labor office contacts, Witold arranged for Stefan's transfer to Harmęże while continuing to gather evidence about the Jewish arrivals. In April, one of his recruits, Jan Karcz, was sent to the penal squad in Birkenau but managed to register as a patient of the camp's rudimentary hospital and reported back via the electricians that he was forming a cell.[50]

Then in early May a transport of Jews was unloaded from cattle cars near the warehouses. Instead of heading for Birkenau, they marched in ranks to the main camp—men, women, and, for the first time, children. The camp was put on lockdown, and Witold and the other prisoners were ordered to lie on the floor. But Teddy, the boxer, managed to stow himself away in a manger by the window of the stable facing the crematorium. He watched the procession of around six hundred Jews, led by a rabbi wearing a yarmulke and tallit around his shoulders, enter the courtyard of the crematorium. The SS guard at the gate struck the rabbi in the face with his rifle, sending his skullcap flying. Then the courtyard gates closed behind the group.[51]

SS-Untersturmführer Maximilian Grabner, the Gestapo chief, a highly strung former policeman from Vienna, appeared on the crematorium roof with several officers and spoke to the gathering below. A truck was parked nearby. He announced that they were to be disin-

Maximilian Grabner, c. 1941.
Courtesy of PMA-B.

fected. "We don't want any epidemics in the camp. Then you will be brought to your barracks, where you'll get some hot soup. You will be employed in accordance with your professional qualifications."[52]

"What is your trade?" he asked one man. "A shoemaker? We need them urgently. Report to me immediately after!"

The first families stepped through the blue-painted doors of the building. The SS men entered with them, joking and reassuring, until the room was finally full, then they slipped away, and the door closed. The first panic set in as the door was screwed shut. Angry, stressed voices escaped from the vents in the concrete roof.

"Don't get burnt, while you make your bath!" Grabner shouted down to those inside.[53]

SS men in gas masks joined him on the roof bearing small tins,

Drawing of crematorium in main camp, by Tadeusz Iwaszko, postwar.

Courtesy of PMA-B.

which they proceeded to open, before positioning themselves over the openings. Someone inside must have caught a glimpse of a masked face, because screaming began.[54]

Grabner made a sign to the truck driver, who turned on his engine and revved the throttle to drown out the noise. The cries were still audible. Grabner gave the order, and the men in gas masks emptied their tins into the space below.

A few minutes passed and the cries grew weak, then silence. The ventilator was turned on and the room unsealed. A detachment of Jews from the penal block started to separate the mass of bodies for burning. The SS ordered the corpses stripped of their clothing and checked for valuables first. The clothes were stuffed in bags; jewelry, watches, and cash were stored in a box. Bags and rucksacks were also emptied. Finally the mouths of the corpses were pried open so that gold fillings and dentures could be removed with pliers. The corpses were stacked for burning and the room scrubbed down. A faint odor of damp bodies remained. Another trainload of men, women, and children was gassed a few days later, and then another.[55]

The killings marked the start of the systematic mass murder of Jews in Auschwitz. The first victims were mostly drawn from nearby towns, and it seems the Nazi leadership initially saw the camp as part of the network of regional killing centers being set up in Poland that spring that mostly targeted Eastern European Jews. Witold heard details from Teddy and the prisoners working the ovens. He recognized the killings as a terrible new development, but with only a dim sense of what was happening elsewhere in Poland, and no clues on the BBC, he couldn't conceive of the Nazis' plan to exterminate Jews because they were Jews. When the Soviets had been gassed, he'd assumed it was because there was no space for them in the camp. The logic was borne out when the gassing had stopped following the construction of new barracks in Birkenau. After hearing about the stripping of the Jewish corpses, Witold came up with a new theory: the Nazis must be killing Jews for plunder. Yet he knew that this evil surpassed anything he had witnessed in the camp.[56]

Around 10,000 Jews were gassed in May. The crematorium team could hardly keep up. After several gassings, the ovens overheated and the chimney began to crack. As dense smoke filled the building, the SS had to rig hoses to extinguish the blaze that had broken out. By the time the camp's fire engine arrived at the scene, the ovens were glowing red and the crew could only spray the outside of the building with water, sending huge clouds of steam into the air.[57]

The cracked chimney seemed to signal to the prisoners the end of mass murder. The remaining bodies were loaded onto trucks and driven to the woods of Birkenau, where they were dumped in a mass grave next to the pits used to bury the Soviets. But it didn't take long for Witold to learn that the gassing had been shifted to a more secluded location. Henryk the electrician reported that a facility of some sort had been prepared in the woods, a redbrick farmhouse to which they were running a 220-volt electric cable from the local village. The house was small and the plot empty save a couple of apple trees just coming into blossom. The SS brought in German contractors to brick up the windows and reinforce the doors and ceiling. In early May, the first groups of Jews were marched there and disappeared between the stands of birch and pine.[58]

Around this time, Henryk befriended several Jewish members of a special work squad known as the Sonderkommando, which the SS had created to assist in the running of the new gas chamber. The Jewish workers were kept isolated from the other prisoners, though they could interact briefly with them at the water pumps. They confirmed to Henryk that groups of Jewish families were being gassed. The SS had refined the operation by having their victims undress themselves before entering the chamber. The Sonderkommando ushered the families inside, and afterward they removed the twisted corpses of men, women, and children burned blue by the Zyklon B gas. The men of the special squad then checked the teeth for gold and hauled the bodies off to the pits.[59]

Witold activated his escape plan to inform Warsaw in mid-May. Stefan Bielecki had been in position in Harmęże for several weeks. Witold asked his artist friend Wincenty to join him. Witold saw something of himself in the charming and oddly vulnerable younger man, who'd taken to heart his order to share and gave any food he received from paintings to friends and Muselmänner. Witold had to remind him at times to take care of himself, but ever since witnessing the massacre of the female political prisoners, Wincenty had been losing the will to live. On one occasion, Witold had found him preparing to commit suicide by charging the electric fence.[60]

He boosted Wincenty's spirits only for his friend to be stricken with the flu and hospitalized. Wincenty recovered, but something still wasn't right with him, and he confided in Witold that he couldn't last much longer. Witold pitched him the escape plan in the second week

Wincenty Gawron, c. 1941.

Courtesy of PMA-B.

of May, and just as he had hoped, the prospect of freedom gave Wincenty a jolt of energy and he threw himself into preparations.[61]

Over the following days, Wincenty obtained some extra bread and a set of civilian clothes to wear under his stripes. In the hospital he'd recorded a diary on stolen notepaper that provided a remarkable snapshot of the camp. "In the evening, beyond the barbed wire, I can see the mountains at which I gaze longingly," he wrote in one entry. "A thousand Jews arrived in the camp and we are confined to quarters. They are given Soviet uniforms and ordered to stand outside all night before marching to [Birkenau] and heaven . . ." He was determined to smuggle the diary and some of his sketches out of the camp, and he persuaded one of the carpenters to fashion him a snug-fitting box of linden wood with a Polish highlander on the lid.[62]

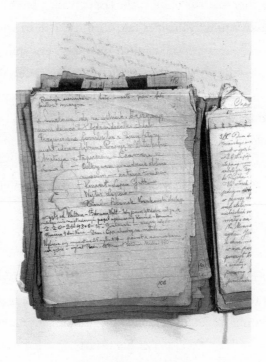

Wincenty's notes, 1942.

On May 22, a Friday, Wincenty tracked down Witold to tell him everything was arranged for his departure the following morning. Witold took him outside for a final briefing on recent developments.

"You need to pass on the information about how the Germans treated the Soviet POWs. But the most important thing is the mass killing of Jews," Witold told him. Wincenty needed to alert headquarters that children and the elderly were being gassed upon arrival in the camp, while others, mostly the young and healthy, were being worked to death in Birkenau.[63]

As he explained it, the Germans were bringing Jews to the camp under the pretext of working in the war industry, but that their real intention was to systematically rob and murder them. "In this way [the Germans] easily walk into the possession of wealth needed to win the war," said Witold. He was missing the larger reality, but his deductions weren't entirely wrong: valuables taken from the dead were meant to be sent to the German central bank to fund the war, while clothes and shoes went to ordinary families; neither measure could allay the spiraling costs of the conflict. Witold told his friend it was vital that the underground inform London at once so the world would come to the Jews' assistance.[64]

Wincenty was silent for a moment, struck by the responsibility Witold was giving him. They locked eyes in the half-light, and that was it.[65]

*

The next morning, May 23, dawned bright and clear. From the window of the hospital block Wincenty saw a column of marching girls that included the fading Rózia. He grabbed his gear, including his paint and brushes, and stashing them under his clothes, hurried outside in time to see Witold marching out of the main gate. The kitchen buggy bound for Harmęże was already waiting for him, and he clambered into the seat beside the kapo, who handed him the reins. At the gate Wincenty's order papers were checked and his transfer to Harmęże confirmed. An SS guard joined them, and they trotted off. The route took them over the railway tracks, and they soon reached the edge of Birkenau. It was the first time Wincenty had seen the place, and its blank rows of barracks scared him.[66]

They turned past the camp and reached the meadows of Harmęże, where a squad of Jewish women was tilling a field beside the road. A couple of them needed the toilet. The SS guards shouted at them to urinate on the ground in front of them. Wincenty winced but consoled himself with Witold's words. "If my plan succeeds, then I will let the whole world know what is happening to the Jews in here," he reflected.[67]

The cart pulled up outside a stolid mansion in the little village. The prisoners were already at work in the ponds and surrounding fields. The kapo spotted Wincenty's paintbrush and told him to paint something, so he sketched a rooster in the yard and made a quick inventory of the building. The prisoners lived on the second floor, where they were locked in every night behind windows with iron grills. The ground floor was mostly workshops and had no bars. The low fence surrounding the building lacked barbed wire.[68]

This might be easier than he had suspected, Wincenty mused, but first he had to speak to Stefan, who returned to the house for midday roll call with the eighty or so other prisoners barracked there.[69]

Stefan, a wiry, intense man with a lopsided face and a lazy eye, recognized Wincenty as one of Witold's confidants, and straight after roll call seized him by the arm and hissed, "Why have you come here? Don't you know that all the men in this barracks are to be replaced with women in two weeks?"[70]

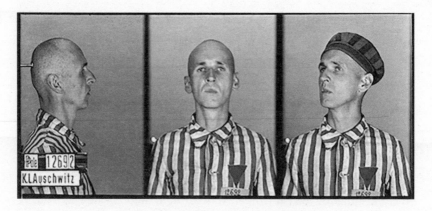

Stefan Bielecki, c. 1941.
Courtesy of PMA-B.

"Don't worry, I'm planning to escape long before that," said Wincenty.[71]

"If so, then that's quite another matter," said Stefan, smiling. "How about tonight?"

"I'm in," said Wincenty. They shook hands and collected their lunch of beet soup and three potato skins as Stefan explained his plan. They would make a dash after supper when the doors upstairs were left open for fifteen minutes for prisoners to use the toilets. The latrine was at the rear of the building, at the edge of thick bush that led down to the Vistula. It was the obvious escape route, which was why Stefan intended to break out from a window at the front of the building and head in the opposite direction for the fish ponds and fields. The terrain was more open, but if they cut across the water they'd confuse the dogs.

Stefan left for the afternoon but returned around 5 P.M. as the shadows lengthened. Wincenty had finished his drawing of the rooster and a brood of hens, much to the delight of the kapo, who rewarded him with a room on the ground floor. As the escape approached, Stefan became more agitated. He briefly pointed out the window in one of

Mansion in Harmęże from which Wincenty and Stefan escaped.

the ground floor rooms used for carpentry. "Our window to freedom," he said. He'd made a habit of tidying up the room during the fifteen-minute toilet break, so the guards were used to seeing him in there.[72]

"Won't the guard be suspicious if I show up too?" asked Wincenty.

"That's what I'm afraid of," he replied. There was an hour before the two of them would have to make their move, and their sense of the risks was growing.

Dinner was a piece of bread, a spoon of marmalade, and some bitter tea. It was Saturday, and an inmate barber was shaving heads on the ground floor. The two SS guards were relaxed, smoking in the hallway as the evening deepened outside. One of them periodically left to escort a prisoner to the toilet. Wincenty and Stefan were so tense it was hard to eat.

Wincenty hurriedly went to his room to get his wooden box, and then there was nothing for it but to try their luck with the guards. Stefan walked past the two SS men and into the carpentry workroom, Wincenty on his heels. The Germans didn't look up, and Stefan quickly closed the door and grabbed a heavy ax from a workbench. He was breathing hard, as he stood there, frozen, waiting to see if a guard followed.[73]

"Drop it!" Wincenty ordered. He clambered onto a desk beneath the window that Stefan had identified. The latch was broken and it opened easily enough. Wincenty slipped through, Stefan right behind him. Together they scaled the fence and started sprinting down one side of the road, trying to stick to the cover of the willow trees that flanked the route. It was almost dark now, and the frogs were croaking. They had reached a bend a couple of hundred yards from the house when Stefan pointed to a small dike that ran perpendicular to the road toward a large pond shining in the gloom. They cut off the road onto the surrounding field when they heard a shout, and saw the two SS guards burst out of the front door and run around the back toward the Vistula, as Stefan had predicted they would. The two escapees stumbled on across the broken field and had reached the reeds of the lake's shoreline when, to their horror, they saw another SS man on a bike bearing down on them from the opposite direction along the water's edge.[74]

"For God's sake," gasped Stefan, and plunged into the water. Wincenty followed. What else could they do? The lake was dark and cold. Wincenty held his breath for as long as he could, knowing they'd surely been spotted, and when he finally poked his head out of the water, clawing in a breath, there was the SS man, not fifteen yards away, peering at him in the half-light.[75]

"Jesus and Mother Mary," Wincenty muttered, and plunged back

Lakes along Wincenty and Stefan's escape route.

underwater, waiting for the end. But when he surfaced again a few moments later, he was stunned to see the man back on his bike and cycling away from them toward the house. He'd forgotten his gun.[76]

Stefan came up gasping for air, saw the retreating guard, and immediately set off through the shallow water to the opposite bank. Wincenty turned to the camp for a moment and shouted, "Up yours!" and followed.[77]

He caught up with Stefan on the far side, and together they set off across the fields at a trot before disappearing into the night.

———

CHAPTER 11

NAPOLEON

WARSAW

MAY 1942

Stefan and Wincenty ran for the next few hours in the dark, following the stars as best they could. At one point they saw the headlights of two SS motorbikes and dropped to their stomachs and hid in the plowed furrows of a field. They reached the Soła after midnight. Clouds had rolled in, and they sought shelter from the cold in a barn for an hour or two before attempting the crossing. The river was stone gray in the predawn. The two men held hands to steady themselves against the current. The water reached up to their chests at one point, and Stefan lost his footing. Wincenty, using his wooden box of notes as a float, managed to reach the far bank and fish him out. Hurrying toward the woods, they stripped off their wet clothes and waited, naked, until nightfall, then continued in their sodden garments.[1]

They moved only at night over the next few days, sticking to the forests and staying in peasant homes when they could. They headed south around Krakow, heading for the hills of Wincenty's home village of Limanowa, where Wincenty led them straight to his sister's place

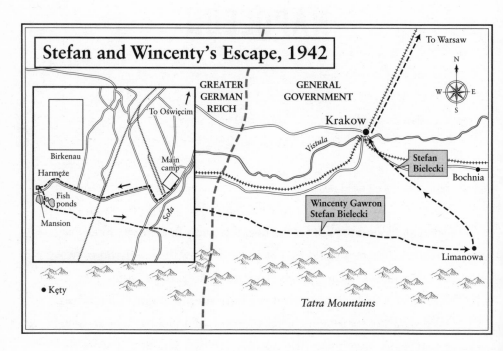

Stefan and Wincenty's Escape, 1942

GREATER GERMAN REICH

GENERAL GOVERNMENT

To Warsaw

To Oświęcim

Birkenau

Harmęże

Fish ponds

Mansion

Main camp

Kęty

Soła

Vistula

Krakow

Stefan Bielecki

Bochnia

Wincenty Gawron
Stefan Bielecki

Limanowa

Tatra Mountains

N
W E
S

John Gilkes

to be reunited with his family. He later recalled the ecstatic details of their first home meal: chicken and potatoes, followed by more chicken, and a glass of home brew to celebrate their return from "the other world." Wincenty was too weak to travel, so Stefan left for Warsaw by himself a few weeks later.[2]

*

The city was in tumult when Stefan arrived at the end of June 1942 and delivered Witold's report to the underground's headquarters. The Germans had resumed their offensive in Russia with a thrust toward the oil fields of the Caucasus, and the central train station was packed with soldiers bound for the front. Rumors swirled through the ghetto that the Jews would be deported to Siberia as soon as the Germans had made their decisive breakthrough. There were wild stories from elsewhere in Poland of Jews being gassed in trucks and specially designed chambers.[3]

By then, the underground leader Rowecki had created a Jewish Affairs Bureau to document and publicize atrocities against Jews and had spent much of the spring piecing together the Nazis' genocidal intentions. A few Jewish survivors had reached the capital and confirmed the existence of execution sites in the Soviet Union and the use of gas trucks at the death camp in Chełmno. Their accounts were compiled in the ghetto by a group of historians, social workers, and rabbis who were in contact with Rowecki through the Jewish labor organization known as the Bund. The underground's paper ran stories about the mass murders in April. Then in May, the Bund had sent Rowecki the first report to lay out the full scale of the killings in the East. The Bund concluded accurately that seven hundred thousand Jews had already died as part of a systematic plan to "annihilate all the Jews of Europe" and demanded an immediate response from the Allies. Rowecki microfilmed the document and in mid-May gave it to his courier Sven Norrman to pass on to London.[4]

In response to the report, the BBC broadcast a speech by the Polish leader Sikorski calling for immediate reprisals to "stay the fury of the German killers and save further hundreds of thousands of innocent victims from inevitable annihilation." The report also made headlines in the *Daily Telegraph* and the London *Times*. The *New York Times* initially featured it at the bottom of a news column but then ran a full-page story. The publicity helped galvanize Jewish groups into action. On July 21, a rally against Nazi atrocities organized by the Jewish American Congress and B'nai B'rith at Madison Square Garden in New York drew a crowd of 20,000. Roosevelt and Churchill both sent statements that were received as declarations of support. But in reality they elided the fact that German ideology toward Jews had become genocidal and instead characterized the targeting of Jews as indistinguishable from German persecution of all Europeans.[5]

"Citizens regardless of religious allegiance will share in the sorrow of our Jewish fellow-citizens over the savagery of the Nazis against their fellow victims," Roosevelt declared. He promised the Nazis would not succeed in "exterminating their victims any more than they will succeed in enslaving mankind" and that a "day of reckoning" would come. Churchill, who had known about mass shootings of Jews for almost a year, stated only that they were among "Hitler's first victims" and at the forefront of resistance to Nazi aggression.[6]

What's more, neither leader considered that the murder of Jews demanded a direct response, such as targeted military action of the kind Sikorski demanded, or humanitarian assistance for the thousands seeking to flee Europe. Indeed, British diplomats were actively trying to prevent refugees from reaching Palestine over fears of destabilizing the British protectorate, while the U.S. State Department stuck to its quotas for migrants from Europe and had even failed to issue its full allocation of visas in 1942. Both governments defended their reticence to Jewish leaders with now-familiar arguments: fear of stirring up anti-Semitism at home and distracting the war effort.[7]

Meanwhile, an interagency committee for the U.S. Office for War Information suggested curtailing atrocity stories altogether because of the "morbid" feelings they inspired. Coverage of the mass murders disappeared from the news. "The Bund should have written that [the Germans] killed 7,000 people," lamented the leader of the Polish socialist party in London. "Then we could provide the news to the British, with a slight chance they would believe us."[8]

The failure of the Bund report to cut through was a profound disappointment to Jewish leaders in Warsaw and likely informed Rowecki's approach to Witold's report on the mass murder of Jews in Auschwitz. He already knew that interest in the camp was limited—Allied officials appeared to have logged the fact that it was a place of special harshness and concluded there was little to be done. For Witold's latest report to register, Rowecki would have to overcome considerable barriers of indifference and skepticism. He needed someone who could see for himself what was happening around the camp and who could then travel to London and serve as a witness.[9]

He had just the man in mind for this dangerous task: a Polish SOE-trained agent named Napoleon Segieda. The thirty-two-year-old corporal had parachuted into Poland in November 1941 to gather evidence of Nazi crimes, among other tasks. In fact, he was supposed to have set off for London months ago, but he had been trapped in the country following the arrest of the courier networks he was to have used on the return leg.[10]

Napoleon was an unlikely spy. He came from a farming family in the village of Lisewo Kościelne on the plains of central Poland but wasn't cut out for rural life. He lacked much of an education and absorbed knowledge with the intensity of a self-taught man. One minute he was propounding Darwin's theories at church (getting himself barred as a result, about which he professed not to care a jot), then he was trying his hand at a crop of cumin seed, which he was convinced would lead to riches (it didn't). When he fell ill around 1935 with tuberculosis he devised his own treatment method, which consisted of running barefoot around the fields at dawn, which he swore cured him. He'd worked as an activist for a political party aimed at improving the lot of peasants named the Peasant Party, then joined the army in the 1930s because that was the best option for escaping rural poverty. War, when it had come, hadn't been a disaster for him; it had brought opportunity.[11]

Napoleon's unit had been captured during the invasion of Poland in 1939 but he had escaped German internment the following year, cycled across Nazi-occupied Europe, and then traversed the Pyrenees midwinter to eventually reach London in May 1941. After volunteering for courier duty, Napoleon had joined a batch of around sixty potential agents from Poland that the SOE was training around Lochailort Castle in the Scottish highlands in the summer and fall of 1941. Two British veterans of the Imperial Shanghai Constabulary ran the boot camp, which included small arms training and martial arts. William "Shanghai Buster" Fairbanks usually introduced the course thus: "What I want you to do is get the dirtiest, bloodiest ideas in your head that you can think of for destroying a human being." One dinner party trick Napoleon learned was how to dive across a table while simultaneously whisking away the linen spread in order to throttle a guest with it. Next had come parachute jump training at the Ringway air base outside Manchester, followed by learning how to send coded messages and brushing up on his German at an SOE facility in Hertfordshire.[12]

Napoleon Segieda, seated left, c. 1939.
Courtesy of Yaninka Salski.

Upon arriving in Warsaw, Napoleon had quickly earned a reputation as a fixer and devised a new method for transmitting intelligence that displayed his fresh thinking. The problem with the underground's network to date, Napoleon concluded, was that every safe house on the route, and every handoff of material from one agent to the next, increased the likelihood of infiltration. So he decided to cut out the chain entirely by stashing messages behind bathroom mirrors on the express train service that ran from Warsaw to Basel on the Swiss-German border. All he needed were operatives at either end with the skills to sneak on and off the train.[13]

Napoleon was on his way back from Switzerland after a test run when he got the order to travel to Auschwitz to check out the latest reports. He set off for the camp around July 18, just as news was breaking that the entire Swedish courier network had also been arrested. Only Sven Norrman had escaped, by virtue of being in Stockholm at the time, and clearly could not return.[14] Napoleon was suddenly the Polish underground's only material link to the outside world.

*

Napoleon was led around the Oświęcim train station by the lanky figure of Wojciech Jekiełek, a local operative who was easy to recognize with his balding pate and English-style handlebar mustache ("the bald eagle," his friends called him). Wojciech belonged to the same Peasant Party as Napoleon and shared his frustrations with Poland's prewar inequality. He'd been an activist before the war in his village, Osiek, a dozen miles from Oświęcim. The sight of Wojciech loping across the fields with a stack of leaflets, or cycling his bike pursued by the family dog, named Hitler for a joke, was a common one.

Since the invasion, Wojciech had built up a network of villagers to combat SS efforts to replace Polish families with German settlers. He'd also established connections with prisoners in the camp via two local women, Helena Płotnicka and Władysława Kożusznikowa, who carried food and medicine for the prisoners. Helena, a forty-year-old mother of five, made bread in her little wooden cottage during the day, when people were at work and the smell of the dozen or so loaves baking was unlikely to attract suspicion. She and the thirty-seven-year-old Władysława then sliced the bread for quick distribution among the prisoners and then set off with their bundles once it got dark. They left their packages in the fields near the camp that were regularly visited by the surveyors and a work squad of gardeners. They'd almost been caught on several occasions, and Commandant Höss had written to the local police complaining about seeing Polish women "laden with sacks

Wojciech Jekiełek, c. 1940.

Courtesy of PMA-B.

and packages" around Rajsko—perhaps in reference to Władysława and Helena.[15]

The plight of the prisoners had also inspired Wojciech to start gathering evidence of the Nazis' crimes. A few weeks before Napoleon's arrival, Helena and Władysława had carried a letter hidden between slices of bread asking for information to be sent back with the surveyors. He had received a letter back from Witold's coconspirator Stasiek saying he would be happy to oblige.[16]

Napoleon and Wojciech didn't linger near the station, which stood opposite several heavily manned SS checkpoints on the roads leading to the camp. Commandant Höss had ordered a lockdown after the latest typhus outbreak, and the air was hot and foul-smelling.

Wojciech led Napoleon via back roads to Osiek, where he lived in a modest two-room cottage outside the village with his wife and sixteen-year-old daughter. The house was surrounded by potato fields and partly hidden from the road by a pear tree.[17]

Wojciech sat Napoleon down at the kitchen table and showed him what material he had gathered about the camp. He likely had Stasiek's most recent report on camp mortality, which recorded that ten thousand Jews had been gassed and their bodies dumped in mass graves. Wojciech also had a collection of letters to show Napoleon from another correspondent. The unknown author called for weapons to be stashed around the camp in preparation for an uprising. As he leafed through the missives he picked up on the author's increasingly desperate tone.[18]

Władysława Kożusznikowa, Helena Płotnicka, and Bronisława Dłuciak (from left), c. 1933.

Courtesy of Krystyna Rybak.

"We will not allow ourselves to get killed like sheep!" declared one. "We can't wait any longer to begin the uprising."[19]

"Bombard this camp!" implored another. It sounded to Napoleon like something particularly dramatic had occurred. But what exactly? He told Wojciech to write back to Stasiek and inform him that a courier from London had arrived and he should send all information he could.

Helena and Władysława set off for the camp a few days later with supplies and a letter from Wojciech requesting evidence of Nazi crimes. Władysława's husband was unhappy at the risks she was taking and begged her to stay home. "No one could stop them once they set their mind on something," recalled Władysława's son, Józef.[20]

The caption on the photograph: "The house of Maria and Franciszek Jekiełek in Osiek. In this house in 1942 the couriers from London Czesław Raczkowski and Napoleon Segieda spent time observing Hitler's crimes in the camp of death in Oświęcim."

Courtesy of Jan Jekiełek and the Klęczar family.

CHAPTER 12

DEADLINE

AUSCHWITZ

MAY 1942

Witold had heard the siren sound the evening of Wincenty and Stefan's escape. Had they been caught? If so, would they inform on the resistance? He couldn't know. At least there were no reprisals from the escape. That didn't mean Witold was safe. The Germans, for most of his eighteen months in the camp, had considered the underground to be little more than a collection of prison gangs. But as Rawicz, Witold's handpicked leader, prepared the plan for an uprising, the SS seemed to suspect the underground's true nature. The first sign of trouble was a locked mailbox that appeared at the camp entrance, in which prisoners could discreetly post tips in exchange for food. Witold ordered one of his men in the smithy to forge a skeleton key that they used to remove evidence incriminating the underground.[1]

Then one afternoon an ashen-faced Kon pulled Witold aside and declared that one of his new recruits in the tannery was likely a Gestapo agent. Kon's sources were among a batch of prisoners who'd shared a cell with the man in Krakow. Two of the group, according to the men, had been conspicuously shot, and the SS had apparently had knowledge of what was discussed in the cell.[2]

Witold confirmed with an inmate clerk working in the camp's Gestapo office that the man was working on "special assignment." Witold had only given the agent an outline of the underground's mission. But there was no getting around the fact that he had been exposed. The question was whether the man had reported yet to the Gestapo. Each moment was vital. They couldn't simply kill the man without raising alarm. Dering suggested instead dosing him with croton oil, a fast-acting purgative. That would get the spy to the hospital, where Dering could try to trick the SS doctors into selecting him for a phenol injection.[3]

That afternoon, the tannery crew cooked up a stew and served the spy a portion laced with the oil. He was clearly unwell by roll call, and made a dash toward the main gate at dismissal. Witold's men intercepted him and marched him over to the hospital, where he was registered as suffering acute meningitis. The SS doctor approved his execution with only a cursory inspection.[4]

Witold still feared the man had given his number to Grabner, the Gestapo chief, but he realized he'd somehow escaped a few weeks later when the Germans resorted to their earlier crude culling of prisoners with a record of resistance or officer rank. The tactic suggested the Gestapo had no real leads on the underground, but the Germans were clearly onto them, and the near-random approach still cost Witold many of his best men.[5]

Then one morning in May, Rawicz was called out for interrogation. He managed to persuade the Gestapo that they were mistaken. But Rawicz was shaken and felt the time had come to launch the uprising, planning for which was now complete. The biggest challenge remained the massive mismatch in firepower. The SS garrison had expanded that spring to 2,500 men, and included a rapid response unit capable of deploying in thirty minutes. Rawicz believed they could count on roughly a third of the garrison being on leave or off duty at any given time. But that would still leave their 1,000 men outnumbered and badly outgunned.[6]

The one element they had on their side was surprise. If they struck in the evening when the squads were returning from work and the camp was in maximum flux, they might have a precious few minutes for one group to overpower the guards at the gate and in the sentry towers, while a second group seized the reserve arms store in the construction office and distributed weapons to the main camp's 9,000 prisoners. Rawicz hoped that the rest of the prisoners would follow their cue and join them. They would then move through the night to Kęty, a town of forested hills twelve miles south of the camp. Rawicz thought that a small contingent of prisoners could then seize the town while the rest escaped into the woods.[7]

Witold considered the plan viable but thought that it could just as easily end in slaughter. Even if they succeeded, the Germans would exact revenge on those left behind. A least a quarter of the prisoners were confined to the hospital block and in no shape to move. Then there were the several thousand prisoners in Birkenau, three miles distant, to consider. Rawicz justified these costs with plans to render the camp inoperable by blowing up warehouses, trains, rolling stock, and the mainline bridge to Krakow.[8]

But Witold still wasn't convinced. The only way to prevent a bloodbath, he believed, was to coordinate their uprising with a diversionary attack by underground forces outside the camp. Rawicz agreed but made clear they couldn't wait indefinitely, not when scores were dying each day. The plan Rawicz sent to Rowecki in May via a released prisoner carried with it an ultimatum: the camp was prepared to go it alone if they didn't hear back from Warsaw by June 1, less than a month away.[9]

*

As they waited, the tensions and the death toll mounted. It wasn't only the daily executions that the prisoners had to contend with. Yet another outbreak of typhus prompted the SS to kill up to a hundred sick patients a day using phenol. Klehr, the adjutant, had devised an efficient killing process in his "operations" room in the convalescent block. One assistant brought in the victim, set him on a stool, and pulled back the shoulders to expose the chest. Then Klehr plunged his needle into the man's heart and emptied the syringe as the victim shuddered and slumped forward. Another assistant dragged the body away. Klehr could dispose of a dozen inmates in half an hour using this method. The killings temporarily cut infections, until word spread that the hospital was to be avoided and that the sick should stay on the blocks for as long as possible.

The underground's response was to fight back using the one weapon that would avoid detection: the infected lice. The idea was probably conceived of by Witold Kosztowny, a nurse and former bacteriologist whom the SS had tasked with preparing typhus vaccines. A partial vaccine had been developed in the 1930s. The process involved infecting individual lice, feeding them human blood, and extracting their typhus-laden feces, which was denatured in phenol, dried, and then turned into a pill. Details of the Auschwitz program are hazy, but it seems that Schwela and the other SS doctors thought they could replicate the pill-making process. Kosztowny was allowed to set up a small laboratory in the basement of the main hospital for harvesting vials of infected lice from patients in the wards. Those vials, the underground realized, could be used as biological weapons.[10]

The challenge was how to hit the Germans with enough lice to cause an infection. The SS had reduced contact with prisoners out of fear of contamination. There were no more card games on the blocks between them and the kapos, and even clean prisoners working in the SS headquarters were nervously edged around. One SS man used his handkerchief to open and close doors in the rooms the prisoners used. Just getting close enough to flick one of the quarter-inch bugs at a guard was likely to raise suspicions. Some prisoners experimented with turning the straw from their mattresses into blowguns to shoot the lice, a dramatic but inefficient means of attack.[11]

The simplest method was to locate an SS cloakroom and empty a jar of lice onto a jacket or cloak. The guards kept themselves carefully buttoned up around the camp, but there was one place where they frequently disrobed: at the SS hospital next to the crematorium. Only the guards and their families could be treated there, and the staff was almost entirely German. The only inmates allowed into the hospital were the janitors. Teddy, the boxer, had taken one of the cleaning jobs, and agreed to launch an attack.[12]

One day, sometime in May, he collected a vial of lice from Kosztowny before work. He arrived at the SS hospital to find a line of coats and jackets in the cloakroom and carefully emptied the vial under several collars. The first German cases of typhus were soon recorded in the camp. Dering targeted Schwela next, the SS doctor who oversaw the phenol injection program. He had caught the German staring at his head oddly one day.[13]

"So perfectly round," Schwela had mused. "I'd like one just like it."[14]

"You can't have this one," Dering had replied lightly.[15]

"We'll see," said Schwela.

Teddy likely did the deed. One day Schwela was complaining about a temperature and sweating profusely under his uniform. The next he was moaning in bed, covered with red spots, and then he was gone, or, as Dering put it, he "moved to the right place for him in hell." It was possible that Schwela had been accidentally infected, but the underground swore that they'd gotten their man. Next they targeted the camp executioner, Gerhard Palitzsch, and starting dumping lice in the beds of hated kapos like Leo, whose death a few weeks later was celebrated across the camp.[16]

The campaign boosted morale but did little to ease the rising anxiety as the date of the uprising approached. On May 27, the SS called out the numbers of 568 prisoners at morning roll call. Fear rippled through the crowd. One hundred and sixty-eight men were immediately marched off toward the penal block for execution. The other four hundred were sent to join the penal company in Birkenau. The blocks came alive with talk of rising up that very night.[17]

Witold urged patience, but he found the wait intolerable. The weather had turned hot. The skies were clear, and the bloom of a jasmine tree near the entrance filled the camp with its scent. They had been ready for weeks. "How soon before we can spring at you?" he thought as he marched past the guards and the straining orchestra at the gate. June 1 arrived with no word from Warsaw. Some men muttered darkly about the underground's leadership, and threatened to take matters into their own hands. It was likely Witold who wrote to Wojciech in Osiek a message saying that they couldn't wait much longer and to bombard the camp.[18]

Then Witold's source in the Gestapo office revealed that the four hundred men sent to the penal company in Birkenau were to be shot in small batches to avoid provoking unrest. Twelve were executed on June 4. Two days later, nine more were killed. The men in the penal company sent Witold a warning that they planned to fight back.[19]

"I inform you that since we must soon become nothing but puffs of smoke, we shall try our luck tomorrow during work. . . . We have little chance of success," one of them wrote. "Bid my family farewell, and if you can and if you are still alive, tell them that should I die, I do so fighting."[20]

Witold felt for the men but saw the bigger picture. A breakout attempt in Birkenau would almost certainly lead to a camp-wide crackdown at the very moment that authorization might be coming from Warsaw. Rawicz agreed that the men in Birkenau needed to wait for Warsaw, and sent the orderly Fred to call the operation off.[21]

Fred managed to wrangle his way onto one of the ambulances the camp authorities often used to ferry Zyklon B to the gas chamber. The penal company was located in one of the stone barracks built by the Soviets in the northeast corner of the camp, separated by barbed

Barracks in Birkenau.

Courtesy of PMA-B.

wire from the endless rows of wooden stables that had been hastily constructed to house the influx of Jewish prisoners. He arrived shortly before curfew. A few Jews lingered outside their blocks, emaciated and dirty. The electric fence had been switched on for the night, and the wires sang with the current.[22]

Some of the men in the penal compound were relieved to hear Rawicz's order. But the majority insisted it was better to die fighting than wait to be shot. In the end, they agreed to delay the action until the following afternoon.[23]

The next morning, June 10, dawned overcast and the air felt heavy. The condemned men started work on a drainage ditch. Few ate at lunch as they waited for a sign. Then suddenly word began to spread that they would rise up at 6 P.M., when the first whistle sounded to return to camp.[24]

The prisoners returned to work. It started to rain. Some guards sheltered under trees. And then the whistle blew early. It was only 4:30 P.M. Was it the end of work or a break? Some of the inmates began to make a dash for it; others remained rooted to the spot. One young prisoner, August Kowalczyk, raised his spade to hit the nearest guard, only for the man to rush off after another escaping prisoner. He took the opportunity to scramble up the causeway, felt the whistle of a bullet, and then dashed over open ground to a patch of trees that he knew was close to the Vistula. With bullets flying around him, he ripped off his prison stripes, reached the riverbank, and plunged into the gray-green waters.[25]

Witold listened powerlessly to the sound of gunshots in the distance. Details emerged the following day. Only August and another prisoner had made it out. The rest were brought back to their barracks and kept under heavy guard. SS-Hauptsturmführer Hans Aumeier, the new deputy commandant, had demanded they name the ringleaders. When no one had answered he'd walked down the line shooting men in the head, pausing only to reload. He killed seventeen in total; his deputy killed three more. The remaining men were ordered to undress. Their hands were tied behind their backs with barbed wire and then they were led through Birkenau to the little red house in the trees to be gassed.[26]

The SS exacted further revenge. More than two hundred prisoners were shot on June 14; 120 a few days later. Each morning new numbers were read. Fear consumed the prisoners. At night they prepared farewell messages for loved ones and discussed whether it was better to die by bullet or gas or phenol. Morale was dangerously low.[27]

*

Eugeniusz Bendera, an inmate mechanic in the SS garage, decided to take matters into his own hands when he was tipped off that his name was on the list. Eugeniusz regularly worked on Commandant Höss's Steyr 220 sedan. The black, six-cylinder, 2.3-liter car was the fastest vehicle in the camp, and he fantasized about stealing it and speeding away to freedom. He shared the dream with his friend Kazimierz Piechowski, or Kazik, who pointed out he'd never make it past the checkpoint guarding the approach to the camp unless he had an SS uniform and could speak German. As it happened, Kazik was fluent. He also knew where the Germans' spare kit was kept. They had a plan.[28]

Witold thought the idea so unexpected that it might work. He arranged for one of his men, twenty-one-year-old Stanisław Jaster, to join them as his courier and had him memorize his next report. He stressed to Jaster that the Allies must be made aware of the Birkenau revolt and the gassing of Jews and be pushed into attacking the camp at once. Witold had likely heard on the BBC about the Polish parachute brigade that was training in Scotland in preparation for an Allied invasion of the continent, because he told Jaster that if two hundred paratroopers landed near the warehouses they could break into weapons stores and arm the other prisoners.[29]

The escape was set for Saturday, June 20, at lunchtime when the warehouse and garage were likely to be empty. Józef Lempart, a monk, had also joined the attempt and gave them a blessing as they assembled on the roll call square at noon. Kazik had arranged a wagon loaded with kitchen waste to serve as their excuse for leaving the camp dump beside the main road, and the guards duly waved them through.[30]

No sooner were the men out of sight than they changed course for the warehouse, entering via a coal chute at the side. The storeroom containing the uniforms was locked, so Kazik kicked the door in. The room contained shelves stacked with SS uniforms. Kazik took a senior sergeant's getup and a gun. They agreed that if they were stopped, he would shoot them to avoid capture. Eugeniusz dashed off to the garage and fetched

Stanisław Jaster, c. 1941.

Courtesy of PMA-B.

the car. He picked up the others at a side door to the warehouse. Kazik took the passenger seat, and they pulled out onto the road.[31]

Eugeniusz saw the barrier three hundred yards away and eased his foot off the pedal. A hundred yards out, there was still no movement from the guards. Kazik flipped open his holster and placed his hand on the gun. Fifty yards out. They could almost see inside the guard post. Eugeniusz was sweating. He brought the car to a stop.

"Kazik, do something," Jaster whispered hoarsely from the backseat.[32]

Kazik leaned out of the window and yelled in German to open the gate. A sheepish-looking guard appeared and casually jogged to the metal barrier and hoisted it upward. Eugeniusz resisted an urge to floor the pedal and drove slowly through. They passed the deputy commandant, Aumeier, riding his horse and gave him a "Heil Hitler." Aumeier returned the salute, and then they were free.[33]

Witold waited anxiously in the camp for the siren to sound. Each passing moment gave him hope. The SS only worked out that the four

Kazimierz Piechowski, c. 1941.

Courtesy of PMA-B.

men were missing at evening roll call. Aumeier let out a tirade of abuse at the assembled inmates as he realized he'd been duped. Then he threw his cap down and suddenly burst out laughing.[34]

But no word came from Warsaw. In early July, the Germans transferred Rawicz to another camp. His departure meant Witold was once again de facto leader of the underground, and the decision about the uprising fell to him. The failed attempt in Birkenau confirmed Witold's fears that an uprising in the main camp without outside aid would end in slaughter. They would have to wait, even if that meant enduring more executions.[35]

Meanwhile, the Germans were transforming Auschwitz from a regional killing facility into the central hub of the Final Solution. Himmler's earlier order to fill Birkenau with Jewish workers had raised the question of what to do with their dependents left behind in their countries of origin. Himmler decided that henceforth entire families would be sent to the camp. A selection of workers would be made upon arrival. Everyone else—mothers and their children, the infirm and elderly—would be gassed. As June ticked into July, the SS prepared to deport 125,000 Jews to the camp from Slovakia, France, Belgium, and the Netherlands. A second farmhouse in the woods of Birkenau was repurposed as a gas chamber in June (dubbed the "white house" on account of its paint). Together with the other chamber, the SS now had the capacity to exterminate an entire transport of around two thousand Jews at once.[36]

The first Jewish transport to be subjected to a selection arrived from Slovakia at the railway branch line a mile from Birkenau's main gate on July 4. The unloading ramp was tightly guarded. The thousand Jews on board were ushered off the train, stripped of their possessions, and lined up for inspection. SS doctors judged that only 372 were fit for work. They were marched off for registration by Polish inmate clerks in Birkenau. The rest headed for the woods.[37]

Witold's cell leader in Birkenau, Jan Karcz, was soon reporting on the almost daily arrival of transports from across Europe. By July 16, Stasiek had compiled figures that put the number of Jewish dead at thirty-five thousand in little more than two months. Witold grasped the sheer horror of the undertaking.[38]

"One wonders what the SS men were actually thinking," Witold wrote later. "There were a great many women and children in the wagons. Sometimes the children were in cradles. They were all to end their lives here together. They were brought like a herd of animals, to the slaughter!"[39]

He talked about a "new nightmare" and saw the crime in existential terms as a crisis for mankind. "We have strayed my friends, we have strayed dreadfully . . . I would say that we have become animals . . . but no, we are a whole level of hell worse than animals."[40]

As the mass murder escalated that July, the camp underground received Napoleon's coded request for evidence of Nazi crimes. Stanisław Kłodziński, a nurse with thick glasses and scholarly manner, was tasked with decoding it. Witold had to decide what to say. He is the likely author of a letter describing the Nazis' systematic program of murder in Auschwitz that July. The letter began with a description of the failed breakout attempt by the penal company and the daily executions that followed. Then the subject turned to the mass gassing of Jews. "In Birkenau the SS cannot keep up with all the dead they're creating. The bodies are stacked up outside the gas chambers for burial in pits."[41]

The letter described the mood of despondency among the prisoners. "Life in the camp is very difficult at the moment, people are prepared

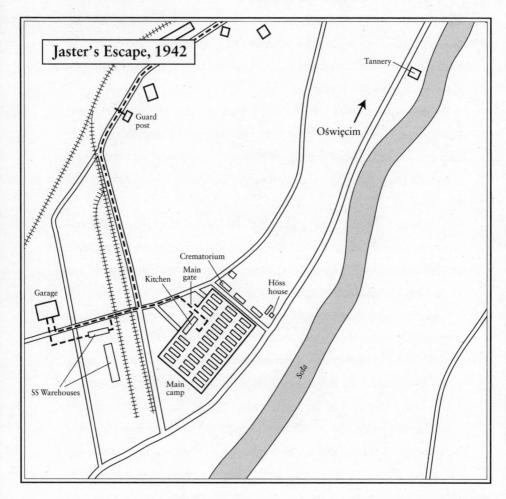

Jaster's Escape, 1942

Guard post

Tannery

Oświęcim

Crematorium

Main gate

Kitchen

Höss house

Garage

Soła

SS Warehouses

Main camp

John Gilkes

Separation of Families and *To the Gas*, by anonymous artist.

Courtesy of PMA–B.

for the worst. People are saying that if we have to die, let's not die like sheep; they say we should do something."

The letter then returned to the theme of an uprising. It doesn't link the operation to ending the mass murder of Jews directly, but the imperative for action is clear. A camp revolt "would echo greatly around the world," the letter concludes. "There is only one thought that stops me: that it would create great repression against the country."

Stasiek also completed his latest report on prisoner mortality around then, and likely included it for sending with the letter. The report included a monthly breakdown on Polish and Soviet deaths and highlighted the thirty-five thousand Jewish dead in Birkenau since May.

Stanisław Kłodziński, prewar.

Courtesy of PMA-B.

Transports arrived every few days bearing Jewish families for gassing, and 3,500 people could be disposed of in two hours, he observed. He wrote that the figures suggested that Auschwitz had become a "death camp."[42]

*

Just as the underground prepared to send the material via the surveyors or one of the gardening details, SS-Reichsführer Heinrich Himmler made his second visit to Auschwitz. Prisoners in the main camp were issued clean uniforms and allowed to wash; the orchestra rehearsed a Himmler favorite: Verdi's "Triumphal March" from *Aida*. On July 18, the healthier-looking inmates gathered in rows in the bright, early-morning sun. A last-minute inspection revealed that one of the prison-

Heinrich Himmler during his visit to Auschwitz, July 17–18, 1942.
Courtesy of PMA-B.

ers was missing a button, and the guilty man, one of the few hundred Jews in the main camp named Yankiel Meisel, was noisily beaten to death by the kapos behind a block. He took a long time to die, his ragged screams filling the still air. Then the orchestra's trumpet struck up the first notes, a black sedan pulled up at the gates, and the SS-Reichsführer emerged, blinking and smiling in the sun.[43]

Himmler had reason to be happy. The German military had launched a major new offensive in the Soviet Union that June to break through Russian lines in the south and capture the oil fields of the Caucasus. Initial progress was good and Himmler could once again dream of German colonies stretching to the Crimea. In the meantime, there was the matter of ridding Europe of Jews. He wanted to see the extermination process in Birkenau for himself. A transport of Dutch Jews had been specially kept for his arrival. He watched as the Jewish families were unloaded, stripped of belongings, and then processed. A group of 449 men, women, and children were selected for gassing in the little white house. He followed them there to observe the disrobing and sealing of the doors, and then heard the screams and then the quiet.[44]

"He did not complain about anything," recalled Commandant Höss. Himmler later attended a dinner party in Katowice hosted by the local gauleiter. There he indulged in a cigar and a glass of wine and revealed to the select group Hitler's plan to kill Europe's Jews, confident that the camp's secret, perhaps the greatest in Nazi officialdom, was safe. A few days later the underground smuggled their package of documents out of the camp.[45]

CHAPTER 13

PAPERWORK

OSIEK

AUGUST 1942

Hidden under prisoner stripes, stashed in a field, and then whisked through the night by smugglers, the underground's reports detailing the start of the mass murder of Jews in the camp reached the safe house in Osiek where Napoleon Segieda, the British-trained agent, was waiting for evidence of Nazi crimes. Napoleon had spent two weeks trying to investigate the camp environs but had been frustrated by the tightened security. He had witnessed enough violence to get a feel for the camp's brutality. Near the train station, he'd seen an emaciated prisoner stumble and fall while marching past with his squad. An SS guard had flipped the man over with his foot and then stepped on his neck until he stopped moving. The rest of the squad moved on, singing "as if from the underworld."[1]

But Napoleon had seen nothing of the scale of the horrors reported in the likely letter from Witold and Stasiek's latest mortality statistics, which revealed a program of industrial killing far larger than he had imagined. He struggled to understand some of their references. Stasiek

Sign warning against entering the camp area.

Courtesy of Mirosław Ganobis.

referred to the "Hammerluft" or "hammer of air" method of killings, which was a reference to the bolt-action gun used to execute prisoners. But Napoleon interpreted Hammerluft to be some sort of sealed chamber that used sudden drops in pressure to kill people. It's not clear where he got the idea from. One explanation may be that he saw smuggled drawings of the new crematorium in Birkenau and concluded that their elaborate ventilation was some sort of pressurized killing system. He also seems to have thought that some of its chambers were wired to produce deadly shocks.[2]

Despite these mistakes, Napoleon concluded correctly that he was in possession of a major Nazi secret: Auschwitz had become an important site for the mass murder of Jews, and that unlike other gassing facilities primarily focused on Polish Jews, the camp had a continent-wide dimension.[3]

Wojciech arranged new papers for Napoleon for his journey to London; every agent jumped into Poland with a fake ID, but sometimes it was judicious to change aliases. Wojciech found the perfect cover: a Polish pastor named Gustaw Molin, from the nearby town of Cieszyn, who had been pressured into signing the Volksliste registry for people of German ancestry and was subsequently conscripted into the army. Molin agreed to let the underground use his orders for movement between Poland and his unit in occupied France; if Napoleon could pass himself off as a German soldier he could travel with minimal checks.[4]

On August 6, 1942, Napoleon set off for Warsaw with his packet of reports for final approval from Rowecki. He found the capital gripped by a new disaster. On July 22, the German authorities had

ID card of Gustaw Molin.

announced that the ghetto's four hundred thousand residents were to be deported to factories in the east. The head of the ghetto's Jewish Council, Adam Czerniaków, learned the horrific truth during negotiations with the SS over the transport of orphaned children: every Jew in Warsaw had been marked for extermination. Shortly before the liquidation began on July 23, Czerniaków took a cyanide pill. "They demand me to kill children of my nation with my own hands," his suicide note read. "I have nothing to do but to die."[5]

German officers and Ukrainian auxiliaries had then sealed the ghetto's entrances and forced its Jewish police, under threat of deportation, to go apartment to apartment and drag people onto the street. Men, women, and children were then marched to a railway line at the edge of the ghetto, where they were warehoused in an open yard and then loaded into cattle cars. On the first day, six thousand Jews were deported, followed by similar numbers every day thereafter.

No one knew where the trains were going, and the next day the Jewish Bund organization sent a spy from the ghetto, Zalman Friedrich, to secretly trace their route. He learned from Polish railwaymen that these prisoners were unloaded at a camp near Treblinka, fifty miles northeast of Warsaw. The barbed-wire enclosure hidden in the woods was too small to accommodate the thousands of people arriving. Yet no one ever left. It seemed likely that they were being murdered en masse. Rowecki received similar reports from his own sources that Warsaw's Jews were being killed on an unprecedented scale.[6]

"The Germans have begun the slaughter of the Warsaw Ghetto," announced the underground's first message to London about the liquidation on July 26. "So far, two trainloads of people were taken away, to meet death, of course."

Rumors circulated that the death camps housed factories for turning fat from the bodies of murdered Jews into soap, an echo of anti-German World War I propaganda. This time it provided a more rational explanation for the Nazis' murders than the fact that they were simply wiping out a people.[7]

In this confused, heated atmosphere, Napoleon delivered his findings about Auschwitz. It's unlikely that Rowecki met Napoleon at this juncture, but he appears to have approved Napoleon's immediate departure to London with the warning to be careful: mass arrests of Polish agents working in France had put everyone on edge.[8]

Napoleon left Warsaw the next day, August 9, with an update on Czerniaków's suicide and the latest murder numbers from the ghetto— one hundred thousand in the first eighteen days of the operation. He also carried microfilms of reports and messages from political parties in Warsaw. There wasn't time to microfilm Witold's likely letter or the latest data from Stasiek, but Napoleon had memorized the key phrases and figures. He was confident of reaching Britain within a couple of weeks.[9]

Napoleon planned to travel to London via Switzerland. He changed trains in Krakow, where he may have boarded one of the military transports that shuttled daily between Vienna and the front in his guise of Wehrmacht soldier Gustaw Molin. The trains traveled mostly at night, and the darkened carriages were usually packed with sleeping men, slumped against windows or collapsed on their rucksacks on the floor. The men were often fractious; Hitler's big push to capture the oil fields of the Caucasus in southern Russia had started to peter out, and the soldiers were facing the prospect of another grueling winter campaign. The Gestapo rarely entered the carriages for fear of stirring the soldiers' anger.[10]

Napoleon arrived at dawn on August 10 in Vienna, where he had an anxious wait until the evening, then caught the connecting train to Zurich. He reached the border station with Switzerland and Liechtenstein at Feldkirch in the early hours of August 11. The passengers were

Napoleon in Warsaw, c. 1942.

Courtesy of Yaninka Salski.

forced to disembark for a visa check at the customs checkpoint. The station lights illuminated the sign over the door that declared EIN VOLK, EIN
REICH, EIN FÜHRER, and the six-foot-high barbed-wire fence extended
past the tracks in either direction. Jews fleeing roundups in Slovakia for
the sanctuary of neutral Switzerland tried to cross the nearby Rhine,
which formed the border between the two countries. Such desperate
lunges for safety occurred most nights, and until that month, the Swiss
had granted entry to more than a hundred thousand foreigners, including around ten thousand refugees. The threat of a Jewish influx from
Nazi roundups elsewhere in Europe had persuaded the authorities to
start turning those they caught over to the Germans.[11]

This was the most dangerous moment of the journey for Napoleon, but the German border police and local auxiliary guards gave him only a cursory pat-down and waved him through in the predawn dark. He must have watched with pleasure the daybreak on the high sides of the Appenzell mountains. In Zurich, he changed trains for the Swiss capital, Bern, which he reached shortly before midday on August 12. From the station, he hastened through the cobbled streets of the Old Town toward the Polish legation at Elfenstrasse 20, keeping his head down.

*

The once-sedate city of Bern had become the center of Europe's spy trade. The offices of the German, British, American, and Soviet spy agencies stood within a few hundred yards of each other, which meant an agent could visit them all in a morning, and some frequently did, playing complicated games of double and triple crosses. The bars and restaurants hummed with shadowy types hawking secrets or offering to act as go-betweens. The Germans tolerated such activities because they saw the value of keeping channels open, even if the means of communication were complex. Wilhelm Canaris, the head of the German Abwehr, or military intelligence, was allegedly having an affair with a Polish agent named Halina Szymańska, whom he was using in turn to put out feelers to the British.[12]

The amount of useful information exchanged in Bern's smoky cafés or quaint backstreets was limited, much of it simply rumormongering and the recycling of old news, while the rewards on offer gave a perverse incentive for fabricating stories. Certainly few agents, if any, carried the payload of intelligence that Napoleon had, and he knew the danger he was in. The legation was notoriously leaky; its messages were intercepted and its phone lines bugged. A single careless disclosure and the Gestapo would be after him.

As it happened, Napoleon wasn't the first source to arrive in Switzerland that summer with news of the Nazis' extermination program. A German industrialist from Breslau named Eduard Schulte had learned from contacts in the Nazi leadership about Hitler's plans to exterminate the Jews and traveled to Zurich at the end of July to pass on information about the plot to a Jewish lawyer friend. The news then made its way via a Zionist organization to the British and American legations in Geneva for dispatch as a telegram to Jewish leaders in the west. Schulte's information was crucial for understanding the systematic nature of the murders and their extension across Europe. But Napoleon alone carried the news that Auschwitz had taken a central role in this expanded killing campaign.[13]

Napoleon hurried over the Kirchenfeld bridge, high over the rushing Aare River, and climbed the hill to the legation to meet the chargé d'affaires, Aleksander Ładoś. It was standard procedure for couriers to report to Ładoś and share their reports, which, if urgent, were sent in code via a radio transmitter that the legation had secretly set up to avoid Swiss and German detection. Napoleon fought his way through the crowd of refugees at the entrance, mostly Jews seeking financial aid or paperwork to avoid being thrown out of the country.[14]

Napoleon was ushered into one of the legation's back rooms, only to be informed by the staff that Ładoś was taking a long weekend in the Alpine resort town of Bex. Napoleon was in a hurry to resume his journey and wouldn't speak to anyone else, so the legation's specialist in Jewish affairs, Juliusz Kühl, arranged to accompany him to Bex in the legation's car.[15]

The three men met in Bex's Grand Hôtel des Salines the following day. The hotel had several ornate dining rooms overlooking the Dents du Midi mountain, with a billiard room at the rear for more discreet conversations. Ładoś was a chain-smoking fifty-year-old with a liberal but morose disposition. He was sympathetic to the plight of the Jews and regularly allowed Jewish groups to use the legation's radio transmitter to send reports to Britain and America. He had also set up a fake passport scheme with Kühl to help Jewish refugees reach Switzerland and flee Europe altogether. Kühl, himself an orthodox Jew from eastern Poland, was also an important conduit for knowledge about the mass murder of Jews due to his work with refugees, and he had cultivated a friendship with the Vatican's chief representative in Switzerland, Filippo Bernardini, whom Kühl regularly briefed over afternoon Ping-Pong matches on the covered patio of the papal nuncio's residence.[16]

In short, the two men Napoleon spoke to were able to grasp the

Juliusz Kühl, c. 1943.
Courtesy of Amud Aish Memorial Museum.

importance of his news and had the means to disseminate the intelligence. Yet Napoleon, wary of leaks, was guarded in what he told them. He revealed what he knew about the Warsaw Ghetto's liquidation and Czerniaków's suicide. Ładoś had possibly already picked up on the story from the messages radioed from Warsaw to London, but Napoleon was able to impress on him the scale of the operation, the role of the Treblinka death camp, and the rumor that Jewish corpses were being turned into soap and fertilizer.[17]

On the subject of Auschwitz, however, Napoleon was silent. In Kühl's account of the conversation, he appears to have discussed the fate of Jewish deportees from Western Europe, explaining that they

Aleksander Ładoś, c. 1935.

Courtesy of Narodowe Archiwum Cyfrowe.

were not being sent to work camps in the East, as the Nazis claimed, but rather to be murdered. But that was all Napoleon would reveal.[18]

*

Napoleon and Kühl returned to Bern after the meeting with Ładoś. Kühl immediately hurried off down the hill to see Bernardini and left word with his secretary, Monsignor Martilotti. Then he wrote up his notes on what Napoleon had said to pass on to a lawyer in Geneva, Abraham Silberschein, who had close contacts to the same Zionist organizations that had received Schulte's earlier information.[19]

Napoleon, meanwhile, prepared to resume his journey. He had thought to set off the very next day using his German papers that would see him through to France. But on Ładoś's advice, he agreed to stay to get the right visas for the onward journey to Spain or Portugal, from where he could travel by plane to London, or else catch a boat. While he waited for the paperwork, he busied himself with his earlier plan to transport messages via the German rail network, but he couldn't get drawn too deeply into the project knowing that he might get his travel documents at any moment.[20]

August dragged on, and his frustrations mounted. Stories about the liquidation of the Warsaw Ghetto appeared sporadically in the press, but they were confused and had little impact. The deportations of Jews from Western Europe gathered more attention and prompted debate as to their final destination. The London *Times* reported on August 8 that Jewish girls from the Netherlands were being "placed on trains and sent to a camp—it is not known what kind of a camp." In fact, more than thirty thousand Jews were deported to Auschwitz in August. But the camp's role remained a secret.[21]

"What are the difficulties in obtaining Portugal visa for Wera [Napoleon's code name]?" asked one missive from London to the Polish legation in Bern on September 17. Then again a few days later: "What's with Wera?"[22]

Another cable observed that it was a pity Napoleon hadn't sent a short, encrypted report. The legation responded that it was taking longer than expected to organize the right paperwork but that Napoleon would soon be on his way. Napoleon understood that the intelligence he had gathered outside Auschwitz was important. But he was one of many British-trained agents working secretly and alone in Poland and had no way of knowing that he carried the one piece of information that could unlock Western understanding of the Nazis' plans and provide an actionable target that might persuade the Allies to intervene militarily. Instead Napoleon waited in Bern with growing frustration for papers that never came as summer turned to autumn.[23]

CHAPTER 14

FEVER

AUSCHWITZ
AUGUST 1942

Train after train trundled with numbing efficiency up to the railway sidings near Birkenau through the summer of 1942. On August 1, 1,007 Dutch and German Jews from the Westerbork transit camp arrived; 200 were immediately gassed; 807 were admitted into camp. The next day 1,052 French Jews arrived from Pithiviers; 779 were gassed. Then a second train came carrying Polish Jews from the Będzin Ghetto; nearly 1,500 were gassed. Two days later, another train of 1,013 Jews from Westerbork saw 316 gassed. Commandant Höss toured the other death camps in Poland around this time and noted proudly that his was the most efficient.[1]

Witold couldn't see the dusty columns marching into the woods, or the stacked bodies. But he had a rough means of tracking the slaughter. Every day a truck pulled into the tannery courtyard where he worked, loaded with leather goods taken from the dead: braces, belts, handbags, shoes, and suitcases bearing name tags to be sorted and either burned or collected for distribution to German families. Pairs of shoes formed ghostly lines in the yard: polished brogues and well-worn loafers, elegant heels and summer plimsolls, little bootlets and, on occasion, great iron perambulators.[2]

The prisoners knew what the shoes meant; some reacted with dread, others made a point of showing they weren't affected. But as the sight became commonplace, the shoes and other items began to represent an opportunity. Valuables were hidden in boot heels and suitcase linings: gold ingots, purses of precious stones, thick rolls of banknotes in various currencies. They were meant to be handed over to the SS for the coffers of the Reich, but soon the camp was awash with loot, or "Canada" as the prisoners called it, an allusion to the imagined wealth of that country. Money lost all meaning. A loaf of bread on the black market went from costing $100 to $200, and then $1,000, while French francs were worthless; prisoners used them for toilet paper.[3]

The SS had orders to crack down on the smuggling, but the guards wanted their piece of the spoils. A form of trade developed, one-sided and dangerous, but which had its uses for the prisoners. As one Birkenau resident noted, "We systematically attempted to soften up the SS men and gave them watches, rings, and money. If they were on the take, they were no longer as dangerous." Höss also wanted a cut. He started making regular trips to the tannery, ostensibly to have his boots shined, but Witold watched from an observation post in the workshop attic as the commandant picked through the goods. "[Höss] took gold, jewels, valuables," recalled Witold, which meant he had to "turn a blind eye to his subordinates' infractions."[4]

The whole camp became gripped by the frenzy. "Once someone has reached for things that are still warm and felt joy in doing so, the bliss of ownership begins to affect him like hashish," wrote one prisoner. Special warehouses for Canada were set up and often staffed by women, selected for their looks, whom the kapos and even some SS men showered with gifts and demanded sexual favors in return. Hidden corners of the warehouses became virtual brothels, lined with silk sheets and down comforters.[5]

Witold refused to touch the plunder. He understood that the owners were dead but he couldn't overcome his distaste for things he considered "stained with blood." Food found in the cases was another matter: chocolates, Dutch cheeses, strings of figs, lemons, sachets of sugar, and little tubs of butter, calories that a few months before would have meant the difference between life and death. "At this time we were eating sweet soups, which contained pieces of biscuits and cakes," he wrote. "They sometimes smelt of perfume when soap flakes were carelessly added."[6]

*

Since the disappointment over the uprising, Witold had struggled to maintain the morale of his men. Warsaw's silence on the subject meant there was no imminent prospect of a revolt, but Witold refused to give up on the idea. Following Rawicz's departure the month before, he'd found a replacement to lead the military side of the underground, a well-meaning air force colonel named Juliusz Gilewicz, who continued to push the plan. The truth was, they needed to believe that they had some control over their fate.[7]

Witold and Stasiek also continued to collect data on the camp's rocketing death toll. They had heard no word from Wojciech in Osiek about Napoleon's mission, but they anticipated an impact shortly. Then one morning in August, Stasiek's number was read out at the roll call. Witold must have feared the worst, but it turned out that Stasiek had simply received a package of food; Höss had recently relaxed the rules on political prisoners getting parcels in the main camp. That evening, Stasiek happily shared the tins of sardines he'd received among his friends, who quizzed him on how it felt to have had his number read out.[8]

"I wanted to go out with my head held high," he told them, "because I knew you'd all be watching!"[9]

But then the next day at lunch, the camp's Gestapo boss, Grabner, fetched Stasiek from his work at a camp-run concrete plant. It seemed the parcel had reminded Grabner of Stasiek's presence in the camp. He was shot half an hour later.[10]

Witold doesn't write about his death subsequently, but it must have been a blow, both personally and in terms of their reporting. He had lost one of his closest collaborators and would have to take on Stasiek's work until a replacement could be found.

Witold hit back in the only way he knew how. After months of searching, his radio expert, Zbigniew, had finally found the parts he needed to finish assembling the shortwave transmitter. To send a signal was to risk revealing their position to the German tracking vans that patroled the area, and the messages were therefore brief. No record of the transmission survives, but it's most likely that they sent recent data collected by Stasiek. In addition to the 35,000 Jews gassed in Birkenau that summer, around 4,000 inmates had died from typhus and a further 2,000 from the Nazi executions and phenol injections. Witold had no way of knowing whether anyone heard the broadcasts, but it was a boost to know that it was out there, and someone on their side might be listening.[11]

*

At the same time, the underground sought to ease the suffering in the hospital by smuggling into the camp ever-increasing amounts of medication. The inmate gardener Edward Biernacki estimated he collected almost two gallons' worth of glucose shots, antibiotics, and painkillers over the summer of 1942, as well as enough typhus vaccine to treat seventy prisoners. Dering insisted Witold take one of these; he was too valuable for the organization to lose, and the risk of infection was growing. In Witold's block, half the prisoners had come down with the fever, including his bunk mate. The latest underground members to contract typhus were the boxer Teddy and Edward.[12]

Dering also tried to protect sick patients by fiddling with their records so it looked like they had only recently been admitted—a long stay in the hospital meant a guaranteed selection for phenol. Even those who had been chosen could sometimes be saved at the last minute by switching out their records for someone who had already died that day. Dering had been working assiduously to cultivate the friendship of one of the new doctors, SS-Hauptsturmführer Friedrich Entress, by helping him improve his surgical skills, in return for exempting his patients from selections—a loophole Dering readily took advantage of that summer.[13]

However, the sight of Dering on such seemingly good terms with an SS doctor had led to concerns in the underground about his loy-

Edward Biernacki, c. 1941.

Courtesy of PMA-B.

alties. Even those aware of his tactics were put off by his increasingly brusque and arrogant manner. The matter came to a head over the use of smuggled medicines. Dering had imperiously used a stash of the underground's morphine to bribe the construction kapo to work on tiling and painting the operating theater. Gienek Obojski, the morgue worker, had then walked in on the construction crew one morning and found a German kapo mixing glucose supplements into his tea. Gienek stormed off to confront Dering.[14]

Both men had short tempers, but Dering knew it wasn't wise to provoke Gienek, who was already rumored to have bashed one kapo's brains out in the hospital morgue and disposed of his body in the crematorium. When Gienek was steaming like this there was no telling what he might do. Dering tried to explain himself, but Gienek's mind was made

Friedrich Entress, c. 1946.

Courtesy of the USHMM.

up. He no longer trusted Dering and stopped delivering him smuggled medicine.[15]

✳

At the end of August, Dering picked up from Entress that a hospital-wide selection was planned to tackle the epidemic. It sounded ominous. Dering went to warn Witold, and the two men set to work removing as many people as possible. Witold found Teddy lying in the convalescent block that evening.

"Get up!" he whispered.[16]

Teddy could hardly move, so Witold returned with two nurses to help him stagger back to his block.

Dering and Witold tried to rescue as many as they could, but the paperwork to discharge each patient took time. As a result, they were able to rescue only a fraction of the patients before curfew.

Dering woke before dawn the following morning and remembered there was a whole ward of the convalescent block he hadn't reached. The patients included a Jewish acquaintance of his, Stanisław Taubenschlag, who was registered in the camp as Aryan. There was just time before reveille for Dering to dress, slip across the street, and shake Stanisław and the others awake.

"Leave the hospital at once," Dering hissed, and promised to take care of their discharge papers.[17]

As he said it, they heard the sound of heavy trucks approaching. Back on the street, Dering saw Entress and Klehr arriving and hurried toward them. The SS doctor was pale and ghostly in the dawn light, his face expressionless. "The whole hospital will be subject to the selection," he said. The chosen would be taken to Birkenau for so-called special treatment. Dering guessed what that meant. He protested that many of the patients on the mend might make a full recovery, especially typhus sufferers whose fever had broken. But Entress waved him away. They would start with the convalescent block.[18]

Entress ordered the nurses to assemble the patients on the pavement for what he called the "transfer to Birkenau" in the waiting trucks. Not everyone understood the significance, and many of those who did were too weak to protest. The orderly Fred Stössel had a long list of numbers, which he started to read out. Those selected clambered up ramps onto the trucks or were slung aboard if they were too sick to walk themselves.[19]

Dering managed to position himself at the ramp and, despite the obvious dangers, pulled out some of those he knew to be almost recovered until Entress spotted him.

"Man, are you crazy?" he shouted. "This is an order from Berlin."[20]

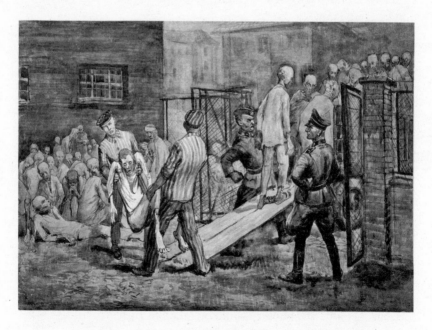

Taking Away Ill Prisoners, by Tadeusz Potrzebowski, postwar.

Courtesy of PMA-B.

Going to the Gas, by Tadeusz Potrzebowski, postwar.
Courtesy of PMA-B.

"They are healthy," Dering yelled back.[21]

"Idiot!" the doctor fumed, but still let him grab a few more before the trucks were full and ready to depart. Entress moved to the next block. But Klehr was checking the numbers. They didn't add up. He cast his eye over to where the block's nursing staff was standing in a group and spotted someone suspicious at the back. He pointed at him.

"What's your number?" he demanded. "You're not a nursing orderly."[22]

The group of nurses parted, exposing a hidden patient named Wiesław Kielar.

"I'm healthy, Herr Oberscharführer, I can work," Wiesław insisted.[23]

Klehr dragged him over to the block wall to wait for the trucks to return. It didn't take long for the rumble of engines to be heard. Dering hurried past as the trucks pulled up.

"Doctor, Doctor!" Wiesław shouted. "Save me! I want to live!"[24]

Dering saw him and shrugged. Fred was already reading out the next list of names, and the first patients were climbing aboard. Then Dering seemed to have a change of mind. "Don't move," he said, "I'll speak to Dr. Entress."[25]

By the time he got back, Klehr had Wiesław by the scruff and was dragging him toward the nearest vehicle. Dering stepped in front of him. "Stop, stop!" he shouted. "Entress wants him." He pointed at Wiesław. Klehr glared at Dering but let his victim go.

"Run," said Dering to Wiesław. "Run as fast as your legs will carry you and report to Dr. Entress."

The morning went on like this. Dering estimated that he saved 112 patients. But 756 were still gassed, almost a quarter of the hospital population, including everyone who had remained on the convalescent block. It was a shattering blow for the underground. That night, the hospital blocks were nearly empty. The silence was broken by sobbing nurses.[26]

Among those saved was the gardener Edward Biernacki, who wrote a secret message to Wojciech in Osiek recounting the days' events.

"So much work, so many sleepless nights," he recounted. "So many people were saved from the cruel disease and now everything is lost."[27]

*

Witold started feeling light-headed a few days after the hospital gassing. He had arranged for a job in the main camp painting instructional images of camp life on the walls. The pigments were swimming before his eyes, his joints ached, and he had a raging thirst that no amount of water could quench. He suspected that the vaccine had failed and he'd caught typhus.[28]

He awoke the next morning with his skin on fire and his mattress soaked. He forced himself to get up for roll call. The weather was warm and muggy, but he was shivering convulsively. His block leader agreed to let him stay in his room, but warned him that another camp-wide delousing was scheduled for that morning. His roommates soon left to be immersed in vats of chlorine solution. Witold remained in his bunk, too weak to move.[29]

The kapos started to search the block for malingerers. Suddenly Dering appeared beside his bunk. He checked Witold's pulse and then lifted up his shirt. He was covered in red pustules—typhus. Dering helped Witold to his feet and put his arm under his shoulder, and they staggered outside past the naked prisoners queuing beside the vats. Dering found his friend a bunk in the surgery as Witold drifted in and out of consciousness.[30]

That night Witold heard shouts and felt a deep throb in his ears. "Air raid!" someone was yelling. "Air raid!" He struggled to organize his thoughts. Could it be true? Were the Allies attacking the camp? Was this the signal he'd been waiting for? The room fell dark as the spotlights turned from the blocks to the night sky. Prisoners clustered at the window.

Witold needed to sound an alert, but there wasn't time to launch the uprising. He felt as if a vast weight pinned him to the bed. The ground shook with the first explosion, which sounded like it came from near Birkenau. Were they targeting the gas chambers? Another dull thud. Somewhere flames were lighting the night sky. He struggled to stay conscious, but found himself floating away in a dream.[31]

Witold remained in a fevered state for the rest of the week. His rash was so pronounced that Dering couldn't hide him on the surgery block without Entress spotting him and demanding to know why he wasn't in isolation. Reluctantly, Dering found Witold a bunk in the quarantine block, where he was packed in with a twisting mass of other prisoners. Dering gave Witold an injection to reduce his fever, and the nurse Stanisław Kłodziński spooned him lemon juice mixed with sugar and helped hide him in one of the bunks during selections.[32]

Witold had moments of lucidity. "In this great mortuary of the half-living," he later wrote of the block, "where nearby someone was wheezing his final breath . . . another was struggling out of bed only to fall over onto the floor, another was throwing off his blankets, or talking in a fever to his dear mother, shouting, cursing someone, refusing to eat, or demanding water, in a fever and trying to jump out of the window, arguing with the doctor or asking for something—I lay thinking that I still had the strength to understand everything that was going on and take it calmly in my stride."[33]

But his fever had yet to peak. A week into his illness, Witold's temperature plunged to ninety-five degrees Fahrenheit, his blood pressure dropped, and he verged on cardiac arrest. He struggled to breathe, and it seemed to him that the air was filled with smoke, black and choking, as if the flames from his inner conflagration had spread beyond him and the whole camp was on fire. The nurses mopped his brow and pressed a sponge to his lips, but there was little they could do except wait for the crisis to ease.

The fever finally broke after ten days. Many of those who survive typhus note the particular ecstasy that follows its passing. But Witold could think only of escaping the isolation ward. He pulled himself to his feet and staggered against the wall, inching his way along it, until one of the nurses coaxed him back into bed.[34]

*

Dering brought him up to speed on the bombing raid: Soviet planes had attacked fields near Rajsko for unknown reasons. Dering also explained that Witold's dreams about smoke had been real. The SS had stopped burying their gassing victims in mass graves, as the corpses were contaminating the groundwater and the stench was alarming citizens outside the camp. Two new crematoria were now planned for Birkenau, but they were still months from completion, so the SS had ordered giant pyres lit for fresh bodies to be burned directly; those already buried were also dug up and burned. The fires raged around the clock, lighting up the night sky and emitting huge clouds of smoke that drifted past the camp as they spoke.[35]

Witold learned more details about the burnings over the following days from Jan Karcz's cell in Birkenau. By September 1942, Karcz had established regular contact with the Jewish workers of the special squad that operated the gas chambers. The three-hundred-odd men had recently moved from strict isolation in the main camp to Birkenau, where only a chain-link fence separated them from the other prisoners. The entrance to their barracks faced a guard post, but around the back the squad members could meet unobserved. Most nights, there was a radiant line of cigarettes along the rear wall "like so many glow-worms," recalled Andrey Pogozhev, one of the hundred or so surviving Soviet POWs, who lived in a neighboring barrack.[36]

A young French Jew named Steinberg had begun sneaking under the fence to join Karcz's underground meetings in Birkenau's hospital block, where the piles of corpses outside the barrack entrance kept the SS away. A representative of the Soviet POWs also attended, and collectively they agreed to coordinate activities and share intelligence. From Steinberg they received the fullest details yet on what was happening out of sight in the birch groves—how the Jews being led to the gas chambers often saw the flames from the nearby pyres through the trees and realized that they were next, but whether for the sake of the children, or their own disbelief, disrobed quietly and entered the gas chambers. Afterward their bodies were slung aboard a waiting rail cart that ran straight to the fires, where another crew worked stoking the flames.[37]

The pyres were usually set beside a mass grave to make disposing of the remains easier. It was a macabre scene even by the standards of Auschwitz: the uppermost layer of bodies could be removed with a hook and a crane, but a few feet down the pits were filled with putrid water, and the submerged bodies had to be fished out and heaved onto the banks. The SS sometimes gave the special squad vodka to ease the horror and also drank heavily themselves, but some refused to work and were shot; others went mad, screaming and raving around the barracks at night about how supernatural beings were about to pluck them from the camp and raise them to the heavens. Suicide was common. In the mornings there was sometimes a curtain of bodies hanging in the latrine. They all knew that they'd seen too much anyway, and that the Nazis were sure to kill them all in the end.[38]

Jan Karcz, c. 1941.

Courtesy of PMA-B.

On the morning of September 17, Karcz learned that the hundred or so surviving Soviets in Birkenau had been stripped of their clothes and locked in their barracks. A short while later, Steinberg appeared to tell him that a special gassing had been ordered for that night at 2 A.M., for which they'd been told they'd get a shot of vodka. He and Karcz concluded that the Soviets were the targets.[39]

Steinberg said that the men in his squad were ready to make a break-out attempt, which if done tonight would give the Soviets a chance to escape. Karcz said he was prepared to rally the Poles in Birkenau, but they'd need to present the operation to Witold and others in the main camp for approval.[40]

The plan the Birkenau cell proposed was rudimentary at best. Karcz's men would rush the guard posts while the Soviets made for the gate. Steinberg and the special squad could use the confusion to slip away into the woods. Many would die, but at least they were seizing their own fates.

That evening, Steinberg and the rest of his unit left early for their night shift. A fog had rolled in from the river. The Soviets had spent the day fashioning crude weapons from bits of wood in their block and were ready. Karcz and his men sat pensively in their bunks, waiting.[41]

Around midnight they heard a train stopping at the sidings a mile away. Then came the sound of trucks. They peered through the cracks in the wooden wall of the barracks and saw a small group of Jews being driven to the gas chamber. They waited. Slowly dawn approached, and they realized the danger had passed. That morning the Soviets' clothes were mysteriously returned, and they were freed to resume work. Whether or not the SS had intended to gas them or simply played some mocking trick was never established.[42]

Witold doesn't record his feelings about the near attempt. But a few weeks later, his belief that condemned men had the right to defend themselves was tested yet again. On October 28, the names of 280 prisoners were read out at roll call. The camp watched them form in ranks. Witold was ready to join them if they rallied. Instead they launched into the Polish national anthem and marched off.[43]

That evening, Witold and the others could see and smell the bloody trail the corpses had made on their way to the crematorium. Birkenau glowed like an ember in the distance. Witold's resolve was starting to falter. He had been a prisoner for two years and lost almost a hundred men to executions, phenol injections, and sickness over the past year, many, like Stasiek, his closest collaborators. He wasn't prepared to launch an uprising and risk a bloodbath and yet at the same time the Nazis' atrocities were escalating at an incredible rate. It was obvious that the Germans meant to kill every Jew they could lay their hands on. The morale of his men had plunged and petty rivalries and squabbles had surfaced as their sense of purpose slipped away. He wasn't sure how much longer he could hold the underground together.

CHAPTER 15

DECLARATION

LONDON
AUGUST 1942

Churchill received horrific accounts of the European-wide roundup of the Jews over summer and autumn of 1942. In southern France, the Vichy government of Marshal Pétain assisted the Germans in emptying internment facilities of Jews. The London *Times* reported from the French-Spanish border that a train left Lyon carrying 4,000 unaccompanied Jewish children to an unspecified location in Germany. Churchill was moved to indict the Nazi deportation of families to the House of Commons as "the most bestial, the most squalid, and the most senseless of all their offences." What he did not know was that the vast majority of these men, women, and children were being sent to their deaths and, in fact, he seems to have accepted the German explanation that they were sending Europe's Jews to labor camps in the East.[1]

The Allied failure to understand Auschwitz's role at the epicenter of the Holocaust allowed officials to continue characterizing the German assault on the Jews as a diffuse phenomenon that could only be stopped by defeating Germany in war. This position prompted senior officials in both governments to downplay genocide and inhibited further investigation.

When the German industrialist Eduard Schulte's warning that Hitler planned to exterminate Europe's Jews reached London and Washington at the end of August, Allied officials responded with disbelief. "We have no confirmation of this report from other sources," noted one British diplomat. "A wild rumor based on Jewish fears," an American official concluded. The U.S. State Department then tried—and failed—to block the telegram bearing Schulte's information from reaching its intended recipient in the States, the influential rabbi Stephen Wise. Even then, U.S. officials persuaded Wise and other Jewish leaders to keep the matter quiet until they could confirm the claim.[2]

The State Department, in turn, opened a modest investigation that involved sending a single representative to Rome in September to verify the information with the Vatican. Pope Pius XII almost certainly knew by the summer of 1942 about the mass murder of Jews and the likely fate of deportees from his bishopric offices in Poland and the papal nuncio in Bern. But he was wary about stirring Hitler's anger against the church and declined to comment.[3]

The Americans appear to have turned next to the Poles. In mid-October, the Polish exile government sent an urgent request to Warsaw for the latest intelligence on the mass murder of Jews. This should have been the moment for the underground leader Rowecki to reveal what he knew about the camp. Witold's messenger Stanisław Jaster had delivered his report on the gassing of Jews in Birkenau in mid-August, and Stasiek's final report, putting the Jewish death toll at thirty-five thousand, had been received and prepared for dispatch. Yet Rowecki remained silent on the killings in Auschwitz. He did mention the camp in a message to Sikorski dated October 3, but only to describe it and other concentration camps as "the manifestation of an extermination policy directed against Poles."[4]

It isn't clear why Rowecki failed to identify Auschwitz's new role as a Jewish death camp. He was certainly frustrated by the lack of response to his efforts to draw attention to the massacres. "The whole world is silent while [we] are witnessing the rapid mass murder of several million people," he had complained to London in September. Rowecki may have calculated that given the West's apparent disinterest in Jewish affairs he needed to focus on the plight of ethnic Poles, whom the Nazis might target next. It's also possible Rowecki was concerned about angering the ultranationalists who considered Auschwitz to be a symbol of Polish— that is, Christian—suffering. He'd asked Sikorski to halt pronouncements on the postwar rights of Jews because they were undermining support for the Polish government among ordinary Poles.[5]

As the American investigation dragged on, Auschwitz's role as a death camp was finally broken on November 20—not by British, American, or Polish intelligence officials piecing together Witold's reports but by a small Zionist organization called the Jewish Agency. Its Jerusalem office had collected the testimony of 114 Palestinian subjects, 69 of them Jewish, whom the Germans had released in a prisoner exchange. One of them, a woman from Sosnowiec in Poland, described the existence of three crematoria in Auschwitz used for gassing Jews. Her testimony was picked up by the London correspondent of the *New York Times*, who wrote a short article that appeared in the November 25 edition of the paper on page 10 under the headline DETAILS REACHING PALESTINE. Reference to Auschwitz was limited to a single line: "Information received here of methods by which the Germans in Poland carrying out the slaughter of Jews includes accounts of trainloads of adults and children taken to great crematoriums at Oswiencim [*sic*], near Krakow."[6]

This was the first reference to Auschwitz as a death camp in the Western media. But there was no follow-up. Instead attention was drawn the same day to a press conference in Washington, D.C., by Rabbi Wise. The State Department had finally concluded its investigation and granted its approval for him to release Schulte's information about Hitler's extermination plans. Wise revealed that two million lives had already been lost.[7]

His statement drew international attention and on December 8 he and four fellow rabbis were ushered into the Oval Office to find the president smoking at his cluttered desk. Roosevelt was friendly and agreed to a rabbinical blessing. Wise read a prepared statement and handed him a detailed summary of the mass murders that also contained a passing reference to Auschwitz. However, Roosevelt showed little interest in such specifics.[8]

"The government of the United States is very well acquainted with most of the facts you are now bringing to our attention," he told the group in the Oval Office. He explained that it was too early to make a pronouncement, and he wondered aloud how effective one would be. Roosevelt didn't reveal his concerns about stoking anti-Semitism at home by focusing on Jewish suffering. The fact that his administration included several high-profile Jews had already led the Nazi regime to repeatedly claim he was in league with them. After less than half an hour the Jewish delegation was politely shown the door.[9]

*

The task of trying to turn the escalating atrocities into Allied action once again fell to Sikorski, who seized upon the interest in Schulte's information to advocate for a formal Allied statement condemning Nazi crimes. On December 2, Poland's acting foreign minister, Edward Raczyński, met his British counterpart, Anthony Eden, to ask him to convene a conference on the Nazis' genocidal program.[10]

Eden was skeptical at first. The Poles, wrote one of his deputies, are "always glad of an opportunity 1. to make a splash at the expense of the minor Allies and 2. to show that they are not anti-Semitic." But pressure from Jewish groups, awkward questions in Parliament, and the steady flow of information about the killings from the Polish government and other sources prompted a rethink. As an official observed, the government would be in "an appalling position" if the atrocities proved real and they had done nothing. Eden hoped that the declaration would put the matter to rest until after the war.[11]

On December 15, Eden presented a draft of the declaration to the cabinet in their subterranean meeting room below Whitehall known as "the hole." Churchill, who had read a note prepared by the Polish government about the mass murders mentioning death camps like Bełżec but not Auschwitz, asked his foreign secretary whether the reports

British foreign minister Anthony Eden conversing
with U.S. secretary of state Cordell Hull.

U.S. Department of State.

about "the wholesale massacre of Jews" by "electrical methods" were true.[12]

Eden replied, "Jews are being withdrawn from Norway and sent to Poland, for some such purposes evidently." Eden was, however, unable to "confirm the method" of killing or their destination. In fact, 529 Norwegian Jews had arrived in Auschwitz the week before, of whom 346 were gassed upon arrival.[13]

*

On December 17, Eden stated plainly to a packed House of Commons that Germany had embarked on a "bestial policy of cold-blooded extermination." He described how Jews were being transported from across Europe to Poland, the Nazis' "principal slaughterhouse," and that "none of those taken away were ever heard from again." The Jewish MP James Rothschild, granted the first question, hoped that Eden's words would offer "some faint hope and courage" for those currently in the Germans' clutches. The House then stood for a minute's silence.[14]

The declaration finally lodged the mass murder of Jews in the public mind. The *New York Times* ran the story on its front page under the headline ALLIES CONDEMN NAZI WAR ON JEWS, and reprinted the statement in full. Edward R. Murrow of CBS News declared, "The phrase 'concentration camp' is obsolete. . . . It is now possible to speak only of 'extermination camp.'" The BBC's European news service broadcast the statement several times a day for a week. News readers were instructed to include "at least one message of encouragement for the Jews." In Germany, the propaganda chief Joseph Goebbels did his best to jam the signals without success. In his diary, he bemoaned the "flood of sob-stuff" he'd heard in the British Parliament.[15]

The scale of the coverage and resulting public outcry took the British government by surprise. The Foreign Office was inundated with requests to help Jews flee to neutral countries and aid those already in refugee camps in places like Switzerland. The MP Eleanor Rathbone called for pressure to be applied to German satellites like Hungary and Romania to either withdraw their cooperation with the Nazis or release their Jews to the Allies—a "frightful prospect," noted one British official, after Romania did indeed offer to release seventy thousand Jews that December. The Foreign Office had no desire to look after thousands of Jewish refugees, especially if that meant an influx into British-controlled Palestine.[16]

The British government also faced fresh calls from the Poles for a retaliatory bombing campaign, given fresh impetus by news of an SS cleansing operation against ethnic Poles in the Zamość region of eastern Poland. Rowecki reported that the Germans were dispatching able-bodied Poles to work camps and the rest to Auschwitz. He mistakenly feared it was the start of the "Jewish method" being applied to the Poles. In fact, Nazi leadership intended to drastically reduce the number of Poles in their territories by up to 85 percent, but wholesale extermination had been ruled out. As one German official observed, "That sort of solution . . . would hang over the German people and deprive us of sympathy everywhere."[17]

Churchill asked the RAF head, Charles Portal, to consider the viability of bombing targets inside Poland. The RAF had enhanced its capabilities in the two years since Portal had first ruled out bombing Auschwitz. Lancaster bombers with a range of 2,530 miles and a bomb load of seven thousand pounds were in service by then. Indeed, a force of Lancasters struck the German submarine yards in Danzig in the spring of 1942. Striking the rail lines leading to Auschwitz and its gassing facilities, where eight hundred thousand Jews would be killed over the next two years, was feasible. But it was at this moment that the British failure to comprehend the significance of Auschwitz was perhaps most tragically revealed. The idea of bombing the camp wasn't discussed that Christmas because no one realized it had been transformed from a target of significant symbolic, if little military importance to the epicenter of a vast, mechanized genocide unparalleled in human history.[18]

Portal acknowledged to Churchill in a memo dated January 6, 1943, that a small-scale attack against a target in Poland was possible, but he characterized it as merely a symbolic gesture that he didn't believe would deter the Nazis. Indeed, he worried it might simply play into Hitler's narrative that the war was being waged at the behest of an international Jewish conspiracy. Portal worried about reprisals against captured British airmen if that was the case, and he wondered too whether an explicit policy of retaliations might call into question the moral underpinnings of the RAF's current operations against German cities as "ordinary operations of war against military (including of course industrial) targets."[19]

Churchill could have overruled him. But he concurred in a clear signal to British officialdom to quietly move on from the matter. The public line was that the Jews would be saved when Europe was liberated, and all resources should be dedicated to that objective. The Americans took a similar approach. The State Department went so far as to instruct the legation in Switzerland to stop sending material from Jewish groups through official channels that might inflame the public. But just as it seemed as if Auschwitz's significance would remain unrecognized, news reached the Polish exile government in London in mid-February that Napoleon was on his way.[20]

CHAPTER 16

BREAKDOWN

AUSCHWITZ

NOVEMBER 1942

Witold was standing in the square with a few men in the early evening as the first winter snow fell in Auschwitz when he heard his name called. He turned to see one of Rowecki's staff officers, Stanisław Wierzbicki, making his way toward them through the gray meltwater. It was Witold's first contact since entering the camp with a member of Rowecki's inner circle. He might be carrying news or perhaps even a message about the uprising. Stanisław gave him a hearty greeting and explained he'd just arrived in the camp. He noted Witold's good health. In Warsaw, he exclaimed, people thought the prisoners were all "walking bags of bones."[1]

Witold winced. He'd come from the tannery, where work now included processing the hair shorn from the corpses of Jewish women in Birkenau for use as mattress stuffing and lining stiffeners for uniforms. He wanted to know how his reports had been received. How had the world responded to news of the mass gassings, phenol injections, and the vast piles of goods plundered from the Jews? Surely they could expect coordinated support for their uprising?[2]

Stanisław confirmed that Witold's messenger, Stefan Bielecki, had made it to Warsaw; in fact, he'd personally driven him to the head-quarters. But no decision had come of it. The truth was, explained Stanisław, that few people gave much thought to Auschwitz. Warsaw was preoccupied with the eastern front. Hitler boasted of an imminent victory in the Soviet Union, but the fighting raged on. Poland needed to be ready to stake its claim for independence in major cities like War-saw and Krakow, not Auschwitz.[3]

Witold nearly laughed in shock. The men standing with him looked as though they had been punched. Their reports, the atrocities—their lives—dismissed with a shrug. Stanisław bid his farewell and left Wi-told with his mind racing over what to do. He couldn't go on pre-tending that the uprising was imminent or ask his men to die in vain without Warsaw's support. But closing down the possibility created a new dilemma. The mission he'd asked each man to risk his life for was suddenly meaningless. Morale was already fragile. Absent a purpose, he worried that the underground would fracture.[4]

His fears were crystalized a few days later when Fred Stössel, the radio operator, submitted to SS orders and began delivering phenol injections to prisoners. Kon confronted Fred immediately.[5]

"Why do you do this dirty work for them?" he demanded.[6]

Fred shrugged. He was mostly injecting the small number of Jews admitted to the hospital, he explained. They were slated to die anyway. "Would you rather die instantly or be clubbed to death over several days?"[7]

"You ask the wrong question," Kon said, "conveniently forgetting that the Germans have set up these camps to exterminate Poles, Jews, and others. Why should we Poles, who are fighting Germans even here in Auschwitz, help them in this terrible scheme?"

Kon couldn't shake the feeling that Fred took pleasure from the power of killing but was unsure how to proceed. A few days later, Czesław Sowul, a member of Stasiek's socialist circle, took matters into his own hands and left a letter in the denunciation box with Fred's name on it—a foolhardy act. Fred had crossed a red line, Witold believed. But he knew enough to have them all killed and may well have simply lost his mind.[8]

Fred was summoned to the Gestapo headquarters the following afternoon, questioned, and sent to the penal block. Over the next few days, he was marched to the Gestapo's headquarters for interrogation. That winter, SS-Oberscharführer Wilhelm Boger introduced the practice of suspending prisoners by their hands and feet and whipping their genitals in order to extract confessions. Each evening Fred returned to the penal block looking more bloodied and desperate. It seemed only a matter of time before he would break.[9]

After a week or so, Fred passed a message through the penal block cleaners that he hadn't betrayed the underground. But he was nearing his limit and requested a dose of cyanide. There was no easy way to smuggle a pill to him; even his food was checked. In the end, an inmate cleaning detail released typhus-infected lice into his cell. Soon Fred came down with the fever, and was brought under guard to the hospital, where Witold's men kept watch. He recovered from the infection only for the SS to lose interest and shoot him.[10]

The socialist faction responded to Fred's transgressions by threatening further action against any orderly deemed too close to the Germans. Some, including Kon, suspected Dering had become a Nazi sympathizer.[11]

That autumn, a new head doctor, SS-Sturmbannführer Eduard Wirths, encouraged his staff to use the abundance of human material available for research. Patients were given experimental drugs for diseases such as trachoma, typhus, tuberculosis, and diphtheria. In many cases, the inmates were deliberately infected and left in agony by a medley of untested drugs they were given. One SS doctor studied the effects of starvation on patients. After interviewing his victims about their diet, he had them photographed, injected with phenol, and then dissected and their livers, spleens, and pancreases preserved in jars.[12]

Dering stood out for his position and willingness to compromise himself in actions large and small—sharing smuggled medicine with kapos, aggressively following Nazi orders to perform unnecessary operations. But it was also true that many nurses acceded to SS orders while secretly working to alleviate the suffering they inflicted with smuggled medicine and food. No one could say with certainty which deed rose to the level of collaboration or what constituted a moral act in an environment where survival depended on complicity with murder. After all, the Germans had directly or indirectly conscripted most prisoners into the operation of the camp's machinery of death.[13]

Prisoners working on the construction of a new crematorium and gas chambers in Birkenau, c. 1943.

Courtesy of PMA-B.

Bernard Świerczyna, c. 1939.
Courtesy of PMA-B.

Witold, for his part, seems to have answered the question of his own complicity by continuing to gather intelligence on Nazi crimes, knowing that his reports would likely be met with indifference. Bernard Świerczyna, one of Witold's men in the storage department, compiled a list of every prisoner death and probable cause in the main camp. The dossier contained sixteen thousand names. At the same time, Witold's intelligence-gathering operation began to reveal the full scale of the mass murder in Birkenau. The victims were never officially registered in the camp, so they based their estimate of 502,000 Jews gassed on the number of trains pulling into the camp (the number was some way off the actual figure of around 200,000).[14]

Then came news that the surveyors had stolen carbon copies of drawings for the new crematoria under construction in Birkenau, which would make the Nazi killing factory even more efficient. The SS architect Walter Dejaco had made a significant modification to earlier designs. The morgues of the two new crematoria had been turned into gas chambers. Instead of chutes for dropping bodies into the basement morgue, steps had been added so that Jewish victims could walk themselves into the chambers. The new facilities would increase the camp's killing capacity to more than six thousand people per day. Construction was expected to be completed in the New Year. The construction office was thrown into quiet chaos for two days when the chief SS architect, Karl Bischoff, discovered that the highly secret drawings had gone missing. Bischoff finally ordered another "original" copy made and hushed up the security breach.[15]

Witold helped engineer a brazen escape that Christmas to deliver

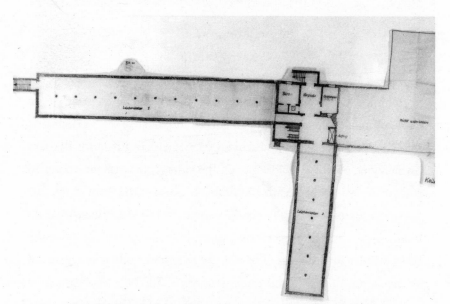

Drawing of Crematorium II stolen by surveyors showing steps leading down into the morgue following its repurposing as a gas chamber.

Courtesy of PMA-B.

the documents to Warsaw. His courier was Mieczysław Januszewski, a twenty-four-year-old naval officer who worked in the labor assignment office. He was joined by Otto, the friendly German kapo who had helped the underground switch work squads. Tannery worker Jan Komski and Bolesław Kuczbara, the camp dentist, completed the party. On December 29, Bolesław donned a stolen SS uniform and with Otto collected a horse-drawn cart loaded with furniture from the carpenters' workshop, ostensibly for delivery to an SS man's home nearby. They picked up Mieczysław and Jan, who hid in two cupboards with the documents. Then they rode out of the camp. The Germans found only the abandoned cart, the prisoners' stripes, and a note in one of their jackets implicating the head kapo Bruno in the escape.[16]

Mieczysław Januszewski, Jan Komski, Otto Küsel,
Bolesław Kuczbara, Andrzej Harat, and his daughter
Władysława after the escape, c. December 1942.

Courtesy of PMA-B.

Witold admired the escapees' wit in doing so—Bruno was subsequently sent to the penal block for interrogation—but the sense of satisfaction was short-lived. The SS soon stepped up its efforts to stamp out resistance. On January 25, a dozen prisoners were brought for interrogation. Further arrests and executions followed. Among those shot were the morgue worker Gïenek Obojski, radio expert Zbigniew Ruszczyński, and the Birkenau cell leader Jan Karcz. Witold ordered everyone to scale back their activities and be wary of new arrivals in their squads. Rumors spread that Grabner's informers had finally uncovered a plot to seize the camp, and that mass executions were imminent. They were all jittery that winter, listening to the screams emanating from the Gestapo office.[17]

One particular scene lingered with Witold. He was returning from a shift at the tannery one night when he was startled to see a dozen men, women, and children standing outside the crematorium. It was cold and the sun had set long ago. Their faces were gray like the road. Witold guessed that they were about to be killed, and they seemed to know it too. Since the gassing operations had moved to Birkenau, the morgue of the old crematorium was sometimes used for executions of political prisoners or Jewish families caught locally. Witold tried not to meet their eyes. But he couldn't help but notice a small boy of perhaps ten, his son Andrzej's age, looking around expectantly. Then the gate to the crematorium opened and he and the others disappeared inside. Muffled shots followed.[18]

Witold lay awake that night thinking of the boy and was overwhelmed with shame. For all his talk of uprisings, he'd failed to act on behalf of a single child. Worse, he knew that this pain, too, would fade, and the boy become faceless and forgotten. He felt the same deadness growing within him as he thought of the murder of the Jews. He was surrounded by evidence of the slaughter in the tannery, but he struggled to identify with the Jewish victims. "Witnessing the killing of healthy people by gas makes a strong impact only when you first see it," he observed.[19]

His sense of emotional distance was underscored by the fact that the treatment of prisoners in the main camp had improved somewhat. The Nazi leadership, facing massive labor shortages, sought to employ inmates in the concentration camp system in war production. In addition to the ongoing construction of the IG Farben factory, dozens of small factories and satellite camps sprang up around Oświęcim. Bathrooms were installed on the blocks and morning roll call abolished. Prisoners now had time to wash and shave. Many began wearing civilian clothes because of denim shortages, with only a red stripe painted on the arm or back marking them as inmates. Commandant Höss even issued an instruction to stop maltreating inmates. The kapos still used their clubs at times, but when they did it was almost as if they had to offer those watching a reminder that this was still a death camp.[20]

*

Witold began to think of escape. Perhaps, he thought, only he could persuade Rowecki to attack Auschwitz. The odds of success were as small as ever. There had been around 170 breakout attempts in 1942, and only a dozen or so had been successful. He had played a hand in ten, but now he struggled to think of a workable scheme. One of his colleagues, a pipefitter, told him of an extensive network of sewers under the camp that might be big enough for a man. To explore the idea, Witold switched squads to the parcel office, which ran a night shift and stood next to one of the manholes leading into the sewers. The single SS man on duty in the office usually dozed off around 2 A.M. Witold obtained a flashlight and a pair of overalls from the clothing department, and slipped out onto the street one night that February.

The manhole he'd identified stood between two blocks, out of sight from the guard towers. The cover came up easily enough. There was a metal grill inside, secured with a padlock that he had to force open. The tunnels led in four directions, following the street grid. They were barely two feet in diameter and were choked with excrement. He started off in a crouch, but the waste had built up in places, forcing him onto his hands and knees, and then his stomach. He slithered inch by inch until the passage narrowed still further and he was in danger of getting stuck. Then he slowly reversed until he emerged into the predawn darkness and prepared for roll call. He repeated this ritual night after night. But eventually he determined that there was no way out.[21]

In early February, Witold's colleagues in the tannery came across a stack of clothes that unmistakably belonged to Polish peasants: clogs,

Sewers of the main camp.
Courtesy of Katarzyna Chiżyńska.

farmers' smocks, and a few simple rosaries. The news was confirmed that evening; a transport of Poles had arrived from the Zamość district of eastern Poland, and half had gone straight to the gas chamber. It was one of the first times that ethnic Poles had been treated to the same extermination process as Jews, and Witold must have wondered if he and the other Polish prisoners were about to become targeted for genocide.[22]

Witold learned on February 23 that thirty-nine Polish boys from Zamość had been separated from their families and brought to the hospital, where they were stripped and left in the washroom. Several children guessed that they were going to die and started crying. The orderlies gathered around them, brought soup, sang songs, and the children quieted down. A nurse, Stanisław Głowa, began to weep. "So we're going to die," one of the older boys let out.[23]

Stanisław tracked down another of the Polish nurses who'd also started administering phenol injections. "If you kill these children, you won't live through the night," he swore. The man ran and hid in one of the blocks. But the children were still injected a few hours later by two SS men. The hospital rang out to cries of "Mummy, Daddy, help me!" and "Dear Jesus, why do we have to die?"[24]

"We had already seen many mountains of corpses in the camp," recalled Witold, "but this one . . . made an impression on us, on even the old inmates." A week later, eighty more Polish boys were injected. He had to get out. But how?[25]

*

Then one morning in March Witold was offered an unlikely means of exiting the camp. News spread that five thousand Polish prisoners, almost half of the main camp's total, were to be transferred to other concentration camps in the Reich and replaced with Jews. Witold figured he was on the list but felt conflicted. He was desperate to leave but realized that transferring to another camp would only delay his mission to Warsaw. In a new camp he'd have to spend months building up his network and figuring out an escape plan. Still, he was tempted.[26]

The first deportation was scheduled for March 10 to the concentration camps of Buchenwald, near the central German city of Weimar, and Neuengamme, outside Hamburg. The SS clearly suspected there would be some effort to resist the transfer among the prisoners who stood to lose desirable work details and their positions in the camp hierarchy. The Gestapo chief Grabner kept the final list of names tightly guarded and ordered an evening selection to give inmates less chance of slipping between barracks or switching numbers. Witold's block was one of the first to be visited. The prisoners waited on their bunks for the kapo to go through the list. Some grumbled at having to learn the ropes of a new camp. Others thought that nowhere could be as bad as Auschwitz. "It means they have given up on tormenting me here," muttered one of Witold's neighbors who'd been selected.[27]

Just as he'd suspected, Witold's number was indeed on the list. He was still surprised by his relief at the thought of leaving. He was moved to a specially designated block with a thousand other men to await transfer. His friend Edek, who'd recently joined the nursing staff, found him early the next morning in one of the rooms. None of the orderlies had been selected to leave, having been classed as essential workers needed to keep the camp running. Edek whispered that he had found a way for Witold to stay. There would be a final medical selection, he explained. Witold could get off the transport by feigning a disability. Overnight, the nurses had built a splint for him to wear around his waist to simulate a hernia—a risky strategy, but Witold agreed to its fitting.[28]

At first light, the transportees were assembled along the Birkenallee for the final review. It was misty, just as it had been on Witold's first morning in the camp. The doctors worked their way slowly down the line, inspecting each prisoner. Witold silently ran through the names of his fallen comrades for a final salute, and knew he owed it to them to stay in the camp and complete his mission.

It was past midnight by the time the doctors reached his row. The medical team took one look at Witold's apparently swollen midriff and dismissed him back to the camp. He exchanged a farewell glance with Kon, who'd been selected for Buchenwald.[29]

Four thousand Poles were shipped out over the following three days. Witold again avoided deportation when 2,500 more Poles were transferred a week later by having himself classed as one of a select group of "indispensable workers" needed to keep the camp running. But his network was gutted, and he was no closer to finding an escape route.[30]

*

In early March, two of the new crematoria and gas chambers opened in Birkenau and were soon put to use murdering Jews from Krakow's ghetto. In the main camp, one of the blocks was converted into a medical laboratory where the SS started chemical and radiation experiments on the sex organs of mostly Jewish men and women to see if a mass-sterilization program was possible for the racially undesirable. The experiments were conducted in high secrecy and the block sealed, but a couple of underground members broke in one night and saw a room of jars containing testicles in a pinkish solution.[31]

"Blasted world," Witold was muttering to himself one afternoon in the parcel office when a young prisoner, Edmund Zabawski, interrupted him.[32]

They fell into conversation, with Edmund doing most of the talking. Witold liked the earnest thirty-year-old. Over the course of several conversations, Edmund revealed that one of his friends was

Edmund Zabawski, c. 1942.
Courtesy of PMA-B.

planning to escape from a bakery outside the camp and that he was thinking of joining him. Witold knew Edmund's friend by sight, a six-foot-four primary school teacher named Jan Redzej who'd come on the same transport as Witold and worked in a squad delivering bread around the camp. Edmund arranged for them to meet after roll call one evening in late March.[33]

It was drizzling in the square when they met. Jan was soaked from his work, his balding pate glistening in the rain, but he flashed them a grin and explained his plan. He collected bread from a bakery that was the perfect location for a getaway, a mile from the camp and in sight of the open fields. It was operated by civilian bakers and a detachment of prisoners. Jan had observed how the civilians left the bicycles they rode to work resting against the wall. His plan was simply to grab a bike each and "go for it."[34]

Witold didn't think that was a good idea, but he saw potential. If they joined the bakery's night shift, he believed, they could slip away under the cover of darkness. Jan agreed to study the bakery more closely and bribed his kapo into letting him switch to the bakers' squad.[35]

Jan Redzej, c. 1941.
Courtesy of PMA-B.

He reported back a few days later. The good news was that there were only two guards at the site. However, the obstacles were formidable. The guards locked and double-bolted the door during work. It was also latched from the outside by the departing shift. There were no other entrances, and all the windows were barred. Jan thought it might be possible to steal one of the door keys; one hung from a guard's belt at all times, but a copy was kept behind a glass front box in an anteroom. The problem was that even if they could acquire the second key and unlock the door, they'd still be stumped by the outer latch.

That "damned latch" made it impossible, concluded Jan. Witold urged Jan to look at the latch again. In the meantime, Edmund asked to join the escape and suggested that they head for his wife's family home in Bochnia, a small town south of Krakow, about a hundred miles from the camp. It would take several days to get there, and they'd have to travel at night to avoid detection.[36]

The next day Jan reported better news. The latch rested on a hook that was bolted through the door with a nut poking through on the inside. If they could gauge the size of the nut they would be able to unscrew it and free the latch. Over the next few days, Jan made an imprint of the nut using a piece of dough, which Witold handed over to a metalworker friend to find the right-sized wrench. The key was trickier, but Jan managed to remove the one on the wall from its box while the guards' backs were turned and made another dough imprint. Witold had a cast made, which Jan tried in the lock. It worked.

The escape was on.[37]

IV

CHAPTER 17

IMPACT

GENEVA
NOVEMBER 1942

Napoleon finally gave up waiting on the legation in Switzerland to sort out his visas and on November 7 he traveled to Geneva, on the French border, to meet a smuggler who swore he had the necessary papers. But the man took his money and then disappeared. Napoleon crossed the border that night by himself and was picked up by French gendarmes a few hours later. The French police released him a week later without charge, perhaps accepting his story of being a Wehrmacht soldier returning to his unit. But during his stay in jail Hitler had moved to occupy the rest of France and seal the border with Spain in reaction to the Allied invasion of North Africa. German troops filled the streets of southern French cities and the Gestapo hunted for Jews and resisters.[1]

Napoleon made it to a safe house in Perpignan in the foothills of the Pyrenees, where the local guide demanded double to smuggle him over the mountain passes to Spain. He had no choice but to pay, only for this man to also disappear. Napoleon struggled over the mountains alone before finally reaching Barcelona a week later, on November 24.

Napoleon planned to stay a few hours and then head south to the British protectorate of Gibraltar. But the city was under heavy police control and he was arrested again. Spain was not officially allied with Germany, but General Francisco Franco, a fascist, was sympathetic to the Nazis' cause. This time there was no quick release.[2]

The Spanish police interned Napoleon for two months in a cell and then transferred him to the Miranda de Ebro concentration camp in Castille, where other foreign nationals caught crossing the border were kept. He arrived at the camp in early January 1943 to join five thousand poorly clothed and ill-fed inmates who spent their days lifting rocks from a nearby riverbed for road construction. Napoleon considered various schemes for escaping, before opting to stage a hunger strike over camp conditions. He persuaded the contingent of several hundred Polish inmates to join, and together they demanded a consular visit from the British, who oversaw Polish affairs in Spain. After two weeks of fasting, the Spanish authorities summoned the British ambassador from Madrid to negotiate. It seems Napoleon arranged a meeting with the diplomat and persuaded him that he was in fact a British-trained agent, thus securing his release.[3]

Napoleon arrived in Gibraltar on February 3, 1943, shortly after news of Germany's catastrophic defeat at Stalingrad broke: some ninety thousand German soldiers had surrendered on the Volga, and a further hundred thousand were lost and presumed dead. Soviet forces had clawed back all the German gains of the previous year and were poised to launch a major counteroffensive. The tide of war was turning.[4]

Napoleon caught one of the merchant ships that sailed regularly between the British enclave and the Firth of Clyde in Scotland, a major hub for Allied shipping, and spent a tense week skirting German U-boat patrols. He finally arrived in the United Kingdom on February 19. The journey he'd expected to require a couple of weeks had taken

John Gilkes

more than six months. "Heartbreaking," he called the delay. The Nazis had killed nearly a quarter of a million Jews in Auschwitz in that time.[5]

*

Napoleon was likely debriefed by the British at the Royal Victoria Patriotic Schools, a vast Gothic building in the southern London suburb of Wandsworth that was used for questioning foreign arrivals. A mild-mannered but firm intelligence officer, Major Malcolm Scott, conducted most of the interviews in fluent Polish (his mother was a Pole). No record of what Napoleon divulged has been located.[6]

Napoleon requested a new name, Jerzy Salski, be entered in police records in order to further conceal his identity, perhaps already with an eye to his next mission. One of the police officers handling his case, a Major J. D. O'Reilly, flagged the request to his superiors.[7]

He was given a curt response: "As you are perhaps aware, we finance Polish SOE to the extent of £600,000 and their activities are *our* activities."

Napoleon was finally released to officials of the Polish interior ministry at the end of February. Over the following days, he revealed what he knew about the mass murder of Jews in the camp, including the facts he had established about the gas chambers and his incorrect theories about the use of air pressure and electrocution to kill. The record doesn't state whether Sikorski sent a message to Warsaw. But it was standard operating procedure to confirm the arrival of couriers, and often led to a back-and-forth. It is clear that Napoleon's arrival marked an influx of intelligence from Warsaw about Auschwitz. On March 3, Rowecki radioed London Witold's news that 502,000 Jews had already died in the camp in 1942. Then on March 12, Rowecki wrote about the opening of the two crematoria in Birkenau that each had the capacity to burn two thousand bodies a day. The same information was sent again to London on March 23. A week later, Rowecki sent a message that the Krakow Ghetto had been liquidated and four thousand of its inhabitants sent to Auschwitz.[8]

The Polish government was shocked by the scale of the deaths, which coincided with the news that barely two hundred thousand Jews were left in the country. Szmul Zygielbojm, one of only two Jews to sit on a thirty-one-man national council, asked the Polish interior ministry to double-check that the figures were right. Both his wife and two children lived in what was left of Warsaw's ghetto.[9]

"I do not know how history will judge us," he told a meeting of the council in March, "but I feel that millions of people in Poland cannot believe, cannot grasp, that we are not in a position to move world opinion here or to do something to end the inhumane suffering."[10]

Zygielbojm called for another Allied declaration in light of the revelations, but there was little chance of that. The British and Americans had no interest in prompting further debate about the mass murders or in supporting rescue measures that might divert resources away from the war effort. In America, the State Department proposed an international conference to discuss the plight of Jews and other displaced persons in a cynical move to delay military and diplomatic action, and the British were quick to back it. When the Polish leader Sikorski continued to push for some form of attack, one Foreign Office official wrote, "We have repeatedly told the Poles, reprisals as such are ruled out." Another diplomat noted, "The Poles are being very irritating over this."[11]

Despite the lack of interest from the British, Napoleon wrote a summary of his findings that was likely shared with the Foreign Office official Frank Savery, a former consul in Warsaw, who dealt with Polish matters and was a key gatekeeper for deciding how intelligence was acted upon. Savery appears to have then brought Auschwitz's role to the attention of the British government's Political Warfare Executive, the government department that oversaw the BBC's coverage—a critical conduit to both policy makers and the British public. In early April the PWE met to discuss whether to include the gassing of Jews in Auschwitz on the news agenda. The debate represented the first time senior British officials had openly acknowledged the camp's role in the gassing of Jews. But they refused to broadcast the report domestically, opting instead to limit reporting to its Polish-language service.[12]

On April 11, the BBC's Polish service prepared to broadcast news about Auschwitz. The walls and ceiling of the makeshift studio in the basement of the BBC's bomb-damaged headquarters were hung with a canvas sheet to improve acoustics, and an oil lamp stood at the door in case they lost power during a raid. The room was usually buzzing with producers rushing around with scripts in multiple languages that were broadcast from the same studio. The text read by the Polish announcer was always carefully checked by British officials, one of whom sat beside a switch during every broadcast, prepared to kill the feed in case of any deviation from the script or if someone "suddenly shouted hurrah for Hitler," as one BBC staffer recalled.[13]

In this instance, the broadcast went smoothly enough, although several errors had crept into the text, perhaps reflecting the fact it had passed through multiple hands. The report began with the announcement that the Germans had liquidated the fifteen-thousand-strong Krakow Ghetto in March. It then explained that the ghetto's inhabitants had been sent to "camps of death" to be murdered. The report concluded that those "remaining were sent by lorries to the concentration camp of Oświęcim, which, as it is known, has special installations for mass murder, that is gas chambers, and iron floors conducting an electric current." The final element might have been drawn from Napoleon's incorrect assumptions about the facilities in Birkenau.[14]

The transmission's impact was limited. Rowecki probably heard the report or at least learned of it, as did the Germans. Before the Polish officials could push the matter further, they were distracted by news from Berlin that a mass grave had been uncovered in the Katyń forests of western Russia. The Germans claimed the grave contained the bodies of three thousand Polish officers shot by the Soviets in 1940. The resulting furor consumed Polish attention, and once again the fate of those who had died or were close to death in Auschwitz became a secondary concern.[15]

＊

Events continued to turn attention away from Auschwitz. On April 19, SS and German police units began an operation to liquidate the remaining sixty thousand Jews in the Warsaw Ghetto. This time, the Jewish resistance fought back, and a grossly mismatched battle began: the Jewish fighters had a few machine guns, handguns, and homemade grenades. The Germans, by contrast, arrived with tanks and heavy weaponry to systematically demolish the ghetto one block at a time.

The slowly unfolding disaster was relayed to London via underground radio. There was little the Polish government or Jewish groups could do but continue to press for action. The politician Zygielbojm made a desperate plea to the Allies to bomb SS units in the Warsaw Ghetto and Auschwitz. The naming of the camp in connection with the mass murder of Jews had finally allowed it to emerge as a target for attack. Zygielbojm knew by then that petitioning the British was pointless, so he put his request to the Americans via a friend in U.S. intelligence. But the U.S. military seemed to have drawn the same conclusion as the RAF about the value and effectiveness of bombing Auschwitz, and Zygielbojm's request was rebuffed.[16]

On May 11, following the razing of the ghetto, Zygielbojm overdosed on barbiturates in his London apartment. Beside his body was found a note.

"By my death," he said, "I wish to give expression to my most profound protest against the inaction in which the world watches and permits the destruction of the Jewish people." Both his wife and son perished in the ghetto.[17]

But Zygielbojm's death passed without much comment, and the plight of the Jews began to slip off the international agenda yet again. The conference the British and Americans had arranged in Bermuda to discuss the refugee crisis in mid-April passed without resolution. Allied attention was consumed by the impending invasion of Italy. On the eastern front, German and Soviet forces were engaged in the greatest tank battle of the war in Kursk. Meanwhile, the trains continued to roll toward Auschwitz: from Yugoslavia, Italy, Greece, France, and

Szmul Zygielbojm, c. 1941.

Courtesy of the USHMM.

the Netherlands. By May 1943, the Chełmno death camp had closed and others were about to, making Auschwitz the singular focus of the Nazis' genocidal urge. In the spring of 1943, two thirds of its eventual million victims were still alive.

Napoleon wanted to return to occupied Europe, but Paweł Siudak of the interior ministry of the Polish government-in-exile saw little value in the proposal.

"[Napoleon] fed us with incredible rumors after his return to the country," Siudak radioed Warsaw in June. "We have ignored these rumors. He will no longer be a courier."[18]

Following this damning verdict, Napoleon was given no further roles disseminating his report. At the same time that Napoleon stood down, another courier named Jan Karski was being prepared for a diplomatic mission to the United States. He had arrived from Poland in November 1942 with compelling eyewitness testimony of the Warsaw Ghetto liquidation and a transit station near the Bełżec death camp. But he had little to say about Auschwitz. The camp had fallen into a gray area, known but unacknowledged.

CHAPTER 18

FLIGHT

AUSCHWITZ

APRIL 1943

Witold and Jan settled on Easter Monday for the escape, when half the garrison would be on leave or drunk. Edmund had dropped out of the escape over concerns about his family's safety. That left Witold to organize the final details over the next few days: civilian clothes stashed in the bakery, money, a pocketknife, cured tobacco to scatter on their trail to throw the dogs off their scent, and bribes for the bakers: apples, jam, honey, and a bag of sugar, and potassium cyanide capsules in case they were caught.[1]

Witold's next task was to arrange a job in the bakers' work squad, but this presented a challenge. He had been classed an indispensable worker in the parcel office in order to avoid deportation to another camp. To seek to change his squad again would look suspicious. Instead, he would have to feign sickness to gain admittance to the hospital and then approach the bakers' kapo and trick him into thinking he had been authorized to switch to his squad. He would have a few hours to escape before his ruse was discovered.

The time had come to inform the remaining underground leadership of his imminent departure. He tried to keep the rationale simple.

"I have had a job to do here. Lately I have had no instructions," he told one of his lieutenants. "I can see no further point in staying here."[2]

"So you think you can choose when you come to Auschwitz and when you leave?" the man replied drolly to the risk Witold was taking.[3]

The Saturday of Easter weekend, April 24, dawned warm and overcast. Upon arriving at the parcel office, Witold began complaining of a headache. That afternoon he stayed in his block and made sure the kapo overheard him talking about pains in his joints and calves, classic symptoms of typhus. The kapo ordered Witold to report to the hospital at once. The nurses gave him a few wry comments when he arrived claiming to have the fever. A couple of them pointed out that he'd already had typhus. But they didn't push him. His friend Edek helped register him without an inspection.

He didn't contact Dering, a sign perhaps of the doctor's growing estrangement. What Witold didn't know was that around this time Dering was under pressure from the SS hierarchy to take part in the radiation and chemical experiments by using his surgical skills to perform hysterectomies or castrations. Dering hadn't decided yet how to respond, but he'd already performed one secret operation to remove the testicles of a German homosexual, and his bad reputation among prisoners had left him feeling increasingly vulnerable. A new kapo, Ludwig Wörl, had taken charge of the hospital and had a clear dislike of the mostly Polish staff, whom he sought to dismiss or move to Birkenau. In their place he installed the first Jewish nurses following a decision to allow Jews to be treated in the hospital. Dering had kept his position but was under attack from all sides.[4]

The following morning, April 25, Witold was woken by Edek.

Witold beckoned him in and explained his plan and that he needed Edek's help to arrange his release.[5]

"Edek, let's not beat about the bush," said Witold. "I'm getting out. Since you got me into the hospital avoiding the usual formalities and you're going to arrange for my release, who are they going to nab after I escape? You. Therefore, I suggest you join me."[6]

"I count on you, sir," said Edek, without asking about the plan.[7]

Witold informed Jan of Edek's inclusion when he visited the hospital that afternoon. Jan grimaced. It was already going to be hard to find a slot for Witold with the bakers, let alone for a second person. But Witold said he'd made the decision. "Well, that's that, then," Jan shrugged.[8]

That evening, Edek made a scene, shouting at Wörl that he was sick of how Poles were being treated in the hospital and he wanted to leave. The kapo snapped, "Then go where you want, you idiot!" Witold listened to the argument from his room on the next floor, and realized it had reached a satisfactory conclusion. A little later he also heard a scuffle and cries, later revealed to be the sound of Edek beating up one of the hated phenol injectors.[9]

The next morning, April 26, Edek went to secure release cards for himself and Witold. This was no easy matter given the fact that Witold was supposedly suffering from typhus and was meant to be kept in the quarantine block for a minimum of two weeks. In the end, Edek came up with the excuse that Witold had been wrongly diagnosed and had really just gotten drunk on smuggled alcohol. They headed over to the bakers' block and found Jan at a table by the window in one of the rooms playing cards with the bakery kapo, a Sudeten German, whom Jan had been buttering up. A half-finished bottle of vodka stood on the table. Witold announced that they'd been sent to him because they were bakers. The kapo looked surprised. Jan leaned over and whispered in his ear.[10]

"Kapo, here's a couple of chumps who've been taken in; they think that they'll fill up on bread in the bakery and that we have an easy job. Let me have them on the night shift and I'll show them what's what."[11]

This was the moment of truth. On cue Witold produced an apple and some sugar, and a little pot of jam he collected from the parcel office. The kapo's eyes lit up.

"All right then, let's see what sort of bakers you are," he said.[12]

They were now on the team. Next they needed to persuade two of the bakers to switch shifts with them. Most of the men were resting on their bunks ahead of the evening's work, which started at 6 P.M. Witold and Edek lay on theirs and began noisily discussing the parcels they'd received for Easter. That got everyone's attention. They handed around some apples and finally persuaded a couple of bakers to give up their shifts. It was late afternoon, barely enough time to arrange additional civilian clothes for Edek from the storage department. He raced to put them on under his stripes. A few minutes later the cry went up for the bakery work squad to fall in.[13]

They passed through the gate as the sun dipped beneath the clouds and the orange light caught the letters of the ARBEIT MACHT FREI sign. A storm was approaching from the south. The old crematoria chimney at the gate was smoking: thirty-three corpses had arrived that day for disposal, and somewhere off in Birkenau the fires were being stoked for the arrival of 2,700 Jews from Thessalonika, Greece.[14]

Four SS guards joined them for the march over to the bakery. There was a new detail for the holiday, and Witold hoped their unfamiliarity with the team would mask the fact that they were newcomers and needed to have an eye kept on them. Unfortunately the new guards were particularly alert, and even the gate guard called out to the crew that they should "be careful."[15]

"Under no circumstances must I walk back through that gate again," thought Witold as he stepped out of the camp.[16]

*

The river beside the road leading from the camp to the bakery was gray and swollen. Three of the guards accompanying the night shift peeled off at the bridge leading into town, probably for some holiday drinking. That left two SS men to supervise them. Witold and his companions reached the bakery at dusk on the night of the escape just as the sky opened and it began to rain. They stopped before a large redbrick building beside a mill house and one of the guards took a key from his leather satchel to unlock the door. As they waited in the rain, the prisoners working the day shift emerged coated in flour. They complained about the downpour as Witold and the other new arrivals entered through a hallway to the changing room. The guard locked the heavy studded door after them, and they heard the latch being fitted from the outside.[17]

The professional bakers had started work earlier and their clothes were already hanging up. Witold and the other prisoners quickly stripped down to their underwear and donned white aprons from pegs beside the door. They headed through a boiler room and down a short corridor toward the main hall. The guards had set up a desk and chairs beside the boiler's open furnace, and there was a narrow cot beside the wall. Witold noted the telephone on the corridor wall that the guards used for making hourly check-ins with the camp headquarters. He had brought a penknife to cut the wires that ran along the ceiling.[18]

The main hall was a long rectangular room with a line of open-faced ovens at the far end. The bakers quickly assigned the night crew their jobs. Witold's task was to mix dough in a large electric blender set on the floor and then shape loaves onto baking trays. He was soon drenched in sweat

Map of the bakery.

Courtesy of Marta Goljan.

and struggling to keep up. Edek shoveled coal into the oven for the first batch of five-hundred-odd loaves and then cleaned out the embers with a stick. After getting repeatedly burned, he let out a cry and fell to the floor.

Jan rushed over.

"Don't worry—nothing happened to me," Edek whispered. "I'm pretending in order to avoid the hard work."[19]

A ginger-haired German, about Edek's age, approached.

"How old are you?" asked the guard.[20]

"Seventeen," said Edek. He was actually twenty-one.

"How long have you been in here?"

"More than two years."

"And you are still alive?"

The German took pity and told him to grab an empty flour bag and lie down in the corridor.

The night shift ran five batches. The plan had been to leave after the first or second batch, around 10 P.M. Witold was about to signal the others to make a move when Jan shot him a worried look; he'd spotted an off-duty SS man and his girlfriend through the window of a storeroom, taking shelter from the rain under the eaves of the roof. They would have to wait for the downpour to ease.

Jan kept checking on the couple, growing more and more agitated.

Edek, lying on his back in the corridor, counted down the minutes as the batches came and went and their odds of escape diminished. It was almost a relief when the guard ordered him to perform a few squats and then fetch coal for the boiler.

The rain finally stopped near midnight and the lovers left. By then, there was only one more batch to fire, and the pace of work slackened. The ginger-haired guard was grilling a sausage over the boiler's furnace. The other German was writing a letter at the desk. The bakers took a short break. It was now or never.

Witold and Jan announced to the bakers that they would go and get the fuel ready, and left for the storage room. Edek joined them with a wheelbarrow for coal. Jan was already dressed in his civilian clothes and had retrieved the wrench from the coal room where he'd hidden it a few days before. On cue, Witold started to chop wood loudly as Jan slipped over to the entrance.

The first task was to unscrew the nut that secured the outside latch to the door. It gave under his weight, and he was able to twist it off and push the bolt through. Next, he turned to the two dead bolts. They were harder to shift. Witold and Edek made as much noise as they could to hide the scrape of the bolts drawing back.

Just then the ginger-haired guard poked his head into the storage room.

"Where's the other one?" he asked.[21]

They froze.

The German made for the entranceway. It seemed certain Jan would be caught, but he had had enough time to dash into the toilet and drop his pants, where and how the SS man found him.

"Oh, there you are," the guard said, still suspicious. He walked over to the door and turned his flashlight on to inspect it. Somehow he failed to notice the bolts were pulled back and the nut for the latch missing. He returned to grilling his sausage at the boiler.

The next task was to disable the phone in the corridor. By then it was almost 2 A.M. The guards were due to check in with their headquarters. Witold hurriedly handed Edek the pocketknife and he set off with the wheelbarrow for the furnace. The ginger-haired guard was facing toward the hallway that contained the telephone but seemed engrossed in the flames and his sausage. The letter writer was asleep on the bed. Edek set down the wheelbarrow as quietly as he could, stepped on the sack of flour he'd been lying on, reached up, and snipped the rubber-coated cable in two places. He caught the falling piece of wire, hastened over to the oven, tossed it into the flames, and immediately realized his mistake as the smell of burning rubber filled the room. The ginger-haired guard ran over and demanded to know what he had thrown on the fire, but seeing nothing, he cursed Edek and returned to the boiler. Edek was about to head back to the entrance when one of the bakers ordered him to fetch water for the dough. He hesitated, knowing the guards could call headquarters at any moment and discover his sabotage. But he had no choice. He started fetching buckets of water from the faucet in the boiler room until an exasperated Witold appeared.

"We leave the bakery immediately," he hissed. "Every second counts."[22]

Edek placed the pail beside the boiler and walked with Witold past the guards and back to the changing room. Witold and Edek grabbed their clothes in a bundle—there was no time to change—and positioned themselves at the door beside Jan, who had the forged key in the lock. It didn't budge. He tried again and then threw his body against the door, Witold and Edek joining in. The door seemed to bend and then suddenly flew open and cold air rushed in. Witold glimpsed the stars and then saw Jan disappearing toward the river. He and Edek tore after him.[23]

Shots rang out. They didn't look back, and two hundred yards out they were shielded by darkness. Witold called for Jan to stop. His plan had been to cross the Soła at the town bridge, and then head back past the camp on the opposite side of the river before striking east toward Krakow, a line of escape the SS would hopefully never suspect. But Jan had set off in the opposite direction away from the camp.

"You said you had a route planned?" asked Jan, bent over and breathing hard, when they finally caught up with him.[24]

Bridge over the Soła River.

I did, said Witold. But it was too late to turn back. They'd have to cross elsewhere. They trotted in single file along the riverbank away from the town. As they jogged, they pulled on their civilian pants and shirts. The bag of tobacco they'd arranged had split. Up ahead, they heard the rattle of a train and then saw a line of lit carriages crossing a bridge over the river. It was the main line to Krakow.[25]

The bridge was almost certainly guarded.

"There's no other way," Witold replied as he headed for the steel-framed span. "We must take the shortest route."[26]

They soon saw the outline of a sentry box atop the railway embankment and dropped to the wet ground, watching. Nothing stirred. After a few minutes they moved closer until they could see that the box was empty.

Witold set off across the bridge, the others in close pursuit. To his right was the outline of Oświęcim's castle; an open field and the curving line of the river lay to the left. The single track of steel they followed crossed an inky void. How many prisoners had traveled in the opposite direction never to return?[27]

They reached the other side and dropped down the embankment to the muddy fields. The Soła meandered beside the railway track for a couple of miles before joining the Vistula. Both the river and the tracks ran east, in the direction they wanted. They planned on crossing the water again to reach the wooded northern shore before dawn. It was slow going along the bank, which was tangled with dead reeds and nettles that were damp from the rain. The riverbank smelled of wild garlic, and they caught a startling whiff of almonds from flowering stands of hagberries. On the other side of the tracks they saw the searchlights play around the chimneys of the vast IG Farben synthetic rubber factory still under construction. Thousands had died in the construction of the factory, which was still not complete. They navigated their way around ditches and drains for the better part of an hour until finally passing the complex.[28]

By then they had run the better part of ten miles from the camp, and the sky was starting to lighten. On the opposite bank they could see the distant trees that promised cover. The river was broader here, and shrouded in early morning mist. Little eddies played on its surface, then disappeared.

"We could use a boat right around now," said Jan.

As luck would have it, they soon came across a waterlogged vessel chained to a stake beside the bank. There were a few farm buildings set back in the trees nearby. The chain had a padlock with a simple bolt. Jan produced his wrench, which fit, and he freed the boat while Witold found an empty can nearby to bail out the interior. They scram-

Vistula at dawn.

bled aboard and pushed off, until they hit a sandbar and had to wade through the last few yards of icy water.[29]

Witold climbed up the opposite bank to find the sun had risen, catching little wisps of fog on the field. A mile of open terrain separated them from the forest. The villages nearby had been ethnically cleansed the year before and now consisted of German settlers. Witold knew they were instantly recognizable as escaped prisoners, with their shaved heads and sodden clothes. Jan took a colored scarf from his pocket and wrapped it around Edek's head and declared that he looked like an exhausted woman.[30]

They hobbled on numbed legs until they heard the wail of the camp siren and the sound of motorbikes in the distance. Jan broke into an adrenaline-charged sprint, with Witold and Edek struggling after him. Jan reached the woods first.[31]

The trees were mostly Scots pine, planted in neat rows by a local

Metków forest, where Witold, Jan, and Edek rested.

landowner. Witold and Edek lost sight of Jan and followed one of the channels until they were deep in the forest's shadow. Suddenly, Jan stepped out from behind a tree, arms outstretched, a big grin on his face.[32]

"Allow me the honor of welcoming you to the open forest!" he declared.[33]

They embraced him and planted kisses on his cheeks. Witold collapsed onto his back on a bed of moss and dried pine needles and gazed up at the trees' tapering trunks.

"The pines whispered, gently waving their huge tops," he wrote later. "Scraps of blue sky could be seen between the tree trunks. The dew shone like little jewels on the bushes and grass . . . In places the sun's rays broke through."[34]

The forest was alive with early morning birdsong, trilling larks and rude crows, and yet what struck him most deeply was the silence, "a

silence far from the roar of humanity . . . far from man's scheming . . .
a silence in which there was not a living soul . . . what a contrast with
the camp in which I felt I had spent a thousand years."[35]

He found a jar of honey and a teaspoon in his pocket, left over
from the parcels, and offered spoonfuls to Jan and Edek. "We were
enchanted by everything," Witold recalled. "We were in love with the
world . . . just not with its people."[36]

*

The feeling slowly passed, wariness returned, and the talk turned
back to their escape. Witold had a dim sense that the border between
the Reich and the General Government must be near, and somehow
they would have to cross it and then make their way to the safe house
in Bochnia, a hundred miles away. They had no food, no money, no
paperwork, and the camp Gestapo had no doubt shared their details
with every police headquarters in the area.

They set off in the afternoon and soon ran into a gamekeeper, who
tried to accost them. They lost him in a dense grove of new pines.
After that, they headed for higher ground, crossing the main road in
the gathering night and then climbing steadily upward to a hardwood
forest of beech and hornbeam. Farther up the hillside, they glimpsed
the limestone walls of a ruined fortress and made for it.

There was no sign of life, but they didn't linger near the building.
Instead they found a nearby gully filled with last year's leaves, which
they used to cover themselves. It was wet and cold. Jan and Edek fell
asleep, but Witold's sciatic nerve was flaring. He lay there shivering and
mulling over their next steps. The border would be heavily guarded,
and they would need a guide to help them cross it, but whom could
they trust? After two and a half years in the camp, he was unsure of the
mind-set of the people he would find. Witold was confident that most

of his countrymen still opposed the Nazis, but how many had been forced through hunger or fear or ambition to make an accommodation with the occupier? The Nazis had long offered protection to Poles with even nominal German heritage, and they had renewed their efforts to enlist more Poles to their cause.

Witold was half dozing around 4 A.M. when he was struck by the memory of a conversation from the year before. A prisoner had told him that his uncle was a priest right on the border. He knew the man's name and thought the town was called Alwernia. It couldn't be far.

Edek was tossing and turning beside him, murmuring about bread and sugar, and then suddenly he leaped to his feet and demanded, "Well? Had [Witold] brought the bread?"[37]

Witold gently coaxed him awake with a smile.

"Don't worry, my friend. Can't you see the wood, the castle, and us sleeping in the leaves? You've been dreaming."[38]

It was time to get up anyway and march while it was still dark. They were stiff, but their joints warmed up as they followed the slope down the forested hillside. As the sky lightened they saw a road through the thinning trees. There was a church and town on the next hill, and the first signs of life on the street. Jan was the best dressed, and naturally bald, so Witold tasked him with asking directions. They watched from a distance as Jan reached the road and caught up with one of the figures. They talked for a moment before Jan cut back toward them. He confirmed that the town ahead was Alwernia. The border was less than a mile away, he explained, and there was a customs post at the town's entrance. They looked up the road and thought they could make out a guard.

The only way to get to the church without being seen was through the woods, but they needed to cross the exposed road first. They scrambled to the other side, and then worked their way from tree to tree to the church.

They were exhausted by the time they reached the back of the building and hunkered down beside an old oak tree. The church bell started to toll.

"It can't be helped, my dear [Jan], you've got to go to the church," said Witold.[39]

Jan got to his feet without complaining and set off, leaving Witold and Edek to doze. He returned alone a few hours later. The priest he'd met had been skeptical about their story. He didn't believe they'd escaped from Auschwitz, and suspected that Jan was trying to entrap him. Witold sent him back again with every detail he could remember about the priest's family, including what his friend had written to them in a Christmas letter. This time Jan came back with the priest, who looked nervous until he saw the pitiful state of Witold and Edek and was convinced of their story. He hurried off and returned with a pitcher of coffee and milk, along with packages of bread, sugar, butter, ham, Easter eggs, and a festive Easter cake.

They opened them one at a time, marveling at each. "What isn't there in these parcels!" cried Edek.[40]

There was even some ointment for rubbing onto joints, and a cigarette for each of them, which they smoked after eating their fill.

It turned out he wasn't the priest they had been looking for, but he knew the family of Witold's friend, and he promised he would do everything he could to help. He knew a guide who could take them across the border to the General Government, but they had to stay hidden until he returned, as there were border guards everywhere.

The priest visited them again at lunchtime with further packages of food, plus a hundred marks, dark berets, and overalls. He told them he'd return with the guide after dark.[41]

*

The three men ate and dozed and waited among the trees for the shadows to lengthen and night to fall. They were dressed and ready when the priest brought their guide and more provisions around 10 P.M. It was clear and moonless. They set off in single file. Their guide was an older man, lean and taciturn, and he led them into the hills without a word, until they reached a wild ravine of felled trees, broken ditches, and bramble patches. The General Government lay one hundred yards away on the other side, he said, and left. The trio picked their way through the tangle and soon hit a road, which they followed until the sky began to brighten and they were forced to hide for the rest of the day in a bush for lack of cover. It was too wet and muddy to sleep, and they were relieved to resume walking again at dusk.

They soon reached the pale expanse of the Vistula. There was a Benedictine monastery on the bluff opposite, overlooking the river and a small town called Tyniec. A ferryman agreed to take them across on a skiff. He eyed them as they boarded. Curfew was coming, he warned. They reached the far shore and hurried through the town. The farmers were bringing the last of the cattle in from the surrounding fields. A doorway opened and a housewife appeared, framed by the warm light of the interior. Jan thought to ask her for milk and bread, but the woman quickly closed the door. They tried again at the far end of the town. The woman in that house was about to shoo them away when her husband appeared beside her. Ignoring his wife's protests, he offered them some beet soup.[42]

"You must come from the works in Germany?" he asked as they entered.[43]

"Yes," replied Jan.[44]

"But at the works you can have hair, and none of you do?" he continued.

Jan said there was a typhus epidemic and they had to shave their heads, but the man clearly didn't believe them. He later mentioned Auschwitz but they didn't allow themselves to be drawn in. He offered to let them sleep in his barn, and Witold, who hadn't slept properly since leaving the camp two nights before, decided to trust him. The next morning, they were quickly on their way.

They continued to skirt around villages for the next few days, occasionally knocking on doors for food or water, never stopping long. They followed the line of the Vistula eastward, and began striking in a more southerly route as they passed Krakow. On May 1 they reached the Niepołomice forest, on the other side of which lay their destination, Bochnia, where they hoped to find Edmund's family waiting for them.

It was a warm spring morning. No one was about, so they followed a curving forest road until they came upon a whitewashed forester's house to the left. Its green shutters were closed, and there was no sign of life. They passed the yard and suddenly spotted a German soldier walking toward them with a rifle slung over his shoulder. They kept moving, trying to keep calm, and had gone a dozen paces when the German shouted "Halt!"

They walked on.[45]

"Halt!" he shouted again and cocked his rifle.

Witold turned back toward him, smiling.

"Everything's good," he said.[46]

A second soldier had come out of the house, but the first, who'd been preparing to fire, now lowered his weapon. He was thirty yards away, the other about sixty.

"Boys, run for it!" yelled Witold and fled. Shots flew after them as they scattered into the forest. Witold hurdled tree trunks and weaved between the bushes, the bullets whizzing past. A moment later, he felt a short, sharp impact on his right shoulder. "Bastard," he thought, but there was no pain and he ran on.[47]

He could make out Edek sprinting to his left and called over to him once they were deep in the woods. They converged and finally stopped. Gunshots rang out in the distance. There was no sign of Jan. Edek inspected Witold's wound: the bullet had passed through his shoulder without touching the bone. Edek quickly dressed the wound with iodine and bandages from a small supply he'd brought from the camp. Three more holes had pierced Witold's trousers and windbreaker without striking him. He'd been unbelievably lucky. There seemed little chance of finding Jan in the forest. They decided to make for Bochnia in the hope that he would, too.[48]

Night was drawing in as they left the forest. They reached a small village on the Raba River, which they crossed by ferry. On the other side they finally saw the lights of Bochnia, an old salt-mining town that had prospered in the nineteenth century as part of the Austro-Hungarian Empire. The Nazis had walled off a section of the city center to make a ghetto but had yet to liquidate it. Witold and Edek walked in silence, thinking about Jan, their spirits sinking.

They slept in a peasant's attic and found Edmund's family home the next morning. His father-in-law, Józef Obora, was working in his garden outside. He gave them a big grin when he saw them, which seemed odd until they ventured inside and found Jan stretched out on a bed in one of the rooms, unharmed and fast asleep, his feet sticking out from under the bedspread. They leaped on the bed to hug him and then spent a few happy hours catching up, eating, and getting to know the Oboras. The conversation turned to the camp and Witold grew restless. Despite his injury and exhausted state, he insisted on meeting someone from the underground that very afternoon, and was only partially satisfied when the local operative he met told him it would take time to see his boss.[49]

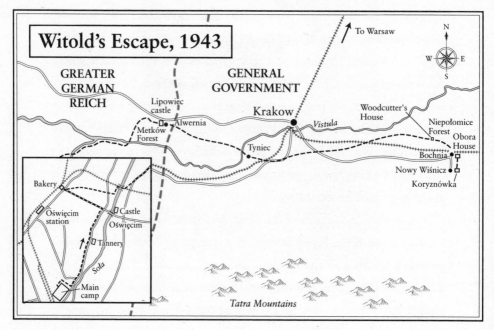

Witold's Escape, 1943

GREATER
GERMAN
REICH

GENERAL
GOVERNMENT

Lipowiec castle

Alwernia

Metków Forest

Krakow

Vistula

Tyniec

Woodcutter's House

Niepołomice Forest

Obora House

Bochnia

Nowy Wiśnicz

Koryznówka

N
W E
S

To Warsaw

Bakery

Oświęcim station

Castle

Oświęcim

Tannery

Soła

Main camp

Tatra Mountains

John Gilkes

Józef Obora, during the war.
Courtesy of Marta Orłowska.

*

A couple of days later, the operative collected Witold and they set off to the next town of Nowy Wiśnicz, while Edek and Jan stayed behind to recuperate. They paused in a forest glade in brilliant sunshine, and Witold thought to ask the name of the commander he was going to meet. Tomasz Serafiński was the reply. It was the very man he had been impersonating in the camp for the past three years.[50]

"Everything okay?" asked his guide.[51]

"It's nothing, I'm just a bit tired," Witold replied. "Let's go a little faster."[52]

They crested a ridge and saw the old castle of Nowy Wiśnicz on the wooded hillside opposite and the little town spread out below it. Tomasz's home lay on the other side of the castle, his guide explained. The Gestapo operated out of a monastery nearby, so they would have to be careful. Witold charged up the hill, convinced that some strange fate had brought him there.

The house was set back from the trees lining the roadside. It was built as a rustic-style summer mansion made of wood, with cedar shingles on the roof, and flowers engraved around the porch entrance. There was a stable to one side and a field beyond. A little sign beside the gate read KORYZNÓWKA in black-and-gold lettering.

The commander's wife, Ludmiła, received them on the veranda at the back of the house. The land sloped down to a river, and there was an orchard and a barn beside a pool.

"I'm here to give Tomasz his name back," Witold announced.[53]

Ludmiła played along when Witold introduced himself as Tomasz to her slight, bookish husband.

"But I'm also Tomasz," said the other man, looking puzzled. He listened as Witold reeled off his own biographical details, and then repeated his Auschwitz number in German, and every change of block or work squad he'd made over the past three years, as he'd done so many times before.[54]

Only after this odd spectacle and a final salute did Witold explain himself.

"There was no knowing how anyone might react to this," recalled Witold. But Tomasz simply opened his arms wide, a slight smile on his open face, and embraced him.[55]

Witold felt at home as they sat at the small dinner table overlooking the orchard. Tomasz was a gentleman farmer like himself who'd studied law in Krakow before settling down to run the family farm. The walls of the house were hung with oil paintings by the artist Jan

Matejko, a relative. Tomasz agreed to host him in the outbuilding, and then they ate—fried rye dough was a family staple—and Witold told him about the camp. He wouldn't need a large force to attack, he explained. Just a modest diversion at the camp gates.[56]

Tomasz thought it was a wild proposal, but he agreed to present his case to the underground in Krakow. He warned that it might take several weeks to arrange. The Gestapo had infiltrated the organization, and half the leadership was in jail or on the run.

When Tomasz left for the city a few days later, Witold set about writing a report to the underground in Warsaw. It was a brief overview of the camp and a description of the underground's structure and organization. His point was clear: the camp contained a force capable of staging an uprising. He demanded immediate action.[57]

Tomasz Serafiński, c. 1940.

Courtesy of Maria Serafińska-Domańska.

Jan and Edek came to visit a week later, and he encouraged them to make a record of the crimes they had witnessed to include with his report. They'd all been shocked to realize how little the public knew of the atrocities the Germans were carrying out in Auschwitz. Hundreds were dying every day in the camp, yet people were focused on the Polish officers killed at Katyń.[58]

"No one protests! No one investigates, no one arrives! Silence! Geneva is silent. No change in the West," Jan wrote in his report. "It is hard to believe that the world, which has reacted to the Katyń massacre, still doesn't realize what is really happening in the German concentration camps."[59]

Jan, Witold, and Edek (from left) outside Koryznówka, c. June 1943.
Courtesy of Maria Serafińska-Domańska.

*

Tomasz presented his case for attacking Auschwitz to the underground leadership in Krakow in late June or early July. The idea was rejected as unfeasible, and some questioned Witold's story. Only a few people had escaped the camp, they reasoned, and none had talked about returning to liberate the place. At one point a map of the camp was consulted, which did not show a bakery. The Krakow leadership concluded that Witold was a German agent and ordered Tomasz to break off contact with him. Tomasz refused, so they threatened him with expulsion.[60]

Witold was incensed when he heard the outcome. Who were these "giants of the organization" anyway? They claimed to be concerned about the plight of prisoners of Auschwitz, but when they were presented with a chance to actually save some of them, they did nothing? They had also refused to arrange false papers, meaning Witold risked immediate arrest at the first checkpoint he encountered. We might as well "break [our] own necks," Witold fumed.[61]

Barn where Witold stayed in Nowy Wiśnicz.

Witold had no choice but to send a message to his former courier Stefan Bielecki in Warsaw asking for Rowecki to attest to his credentials. A few days later Stefan showed up at Nowy Wiśnicz with fake paperwork for Witold's identity and a cyanide pill. Stefan confirmed that no decision was imminent on the uprising. He also brought word that his family was safe and anxious to see him. In fact, Stefan had promised Eleonora he'd bring him home immediately. But Witold had no intention of going.[62]

A few weeks later, Tomasz arranged a meeting for Witold with Andrzej Możdżeń, the local head of sabotage, who said he could rally 150 soldiers to attack Auschwitz. The challenge, Możdżeń explained, was to stage the men and weapons close enough to strike, which might take weeks to prepare. Witold wasn't sure the underground could wait. He already feared that the SS had retaliated against them for his escape. The Gestapo chief Grabner sent one of his men from Auschwitz to Nowy Wiśnicz to arrest Witold. Luckily he was not in the house, and Tomasz was able to convince the officer it was a case of mistaken

Witold ID arranged after his escape from the camp.
Courtesy of PMA-B.

identity, aided by the fact he looked nothing like the camp photo of Witold that the SS man had brought.[63]

It was a close call that only emphasized the need to strike quickly against the camp. Witold asked Możdżeń if he could organize three cars to carry about a dozen men and assorted weapons to the camp for an immediate attack. They'd dress as SS men to bluff their way into the camp and then blast their way back out again. Witold knew it was a suicide mission, but felt he owed it to the people he had left behind.[64]

The Obora family with whom Jan and Edek were staying were still in touch with Edmund Zabawski in the camp, to whom they sent reg-

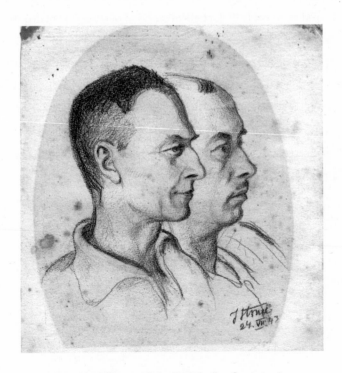

Witold and Tomasz, July 1943, by Jan Stasiniewicz.
Courtesy of Maria Serafińska-Domańska.

ular parcels with messages inside. Witold wrote down his plan in code along the edge of a napkin that was used to wrap a parcel of bread husks, garlic, and onions intended for Edmund. "We can arrive in three cars and break into the camp," went the message. "Let us know."[65]

The reply arrived a few weeks later. "Elżunia's friends shouldn't go anywhere by car and should stay at home to work." Another note added the explanation, "Autumn is coming and it's too cold for you to come, and too early for somebody to take care of us."[66]

The underground clearly still functioned, but they would need more than three cars. Witold decided to travel to Warsaw himself to lobby the underground to take action. Word had likely reached him of turmoil in the leadership: the Gestapo had arrested Rowecki at the end of June, and then on July 4, the Polish head of state, Sikorski, died in a plane crash in Gibraltar.

A few days before his departure in August, Witold received a letter from Stefan, which he tore open, but there was no mention of an uprising. Instead Stefan wrote that the underground headquarters in Warsaw was "very favorably disposed" to giving him a medal for his underground work. Witold threw the letter away in disgust. He didn't want a ribbon. He wanted action.[67]

CHAPTER 19

ALONE

WARSAW

AUGUST 1943

Witold returned to Warsaw on Monday, August 23, nearly three years after volunteering for Auschwitz, to find the city in the grip of a bloody guerrilla campaign. The underground had started assassinating Nazi officials and bombing German-owned businesses. In response, the SS had ordered a hundred Poles shot in the street for each incident. The victims' cries of "Long live Poland" had become so frequent that some German units carried gypsum to stuff into their victims' mouths. There was no doubt that the Germans were still in control, but perhaps not for much longer following the devastating loss of Stalingrad and the Allied invasion of Italy in July.[1]

Witold's first step was to inform Eleonora that he had returned and to set up a meeting with the underground leadership. His journey to her flat in Żoliborz took him past what was left of the ghetto. Himmler had ordered the remaining buildings of the quarter to be razed following the Jewish uprising and the land turned into a park bearing his name. In Żoliborz, the citadel was prickled with German antiaircraft guns, and Witold saw several fresh craters where Soviet bombs had fallen.[2]

Eleonora was expecting Witold and made sure the blinds were down. Curfew was approaching, and German patrols shot at anyone they saw in the window once it got dark. Witold was anxious for news of Maria and the children. Over a quiet dinner Eleonora shared what she knew of their life in Ostrów Mazowiecka. A German official had recently commandeered the family home and forced Maria to move to the attic and serve as his housekeeper. They were safe, but it was too risky for Witold to visit. Eleonora suggested they meet in the vacant apartment on the floor above hers. Maria came to Warsaw every few weeks to collect stationery supplies for a bookshop she helped run in Ostrów Mazowiecka. Eleonora gave Witold the address of the stationery store where Maria shopped to leave a message.[3]

In the meantime, Witold needed to convince the underground's new leader, General Tadeusz Komorowski, to authorize an attack on the camp. Tightened security and the paranoid atmosphere made it difficult to arrange a meeting. His messenger, Stefan Bielecki, suggested he start work in the underground's operational wing that carried out targeted killings and sabotage of German supply lines. That group would likely plan any Auschwitz operation. But even meeting the wing's head, Karol Jabłoński, proved difficult. Witold needed to have his credentials checked and rechecked, with each message passing through a web of safe houses and couriers.

While he waited, Witold took a job with the team that drew up lists of informers to be executed. The underground had created a court for trying those suspected of collusion. The idea was to create a semblance of due process, but mistakes were made frequently. Witold's own courier, Stanisław Jaster, who'd delivered early news of the gassing in Birkenau, had been executed as an informer. It was a frustrating time for Witold. The camp's leadership in Auschwitz was in peril, and thousands perished each day. Yet Witold's discussions in Warsaw confirmed what he'd already picked up in Nowy Wiśnicz: few seemed to know there was an underground in Auschwitz capable of rising up. Even fewer talked about the camp's role in the mass murder of Jews. If anything, the anti-Semitic attitudes Witold had encountered in Warsaw early in the war were more widespread. Vitriolic editorials appeared in the right-wing press, and gangs of blackmailers roamed the streets looking for any of the estimated twenty-eight thousand Jews in hiding. The Nazis offered high rewards for any information and shot any Jews that they caught, along with the Polish families who sheltered them.[4]

The underground officially condemned the blackmailers and ran a significant relief operation for undercover Jewish families. But its leadership generally avoided confronting the anti-Semitic elements of the resistance for fear of upsetting the fragile alliance it felt necessary to reclaim Poland's independence. There was nothing Witold could do but wait for Jabłoński and hope to persuade him of the merits of an Auschwitz operation.[5]

*

In the meantime, Witold was finally reunited with Maria. Instead of leaving her a message at the stationery store he decided to surprise her in person. He bought a few presents: a navy-blue dress adorned with little butterflies, a delicate nightdress, and a small bottle of perfume. For several days he hung around the street, waiting for her to show up. At last, she came and he whisked her off to the flat above Eleonora's. How often had he imagined this moment or yearned to share his experiences? When they were finally in each other's arms, he didn't talk about the camp, or the war. For the moment, he tried to forget.[6]

The next morning, Witold wrote letters to his children, Andrzej and Zofia, for Maria to take home. They were formal and spoke of the need for good manners. But before Maria left, he seems to have dashed off a lighter-hearted note to Zofia. He wanted to write her a poem, he told her, but there wasn't enough time. Maria had told him about a garden Zofia had planted by herself. Witold asked her to take care and not "fly like a little butterfly" in the cold.[7]

Maria returned a couple of weeks later bearing Zofia's reply and a flower from her garden. "It's nice to see you're such a good farmer," he wrote her back. "And that you love the worm, beetle, pea or bean and everything that lives." They are qualities he shared with her, he wrote. Andrzej hadn't written, he noted. "I'm sure I could find something in common with [Andrzej]—if he'd only write," he added. Maria and Witold discussed bringing the children to Warsaw for a visit, but they both knew that might prove impossible amid the worsening violence.[8]

In September 1943, the appointment of a new German police chief heralded a fresh crackdown. On October 1, twenty-two men and women were executed in the ruins of the ghetto. Two days later, the SS rounded up 370 men and women in Żoliborz. Their execution was announced over the loudspeakers around the city. "There isn't a day without shooting in different parts of the city," wrote the diarist Ludwik Landau. "The rattle of machine guns and automatic pistols doesn't stop." The underground fought back, with further assassinations and bomb attacks. The streets were deserted for days at a time.[9]

*

Witold was finally granted a meeting with Jabłoński on October 29. He was confident, as he made his case, that his plan was militarily sound. A diversionary attack on Auschwitz by an underground unit outside the gates followed by a camp-wide uprising would allow a siz-able proportion of the prisoners to escape. He likely outlined the ugent moral imperative to attack the camp.[10]

Jabłoński assured Witold that he knew all about Auschwitz.

"After the war I will show you how thick are the Auschwitz files in our archives," he said. "All yours are there too."[11]

Witold responded that the thickness of the files brought no relief to those in the camp.

But Jabłoński was definitive: there would be no attack. In his view, the underground needed to concentrate their forces on a nationwide revolt; when German forces retreated they would emerge from hiding and declare Polish independence. Jabłoński was also worried about the threat posed by Soviet forces, which were advancing quickly. Stalin had broken off diplomatic relations with the Polish exile government after news of the Katyń massacre broke, suggesting that the Soviets intended to supplant the Germans as a new occupying force. What was more, there was no sign that the Allies would support the Poles against the Soviets. Every weapon they had needed to be preserved for the crucial battles to come.

Jabłoński did leave open the possibility of conducting an operation outside the camp, but only after major cities had been secured. "I can assure you that we will contact you as soon as this matter becomes live," Jabłoński concluded.[12]

Witold's only hope was to go over Jabłoński's head to Komorowski. But the underground leader wouldn't see him, and the staff member he did meet confirmed what Jabłoński had said. Witold's request was passed on to the underground commander for the district around the camp to make a final assessment. The conclusion was that the under-ground could hold the gates open for half an hour, enough time for only a fraction of the prisoners to escape. Given the likely reprisals for those who remained, the action would only be worth it if the Germans tried to liquidate the camp.[13]

Witold had no choice but to accept the underground's decision. Shortly after the meeting he sent another letter to the camp, probably via the Zabawski family, explaining the rejection of the uprising plan. Around that time, he learned that the majority of the camp's underground leadership had been rounded up and shot. He was devastated by what he saw as his failure to persuade the underground to take action. He understood the practical objections to the mission that Jabłoński had raised and belatedly seemed to realize that the only way to overcome them was to focus on the moral case for attacking the camp. After all, the imperative to face down such evil was what had kept his men fighting and had formed the basis of his reports.[14]

Yet he struggled to find the words to explain himself. He wanted people to feel the righteous anger that he had felt upon arriving in the camp. But when he talked about the camp's horrors to friends that autumn, they closed down or changed the subject or, worse, tried to commiserate. He didn't want pity but rather understanding. Witold found it difficult to connect with ordinary people now. Their ideas seemed so small to him. "I can no longer relate to my friends or other people," he wrote later. "I didn't want to be different but I was, after that hell."[15]

He sought out former prisoners—"People of Oświęcim," he called them. Sławek, his first bed mate, had been released from the camp in 1941 and lived in the same building as Eleonora. He made good on his old promise and prepared the dish he had dreamed of that first winter in the camp: potato pancakes heaped with sour cream. Witold didn't have to explain himself to Sławek; he didn't fuss over the small stuff, either.[16]

Witold also stayed with another former prisoner, Aleksander

Paliński, Olek for short, who lived in a block of flats in Żoliborz with his wife, Ola, and their sixteen-year-old daughter. The family ran a small kitchen out of their two-room apartment on the second floor. Ola cooked bone broths and traditional cabbage soup, which she served with fried potatoes. Occasionally she acquired minced chops or veal from the countryside, which she made into schnitzel.

Witold and Olek talked for hours. Olek had been gregarious before the war, running a children's puppet theater for which he built elaborate sets and played music. But his old spark hadn't returned since he'd been released from the camp nearly a year before. He and Ola were having difficulties. Talking with Witold about the camp was a relief.[17]

Together, they tracked down the families of friends who had died in Auschwitz. But the families often refused to believe that their loved ones were dead, and those who did found little solace in the news that they had died in service to the underground. Sometimes Witold had to explain why it was that he had survived.[18]

Around then, Witold started work on a new report about Auschwitz to capture his evolving thinking. He began with an assessment of the underground's size and strength and gave the numbers of the killed, including the latest figures of Jewish dead. For the first time he told the story of his experience through scenes, thoughts, and impressions. The camp's sights and sounds and smells flowed onto the page. Sometimes he reverted to military-speak, but he kept returning to the moments of individual bravery he had witnessed. His hope was to connect the reader to the moral universe of the camp. His recent conversations with the families of prisoners shaped his thinking. "Perhaps some families can then find images of their loved ones in my story," he wrote in his introduction. "T h i s i s w h y I w r i t e [Witold's extra spacing]."[19]

*

Witold continued to work for the underground through the autumn and winter of 1943 and extracted some funding from headquarters to support former prisoners and their families. Among those he gave money to was Olek's neighbor Barbara Abramow-Newerley, whose husband, Igor, was in the camp. She needed the money both to pay for care packages for Igor and to support several Jewish families that she and Igor protected. Barbara was herself Jewish but lived under her husband's Catholic name. She guarded her secret carefully and hadn't told her seven-year-old son about his mixed heritage, but her friends all knew she'd grown up in a Jewish orphanage called Dom Sierot.[20]

Witold learned that Barbara was in trouble one day that autumn. She asked him over to her flat, clearly distraught and close to tears. A

Barbara Abramow-Newerly.
Courtesy of Jarosław Abramow-Newerly.

week or so before, Barbara explained, there had been a knock on the apartment door. It was a man claiming to be a friend of one of the Jews whom Igor had rescued before his arrest. The man said he'd come to collect money on the behalf of their mutual acquaintance. Barbara had given him some money and he'd left. But then a few days later he'd come back again and said that Igor's friend was dead, but that he still wanted money. He was a Jew himself, he explained, and needed cash. Then he threatened to report her to the Gestapo if she didn't cough up.[21]

"Barbara, please calm down," Witold told her. "We will take care of it. For now, you will receive the money and then we will see."[22]

The blackmailer got the money when he returned, but that was the last time he showed up. His fate is not clear, but it seems likely that Witold arranged for his execution.[23]

*

The onset of winter brought a lull in the roundups and shootings, and Witold's thoughts turned increasingly to seeing his family. That late November or early December, Maria bundled Andrzej and Zofia onto a bus to Warsaw. Witold was waiting for them at Eleonora's. For the occasion, Eleonora had made molded red jellies, which she kept in the bathtub filled with cold water to make them set. It had been more than three years since Witold had last seen his children. Andrzej was eleven years old, tall and awkward. Zofia, one year younger and still a girl, was bright and pretty. They hugged.

Andrzej had brought a small pop gun to show Witold, but soon dashed outside to play "Germans and Poles" with Eleonora's son Marek. Zofia lingered. She thought her father looked thinner, older, and at one point she caught him looking pensive and fiddling with something in his pocket. When she asked him what it was, he pulled out a small crust of bread. He explained he kept it just in case.[24]

It was dark when they ate. The children had a mattress on the kitchen floor, while Witold and Maria retired upstairs. The next morning, Witold took them out early for a walk to "teach them a few tricks," he explained. He demonstrated how to use the reflection of shop windows to see if they were being followed or to pretend to tie their shoelaces so they could survey the street. Their father presented it as a game, and it was, but they could detect a seriousness in his instruction. Andrzej wanted to ask him what he'd been doing all those years, but he sensed it was not a topic to be discussed.[25]

It's not clear if they met again at Eleonora's for Christmas, but it's unlikely. After the lull, the city swiftly returned to chaos. The underground launched eighty-seven attacks in December, forcing the Germans to barricade office buildings and keep off the streets unless armed or walking in groups. From the scaffolding of a building site in the center of town, a giant puppet of Hitler was hung to the delight of residents. The SS reprisals were typically bloody. "We are still afraid of the Germans," observed one diarist. "But now the Germans are afraid of us."[26]

Witold continued to work on his report. In December, Edek arrived from Nowy Wiśnicz with the latest news from the camp. The camp underground's leadership had reconstituted itself around several Austrian and Polish Communists, and though several of Witold's friends had retained influential positions in the camp, the organization was much reduced. Even if he had support for an uprising, he wasn't sure whether the new leaders could pull it off or were committed to the idea.[27]

As Witold's links to the camp frayed, his priorities shifted. In early 1944, he was introduced to the head of the Warsaw underground's sabotage wing, Emil Fieldorf, who was preparing a group to resist the

Soviets ahead of their occupation of the country, as now seemed increasingly likely. At that point, the Polish leadership still believed they had Allied backing for their independence. But then in February came the news of a speech by Churchill to the British Parliament announcing that he had effectively agreed to cede most of eastern Poland to Stalin in an apparent sop to the Soviet leader because of repeated delays to the Allied invasion of France. "I have an intense sympathy with the Poles," Churchill told Parliament, "that heroic race whose national spirit centuries of misfortune cannot quench, but I also have sympathy with the Russian standpoint." He added that he was sure Stalin would honor the independence of what remained of Poland and hoped that Poles and Russians would still be able to fight on together against their shared enemy.[28]

"A disgraceful and immoral betrayal," declared the main underground newspaper in Warsaw.[29]

Around March of that year, Fieldorf approached Witold to join an anti-Soviet cell. Witold was reticent at first. He had just been reunited with his family. The Germans were on the verge of defeat, and he'd no doubt longed for peace. How could he tell Maria that their future was once again postponed? But as he had always done, he chose nation over family. He took the oath and swore in the name of God and Poland to fight to the death if need be.[30]

Shortly thereafter, he met up with Maria and Eleonora in the little town of Legionowo, fifteen miles north of Warsaw, where some of Maria's relatives lived. They went for a picnic. It was a short walk to the woods, and the Vistula was a couple of miles away. The sun was out but it was still cold. Maria wore the blue dress with butterflies that Witold had bought her in Warsaw, while Witold had on a white shirt buttoned to the neck and a pair of woolen plus-fours. Someone

Witold and Maria in Legionowo, c. May 1944.

Courtesy of the Pilecki family.

had brought a camera, and Witold agreed for his and Maria's photo to be taken.

He didn't tell Maria about his new oath. But when she got home to Ostrów Mazowiecka, she found a picture of their picnic in her blazer pocket. Somehow Witold had developed the film and hidden it there as a memento for when he was gone.[31]

CHAPTER 20

UPRISING

WARSAW

JULY 1944

In July 1944, Witold finished compiling his tenth report on the camp in four years, certain that most of his comrades were dead. The Germans had occupied Hungary that spring and were in the midst of deporting half of the country's eight hundred thousand Jews to Auschwitz. Up to five thousand were gassed each day, outstripping the capacity of its crematoria. The camp authorities were burning bodies in giant funeral pyres again.[1]

Witold believed he had failed, but in fact the West was finally acknowledging the camp's significance. Two Slovak Jewish prisoners had escaped from the camp in April 1944 and had prepared a report while in hiding in Slovakia that described the operation of the gas chambers in Birkenau and the impending destruction of Hungarian Jews. The material was brought to Switzerland, where it was publicized and sent to Allied capitals. This report has been credited for capturing the attention of Western leaders. But the intelligence Witold had smuggled out of Auschwitz laid the groundwork for its acceptance. Churchill read the Slovakian account on July 5 and wrote Eden the next day: "What can be said? What can be done?" He urged the RAF to bomb the camp. The American military considered its own operation to attack Auschwitz at the behest of the War Refugee Board, which Roosevelt had belatedly set up to coordinate rescue efforts.[2]

The accumulating weight of evidence meant that by July enough people in the West knew of the mass murders to create a collective sense that something should be done. Even so, the Allies finally rejected the proposal to bomb the camp as too difficult and costly. Some Jewish groups wanted to enlist the Polish underground to attack the camp— the very strategy Witold had been advocating—but U.S. officials judged that the Poles lacked the strength to mount an offensive. In the end, Churchill and others fell back on their earlier arguments of needing to focus on defeating the Germans, whose collapse they believed was imminent in the wake of the Allied landings on the beaches of Normandy in June and the Soviet breakthrough in Byelorussia and rapid advancement through Poland in July.[3]

Witold secured a meeting with the underground leadership on July 25 to present his report along with statements from Edek, Jan, and several of his former couriers whom he had tracked down in Warsaw. He intended to present a record of his mission, but the material read like an indictment of the underground's abdication of its duty to bring down the camp. Komorowski was too busy to meet and passed him off to a deputy, Jan Mazurkiewicz, who told Witold he would get his chance to fight the Germans in the impending battle for Warsaw.[4]

The Soviets were expected to reach the east bank of the Vistula and surround Warsaw any day. Komorowski had initially planned uprisings against the Germans in major cities as a show of independence. But Stalin displayed no interest in making concessions to Polish sovereignty. As Stalin saw it, Russia had borne the brunt of the war and should set the terms of the postwar settlement, which included Poland as a client state. Indeed, when the Polish underground did rise up, they were subsequently arrested by the Soviet secret police.[5]

Komorowski was now faced with the choice of surrendering to the Soviets or trying to seize the city in the hope of gaining the support of the Allies and some leverage over Stalin. Timing was crucial. They needed to wait until the Soviets were almost upon them and the Germans were on the point of fleeing. They might have only hours to secure the city before the Soviets reached them. However, if they attacked too soon they would have to take on a German garrison of thirteen thousand men with only enough supplies and ammunition for a few days of fighting.[6]

That July, German troops were drifting back through Warsaw, a few at first and then a steady flow of dirty and bedraggled men carrying their injured with them. Crowds of Poles gathered in the hundred-degree heat on Jerozolimskie Avenue to watch.[7]

"It was an unforgettable spectacle," recalled Stefan Korboński. "The July sun shed so much light on this procession of misery that one could see every hole in the uniforms, every stain on the bands, every spot of rust on the rifles."[8]

A few girls waved handkerchiefs and called out in mock sadness, "Good-bye, good-bye, we will never see you again!" Policemen who heard them did nothing to intervene.[9]

German authority appeared to disintegrate as shops shuttered, offices closed, and the barking loudspeakers fell silent. SS men and off-duty soldiers drank in the street, declaring to one passerby that they were "sick of this war!" German moving vans and trucks piled with furniture clogged the roads heading west. Rumors spread that capitulation was imminent.[10]

Witold's supervisor ordered him to avoid the fighting and prepare for the Soviet occupation. But Witold was determined to fight the Germans. The next morning he bundled a copy of the report in an air-tight box and buried it in a friend's garden in Bielany, in the far north of the city, then prepared for battle.[11]

*

Soviet reconnaissance planes started buzzing over Warsaw toward the end of July. The authorities announced that women and children should leave the city, sparking panic in the German quarters. The roads jammed with fleeing families, and the Nazi governor, Ludwig Fischer, took off in his private plane. Prisoners were released from Mokotów Prison. The Communist-backed radio station urged the Poles to rise up.[12]

Then, as suddenly as it began, the retreat stopped. Hitler, who had survived an assassination attempt on July 20, declared that Warsaw would be held at all costs and dispatched eight thousand frontline troops and two hundred Panzers to launch a counteroffensive. Over the following days, fresh German troops paraded through the city center and massed on the east bank of the Vistula. City officials returned and shops reopened. The loudspeakers spluttered into life and ordered all working-age Poles to report to the main square to build antitank ditches. Komorowski, on the advice of his intelligence chief, Colonel Kazimierz Iranek-Osmecki, decided to postpone the uprising.[13]

The German counteroffensive against the Soviets began on July 31. The city vibrated to the sounds of distant artillery and mortar fire. The underground leadership was on tenterhooks, unsure of the battle's outcome. In the confusion Komorowski received flawed intelligence that the Soviets had already swatted the Germans aside and that the shell-fire heralded the Red Army's imminent arrival. He impulsively sent messengers across the city to rally the underground to rise up the next day. Iranek-Osmecki, returning from a fact-finding mission, learned of the order and rushed to alert Komorowski that the Germans weren't fleeing and had fought the Red Army to a standstill.[14]

"Too late," Komorowski said, and slumped into a chair, drained.[15]

Curfew was in an hour, and by morning every commander would be moving into position. "We cannot do anything more," he said, and rose to his feet.

*

Witold awoke on August 1 to hear the fighting on the opposite bank of the Vistula. He had arranged to meet Jan near Komorowski's headquarters around midday. He hid his handgun and spare bullets under a light jacket and set off. The streets were full of would-be insurgents, their guns and supplies hidden under heavy coats or in rucksacks and travel suitcases as they made their way into position. The Germans stopped one group, and a gun battle broke out that echoed through the surrounding streets and then died away.[16]

Witold and Jan were still making their way through the rainy streets when the uprising began around five with an explosion of gunfire. Many fighters hadn't made it to their units in time and simply attacked the nearest target. Those without guns used rocks to smash German shop windows. Teenagers dragged a German from a car and rifled through the vehicle. There was a cry of excitement as a fourteen-year-old boy held up a grenade.[17]

Witold and Jan fell in with a group on Chłodna Street. They cut through the partially dismantled ghetto and ducked for cover amid stacks of bricks as German gendarmes fired at them from a nearby police station. A small group of fighters was gathering to attack, but they scarcely had a gun between them.[18]

A couple of German snipers shot from the roofs, and the group scattered. Witold and Jan made for a nearby restaurant on Twarda Street, ducking between doorways for cover. Bodies were strewn across the street. They found an officer, Major Leon Nowakowski, surrounded by staff on the ground floor of the building. Witold didn't reveal his name and rank to Nowakowski, and the commander didn't ask too many questions. He told Witold and Jan to form a platoon.[19]

The fighting quieted as darkness fell. Hitler's troops had been taken by surprise, and the center of Warsaw and the Old Town were largely in the hands of the insurgents, along with the southern suburbs of Czerniaków and Mokotów. They had also taken the power station at Powiśle and supply depots around Umschlagplatz, the staging area once used to deport Warsaw's Jews.[20]

But contrary to Polish hopes, the Germans hadn't fled and indeed retained control of the police headquarters, governor's office, and key

Leon Nowakowski, c. 1944.

Courtesy of the Warsaw Uprising Museum.

rail and road links over the Vistula. Indeed, the local commander in the area didn't even consider the uprising serious enough to divert troops from their counteroffensive against the Soviets; instead he left it to the SS to put down the revolt. Himmler had been informed of the "disturbances" at 5:30 P.M. His first act was to telephone the Sachsenhausen concentration camp, where the underground leader Stefan Rowecki had been held since his capture, and order his execution. Next he informed Hitler.

"The timing is unfortunate," admitted the Reichführer-SS, "but from a historical perspective what the Poles are doing is a blessing. After five or six weeks we shall leave. But by then Warsaw will be liquidated; and this city, which is the intellectual capital of a 16- to 17 million strong nation . . . will cease to exist." That evening, Himmler announced that the city would be razed and that "every citizen of Warsaw is to be killed including men, women, and children."[21]

*

The next morning, August 2, Witold and Jan joined a small group of men in the city center to hunt down German snipers. It was slow work, but after several hours of sneaking around the roofs they killed them all. The underground radio was reporting, erroneously, that the Soviets were almost in the city and people flooded ecstatically onto the streets. Polish flags appeared in windows and the loudspeakers on streetcorners played the national anthem for the first time in nearly five years. The music soared above the crackle of explosions and gunfire. "People are crazy with joy," recalled one man. "They hug one another with tears of excitement and are very emotional." Underground commanders warned that conditions were still dangerous. "It may be necessary to write propaganda to dampen the enthusiasm and remind people that the Germans are still in the city," noted one officer. Barricades were hastily built out of paving stones, bricks, tiles, wood, heavy furniture, a child's stroller.[22]

On day three of the uprising, Nowakowski ordered Witold and a dozen men to attack the main mail distribution center at the corner of Żelazna Street and Jerozolimskie Avenue, a major thoroughfare that led to one of the bridges over the Vistula. By securing the corner, they could fire directly at German convoys trying to reach their besieged headquarters or troops fighting against the Soviets over the Vistula. The main line to Krakow also ran beside the road to the nearby train station.

Witold quickly flushed out the building's defenders and prepared to seize a hotel on the other side of Jerozolimskie Avenue in order to block the street entirely. Bullets zipped down Żelazna Street as Witold prepared to cross. Before they could make a run for it they heard the grate of Panzer tracks and saw a column of tanks approaching. The lead tank herded a group of terrified civilians in front of the convoy to serve as human shields. The Germans shelled the mail distribution center, but no one shot back. What could they do? Witold waited for them to pass and then charged across Jerozolimskie Avenue and burst through the front door of the hotel to find the Germans had scrambled out the back of the building. One of the men with Witold ran to the roof and raised a Polish flag, immediately attracting a barrage of fire from the buildings farther up the street.[23]

Witold continued to attack along Jerozolimskie Avenue in the direction the tanks had taken toward the city center. A few doors down, the Germans had barricaded the entrance to a building that housed a military institute for making maps. Witold charged the sandbag wall, yelling at the top of his lungs, and the defenders fled. In a courtyard at the back were a couple of parked cars containing guns and ammunition.[24]

The flag raised over the government-run hotel captured by Witold.
Courtesy of the Warsaw Uprising Museum.

Witold's men encountered stiffer resistance in the next building, a local district office where the Germans had barricaded themselves on the third floor. The insurgents tried the stairwell, but were met by a hand grenade that killed two and injured three more, forcing them to retreat to the institute with the bodies.[25]

They rested briefly but soon heard tanks rumbling toward them from the river. Witold watched the vehicles' steady progress toward their position through a hail of homemade insurgent bombs. There was no time to build a barricade, but Witold had found a room filled with barrels of Sidol, a cleaning chemical. The substance had no explosive properties, but the Germans might not know that. He and Jan rolled them out into a line that spanned the street and watched as three tanks stopped a safe distance away. The Germans shot at the barrels but soon gave up and drove away.[26]

Witold had succeeded in carving out a parcel of territory, but he suspected they'd made all the easy gains they were going to. The Germans had fortified hospital buildings beside a nearby park, which gave them clear lines of fire to Witold's position.

Furthermore, the city's water supply had also been shut off, so they had to ferry water from a brackish well that had been dug on the opposite side of the street. They had little food, and most worrisomely were running low on ammunition. That night Witold and his men fought their thirst as they dug graves in the courtyard of the institute, wrapped their two fallen comrades in curtains, and buried them with handwritten messages.[27]

Elsewhere, the underground had consolidated its hold over large areas of the city at great cost. Two thousand fighters had died, a tenth of their force, without seriously denting the German garrison, which had lost five hundred men. And still there was no sign of the Soviets. But spirits remained high behind the hastily constructed barricades. Soup kitchens opened to feed civilians and off-duty uprisers. In the city center, there were Chopin recitals in one of the cafés on Nowy Świat Street and lectures and performances at the Palladium theater. "Morale is fantastic," Komorowski radioed London that night from the Old Town.[28]

Day four brought Messerschmitt fighter planes, scouting for Soviet resistance. When they met none, a squadron of German Stukas roared in and dropped several tons of incendiary bombs over the Old Town, sending up vast plumes of black smoke that drifted down Jerozolimskie Avenue.

Witold took the opportunity to attack the Germans holed up in the nearby district office. The skirmish ended with another grenade down the stairwell that killed a sergeant and injured two more men. They just had time to drag the casualties back to their base at the institute when they heard the cry of "Tanks!"[29]

This time, the Germans had sent eighty-odd Panzers against Witold's barricade. They indiscriminately shelled buildings as they advanced. Infantrymen followed on either side. The front of the institute took a direct hit, sending a fireball through the ground-floor rooms that miraculously failed to hurt anyone. Jan battled through the flames to shoot back and found German tanks rumbling past the dismantled barricade. Witold didn't think that the same cleaning fluid ruse would work twice. That night they buried the dead sergeant in the courtyard.[30]

Half a dozen men attacked the district office the next day only to be repulsed again. Jan set off with some men to try to approach the building from the rear. A short while later, Witold was horrified to see Jan being half carried, half dragged back into the building, shot by a sniper, bleeding heavily and struggling to breathe. He died an hour later. It took two men to lift his large frame into a shallow grave in the courtyard.[31]

A sapper unit showed up in the afternoon with enough dynamite to blast the Germans out of the district office. They laid a charge on the ground floor and triggered an explosion that ripped through the building. A dozen or so Germans emerged from the rubble, three SS men among them. The leader of the group had shot himself rather than be captured. Witold's men threw his body out the window onto the street and wanted to shoot the remaining SS men. But in the end they ferried the Germans to headquarters, where they were put to work digging wells and latrines.[32]

Witold went back to the shattered district office and retrieved a few pistols, a machine gun, a shotgun, and some food, butter, cream, and

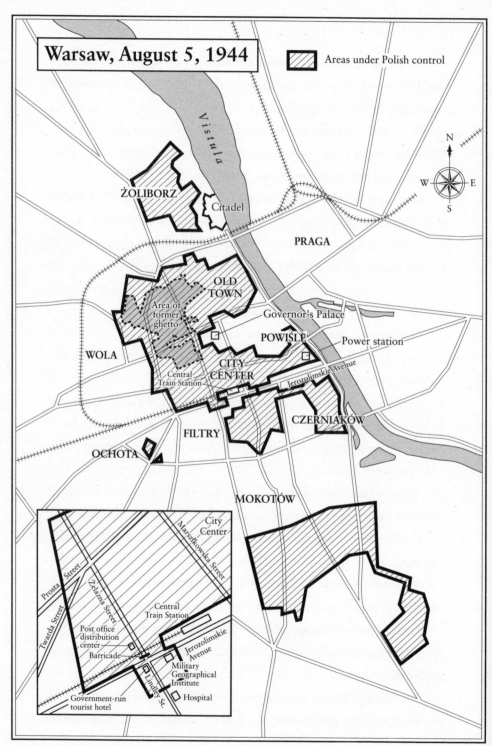

Warsaw, August 5, 1944

Areas under Polish control

Vistula

ŻOLIBORZ

Citadel

PRAGA

OLD TOWN

Area of former ghetto

Governor's Palace

POWIŚLE

Power station

WOLA

CITY CENTER

Central Train Station

Jerozolimskie Avenue

FILTRY

CZERNIAKÓW

OCHOTA

MOKOTÓW

City Center

Marszałkowska Street

Prosta Street

Żelazna Street

Twarda Street

Central Train Station

Post office distribution center

Barricade

Jerozolimskie Avenue

Military Geographical Institute

Lindley St.

Hospital

Government-run tourist hotel

John Gilkes

bacon, which he shared with his companions. The sappers had brought word of brutal German reprisals: an SS battalion under the overall command of SS-Obergruppenführer Erich von dem Bach-Zelewski had arrived that morning in the western suburb of Wola. SS men went from apartment to apartment shooting civilians. Within a few hours they'd killed two thousand people.[33]

That night four Liberators and a Halifax bomber manned by Polish crews from Allied air bases in Foggia, Italy, flew over the city. German spotlights quickly caught the planes and anti-aircraft batteries opened up, but the guns were aimed too high. By the time they'd adjusted, the aircraft had dropped their loads by parachute. There were cheers from the insurgents, but most of the boxes of weapons drifted past their positions toward the Jewish cemetery.[34]

The next morning, day six, Witold received reinforcements: eight teenagers arrived wearing oversized firefighter outfits. The oldest, Jerzy Zalewski, eighteen, had a machine gun. Witold had managed a shave that morning, and he came downstairs to greet the arrivals.

Jerzy gave a salute, clipped his heels, and announced that he had orders to continue attacking toward the train station. His mission was to capture a church.

"Impossible," said Witold. "You'd need everyone we've got."[35]

Jerzy insisted those were his orders. Witold gave in and offered two men.

The teenager came back a few hours later to report no casualties, but also no progress. Witold gave the lad a wry smile.

That afternoon, Witold attacked one of the German-held buildings near the park but was beaten back, with two men killed and three wounded. They had weapons but not enough ammunition to attack further. There were no more Halifaxes that night, or the next. From the western suburb of Wola came horrific stories of German massacres. The SS men were emptying buildings and either shooting the residents on the spot or funneling them toward execution sites to be dispatched in large groups. In three days, the SS had killed more than forty thousand people. After finally clearing insurgents from around the government buildings on August 9, the SS commander von dem Bach-Zelewski ordered a halt to the killings. He claimed after the war that this was for humanitarian reasons.[36]

Witold's men had been hunkered down in the institute for several days, returning fire only when they had to. Smoke engulfed the city in a gray haze that reduced visibility to a dozen yards; the nights were black and hot. They were extremely thirsty. They tried digging their own well, but soon gave up to prepare barricades. Witold took up position in a building overlooking the park with seven men in anticipation of an attack, but despite the ominous crunching of tank tracks nearby and the scream and thud of shellfire, they'd been spared.[37]

Then, around 4 P.M. on August 12, three tracked vehicles suddenly burst through the haze. The first leveled its cannon toward the barricade and fired. The blast forced Witold back from the window. By the time he returned, a German force of Russian mercenaries was rushing the building. Witold shot at them, but that only drew the attention of a tank, which fired at him. The percussive force of the explosion knocked him off his feet. A moment's quiet followed, broken by the sound of the building's entrance door being kicked in.[38]

Witold scrambled to his feet and raced to the stairwell, but the Russian mercenaries were inside, and the best he and the others could do was fight a rearguard action room by room. They managed to hold off the offensive until darkness fell and the assault finally eased. By then, they were down to their last rounds. Witold sent a runner across Jerozolimskie Avenue to headquarters with a request for more ammunition. Around 2 A.M., the answer came back: headquarters had nothing to spare, and they should abandon their position. There was nothing to do but scramble in pairs back across Jerozolimskie Avenue and through the small entrance at the base of the barricade.[39]

Witold joined the others in the basement of an apartment block for railway workers. It was the only place free from the threat of snipers. Rows of insurgents, mostly kids in outsized police and military outfits, dozed in the low light. Witold tried to sleep as the ground shook with distant explosions. Half of the forty fighters who'd joined him on the other side of the street were dead. At best, they'd managed to block the passage of tanks on Jerozolimskie Avenue for a few days.

The next morning, Nowakowski appointed Witold deputy commander of a company guarding the barricade facing Jerozolimskie Avenue. From the top of the rubble battlements, Witold watched the Russian mercenaries occupying his old positions. The Polish flag atop the hotel was torn down, and a loudspeaker was set up in one of its windows. It crackled into life at midmorning. A Russian-tinged voice urged them in Polish to give in.

"We have food and water," the voice announced. "We won't harm you."[40]

After a ten-hour shift on the barricade, Witold retreated out of sniper range. He found civilians out on some of the more sheltered streets. Thousands of residents had taken refuge in the city center to escape the massacres elsewhere. As the days and weeks passed, food became scarce, and ever larger crowds gathered at makeshift wells to draw water. By early September, a month into the uprising, no one shouted encouragement to the insurgents anymore; they were more likely to snap at them. "You bandits, leave us alone," declared one woman.[41]

The discipline of some insurgents broke down. Heavy drinking and acts of theft and looting became increasingly common. On September 12, one gang of armed men discovered a dozen or so Jewish men and women who had been in hiding in an underground shelter since the liquidation of the Warsaw Ghetto. The gang burst into the shelter, robbed the cowering men and women, and then shot some of them. Two Jews are known to have survived and four others in their party witnessed events from a nearby courtyard. The underground ordered an investigation, but no action was taken.[42]

*

The Polish underground managed to hold out for another six weeks. But the German's military superiority was overwhelming. One Polish-held neighborhood after another fell, and surrender appeared inevitable. There was a brief flurry of excitement when Soviet forces finally routed the Germans from the eastern shore of the Vistula in mid-September. A Soviet-trained force of around 1,600 Polish soldiers crossed the river by boat to link up with the uprisers. But without Soviet air or artillery support they were quickly beaten back. They were little more than a gesture on Stalin's part to defuse pressure from Churchill to assist the Poles. The Soviet leader intended to let the Germans finish crushing the Poles before he ordered his troops in.

Komorowski made a brief tour of the front line on September 22, the fifty-third day of the battle for Warsaw, and concluded they couldn't hold out any longer. The Germans were pushing for a cease-fire and talks. Komorowski finally agreed to a temporary cessation. A Polish envoy and interpreter holding a white flag crossed over the barricade at Żelazna Street that Witold was guarding. He watched as the Polish negotiators were met by five German officers in a limousine to be whisked away to von dem Bach-Zelewski's villa outside the city. Himmler had come up with the delusional notion that Komorowski would agree to fight the Soviets.[44]

The Polish delegation returned a few hours later; the German commander had readily agreed to Komorowski's terms: Polish fighters would be granted combatant status and sent to POW camps. Civilians would be processed at the Pruszków facility and sent to work camps. As soon as the men were back behind the barricades, the bombardment resumed; the Germans wanted to keep the pressure up until Komorowski signed the capitulation agreement.

The next morning, day fifty-four, Witold was woken at dawn by one of the officers. He'd recently taken charge of his company after the commanding officer was shot in the leg.[45]

"Get up, Witold, you have a guest!"[46]

"I assume you already know about the capitulation?" Witold asked.[47]

He grabbed his gun from beside the dirty couch he'd been resting

Tadeusz Komorowski shakes hands with Erich
von dem Bach-Zelewski after capitulating.

Courtesy of the Warsaw Uprising Museum.

on, only to see his old camp mate Wincenty Gawron rushing over to embrace him. Wincenty was almost in tears. He'd been hiding in the sewers since escaping the fighting in the Old Town. The lull in the battle had finally brought him to the surface.

"I don't want to surrender," said Witold, "but we have no more food or ammunition. I can't even offer you breakfast."

On October 1 a twenty-four-hour cease-fire was called to allow civilians to depart. No one believed it at first, but one by one they emerged from the rubble, dirty and unkempt, blinking in the light. A crowd made its way down Jerozolimskie Avenue. Some Polish fighters stood atop the barricades and jeered at those leaving, calling them quitters. Sixteen thousand civilians left that day and the next, only a fraction of the ninety thousand still trapped in the city center.[48]

The following day, October 2, Komorowski signed the capitulation order. Witold's battalion was summoned onto Żelazna Street before dawn on October 4 to hear the notice read out. They couldn't see each other's faces in the dark.

The uprising against the Germans that Witold had first planned for in the heady days after the invasion, then dreamed of for so long in the camp, had finally ended in defeat in the waning days of the German occupation. More than 130,000 people died in the fighting, most of them civilians. Of the 28,000 Jews hiding in the city, fewer than 5,000 survived. Warsaw lay in ruins.[49]

"Make your peace with God, as no one knows what is in store for us," the priest said.[50]

Witold fell to a knee with the others and prayed.

CHAPTER 21

RETURN

WARSAW
OCTOBER 1944

Witold followed the long line of prisoners as they wound their way out of the shattered city. Their destination was a temporary transit camp in a former cable factory at Ożarów, where Witold was startled to see Eleonora in the crowd gathered at the entrance. They managed to exchange a few words. She'd been stuck outside the city during the uprising and was desperately searching for her son.[1]

Witold asked her to bring him civilian clothes in case he had a chance to escape. But that night he was loaded onto a train bound for a POW camp near Lamsdorf, in Silesia. They were greeted by a crowd of local Germans yelling "bandits," who threw stones and beat several prisoners as they marched through the rain toward the camp.

As Witold reached its gates, he saw two planes take off from a nearby airfield and collide, producing a spectacular fireball. The Poles cheered, and the German sentries opened fire. Some prisoners dropped to the floor; others hid in the furrows of a nearby potato field until they were eventually rounded up and brought into the camp, where they were left in the yard overnight to be registered. The next morning they were robbed of their belongings and then locked up in a concrete barrack without windows, mattresses, or bedding.[2]

Witold spent a week in the camp. Then he and the other officers were transferred by train to a facility in Murnau, southern Bavaria. Murnau's proximity to Switzerland meant the Red Cross visited often, and the Germans treated it as a model camp. The five-thousand-odd prisoners were well fed and had no work duties. During the day, they organized talks, lectures, and soccer games in the yard. In the evenings, they put on plays, for which the guards helped organize costumes, wigs, cosmetics.[3]

The prisoners followed the final days of the war on several camp radios. In early October, Soviet troops swept into Hungary and Slovakia and reached the borders of the Reich proper in East Prussia. Hitler fled his wartime headquarters at Rastenberg for Berlin the following month. In the West, American forces under General Dwight Eisenhower were briefly held up by a German counterattack in the Ardennes forest over Christmas, but by January 1945 their progress resumed.

Then came the news the camp had been waiting for and dreading. On January 17, Soviet-led forces captured Warsaw, and Stalin moved swiftly to install Polish Communists in the capital to head a new administration.

The underground's new leader, General Leopold Okulicki, realized the organization was too weak to oppose the Soviet occupation and announced the dissolution of the secret army. In London, the Polish exile government fell into disarray after its leader, Stanisław Mikołajczyk, opened talks to join the new administration in the hope of preserving some sort of Polish autonomy. The other exiles remained opposed to Stalin, but the British and Americans no longer took them seriously. At the Yalta Conference in February, Churchill and Roosevelt acquiesced to Stalin's plan to seize the eastern third of Poland for the So-viet Union, including the historic Polish cities of Lwów and Wilno. Witold's family home was now in the Byelorussian Soviet Socialist Republic. In recompense, Poland would receive some German terri-tory and the promise of elections at some point in the future. Under the deal, six million Poles and 11 million Germans were to be forced from their homes—a scale of ethnic cleansing that went beyond anything yet seen in the war.[4]

The commander of a Polish contingent in Italy, General Władysław Anders, called on Poles to oppose the Communist takeover and rally to him. The prisoners in Murnau debated whether to carry on the fight for Poland's freedom. Most prisoners, though, wanted to put the war behind them and go home as soon as they were liberated.

In March, American and British forces crossed the Rhine at mul-tiple points. Cologne fell, followed by Frankfurt. Then, on April 29, they awoke to shots directly north of the camp, in the direction of Mu-nich. The prisoners assembled in the roll call square and watched as an American reconnaissance plane circled overhead and tipped its wings. In the early afternoon, the guard commander, Captain Oswald Pohl, ordered his men to stack their weapons and place white flags in the yard. He informed the prisoners that the guards planned to surrender but he warned them that a die-hard SS unit was on its way to liquidate the camp.[5]

They heard the crunch of three American M5 tanks approaching. Then came the roar of half a dozen SS vehicles from the opposite di-rection. The SS reached the gates first, but the tanks were immediately upon them. The Nazi officer in the lead car drew his gun and started shooting. The lead tank responded with its 76 mm cannon, hitting the German and his driver. The prisoners ran to the fence to watch the battle only to scatter as the bullets flew. The SS fled, pursued by two tanks. A third approached the camp. The gates were opened, the tank pulled in, and the gunner popped his head up. He was from Poland originally. "You guys are free," he said in Polish.[6]

＊

Germany surrendered eight days later, on May 7, to jubilation in the camp. A few days later the Warsaw Uprising leader, Komorowski, newly released from German custody, visited and told them to remain in place and await further instruction. Allied forces were struggling to deal with the millions of forced laborers and prisoners being freed across Germany. As the days and weeks passed, some of his colleagues slipped away with the crowds drifting past the camp. But Witold felt bound to his oath to fight the Soviets and waited.[7]

It wasn't until July that one of Anders's officers appeared with orders for Witold and several dozen others to accompany him to Italy. They traveled first to the port of Ancona, where elements of Anders's II Corps, which had fought under British command during the Allied campaign in North Africa and Italy, was stationed. The British wanted to demobilize the force, which numbered fifty thousand. Anders had angrily informed the Brits that most of his men came from eastern Poland in the territory now incorporated into the Soviet Union and thus didn't have a home to go to and that those who did return had been arrested by the new Communist regime.[8]

In Ancona, Witold met with Colonel Marian Dorotycz-Malewicz, the head of intelligence for II Corps. They discussed the idea of creating an underground intelligence network in Poland. The colonel informed Witold that he would need approval from Anders and instructed him to wait in Porto San Giorgio, a town a couple of hours south along the Adriatic coast, which served as an R&R post for the Poles. Witold was directed upon arrival to a villa on the beach.

After settling in, he joined other Polish soldiers strolling on the beach. He took off his shoes and felt the warm water against his toes, and the soft easterly breeze on his face. He tried to savor the moment, but he was already mentally back in the camp, the scenes rising unbidden and triggered by the smallest things: a face on the street, a turn of phrase, the stars at night. Everything seemed to revolve around the camp and there was no way to free himself from the feelings that came with each remembering: anger, remorse, and guilt.

Finally, he procured a pad of paper and started writing another report. He intended this one, like the others, to serve as a record of his time in the camp, but he was also ready to give freer rein to his emotions.

"So, I am to write down the driest of fact, which is what my friends want me to do," he wrote in the introduction. "Well, here I go . . . but we were not made of wood, let alone stone . . . though I often envied it;

The beach at Porto San Giorgio.

one still had a heart beating, sometimes in one's mouth, and certainly running around one's brain was the odd thought which I sometimes with difficulty grasped."

He had few other duties that August and wrote in the cool, bright mornings. A soldier friend of his from Warsaw, Jan Mierzanowski, came down to visit from barracks in the town of Imola. He recalled Witold emerging onto the beach in the afternoons with a stack of papers under his arms, each page marked with his looping script. For a few lira the two men would rent a pedalo, a twin-hulled contraption that had a deck chair mounted forward and a seat for rowing that pulled back and forth with each stroke. Jan took the oars as Witold sat atop the chair and read aloud from his papers. Witold also en-

Maria Szelągowska, closest to camera, prewar.
Courtesy of the Woyna-Orlewicz family.

listed an intelligence officer he'd known in Warsaw and reconnected with in Murnau, Maria Szelągowska, to type up his manuscript. She was smart, university educated, and committed to Poland's cause. They bonded emotionally through their work and Maria seems to have helped Witold open up about his camp experiences in his writings.[9]

Finally, in early September, Witold was summoned by Anders to Rome to discuss his proposals. He proposed that Maria join him on the mission as a secretary and that a friend of his from the uprising, Bolesław Niewiarowski, serve as his courier to Anders. The general approved his mission and set a departure date for the end of October. A few days later Witold was back in Porto San Giorgio and writing with renewed vigor. "I must use shorthand owing to the decision I've just made," he noted in the text.[10]

Witold's time was increasingly taken up with preparing their journey to Poland. The route needed organizing; documents had to be forged. It was clear that this time he would have to approach his underground work differently. Against the Germans he could count on the near-universal support of the people, but against these Polish Communists he could not be so sure. Witold planned on operating in small circles of acquaintances to solicit material. He wouldn't recruit anyone or even necessarily reveal his role. That way he could avoid directly implicating his friends while involving them in the cause.[11]

As their departure date neared, Witold was completing several pages of manuscript a day while simultaneously line-checking what Maria had already typed up. There was no time to produce a clean copy, so after rudimentary editing they cut off the margins to remove his comments and pasted pages together. By the time he returned to Rome for final instruction on October 21, Witold had 104 typed pages in his bag, which he duly handed over to the Polish ambassador to the Vatican, Kazimierz Papée, for safekeeping.[12]

*

A few days later he, Maria, and Bolesław set off for Poland. They crossed the Alps into Germany by bus or train. Bolesław appeared to get cold feet at the German border, so Witold and Maria carried on without him into Soviet-controlled Czech territory on their way to Prague. Czech militia were ethnically cleansing the Sudeten border region of its majority German population, and they passed a seemingly endless procession of bowed heads. Some Germans wore armbands emblazoned with the letter *N*, symbolizing the Czech word for "German." Soviet soldiers with sticks drove them on like cattle, swearing at

Jan Mierzanowski, Maria Szelągowska, and Witold in Rome.
Courtesy of the Pilecki family.

them and drinking vodka. Sometimes they grabbed a woman to rape beside the road.[13]

Witold and Maria stayed for a few days in Prague and then carried on to the Polish border, where they encountered lines of Poles seeking reentry. Once over the border, they got papers stamped at the nearest repatriation office under the watchful eye of the new Polish secret police, known as the Urząd Bezpieczeństwa, or UB. They then carried on to the mountain resort of Zakopane, where Maria had friends and they could take their bearings.[14]

The country was in tumult. Soviet forces and the police patroled the streets during the day, but at night the last radical fringes of the underground emerged from the woods. They attacked Polish officials of the new Communist regime and burned police stations and cars. There were more than five hundred assassinations a month across the country, and a full-blown insurgency raged in some areas. A police report from one district in Silesia captured the scale of the lawlessness over a fortnight that autumn: 20 murders, 86 robberies, 1,084 cases of breaking and entering, 440 political crimes, 92 arsons, and 45 sex crimes.

Meanwhile, a public health crisis was brewing. Hunger was widespread. Soviet forces had requisitioned most of the harvest, and they impeded the work of an international relief agency as it distributed supplies. Desperate hordes ransacked shops and warehouses looking for food or items to barter. Typhus and dysentery were endemic, and there were more than 250,000 cases of venereal disease, mostly as a result of rape by Soviet soldiers.[15]

Witold and Maria left a few days later for Nowy Wiśnicz, where Witold had stayed after his escape, but the Serafińskis' little wooden cottage was deserted. In neighboring Bochnia, Witold spoke to the Obora family, who'd hosted Jan and Edek, and got a sense of the challenge they faced. Józef, the father, was opposed to the Communists, but he had little work. Many of his friends were taking jobs with the new regime. He was tired of fighting.

They reached Warsaw in early December. This was Witold's first chance to take in the scale of the destruction. Hitler had ordered the city's demolition, and German sappers had dynamited the few buildings left standing after the uprising, leaving 90 percent of the city in rubble. Some officials of the new regime had discussed simply leaving Warsaw in ruins as a symbol of the war, but Stalin had concluded that rebuilding the city better served its purposes.[16]

The city had lost more than half of its million residents during the war, and survivors were flocking back. Small marks of habitation were visible where a family had carved out a niche: a clothesline between broken walls, a line of smoke from the upper floor of a roofless tenement, a toy outside a cave of rubble. Even in the cold of December, the stench of unburied bodies and open sewers and latrines was strong. A giant picture of Stalin hung above the only undamaged bridge over the Vistula.[17]

Witold tried to locate members of the anti-Soviet organization he'd joined before the uprising, but most were dead, arrested, or displaced. Indeed, the Soviet secret police and their Polish proxies had detained forty thousand former members of the underground since the end of the war and deported most of them to the gulags of Siberia. He eventually tracked down an old recruit, Makary Sieradzki, who agreed to host him in his remarkably undamaged apartment on Pańska Street in the city center.[18]

Over the next few weeks Witold turned the apartment into his operational headquarters. He acquired a typewriter on the black market to produce reports and found a carpenter to build him a secret compartment in the floor. Another preserved building nearby housed a photography store that agreed to produce microfilms. With Maria's help, he started reaching out to friends and acquaintances who'd taken jobs in various government ministries and gently pushed them for useful information. Intermittently, he wrote reports for Anders that captured the dissonances of living under Soviet rule.[19]

He had returned thinking he would find a Soviet republic. But he was surprised to discover how much of Poland endured and seemed to thrive under the new order. Churches opened their doors to the homeless, women's groups ran soup kitchens, and scout troops helped the soldiers clear away rubble. The former Polish leader Stanisław Mikołajczyk urged the country to unite behind reconstruction. Witold felt his opposition to the regime softening.[20]

*

Predictably, his thoughts turned to Auschwitz. He thought about publishing his memoir and raised the matter with a former block mate from the camp, Witold Różycki, whom he bumped into on the tram that March. The two men agreed to visit Auschwitz in the hope of finding closure. After its liberation, the camp had been used to house German prisoners, but in March 1946, the Polish regime had announced it would be turned into a permanent memorial.

Before setting off, Witold visited his family in Ostrów Mazowiecka. His contact with his wife, Maria, had been limited to a few letters. The family was sharing a small wooden house with Maria's sister and her husband, Bolesław Radwański, on the outskirts of town. Most of the Radwańskis had either taken jobs with the Communist regime or joined the party. Witold played a few games with Zofia and Andrzej in the yard, but they were twelve and fourteen years old now and no longer children. The war had cost him, and them, their bond. He didn't tell Maria about his latest mission, but she knew he was working for the underground and that she couldn't persuade him to quit.[21]

Witold and Różycki left a few days later for Auschwitz. Thousands made the pilgrimage that spring of 1946. Some came in search of loved ones or to pay their observances to the dead. Others were former prisoners who wanted to see the place that consumed their thoughts. A few stayed in the barracks and served as unofficial tour guides. One of the blocks contained items salvaged from around the site. Its basement was divided into small alcoves: a pile of children's slippers in one, human hair in another, prosthetic limbs in a third. The fact that these items belonged to murdered Jews who comprised the vast majority of the camp's victims was not hidden, but since most visitors were ethnic Poles the exhibitions foregrounded Polish suffering and were framed in Christian terms; the same block that contained the Jewish items had an illuminated cross in the hallway. The penal block was also open. Stacks of flowers and candles in jars were arranged at the base of the wall where so many of Witold's friends had been shot.[22]

In Birkenau, Witold saw what was left of the gas chambers and crematoria he'd reported on. The Nazis had blown up the buildings in an attempt to hide their crimes, but the ruined structures were plainly discernable. Most of the stables had been dismantled for use as temporary accommodation elsewhere and the mounds of Jewish clothes in the warehouses distributed among the needy. A couple of guards scared off any looters who came to pick through the mass graves in the woods looking for gold.[23]

Witold observed the scene without comment. He'd come looking for answers but found none.

*

Witold returned to Warsaw and began to write a first part to his memoir, which traced his early years and which he provisionally titled "How I Found Myself in Auschwitz." He had moved into a little flat on

Skrzetuskiego Street, on the southern outskirts of the city. The place was empty during the days. He tapped away at his portable typewriter beside the window and was soon lost in memories of Sukurcze: the hollowed-out trunk of a fallen linden tree, where he played as a child; his great-grandmother's bedroom, which had been left untouched since the day she died, like a dusty museum piece. Sometimes Witold headed into the town center to see his son, Andrzej, whose scout troop from Ostrów Mazowiecka was being bussed into the city on weekends to clear rubble. Witold didn't approach; he simply watched the boys heaving barrows of debris from a distance.

He still met Maria Szelągowska for underground work, but they'd received no further instructions and he did little reporting. Then one morning in June, they were at the flat when a messenger of his, Tadeusz Płużański, showed up at the door. He had come from Rome and looked anxious. Headquarters had information that the secret police were on to Witold and that an emissary of Anders, Jadwiga Mierzejewska, had come to Warsaw to select his successor.[24]

Witold was stunned, but there was no point in arguing with Tadeusz. Witold said he needed time to think. Tadeusz agreed to cover for him and tell Anders's emissary that he was in the woods meeting partisans. The next time Witold saw his wife he raised the idea of leaving for Italy. It would mean a life of exile. Witold confessed that fleeing felt like a betrayal of his oath to fight for Poland. Maria agreed. This was their home.[25]

But to stay, Witold needed to prove his worth to Jadwiga. That summer he filed several reports, including one on a pogrom in the southern town of Kielce in which a mob and local officials murdered thirty-seven Jews and injured thirty-five more. Three hundred thousand Polish Jews of the once three-million-strong community had survived the war. Those who remained or had returned home were subjected to abuse and violence by a contingent of Poles who blamed Jews for the Communist takeover of the country. "A tragedy," Witold called the episode in his report.

He finally met Jadwiga in September at the back of the photography shop. She was adamant he leave the country, but he persuaded her to let him remain until his replacement could be found, and he promised to send more reports on the Communists' tightening grip.[26]

That Christmas saw a new level of terror as Stalin enjoined Polish Communists to break the remaining opposition to their rule ahead of elections scheduled for January 1947. Thousands of people were jailed and the officials of rival parties beaten up. The rigged election saw the Communists and their allies capture 80 percent of the vote, after which Poland effectively became a single-party dictatorship.[27]

Witold had never given serious consideration to using violent means to oppose the Communists, but his courier, Tadeusz Płużański, had other ideas. He had started gathering material on secret police operatives. That winter, Tadeusz proposed that they assassinate the head of the secret police, Józef Różański. Tadeusz had obtained his address, phone number, and daily schedule to plan an attack. Witold was skeptical, saying only that they'd need London's permission to proceed. Some weeks later Witold noticed an unmarked car outside the apartment where they worked. The next day the vehicle appeared again. He tried to rationalize the situation. The secret police often put people under surveillance—it usually meant they didn't have enough information to make an arrest, and they used the tactic as a warning.[28]

He dismissed the affair and returned to his reports and the completion of his memoir. That spring he wrote a short introduction in which he reflected on his work to make the world comprehend what he had witnessed in Auschwitz. He had blamed other people for failing to heed his messages. But there is, implicit in the tortured prose that emerges, a recognition that the horrors of the camp might never be comprehensible, even to a prisoner like himself who had suffered within its walls. Perhaps this gave him a measure of relief. For what emerges from these passages is a sense that Witold's orientation had shifted. No longer did he need his readers to understand an evil that defied comprehension. Instead he asked them to look within themselves for that which they could share with those who suffer.

"I have listened to many confessions of my friends before their deaths," he wrote around then. "They all reacted in the same unexpected manner: they regretted they hadn't given enough to other people, of their hearts, of the truth . . . the only thing that remained after them on Earth, the only thing that was positive and had a lasting value, was what they could give of themselves to others."[29]

Witold, c. 1946.
Courtesy of the Pilecki family.

*

Witold sometimes went weeks without seeing his fellow collaborators. But in early May he met Tadeusz at the apartment. Two days later he returned. It was evening, and the lights were on. He climbed the stairs and knocked. Makary answered, so Witold opened the door and stepped inside. Makary and his wife were in their room with men in dark suits standing beside them. Then he felt his arms seized and before he knew it two men were marching him downstairs to a waiting car. He was brought to a nondescript office building in the city center, and led to a small, whitewashed room on the first floor that contained a desk and two chairs. On the desk were a pen and paper. He was politely asked to take a seat, and his captors left, locking the door behind them.[30]

There is no record of what happened next, but it's likely he was visited by the secret police chief Różański. Różański's usual tactic was to claim he knew everything about his subject's crimes and that any co-conspirators were already talking. Witold may have learned then that Tadeusz had been detained the day before. The pen and paper were for Witold's confession.

After Różański came a slim, handsome man named Eugeniusz Chimczak, the chief interrogator. Until then, his captors had been civil, courteous even. Chimczak's job was to break his victim's spirits. His favorite tool was a simple metal-covered ruler, which he used to slap and stab. Other methods included "plucking the goose," by tearing out hair, pulling off fingernails, stubbing cigarettes out around the mouth and eyes, and slowly tightening a metal band fastened around the head until the victim fainted. Witold was soon transferred to another prison in the Mokotów district, where the torture continued.[31]

On May 12, the public prosecutor charged Witold with treason. Witold tried to bargain for information and offered up his reports and writings in return for his family's safety. In his despair, Witold wrote a confession that took the form of a poem to Różański, in which he likened himself to a plague bearer, wandering around the city, infecting those he met with his disease.

"I'm writing this petition, / For me only to be punished / by the sum of all penalties, / because even if I lose my life / I prefer that to living with this wound in my heart."[32]

Days came and went, light and then dark, pain and then the memory of pain. Between May and November 1947, Witold was interrogated more than 150 times. He told them the truth, he told them lies, he told them what he thought they wanted to hear. Then he signed what they told him to sign and was returned to his cell.

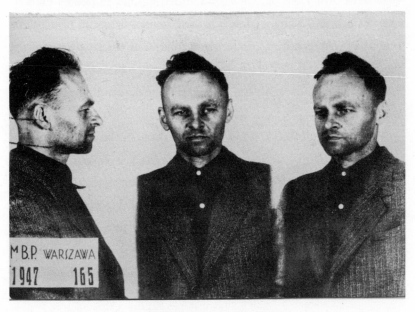

Witold's arrest photo, May 1947.

Courtesy of the Pilecki family.

He saw no one else. Occasionally he heard screams from a distant cell. Sometime after Christmas, he was hauled out of his room to serve as a witness in a trial of a priest he'd worked with. He was brought shuffling into the courtroom, unable to raise his head, likely because his collarbones had been broken. He stood, head bent, arms limp at his sides, and spoke a few words before being dismissed back to his cell.[33]

In February formal charges were brought against him and seven of his associates, including Maria Szelągowska, Tadeusz Płużański, and Makary Sieradzki. A trial date was set for March 3. The state appointed him a token defense attorney. The man was well-meaning and agreed to contact his family on his behalf. Witold had no visitation rights, but the lawyer said that Maria could attend the parts of the trial that were open to the public and speak to Witold before the hearings.

Witold's case was to be one of the country's first Soviet-style show trials. After the election, the Communist regime wanted to demonstrate its power. As the trial date neared, government-run newspapers were filled with headlines declaring Witold to be the ringleader of the "Anders gang" and in the pay of Western imperialists. "Traitors," declared a state radio announcer, "threatening society and our wonderful youth."[34]

Witold was allowed to shave and wash ahead of the trial, which was to be recorded and broadcast on the radio. He arrived at the military district court on Koszykowa Street in a black suit and tie and with a heavy police guard. The courtroom was crowded. He sat on a wooden bench beside the seven other defendants. He saw his wife and Eleonora in the audience.

The prosecutor, Czesław Łapiński, a smooth-faced former underground officer, read out the list of charges against him: treason against the state, plotting the assassination of UB officials, failure to report himself to the authorities, use of forged documents, and illegal pos-

Witold's cell in Mokotów Prison.

session of firearms. Witold stared ahead impassively. Any one of those charges carried a heavy prison sentence; treason was punishable by death. Finally the judge called Witold to the stand to answer the charges. In a low, barely audible voice he admitted to hiding weapons and using fake documents. But he denied working for a foreign power, or that he'd planned to kill secret police officers.

During a break Maria and Eleonora were briefly allowed to approach him. Eleonora asked if they could do anything.[35]

"Auschwitz was just a game compared to this," he told them. "I'm very tired. I want a swift conclusion."[36]

The trial carried on for another week and consisted mostly of Łapiński reading out their signed confessions. But on the final day, Witold was given an opportunity to respond. He rose slowly to his feet, keeping his battered hands hidden from Maria and Eleonora. His attorney usually advised clients to beg forgiveness of the court. But

Witold refused. "I tried to live my life in such a fashion," he told the courtroom, "so that in my last hour, I would rather be happy than fearful. I find happiness in knowing that the fight was worth it." He reiterated the fact that he was a Polish officer following orders.[37]

Four days later, Witold was sentenced to death. His attorney lodged an appeal and assured Maria it might be possible to reduce the punishment to life imprisonment if they could sway the country's leaders. The appeal was denied ten days later. Some of Witold's former Auschwitz friends banded together to sign a petition to the Polish prime minister, Jósef Cyrankiewicz, an ex-prisoner himself. They cited Witold's extraordinary work and patriotism. But Cyrankiewicz was unswayed, and the man who organized the petition, Wiktor Śniegucki, was promptly fired from his job.[38]

Maria also wrote to the president, Bolesław Bierut, directly, begging him on behalf of her children to spare Witold's life.

Witold in the dock, March 1948.
Courtesy of Narodowe Archiwum Cyfrowe.

"We have been living in hope for a peaceful life together with him for a long time," she pleaded. "We not only love him, but we worship him. He loves Poland and this love overshadowed all others."[39]

Bierut too upheld the verdict. Witold was collected from his cell on May 25, an hour after sunset. The jailers read his sentence aloud, gagged him with a white scarf, then took him under the arms to lead him outside. It had rained that morning, but the clouds were lifting and the sky was still light in the west. They brought him to a small, single-story building on the prison grounds. As they neared the dimly lit building, Witold insisted on walking unaided.

The executioner, Piotr Śmietański, was waiting inside. A priest and a doctor in a medical smock stood to one side. Witold was ordered to stand against the wall. Then Śmietański raised his pistol and shot him in the back of the head.[40]

EPILOGUE

Poland's Communist government arrested eighty thousand members of the underground over the next four years. The regime considered Witold's family to be enemies of the state, and Maria retreated into obscurity as a cleaner in a church orphanage. The regime sealed Witold's papers in the state archives, and Prime Minister Józef Cyrankiewicz fashioned an official history of Auschwitz that presented its Communist inmates like himself as heroes in a global struggle against fascism and imperialism. The Holocaust was barely mentioned in this telling, and Witold's group was characterized as a proto-fascist side note.[1]

A former underground leader, Tadeusz Pełczyński, brought the report Witold had written in Italy to London, and there was talk among the exiles of searching out a publisher. But they found little interest. The public shock that had followed Allied liberation of the concentration camps in 1945 had faded, and the Cold War dominated political discussion. Witold had been effectively deleted from history.

His story remained hidden until the 1960s, when Pełczyński shared the report with the Polish historian and fellow exile Józef Garliński, whose 1975 book, *Fighting Auschwitz*, finally attested to Witold's role in the creation of the camp underground. But it wasn't until the collapse of the Soviet Union in 1989 and the opening of the state archives in Warsaw that the academic Adam Cyra and Witold's sixty-year-old son, Andrzej, gained access to a large leather briefcase containing Witold's report from 1943–44, his memoir of his early life, additional notes, interrogation files, and the crucial key to his coded references. It was the first time that the family had had a chance to read about Witold's mission in his own words.[2]

Cyra published one of the first biographies of Witold in Polish in 2000 based on the material and new testimony from Eleonora, Wincenty, and Kon. The book helped establish Witold's status as a national hero in Poland. But Witold's writings were not fully translated, and his story remained almost unknown in the West, where Auschwitz was better known for its central role in the Holocaust and as the setting for one of mankind's darkest acts.[3]

Yet Witold's story is essential for our understanding of how Auschwitz came into being and obliges us to confront how we respond to evil in our own time. Witold entered Auschwitz before the Germans understood what the camp would become. This meant that Witold had to come to terms with the Holocaust even as the camp was trans-

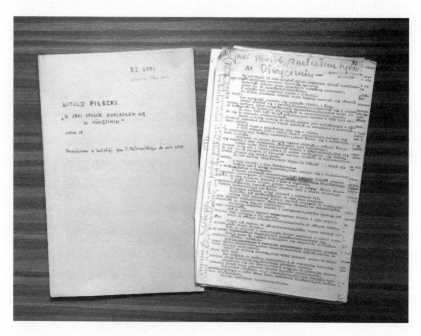

Witold's report written in Italy in 1945.

formed into a death factory before his eyes. At times he struggled to make sense of events, resorting to placing extraordinary atrocities in the context of the familiar. But Witold, unlike most prisoners or the long chain of people who handled his reports between Warsaw and London, refused to look away from what he could not understand. He engaged, and in doing so felt compelled to risk his life and act.

Witold's story demonstrates the courage needed to distinguish new evils from old, to name injustice, and to implicate ourselves in the plight of others. But I think it's important to observe that there were limits to how far Witold's empathy could reach. Witold never came to see the Holocaust as the defining act of World War II or the suffering of Jews as a symbol of humanity. He never let go of his Polishness or his sense of national struggle. At times in his 1945 report he is brutally frank about the difficulty he felt in identifying with the

Marek Ostrowski and Andrzej Pilecki in the apartment
from which Witold was captured, 2017.

gassing of the Jews, as his focus was on survival of his country, his men, himself.

Patriotism of this strength can seem outdated or worrisomely like the preserve of a far right rising on a tide of nationalism. But we must also reckon with the fact that Witold's patriotism furnished him with a sense of service and a moral compass that sustained his mission in the camp. Ultimately he couldn't save his comrades, or the Jews. He makes no apologies for that fact, but neither does he hide his failure. Rather, he suggests in his final writings that we must come to understand our limits, even as he exhorts us to see past them.

Above all, he asks us to trust one another. Witold's defining quality was his ability to place his faith in other people. In the camp, where the SS sought to break the prisoners down and strip them of their values, the idea of trust had revolutionary potential. So long as the prisoners could believe in the greater good, they were not defeated. Witold's men perished in many terrible and excruciating ways, but they did so with a dignity that Nazism failed to destroy.

Witold died knowing that he had failed to deliver his message. My hope is that this book will help us hear him.

ACKNOWLEDGMENTS

This book would not have been possible without my editor at Custom House, Geoff Shandler, whose support, keen advice, and patience have helped bring Witold's story to life. Liate Stehlik, my publisher, has shared my passion for Witold's story over the past three years and I'm grateful to her and the HarperCollins team for the platform they have provided. Many thanks to Vedika Khanna, assistant editor, and Nyamekye Waliyaya, the head of production, and David Palmer, for turning the manuscript into a book. My U.K. editor at Ebury, Jamie Joseph, offered astute edits and encouragement. The book was first conceived of with the help of my wonderful agents Larry Weismann and Sascha Alper. I am grateful to Clare Alexander, my agent in the United Kingdom, for her support throughout my career. Jacob Levenson edited (and reedited) each draft of the manuscript, never gave up correcting my prose, and helped me discover Witold's humanity.

Marta Goljan led my research team and joined me in following Witold's footsteps from Krupa to the camp and beyond. She and Katarzyna Chiżyńska spent two years in Oświęcim tracking down and translating hundreds of prisoner accounts and memoirs. Along with Luiza Walczuk in Warsaw, they helped locate and interview dozens of camp survivors and their families, and in the process introduced me to the joys of Polish culture. I'm especially grateful to Katarzyna for her amazing work pulling the book together in its final stages. Ingrid Pufahl was my wise and brilliant researcher in Washington, D.C., who invariably found answers to my many obscure requests. Many thanks also to the rest of the team: Hannah Wadle, Irina Radu, Alexandra Harrington, Karianne Hansen, Iga Bunalska of the Auschwitz Study Group, and Anna Łozińska and Paulina Wiśniewska and the staff of the Pilecki Institute. Filip Wojciechowski offered his insights and many fine runs through Warsaw.

I am hugely grateful to Piotr Cywiński and Andrzej Kacorzyk for opening the doors to my research at the Auschwitz-Birkenau State Museum. Piotr Setkiewicz at the research department fielded my endless queries with good humor, and offered his insights on each stage of the manuscript. Adam Cyra was my first guide to Witold's story and generously shared his own research and findings. Wojciech Płosa and Szymon Kowalski ensured I never got lost in the archives. Thanks also to Jerzy Dębski, Jacek Lachendro, Agnieszka Sieradzka, Anna Walczyk, Agnieszka Kita, Sylwia Wysińska, Halina Zdziebko, Roman Zbrzeski. Mirosław Obstarczyk helped me see the camp through Witold's eyes. Special thanks to Krystyna Bożejewicz at the Polish Underground Study Trust in London for fielding many requests and Jarek Garliński for first encouraging me to write the book. On behalf of my research team I'd also like to thank Klaudia Kieperka from The Polish Institute and Sikorski Museum in London, Ron Coleman, Megan Lewis and Rebecca Erbelding at the United States Holocaust Memorial Museum, Alla Kucherenko at Yad Vashem, Dovid Reidel of the Kleinman Holocaust Education Center, Jacek Syngarski of Archivo Polonicum, Freiburg, Fabrizio Bensi of the International Committee of the Red Cross, Geneva, Gerhard Keiper of the Political Archive, German Federal Foreign Office, Carina Schmidt and Peter Haberkorn at Hessian State Archive, and Johannes Beermann of the Fritz-Bauer Institute in Frankfurt.

Over the course of my research I have had the great privilege of getting to know Witold's family. Andrzej Pilecki and Zofia Pilecka-

Optułowicz spent hours sharing with me memories of Witold. Their great warmth, generosity, and frankness gave me an early insight into their father's character. Andrzej joined me on several stages of the research, most memorably overnight in Alwernia's seventeenth-century Bernardine monastery, where Witold, Jan, and Edek had been well fed after their escape. When Andrzej couldn't be with us, he made sure we were properly taken care of. Marek Ostrowski has also become a dear friend and mentor. Special thanks also to Dorota Optułowicz-McQuaid, Beata Pilecka-Różycka for many fine cakes, Elżbieta Ostrowska, Tomasz Ostrowski, Edward Radwański, Lidia Parwa, Stanisław Tumielewicz, and Krysztof Kosior. David McQuaid helped me piece together some of the gaps in Witold's story and understand his connections to our own time.

I was also honored to interview those who knew Witold or shared in the struggle of those times: Kazimierz Piechowski, Bohdan Walasek, Jerzy Zakrzewski, Jerzy Bogusz, Janusz Walendzik, Mieczysław Gałuszka, Zofia Zużałek, Jacek and Ryszard Stupka, Józefa Handzlik, Anna Czernicka, Stefan Hahn, Mieczysław Mastalerz, Kazimierz Albin, and Zofia Posmysz. I am indebted to the families of those connected to Witold's story for sharing their time, memories, and private papers: Maria and Szymon Świętorzecki, Marek and Barbara Popiel, Yaninka Salski, Jarosław Abramow-Newerly, Daniel Piechowski, Jan Tereszczenko, Piotr Woyna-Orlewicz, Ewa Biały, Adam Wojtasiak, Zofia Wiśniewska, Maria Serafińska-Domańska, Stanisław Domański, Jan Dembinski, Jan Jekiełek, Krystyna Klęczar, Wiesław Klęczar, Kazimierz Klęczar, Andrzej Molin, the Stupka family, the Kożusznik family, Krystyna Rybak, Robert Płotnicki, Jacek Dubois, Bożena Sławińska, Henryk Bleja, the Harat family, Beata Ciesielska-Mrozewicz, Felicjan Świerczyna, Piotr Wielopolski, the Mikusz family, Krzysztof Nahlik, Jan Chciuk-Celt, Stefan Pągowski,

Tadeusz M. Płużański, Marta Orłowska, Wanda Janta, Ryszard Stagenalski, and Stanisław Mróz.

Thank you to the following for looking over various stages of the manuscript: Anthony Polonsky, Robert Jan van Pelt, Nikolaus Wachsmann, Dariusz Stola, David Engel, Bernard Wasserstein, Yehuda Bauer, Wojciech Kozłowski, Hanna Radziejowska, Rafał Brodacki, Jeffrey Bines, Staffan Thorsell, Wojciech Markert, Kate Brown, Magdalena Gawin, Anna Bikont, Francis Harris, Rufus and Cherry Fairweather, Adam Fairweather, and Suzannah Lipscomb. I'd also like to thank the following for their insights and assistance: Mikołaj Kunicki, Krzysztof Szwagrzyk, Andrzej Kunert, Wojciech Frazik, Wiesław Jan Wysocki, Zygmunt Stanlik, Mieczysław Wójcik, Anna Początek, Jadwiga Kopeć, Olga Ivanova, Aliaksandr Paskievic, Leon Lauresh, Francois Guesnet, Wojciech Hałka, Małgorzata Zalewska, Elżbieta Przybysz, Marek Księżarczyk, Piotr Cuber, Mirosław Ganobis, Artur Szyndler of the Auschwitz Jewish Center, Bolesław Opaliński, Krzysztof Kredens, Alfred Wolfsteiner, Annett Bresan of the Sorbian Cultural Archive in Bautzen, Melaney Moisan, Martin Lohman, Bob Body, Heidi Rosskamp, Rolph Walker, Joan and Tom Fitzgibbon, and Michal Teital.

I was assisted in re-creating Witold's escape route by Bogdan Wasztyl, Mirosław Krzyszkowski, Zbigniew Klima and Marcin Dziubek of Stowarzyszenie Auschwitz Memento, Piotr Grzegorzek on the banks of the Soła, Bolesław Opaliński in Alwernia, Zbigniew Kumala in the Niepołomice Forest, Stanisław Kobiela in Bochnia. Special thanks to Ales Hitrun and Piotr Kubel for showing me Witold's home in Krupa, Łukasz Politański the battle scene in Wolbórz, Jacek Szczepański and Jacek Iwaszkiewicz the family holiday home in Legionowo, and George Dernowski and Maria Radożycka Paoletti the glorious beach of Porto San Giorgio. Thanks also to Jacek Zięba-Jasiński, who introduced my brother Adam and me to the Tatra courier routes, for which we are grateful.

None of this would have been possible without my wife, Chrissy, who put up with my long absences unflaggingly, listened to my stories about archives diligently, and pushed me to deepen my understanding of Witold with her edits. She and my three wonderful daughters, Amelie, Marianna, and Tess, are a constant reminder of what Witold was fighting for.

CHARACTERS

Abramow-Newerly, Barbara (1908–1973)—Music teacher in Warsaw whom Witold saved from a blackmailer on account of her Jewish ancestry. Her husband, the writer Igor Abramow-Newerly, was imprisoned in Auschwitz, and Witold supplied funds to Barbara for his support.

Bach-Zelewski, Erich von dem (1899–1972)—SS officer who supported the creation of a concentration camp at Auschwitz. As police chief in occupied Belarus, he oversaw the work of Einsatzgruppen-B, which was responsible for the mass murder of tens of thousands of Jews in 1941. In subsequent antipartisan operations in the region, his forces killed an estimated 235,000 people. In 1944, von dem Bach-Zelewski oversaw the suppression of the Warsaw Uprising at the cost of an estimated 185,000 lives. He escaped punishment at the Nuremberg trials after agreeing to testify against his colleagues. In 1951, Bach-Zelewski was sentenced to ten years in a labor camp for the murder of political opponents in the early 1930s. He died in prison in Munich without facing charges for crimes in Poland and the Soviet Union.

Bendera, Eugeniusz (1906–1988)—Polish mechanic who entered camp in January 1941 and worked in the SS garage. After learning he was due to be shot, he hatched a plan with Kazimierz Piechowski to steal an SS staff car and escape the camp.

Bernardini, Filippo (1884–1954)—The Papal Nuncio in Bern who relayed Holocaust evidence to the Vatican that likely included some of the material carried by the courier Napoleon Segieda on his journey to London.

Bischoff, Karl (1897–1950)—SS officer and architect who ran the camp's construction office, which was responsible for the building of Birkenau and its gas chambers. He escaped punishment after the war.

Bock, Hans (1901–c. 1944)—German kapo in charge of prisoner admissions to the hospital. He died of a likely morphine overdose in Birkenau around 1944.

Chimczak, Eugeniusz (1921–2012)—Secret police interrogator for Poland's Communist regime after the war. He led the investigation and torture of Witold following his arrest in 1946. In 1996, he was sentenced to 7.5 years in prison for his crimes but spared jail on health grounds.

Ciesielski, Edward "Edek" (1922–1962)—Arrested as a high school student and sent to Auschwitz April 1, 1941, Edek was recruited by Witold to the underground in the summer of 1941 and later escaped the camp with him. He was severely wounded in the Warsaw Uprising but survived, and later he wrote the first account of the underground. He died of a stroke before its publication in 1966.

Dalton, Hugh (1887–1962)—A Labour Party politician who joined Churchill's cabinet in 1940 as minister for economic warfare. In July of that year, he set up a clandestine organization called the Special Operations Executive to carry out subversion and sabotage activities on the continent. The SOE became the main point of contact for the Polish government-in-exile, and coordinated airdrops of equipment and agents like Napoleon Segieda into Poland.

Dering, Władysław (1903–1965)—Polish gynecologist whose arrest for underground activity in Warsaw and dispatch to Auschwitz in June 1940 was a spur to Witold's mission. He was Witold's first recruit in the camp, and he used his position in the hospital to save prisoners. In May 1943, Dering participated as a surgeon in the Nazis' experiments in sterilization using X-rays and chemical injections. He also participated as a surgeon in 115 castrations and hysterectomies of mostly Jewish victims. In 1944, Dering signed the Volksliste to confirm his status as an ethnic German and was released from the camp. After the war, he went to work for one of the SS doctors responsible for the program, Carl Clauberg, in his private clinic in Königshütte, Silesia. In 1947, the Polish government opened an investigation against him as a potential war criminal, prompting Dering to flee to London. At a subsequent war crimes trial in 1948 he was cleared of the charge, which he denied. Dering's case was the subject of further legal action in 1964, when he sued the author Leon Uris and his publisher William Kimber over a book that referred to a "Dr. Dehring" who had performed over 16,000 "sex operations in the camp." During the trial, Alina Brewda, a Jewish doctor who had known Dering before the war, and worked as a nurse in the camp, recounted that she had also been ordered to take part in the operations but had refused. The judge subsequently ordered the publisher to pay Dering a halfpenny in damages, the smallest coin of the realm. Dering was also required to pay legal costs for the defense of £25,000.

Diem, Rudolf (1896–1986)—Polish doctor who entered the camp in February 1941. As a nurse in the hospital, he opposed SS attempts to enlist Polish nurses in murderous practices.

Dipont, Marian (1913–1976)—Polish doctor who entered the camp in August 1940 and joined the hospital nursing staff. He was released in September 1941, and likely carried news of the SS gassing of Soviet POWs and hospital patients to Warsaw.

Dubois, Stanisław "Stasiek" (1901–1942)—Polish politician and writer who entered the camp in September 1940 and worked alongside Witold gathering evidence of Nazi crimes in the camp. His reports on prisoner mortality in the camp in June and July 1942 contained the first data on the Holocaust in Auschwitz to reach Warsaw and London.

Eden, Anthony (1897–1977)—British foreign secretary who announced the existence of the Holocaust on behalf of the Allies but subsequently proved reluctant to endorse rescue measures for Europe's Jews over concerns about their impact on the war effort.

Entress, Friedrich (1914–1947)—SS doctor in the camp hospital from December 1941 who played a key role in selecting patients for phenol injections. He was arrested by U.S. forces in 1945, convicted of war crimes, and executed in 1947.

Frank, Hans (1900–1946)—Governor of German-occupied Poland following the invasion. He was executed after standing trial for war crimes at Nuremberg.

Fritzsch, Karl (1903–1945)—Deputy commandant of Auschwitz who pioneered the use of the Zyklon B pesticide to gas inmates. He is believed to have died in Berlin.

Gawron, Wincenty (1908–1991)—Polish artist and wood engraver whom Witold recruited in the camp and used to pass on early warnings about the start of the Holocaust in Auschwitz. He later fought in the uprising before emigrating to the United States, where he worked as a carpenter and an engraver in Chicago.

Gawryłkiewicz, Mieczysław (1898–c. 1944)—Witold's commanding officer during the German invasion of Poland.

Goebbels, Joseph (1897–1945)—German minister of propaganda, committed suicide.

Grabner, Maximilian (1905–1948)—The head of the camp's Gestapo unit tasked with eliminating underground members. He directed some of the first gassings of Jewish families in Auschwitz. In 1943, he was arrested as part of an SS investigation into corruption in the camp and subsequently sentenced to twelve years in prison for carrying out extrajudicial killings in the penal block (a bizarre charge given the mass murder of Jews in the camp). After the war he was arrested by U.S. forces and handed over to the Polish authorities to stand trial in 1947. He was executed in 1948.

Himmler, Heinrich (1900–1945)—German police chief and head of the SS who oversaw the concentration camp system. He visited Auschwitz in

March 1941 to authorize its rapid expansion ahead of the invasion of the
Soviet Union, and again in July 1942 to observe the selection and gassing
of a transport of Dutch Jews. Committed suicide.

Höss, Rudolf (1900–1947)—Commandant of Auschwitz during Witold's
time in the camp. Tried by Polish authorities in 1947 and hung in Auschwitz in April of that year.

Jabłoński, Karol (1903–1953)—Polish officer and head of sabotage operations in Warsaw to whom Witold pitched the idea of attacking Auschwitz.

Jaster, Stanisław (1921–1943)—High school graduate who entered the
camp in November 1940. He escaped the camp in an SS car in June 1942
and carried a report from Witold about the mass murder of Jews in Birkenau to Warsaw. He was later executed by the underground for allegedly
being an informer. There is no evidence to suggest he was.

Jekiełek, Wojciech (1905–2001)—Polish social activist in the small town of
Osiek, outside the camp, who created an underground network to smuggle prisoners food, medicine, and messages. He collected data on Nazi
crimes in the camp and passed material to the courier Napoleon Segieda.

Karcz, Jan (1892–1943)—A cavalry officer who created an underground cell
in Birkenau that reported on the mass murder of Jews in Birkenau.

Karski, Jan (1914–2000)—Polish courier who brought an eyewitness account of liquidation of the Warsaw Ghetto and a transit point outside
the Bełżec death camp to London. In 1943, he traveled to Washington,
D.C., and presented his testimony to President Roosevelt.

Kielar, Wiesław (1919–1990)—Polish student who arrived in Auschwitz on
the first transport in June 1940. He subsequently worked as a nurse in the
hospital, where he witnessed the gassing of patients and Soviet POWs in
September 1941.

Klehr, Josef (1904–1988)—Austrian cabinetmaker who served as a non-
commissioned officer in the camp's hospital. He helped pioneer the use of

phenol injections to kill patients. He was also employed in the so-called disinfection unit that worked in the gas chambers of Birkenau. Klehr initially escaped prosecution at the end of the war, eventually standing trial in Frankfurt in 1963. The court convicted him of murder in 475 cases, assistance in the joint murder of at least 2,730 cases, and sentenced him to life imprisonment plus an additional fifteen years.

Kłodziński, Stanisław (1918–1990)—Medical student and activist who entered the camp in April 1941 and joined the underground. He worked as a hospital orderly and cared for Witold after he fell ill with typhus. Kłodziński decoded the messages of Napoleon Segieda and Wojciech Jekiełek that reached the camp in 1942.

Komorowski, Tadeusz (1895–1966)—Polish officer who assumed military control of the underground following the arrest of Stefan Rowecki in 1943. Komorowski made the decision to launch the Warsaw Uprising.

Korboński, Stefan (1901–1989)—Polish underground leader and memoirist.

Kosztowny, Witold (1913–?)—Polish biologist who arrived in the camp in June 1940 and subsequently worked in the hospital. At the request of the SS he set up a laboratory that bred typhus-infected lice for use as a vaccine. He subsequently deployed lice to attack kapos and SS men.

Kożusznikowa, Władysława (1905–1976)—Housewife from the village of Przecieszyn, near the camp, who worked with Helena Płotnicka to deliver supplies to prisoners. In July 1942, she delivered Napoleon Segieda's call for testimony about Nazi crimes.

Krankemann, Ernst (1895–1941)—German barber sentenced to indefinite detention over spousal abuse claims in 1935. He was among the first kapos to arrive in Auschwitz, where he ran the penal company of Jews and priests. He was likely murdered by prisoners on a transport bound for gassing at a facility outside Dresden.

Kühl, Juliusz (1913–1985)—Polish Jew and embassy official in Bern, Switzerland, who oversaw Jewish affairs and who likely chaperoned the courier Napoleon Segieda to meet the head of the legation, Aleksander Ładoś.

Küsel, Otto (1909–1984)—A German kapo in Auschwitz in charge of labor assignments. He saved Witold's life by offering him a stove-fitting job. He helped the underground switch between squads and tried to spare sick prisoners the worst jobs. He later joined one of the escapes in 1942 that smuggled Holocaust material out of the camp. Originally a drifter from Berlin, Otto was arrested by the German police for stealing and ended up in the concentration camp system. He was among the first kapos to arrive in the camp in May 1940.

Ładoś, Aleksander (1891–1963)—Polish diplomat and head of the legation in Bern, Switzerland, during the war. He was likely briefed by the courier Napoleon Segieda on the liquidation of the Warsaw Ghetto. He helped issue false passports from Latin American countries for fleeing Jews.

Norrman, Sven (1891–1979)—A Swedish courier for the Polish underground who carried reports about the SS's first gas experiments on Soviet POWs and hospital patients in Auschwitz from Warsaw to Stockholm. Norrman worked in Warsaw before the war as the country manager of the ASEA engineering firm. In May 1942, he smuggled out the first major report on the mass murder of Jews in German-occupied territories in the East.

Nowakowski, Leon (1908–1944)—Polish officer who commanded Witold's unit during the Warsaw Uprising.

Obojski, Eugeniusz "Gienek" (1920–1943)—An apprentice cook in Warsaw before the war, he arrived in the first transport to Auschwitz in June 1940 and was put in charge of the hospital's morgue. He was one of Witold's first recruits and an important smuggler of medicine and supplies into the camp, including the underground's short-lived radio transmitter.

Obora, Józef (1888–1974?)—Polish businessman from Bochnia who sheltered Witold, Edek, and Jan after their escape from the camp.

Ostrowska, Eleonora (1909–1995)—Witold's sister-in-law and his point of contact in Warsaw during his time in Auschwitz. She hosted the inaugural meeting of Tajna Armia Polska in her flat and was an active member of the underground throughout the war.

Paliński, Aleksander "Olek" (1894–1944)—A Polish clerk and musician from Warsaw who entered the camp in January 1941, Aleksander was recruited by Witold and later served as a messenger for him upon his release in 1942. Witold stayed with the Palińskis after his escape and worked with Olek to send aid to prisoners still in the camp.

Palitzsch, Gerhard (1913–1944)—SS officer and the camp's executioner. His wife died of typhus in 1942. He had sexual relations with at least one Jewish female prisoner and was transferred from the camp in 1943. He is thought to have died outside Budapest in 1944.

Piechowski, Kazimierz "Kazik" (1919–2017)—Polish student who entered Auschwitz as one of its first prisoners in June 1940. He escaped the camp dressed as an SS soldier in a German staff car in June 1942 with Eugeniusz Bendera, Józef Lempart, and Stanisław Jaster, who carried a report about the mass murder of Jews in Birkenau.

Piekarski, Konstanty "Kon" (1913–1990)—Polish engineering student and officer who arrived in Auschwitz on the same transport as Witold and was recruited by him into the underground in 1940. He helped Witold steal a radio transmitter from the SS construction office.

Pietrzykowski, Tadeusz "Teddy" (1917–1991)—Polish professional boxer and early recruit of Witold's in the camp. He defeated the German kapo Walter Dunning in a boxing match. He later witnessed one of the first gassings of Jews in Auschwitz and used lice infected with typhus to attack SS officers and kapos.

Pilecka, Maria (1899–1991)—Witold's wife.

Pilecka, Zofia (born 1933)—Witold's daughter.

Pilecki, Andrzej (born 1932)—Witold's son.

Płotnicka, Helena (1902–1944)—Housewife from the village of Przecieszyn, near the camp, who worked with Władysława Kożusznikowa to deliver supplies to prisoners. In July 1942, she delivered Napoleon Segieda's call for testimony about Nazi crimes. She was later arrested and brought to Auschwitz, where she died of typhus.

Płużański, Tadeusz (1920–2002)—Polish courier who carried Witold's reports on the Communist takeover of postwar Poland to the exile leader General Władysław Anders. His plan to attack members of the Polish secret police likely led to Witold's arrest. He was tried at the same time as Witold in 1948 and sentenced to death, later commuted to life imprisonment. He was released from prison in 1955.

Porębski, Henryk (1911–?)—Polish electrician who entered the camp in October 1940 and established the first links between the underground in the main camp and the Jewish squad that worked in the gas chambers of Birkenau.

Portal, Charles (1893–1971)—Head of the Royal Air Force, he considered and rejected Witold's first call to bomb the camp in 1941 and subsequent requests from the Polish government for greater air support for the underground.

Rawicz, Kazimierz (1896–1969)—Polish officer who entered the camp in January 1941 and united the underground's factions at Witold's request. In 1942, he devised a plan to stage an uprising to destroy the camp and enable a mass breakout.

Redzej, Jan (1904–1944)—Polish primary school teacher who entered the camp on the same transport as Witold and later conceived of the idea of escaping from the camp from an outside bakery. He died fighting alongside Witold in the Warsaw Uprising.

Romanowicz, Michał (?–1940)—A cavalry officer and an early recruit of Witold's who helped him switch work details and arranged the transmission of his first report from the camp via Aleksander Wielopolski.

Rowecki, Stefan (1895–1944)—Polish officer and leader of the underground in Warsaw until his arrest in 1943. He conceived of Witold's original mission to Auschwitz and later sent the courier Napoleon Segieda to the camp to investigate his reports.

Różycki, Witold (1906–?)—A Polish officer who entered the camp on the same transport as Witold. After the war, he accompanied him to Auschwitz.

Ruszczyński, Zbigniew (1914–1943)—Polish architect who entered the camp in 1941 and hatched the plan to steal a radio transmitter from the SS construction office.

Savery, Frank (1883–1965)—A British diplomat and consul in Warsaw in the 1930s. As acting head of the Foreign Office department that ran the Polish file during the war, he was a crucial gatekeeper for intelligence reaching London from Warsaw. He was likely the first Western official to grasp Auschwitz's central role in the Holocaust.

Schwela, Siegfried (1905–1942)—SS doctor who worked in the camp's hospital from 1941. He was a pioneer of injecting patients with phenol and took part in early gas experiments. He was likely killed by prisoners using typhus-infected lice in 1942.

Segieda, Napoleon (1908–1988)—Polish soldier before the war, who reached Britain in 1941 and was selected as courier. After training by the British Special Operations Executive as a courier, he parachuted into Poland in 1942. He subsequently investigated reports of Nazi atrocities in Auschwitz and returned to London to deliver his findings in February 1943.

Serafiński, Tomasz (1902–1966)—Polish lawyer and gentleman farmer whose identity card Witold used upon registering in the camp. After his escape from the camp, Witold stayed at his home in Nowy Wiśnicz. Tomasz presented Witold's plan to attack the camp to the underground in Krakow but was rejected. Later he was expelled from the organization for his support of Witold.

Schulte, Eduard (1891–1966)—German industrialist who was one of the first people to inform the Allies about the systematic extermination of the Jews in occupied Europe.

Siegruth, Johann (1903–1941)—One-armed German kapo in the warehouses beside Auschwitz. He was likely killed by prisoners in 1941.

Sieradzki, Makary (1900–1992)—Polish civil servant and underground member who sheltered Witold upon his return to Poland in 1945. He was later tried alongside Witold and sentenced to fifteen years in prison.

Sikorski, Władysław (1881–1943)—Polish general and former prime minister who became the leader of Poland's exile government in 1940.

Staller, Alois (1905–?)—A German kapo in Auschwitz who ran Witold's first block and selected him as a room supervisor. Staller was a former factory worker and Communist from the Rhineland. He had been arrested for putting up anti-Nazi posters in 1935 and detained indefinitely in Sachsenhausen a year later.

Stössel, Alfred "Fred" (1915–1943)—Ethnic German Pole who worked as a nurse in the camp's hospital. Witold entrusted him with guarding the underground's radio transmitter. He was later denounced to the SS by the underground for taking part in the phenol injecting of patients and executed.

Stupka, Helena (1898–1975)—Oświęcim resident who established the first links with inmates.

Surmacki, Władysław (1888–1942)—A Polish officer and engineer whose arrest in Warsaw for underground work and dispatch to Auschwitz in August 1940 prompted Witold's mission. In the camp, Surmacki worked as an inmate-surveyor in the construction office and established the underground's first links with the outside world via Helena Stupka.

Świętorzecki, Karol (1908–1991)—Karol was an early recruit of Witold's in the camp. They arrived on the same transport and worked in the same block as room supervisors. Witold used Karol to distribute news around the camp that was gleaned from the underground's illegal radio monitoring. Karol served as a messenger for Witold upon his release from the camp in May 1941.

Szelągowska, Maria (1905–1989)—Polish chemist and underground worker. In 1945, she helped Witold type up and edit his 1945 report. She later worked with him in Warsaw gathering intelligence and preparing reports for sending to the exile leader Władysław Anders. She was tried at the same time as Witold in 1948 and sentenced to death, later commuted to life imprisonment. She was released from prison in 1955.

Szpakowski, Sławomir "Sławek" (1908–?)—A postcard painter from Kielce who was arrested at the same time as Witold. The two men shared a mattress for their first few weeks in the camp and worked together on a demolition crew. He was released from the camp in 1941.

Trojnicki, Ferdynand (1895–?)—A Polish officer before the war and member of Tajna Armia Polska, Ferdynand was an early recruit of Witold's who helped arrange a job for him in the carpentry unit. He was subsequently released from the camp in November 1941 and likely brought news of Soviet gas experiments and creation of the Birkenau camp to Warsaw.

Westrych, Wilhelm (1894–1943)—Ethnic German from Poland who worked as the kapo of a carpentry workshop in Auschwitz. He gave Witold a job on this squad and shielded him from other kapos.

Wielopolski, Aleksander (1910–1980)—Polish engineer and member of the so-called Musketeers underground cell. He was arrested during the same roundup as Witold and sent to the camp. He was released in October 1940 carrying Witold's first report about the camp.

Wietschorek, Leo (1899–1942)—German kapo who ran punishment drills with prisoners. He was notorious for raping teenage boys in the camp and murdering them. He was likely killed by prisoners using typhus-infected lice in 1942.

Wise, Stephen (1874–1949)—American Jewish rabbi who received an early warning about Hitler's order to exterminate Europe's Jews in August 1942. He agreed not to publicize the information until a U.S. State Department investigation could confirm the details. In November 1942 he gave a press conference announcing that the Germans had killed two million Jews.

Włodarkiewicz, Jan (1900–c. 1942)—Polish officer who fought as a partisan with Witold in the weeks after the German invasion. In November 1939 he formed an underground cell in Warsaw with Witold known as Tajna Armia Polska. He suggested Witold's name to the underground leadership for the mission to Auschwitz.

Zabawski, Edmund (1910–?)—Teacher from outside the town of Bochnia in southern Poland. He introduced Witold to his fellow escaper Jan Redzej and contacted his family on Witold's behalf to shelter them upon leaving the camp. He later passed on to the underground leadership Witold's plans to attack the camp.

NOTES

Note on Text

1. Figures courtesy of Wojciech Płosa.
2. Pilecki, *The Auschwitz*, loc. 521; Pilecki, [List], October 19, 1945, PUMST, BI 6991, p. 2.

Chapter 1: Invasion

1. Pilecki, [Pod Lidą], Materiały, vol. 223c, APMA-B, p. 36; Dmytruk, "Z Novogo," cited in Brown, *A Biography*, loc. 954; Tumielewicz, [Kronika], p. 229; Lacki, "Burza," pp. 229–30; Pilecka, [Dzieje], vol. 223c, APMA-B, p. 104; Pilecki, [W jaki], PUMST, p. 8.
2. Kochanski, *The Eagle*, p. 57; Wilmot, [Notes], LHCMA, LH 15/15/150/2.
3. General mobilization took place on August 30, but covert mobilization had begun August 24. Kochanski, *The Eagle*, p. 57; Pilecki, [W jaki], PUMST, BI 6991, p. 8; Лаўрэш, "13 траўня," pp. 15–9; Лаўрэш, "Ліочына," p. 76; Brochowicz-Lewiński, [Raport], CAW, I.302.4. 466.
4. Pilecki, Interview, May 21, 2016.
5. Gawron, *Ochotnik*, p. 68; Pilecki, Akta sprawy, Protokół przesłuchania podejrzanego Tadeusza Płużańskiego, Materiały, vol. 223, APMA–B, p. 197; Pieńkowska, [Wspomnienia], p. 12; Budarkiewicz, "Wspomnienia," in Cyra, *Rotmistrz*, p. 24.
6. Tracki, *Młodość*, p. 112; Pilecka, [Dzieje], Materiały, vol. 223c, APMA-B, pp. 94–96; Pilecki, [Życiorys], Materiały, vol. 223c, APMA-B, no pages given; Tracki, *Młodość*, pp. 178–79, p. 185. The Sukurcze estate was inherited on his mother's side. The Pileckis' land was mostly confiscated by the Russian state after his grandfather's participation in the 1863 January Uprising against Tsar Alexander II; Cyra, *Rotmistrz*, p. 22.

7. For cooperative details see AAN, 2/213/0/9/8498, and AAN, 2/213/0/9/8499; Pilecka-Optułowicz, Interview, July 14, 2016; Pilecki, Krzyszkowski, Wasztyl, *Pilecki*, p. 30; Pilecki, Interview, February 1, 2016; Pilecki, Krzyszkowski, Wasztyl, *Pilecki*, p. 30; Tracki, *Młodość*, p. 187, pp. 188–91.

8. Kochanski, *The Eagle*, pp. 30–32; Bikont, *The Crime*, pp. 11–26, Ringelblum, *Polish*, p. 11; Brzoza, Sowa, *Historia*, p. 135; Brown, *A Biography*, loc. 534; Лаўрэш, "Яўрэі," pp. 141–54; Лаўрэш, "Лідчына," p. 64; Gelman, *Jewish*, cited in Manor, Ganusovitch, Lando, *Book of Lida*, p. 83; Ярмонт, *В тени*, pp. 93–94, cited in Лаўрэш, "Лідчына," p. 76.

9. Pilecki, [W jaki], PUMST, BI 6991, p. 7; Pilecki, Interview, February 2, 2016; Gombrowicz, *Polish*, p. 32. Witold evicted a Jewish tenant who'd leased the estate's land in 1922. There is no evidence to suggest racial animus behind the incident. Pilecka, [Dzieje], Materiały, vol. 223c, APMA-B, pp. 15–18. Cooperatives in Poland had a role in boosting the economic interests of their communities, which often had an ethnic dimension. Piechowski, *Byłem*, pp. 17–18.

10. Markert, 77, p. 53; Pilecki, Interview, October 10, 2017; Pilecka-Optułowicz, Interview, May 17, 2016.

11. Pilecki, Interview, February 1, 2016, and October 10, 2017.

12. Pilecki, Interview, October 10, 2017.

13. Pilecki, Interview, May 21, 2017; Pilecki, [Pod Lidą], Materiały, vol. 223c, APMA-B, p. 26.

14. Pilecki, Interview, February 1, 2016. Since the Polish Army was caught in midmobilization and never fully mobilized, it was outnumbered 1.5:1 in infantry, 3:1 in artillery, and 5:1 in tanks. Perhaps slightly more than 700,000 Polish troops made it into battle, mostly in piecemeal and disorganized fashion, compared with roughly one million Germans. Komisja, *Polskie*, vol. 1, part 1, p. 191, p. 247; Kochanski, *The Eagle*, p. 46, pp. 55–57; Thomas, *German*, p. 8.

15. Pilecki, [W jaki], PUMST, BI 6991, p. 2, p. 8; Gawron, *Ochotnik*, pp. 86–99.

16. Witowiecki, *Tu mówi*, p. 54, Markert, 77, p. 55; Jezierski, [Wspomnienia], CAW, I.302.4.466.

17. Witowiecki, *Tu mówi*, p. 54; Naruszewicz, *Wspomnienia*, p. 177. For travel in freight cars see also Bujniewicz, *Kolejnictwo*, p. 58.

18. Szpilman, *The Pianist*, p. 22; Richie, *Warsaw*, pp. 110–14.

19. Witowiecki, *Tu mówi*, p. 76; Gnatowski, [Wspomnienia], CAW, I.302.4.466.

20. Blum, *O broń*, pp. 20–41; Jezierski, [Wspomnienia], CAW, I.302.4.466. Special thanks to David McQuaid and Łukasz Politański for ascertaining the right dates for when Witold reached Piotrków Trybunalski.

21. Pilecki, [W jaki], PUMST, BI 6991, p. 8.

22. Pilecki, [W jaki], PUMST, BI 6991, p. 8; Schmidtke, [Wspomnienia], CAW, I.302.4.466.

23. Stoves, *Die 1.*, p. 57.

24. Stoves, *Die 1.*, p. 57; Pilecki, [W jaki], PUMST, BI 6991, p. 8; Blum, *O broń*, pp. 20–41; Jezierski, [Wspomnienia], CAW, I.302.4.466.

25. Blum, *O broń*, pp. 20–41; Witold doesn't write much of the scene in his memoir. "Tanks on the road. My horse is dead." But the very terseness is revealing. In the margins he also wrote in blue pencil, "I made an oath that night, harder for me than any other decision." He doesn't say what that oath might be, but knowing Witold he likely swore to fight on to the bitter end. Pilecki, [W jaki], PUMST, BI 6991, p. 9.

26. Pilecki, [W jaki], PUMST, BI 6991, p. 9.

27. Kochanski, *The Eagle*, p. 69; Wilkinson, *Foreign*, p. 72.

28. Kochanski, *The Eagle*, pp. 48–49; Pilecki, [W jaki], PUMST, BI 6991, p. 9.

29. Wilkinson, *Foreign*, p. 73.

30. Pilecki, [W jaki], PUMST, BI 6991, p. 10.

31. Pilecki, [W jaki], PUMST, BI 6991, p. 10. A group of British soldiers from the military mission were trying to rescue people from the rubble and managed to extract the Polish wife of the embassy's postmaster. It took several more days for the delegation to exit the country. Colin Gubbins, who was to play an important role in Witold's story, was among the party. Wilkinson, *Foreign*, p. 77.

32. Pilecki, [W jaki], PUMST, BI 6991, p. 10; Karski, *Story*, p. 11. Karski's name before the war was Jan Kozielewski, but he is better known by his *nom de guerre*, which he subsequently adopted.

33. Pilecki, [W jaki], PUMST, BI 6991, p. 11.

34. Pilecki, [W jaki], PUMST, BI 6991, p. 11.

35. Kochanski, *The Eagle*, pp. 76–79.

36. Kochanski, *The Eagle*, pp. 89–90.

37. Pilecki, [W jaki], PUMST, BI 6991, p. 11; Pilecki, Interview, March 11, 2016.

38. Pilecki, [W jaki], PUMST, BI 6991, p. 13.

39. Pilecki, [W jaki], PUMST, BI 6991, p. 13.

40. Pilecki, [W jaki], PUMST, BI 6991, p. 13.

41. Widelec, *Diary*, cited in Margolis, *Memorial*, p. 422; Lewitt, *When*, cited in Margolis, *Memorial*, p. 442; Nejmark, *The Destruction*, cited in Margolis, *Memorial*, p. 445; Dekel, [Browar], p. 15, p. 101; Hodubski, Protokół, Ostrów Mazowiecka, August 5, 1947, IPN, Bl 407/63, K 296/47, GK 264/63,

SOŁ 63, pp. 0343–44; Słuchoński, [Wspomnienia], IP, 019 Sluchonski_ Artur_2_skan_AK; Pilecki, Interview, March 11, 2016.

42. Pilecki, Interview, March 11, 2016.
43. Pilecki, [W jaki], PUMST, BI 6991, p. 14.

Chapter 2: Occupation

1. Pilecki, [W jaki], PUMST, BI 6991, p. 14.
2. Nowak, *Courier*, p. 58; Richie, *Warsaw*, p. 147; Goebbels, *Diaries*, p. 37; Landau, *Kronika*, vol. I, p. 48; Korboński, *Fighting*, p. 7; Bryan, *Warsaw*, p. 19, p. 25; Goebbels, *Diaries*, p. 37. Bryan estimated that between ten thousand and thirty thousand shells hit the city daily. Bryan, *Warsaw*, p. 24; Goebbels, *Diaries*, p. 37.
3. Frank, *Extracts*, p. 368, cited in O'Connor, *Butcher*, loc. 2008.
4. Olsson, *For Your*, p. 203.
5. Snyder, *Black*, loc. 423; Lukas, *Forgotten*, loc. 72. The first group of forced labor in Germany was drawn from Polish POWs. Herbert, *Hitler's*, pp. 61–94. The use of POWs for labor was prohibited under the Geneva Convention, but following the German dismantling of the Polish state, the prisoners were "released" from their status. Tooze, *Wages*, loc. 6701. Two hundred thousand more workers from Poland had arrived in Germany by the spring of 1941; Frank, *Extracts*, p. 110, cited in Kochanski, *The Eagle*, p. 98.
6. Snyder, *Black*, loc. 196; Hilberg, *The Destruction*, pp. 64–74; Winstone, *Dark*, loc. 1693.
7. Pilecki, [W jaki], PUMST, BI 6991, p. 14; Bartoszewski, *1859*, p. 91; Sobolewicz, *But I*, p. 70; Lukas, *Forgotten*, loc. 942. Polish poisoning attempts became sophisticated over time. See Rowecki, [Meldunek], August 13, 1941, in Iranek-Osmecki et al., *Armia*, vol. II, p. 36; Ostrowska, [Wspomnienia 1], p. 2; Malinowski, *Tajna*, p. 27; Nowak, *Courier*, p. 59; Frank, *Extracts*, p. 5896; Bartoszewski, *1859*, p. 99.
8. Ostrowska, [Wspomnienia 1], p. 2; Ostrowski, Interview, May 1, 2016; Ostrowski, Interview, October 10, 2017.
9. Ostrowski, Interview, May 1, 2016; Tereszczenko, *Wspomnienia*, p. 83.
10. *Znak*, [Deklaracja], AAN, 2/2505/0/-/194, p. 3; Tereszczenko, Interview, November 1, 2016; Ostrowska, [Wspomnienia 1], p. 3.
11. Pilecki, [W jaki], PUMST, BI 6991, pp. 14–15.
12. Pilecki, [W jaki], PUMST, BI 6991, p. 14; Malinowski, *Tajna*, p. 29.
13. Garliński, *Fighting*, p. 43; Nowak, *Courier*, p. 71; Korboński, *Fighting*, p.

NOTES · 415

11, p. 157; Thorsell, *Warszawasvenskarna*, p. 134; Szarota, *Okupowanej*, pp. 223–25.

14. Korboński, *Fighting*, p. 183; Szpilman, *The Pianist*, p. 48; Garliński, *Fighting*, p. 43; Nowak, *Courier*, p. 71; Korboński, *Fighting*, p. 11.

15. Korboński, *Fighting*, p. 219; Gistedt, *Od operetki*, p. 92.

16. Pilecki, [W jaki], PUMST, BI 6991, p. 14; Unknown author, [Zasady konspiracji], AAN, 2/2505/0/-/194.

17. Rablin, Oświadczenia, vol. 29, APMA-B, p. 82.

18. Rablin, Oświadczenia, vol. 29, APMA-B, p. 82.

19. Pilecki, [W jaki], PUMST, BI 6991, p. 14; Unknown author, [Zasady konspiracji], AAN, 2/2505/0/-/194.

20. Korboński, *Fighting*, p. 183; Szpilman, *The Pianist*, p. 48; Garliński, *Fighting*, p. 43; Nowak, *Courier*, p. 71.

21. Malinowski, *Tajna*, p. 100.

22. Szpilman, *The Pianist*, p. 54; Dwork, van Pelt, *Auschwitz*, p. 144.

23. Tooze, *Wages*, loc. 6789; Szpilman, *The Pianist*, p. 54; Szarota, *Okupowanej*, p. 203. See *Ziemniaki na pierwsze . . . , na drugie . . . , na trzecie* (Potatoes for the first meal . . . for the second meal . . . for the third meal) by Zofia Serafińska or *Sto potraw z ziemniaków* (One hundred potato dishes) by Bolesława Kawecka-Starmachowa; Pilecki, [Raport 1945], PUMST, BI 874, p. 5.

24. Allen, *The Fantastic*, loc. 212. Several ghettos had already been created in Poland at this point, the first in Piotrków Trybunalski in October 1939. Winstone, *Dark*, loc. 1856; Frank, *Extracts*, p. 5896.

25. Pilecki, [W jaki], PUMST, BI 6991, p. 14; Bartoszewski, *1859*, p. 70.

26. Malinowski, *Tajna*, p. 53, p. 100; Nowak, *Courier*, p. 63.

27. Malinowski, *Tajna*, p. 39; Zwerin, *Swing*, p. 64.

28. Zwerin, *Swing*, p. 64.

29. Pilecki, interview, May 17, 2016; Pilecka-Optułowicz, Interview, May 17, 2016; Łapian, Interview, May, 15, 2017.

30. Pilecki, Interview, May 16, 2016.

31. Szwajkowski, [Zeznania], IPN, S/139/12/Zn, pp. 137–42; Zawadzki, [Zeznania], IPN, S/139/12/Zn, pp. 124–28; Roth, *Murder*, cited in Zalc, Bruttman, *Microhistories*, p. 227; see footnote 55 for anti-Semitic attitudes; Gutman, Krakowski, *Unequal*, p. 48; Zimmerman, *The Polish*, p. 74, p. 83.

32. Gross, *Polish*, p. 254; Tereszczenko, *Wspomnienia*, p. 85; Tereszczenko, Interview, November 1, 2016.

33. *Znak*, 06.05.1940/6–7, cited in Malinowski, *Tajna*, pp. 12–15. A later edition

of *Znak* rejected the Nazis' brutal treatment of Jews, which the writers felt was alien to the Polish culture. Nonetheless, "nothing changes the fact, that Jews are in Poland an element unwanted and even harmful, and the elimination of their influences from our national life will still be our main purpose." *Znak*, 1940/27, AN, 1925, pp. 3–4.

34. Pilecki, [W jaki], PUMST, BI 6991, p. 15; Tereszczenko, Interview, November 1, 2016; Nowak, *Courier*, p. 39. Nowak, who went on to become one of the most celebrated couriers of the war, had been an early contributor to *Znak*, but stopped working with them because of their political stance. He noted in his memoir at one point, "Genuine ideological motives were quite frequently mixed with the ambitions of individuals planning for their personal and political post-war futures" (Nowak, *Courier*, p. 67). Jan Włodarkiewicz's own views on Jews are not recorded, but it's likely they aligned closely with those espoused in *Znak*.

35. *Znak*, May 1940/6–7, cited in Malinowski, *Tajna*, pp. 12–15; Faliński, "Ideologia," pp. 57–76; Kochanski, *The Eagle*, p. 97; Pilecki, [W jaki], PUMST, BI 6991, p. 15; Pilecki, Wspomnienia, vol. 179, APMA-B, p. 312.

36. Pluta-Czachowski, . . . *gdy przychodzi* . . . , cited in Szarota, *Stefan*, p. 91, p. 86; Rakoń, [Meldunek nr. 15], in Czarnocka et al., *Armia*, vol. I, p. 194. The courier Jan Karski makes a similar point in his reporting to the underground in 1940 (Karski, cited in Zimmerman, *The Polish*, p. 73).

37. Zimmerman, *The Polish*, p. 67.

38. Favez, *The Red*, pp. 136–37; Zimmerman, *The Polish*, p. 67; Fleming, *Auschwitz*, p. 32; Wood, *Karski*, loc. 1109; Winstone, *Dark*, loc. 1244.

39. Pilecki, [W jaki], PUMST, BI 6991, p. 14.

40. Pilecki, [W jaki], PUMST, BI 6991, p. 15; Pilecki, Wspomnienia, vol. 179, APMA-B, p. 313.

41. Pilecki, [W jaki], PUMST, BI 6991, p. 15.

42. *Znak*, 15.07.1940/14, cited in Malinowski, *Tajna*, pp. 173–75; Znak, [Deklaracja], AAN, 2/2505/0/-/194, pp. 2–3. Jan's declaration made no specific reference to Jews, but its language is typical of nationalists of the time—he sought to define Polishness along religious and sectarian lines. Pilecki, [W jaki], PUMST, BI 6991, p. 15; Pilecki, Wspomnienia, vol. 179, APMA-B, p. 313.

43. Malinowski, *Tajna*, p. 70.

44. Winstone, *The Dark*, loc. 1329; Lasik et al., *Auschwitz*, vol. I, pp. 49–50; Bartoszewski, *1859*, p. 157; Cyra, *Rotmistrz*; Pieńkowska, [Wspomnienia 1], AAN, 2/2505/0/-/194, p. 2.

45. Malinowski, *Tajna*, p. 88; Cyra, "Dr Władysław," p. 74; Kantyka, Kantyka,

Władysław, in *idem, Oddani*, p. 266. Only the woman's surname, Żurawska, is known.

46. Malinowski, *Tajna*, p. 54, p. 88; Ostrowska, [Wspomnienia 1], p. 4; Wachsmann, *KL*, pp. 7–9; Tabeau, [Sprawozdanie], in *Zeszyty* (1991), p. 105; Wachsmann, *KL*, p. 191.

47. Wachsmann, *KL*, pp. 6–9. Auschwitz was originally conceived as a transit facility for Polish laborers traveling to the Reich, but it seems that the camp was quickly repurposed to serve as a more conventional concentration camp. Rees, *Auschwitz*, loc. 643; Steinbacher, *Auschwitz*, p. 22, Dwork, van Pelt, *Auschwitz*, p. 166.

48. Malinowski, *Tajna*, p. 54, p. 88; Ostrowska, [Wspomnienia 1], p. 4. It's not clear exactly how many prisoners had died in Auschwitz by the end of August. Records are incomplete, and only the name of one murdered inmate has been preserved.

49. Pilecki, [W jaki], PUMST, BI 6991, p. 15; Malinowski, *Tajna*, p. 100. Malinowski says the meeting took place at the end of August, but this contradicts the timeline.

50. Pilecki, [W jaki], PUMST, BI 6991, p. 15.

51. Pilecki, [W jaki], PUMST, BI 6991, p. 15; Ostrowska, [Wspomnienia 1], p. 4; Gawron, *Ochotnik*, p. 114; Pilecki, Akta sprawy, Zeznanie w śledztwie Witolda Pileckiego, ASS MON, vol. 1, p. 74.

52. Pilecki, [W jaki], PUMST, BI 6991, p. 15.

53. Malinowski, *Tajna*, p. 54; Gawron, *Ochotnik*, p. 114.

54. Pilecki, [W jaki], PUMST, BI 6991, p. 15.

55. Pilecki, [W jaki], PUMST, BI 6991, p. 15; Pilecki, Interview, February 1, 2016.

56. Winstone, *The Dark*, loc. 1371; Pilecki, [W jaki], PUMST, BI 6991, p. 15; Landau, *Kronika*, vol. I, pp. 635–36; Ostrowska, [Wspomnienia 1], p. 3.

57. Pilecki, [W jaki], PUMST, BI 6991, p. 15; Pilecki, Wspomnienia, vol. 179, APMA-B, p. 313.

58. Dering, [Wspomnienia], p. 11; Malinowski, *Tajna*, p. 33.

59. Pilecki, [W jaki], PUMST, BI 6991, p. 15; Pilecki, Interview, February 1, 2016.

60. Pilecki, Interview, February 1, 2016; Ostrowski, Interview, March 9, 2016.

61. Pilecki, [Raport 1945], PUMST, BI 874, p. 46.

62. Cyra, *Rotmistrz*, p. 45; Ostrowska, [Wspomnienia 1], p. 5.

63. Ostrowski, Interview, March 9, 2016; Ostrowska, [Wspomnienia 1], p. 5.

64. Ostrowska, [Wspomnienia 1], p. 5.

65. Ostrowska, Wspomnienia, vol. 179, APMA-B, p. 148; Gorzkowski, *Kroniki*, p. 51.

66. Pilecki, [Raport 1945], PUMST, BI 874, p. 1; Bartoszewski, *Mój*, pp. 12–14.

Chapter 3: Arrival

1. Czech, *Auschwitz*, p. 29; Bartoszewski, *Mój*, pp. 14–16; Korboński, *Fighting*, p. 49; Pilecki, [Raport 1945], PUMST, BI 874, p. 1; Bartoszewski, *Mój*, pp. 16–17; Kowalski, *Niezapomniana*, pp. 154–58; Ptakowski, *Oświęcim*, pp. 12–13; Redzej, [Raport 1943], AAN, 202/XVIII/1, p. 34.

2. Pilecki, [Raport 1945], PUMST, BI 874, p. 1.

3. Pilecki, [Raport 1945], PUMST, BI 874, pp. 1–2; Piekarski, *Escaping*, pp. 8–12; Redzej, [Raport 1943], AAN, 202/XVIII/1, p. 34; Bartoszewski, *Mój*, p. 18; Nowacki, Wspomnienia, vol. 151, APMA-B, p. 133.

4. Pilecki, [Raport 1945], PUMST, BI 874, p. 2; Kowalski, *Niezapomniana*, p. 161; Bogusz, Interview, December 19, 2015; Pilecki, [Raport 1945], PUMST, BI 874, p. 4.

5. Pilecki, [Raport 1945], PUMST, BI 874, p. 3.

6. Pilecki, [Raport 1945], PUMST, BI 874, p. 3; Kowalski, *Niezapomniana*, p. 163; Stapf, Wspomnienia, vol. 110, APMA-B, p. 75–81.

7. Pilecki, [Raport 1945], PUMST, BI 874, p. 3.

8. Pilecki, [Raport 1945], PUMST, BI 874, p. 4; Stapf, Oświadczenia, vol. 29, APMA-B, p. 89; Albin, Interview, May 21, 2016; D-Au-I-2, *Häftlings-Personal-Karte*, v. 7, APMA-B, p. 234; Pilecki, [Raport 1945], PUMST, BI 874, p. 4.

9. Pilecki, [Raport 1945], PUMST, BI 874, p. 4; Bartoszewski, *Wywiad*, p. 46; Kowalski, *Niezapomniana*, pp. 164–65.

10. Lasik et al., *Auschwitz*, vol. I, pp. 66–68; Nowacki, Wspomnienia, vol. 151, APMA-B, p. 133.

11. Pilecki, [Raport 1945], PUMST, BI 874, p. 4; Piekarski, *Escaping*, p. 16.

12. Siedlecki, *Beyond*, p. 149; Pilecki, [Raport 1945], PUMST, BI 874, p. 4; Redzej, [Raport 1943], AAN, 202/XVIII/1, p. 36a; Ciesielski [Raport 1943], AAN, 202/XVIII/1, p. 55; Bartoszewski, *Mój*, p. 20; Świętorzecki, Oświadczenia, vol. 76, APMA-B, p. 95; Nowacki, Wspomnienia, vol. 151, APMA-B, p. 65.

13. Kowalski, *Niezapomniana*, p. 166; Fejkiel, *Medycyna*, in Bidakowski, Wójcik, *Pamiętniki*, p. 412; Pilecki, [Raport 1945], PUMST, BI 874, p. 4.

14. Dering, [Wspomnienia], p. 9; Piekarski, *Escaping*, p. 23; Kowalski, *Niezapomniana*, p. 166.

15. Gawron, *Ochotnik*, p. 17; Paczyński, Oświadczenia, vol. 100, APMA-B, p. 95; Piekarski, *Escaping*, p. 22; Głowa, Wspomnienia, vol. 94, APMA-B, p. 117.

16. FBI, FAP 1, HA 29, Bl. 4908–14; NRW, W, GSTA Hamm 3369,3367 Q 211 a.

17. Fejkiel, *Medycyna*, in Bidakowski, Wójcik, *Pamiętniki*, p. 413; Świętorzecki, Oświadczenia, vol. 76, APMA-B, p. 95.

18. Wachsmann, *KL*, pp. 60–63.

19. Rees, *Auschwitz*, loc. 425.

20. Iwaszko et al., *Auschwitz*, vol. II, p. 66; Szczepański, video recollection, July 14, 1995, APMA-B, V-246.

21. Pilecki, [Raport 1945], PUMST, BI 874, p. 4.

22. Pilecki, [Raport 1945], PUMST, BI 874, p. 19; Redzej, [Raport 1943], AAN, 202/XVIII/1, p. 45a; Piekarski, *Escaping*, loc. 325; Piekarski, *Escaping*, p. 25; Siedlecki, *Beyond*, p. 155. Fritzsch supervised roll calls in his role as Schutzhaftlagerführer or Leader of the Protective Custody Camp.

23. Fejkiel, *Medycyna*, in Bidakowski, Wójcik, *Pamiętniki*, p. 419.

24. Bartoszewski, *Mój*, p. 20; Fejkiel, *Medycyna*, in Bidakowski, Wójcik, *Pamiętniki*, p. 419.

25. Bartoszewski, *Mój*, pp. 21–22.

26. Szczepański, video recollection, July 14, 1995, APMA-B, V-246; Iwaszko et al., *Auschwitz*, vol. II, p. 70; Kowalski, *Niezapomniana*, p. 223; Siedlecki, *Beyond*, p. 155; Ciesielski, [Raport 1943], AAN, 202/XVIII/1, p. 7; Redzej, [Raport 1943], AAN, 202/XVIII/1, p. 34, p. 34a; Piekarski, *Escaping*, p. 27.

27. Siedlecki, *Beyond*, p. 155; Kowalski, *Niezapomniana*, p. 233; Langbein, *People*, p. 133; Langbein, *People*, p. 65; Siedlecki, *Beyond*, p. 155; Pilecki, *The Auschwitz*, loc. 563; Pilecki, [Raport 1945], PUMST, BI 874, p. 3.

28. Langbein, *People*, p. 70; Wachsmann, *KL*, p. 501. See Gawron, Wspomnienia, vol. 48, APMA-B, pp. 9–13 and p. 38 for description of Jewish prisoners being denounced by fellow Poles.

29. D-Au1-2, 1-5, APMA-B, cited in Czech, *Auschwitz*, p. 373; Iwaszko et al., *Auschwitz*, vol. II, p. 372, p. 374.

30. Iwaszko et al., *Auschwitz*, vol. II, pp. 371–80.

31. Kowalski, *Niezapomniana*, p. 188, p. 191; Siedlecki, *Beyond*, p. 152.

32. Wachsmann, *KL*, p. 497; Bielecki, *Kto ratuje*, p. 130; Smoleń, "Czarna," p. 4; Kowalski, *Niezapomniana*, p. 175.

33. Müller, *Eyewitness*, p. 5; Langbein, *People*, p. 70.
34. Piekarski, *Escaping*, p. 85; Świętorzecki, Interview, February 14, 1972.
35. Piekarski, *Escaping*, p. 33; Ziółkowski, *Byłem*, p. 31; Kowalski, *Niezapomniana*, p. 234.
36. Kowalski, *Niezapomniana*, p. 233; Szpakowski, Interview, January 31, 2017; Wachsmann, *KL*, p. 501.
37. Iwaszko et al., *Auschwitz*, vol. II, pp. 294–96; Favez, *The Red*, p. 27, pp. 137–41.
38. Lasik et al., *Auschwitz*, vol. I, pp. 66–68; Nosal, Oświadczenia, vol. 132, APMA-B, p. 165; Bartys, Oświadczenia, vol. 63, APMA-B, p. 135.
39. Piekarski, *Escaping*, p. 21.
40. Piekarski, *Escaping*, p. 21.
41. Piekarski, *Escaping*, pp. 30–32.
42. Piekarski, *Escaping*, p. 30.
43. Iwaszko et al., *Auschwitz*, vol. II, p. 311; Diem, Wspomnienia, vol. 172, APMA-B, p. 11, p. 14, p. 30.
44. Iwaszko et al., *Auschwitz*, vol. II, p. 61; Bartoszewski, *Mój*, pp. 36–38; Fejkiel, *Medycyna*, in Bidakowski, Wójcik, *Pamiętniki*, p. 461; Kowalski, *Niezapomniana*, pp. 172–73.
45. Szczepański, video recollection, July 14, 1995, APMA-B, V-246.
46. Urbanek, Oświadczenia, vol. 44, APMA-B, p. 8; Ciesielski, Wspomnienia, p. 40; Pilecki, [Raport 1945], PUMST, BI 874, pp. 5–6; Dering, [Wspomnienia], p. 70; Dembiński, [Raport], PUMST, A. 680, p. 593.

Chapter 4: Survivors

1. Kowalczyk, *Barbed*, p. 112; Pilecki, [Raport 1945], PUMST, BI 874, p. 11.
2. Iwaszko et al., *Auschwitz*, vol. II, pp. 312–15; Fejkiel, *Więźniarski*, pp. 46–49; Piekarski, *Escaping*, p. 36; Strzelecka, *Voices*, vol. 3, p. 10; Dering, [Wspomnienia], p. 24; Diem, Wspomnienia, vol. 172, APMA-B, p. 45, p. 77, p. 122.
3. Iwaszko et al., *Auschwitz*, vol. II, p. 216; Langbein, *People*, pp. 50–84; Fejkiel, *Więźniarski*, p. 216.
4. Dering, [Wspomnienia], p. 11, p. 14, p. 41.
5. Pilecki, [Raport 1945], PUMST, BI 874, p. 20; Czech, *Kalendarz*, p. 19. A Jewish prisoner, Dawid Wongczewski, appears to have died during the roll call, the camp's first known Jewish victim. This formula is from an SS study carried out by Dr. Hans Münch between 1943 and 1944, although he only wrote up the

results in 1947 while awaiting trial in Poland for war crimes. Münch, *Analyzis*, Materiały, vol. 35, APMA-B, p. 93; Collingham, *The Taste*, loc. 293.

6. Pozimski, Wspomnienia, vol. 52, APMA-B, p. 165; Dering, [Wspomnienia], p. 14; Wachsmann, *KL*, p. 209; Piekarski, *Escaping*, pp. 37–38; Redzej, [Raport 1943], AAN, 202/XVIII/1, pp. 34a–35, p. 37; Albin, *List*, p. 54; Świętorzecki, Oświadczenia, vol. 76, APMA-B, p. 96; Pilecki, [Raport 1945], PUMST, BI 874, p. 35; Bartoszewski, *Mój*, p. 32; Piątkowska, Wspomnienia, vol. 66, APMA-B, pp. 116–19; Butterly, Shepherd, *Hunger*, p. 134.

7. Lasik et al., *Auschwitz*, vol. I, p. 171; Piekarski, *Escaping*, p. 23, p. 28; Świętorzecki, Interview, February 14, 1970.

8. Pilecki, [Raport 1945], PUMST, BI 874, p. 6; Dering, [Wspomnienia], p. 70.

9. Piekarski, *Escaping*, p. 35.

10. Iwaszko et al., *Auschwitz*, vol. II, pp. 378–80; Świętorzecki, Oświadczenia, vol. 76, APMA-B, p. 96; Piekarski, *Escaping*, p. 35; Kowalski, *Niezapomniana*, p. 177; Ciesielski, [Raport 1943], AAN, 202/XVIII/1, p. 6; Radlicki, *Kapo*, pp. 64–65; Siciński, "Z psychopatologii," pp. 126–30; [Krankemann], HHStAW Fonds 430/1, no. 9402.

11. Pilecki, [Raport 1945], PUMST, BI 874, p. 6; Ciesielski, [Raport 1943], AAN, 202/XVIII/1, p. 7.

12. Pilecki, [Raport 1945], PUMST, BI 874, p. 6.

13. Pilecki, [Raport 1945], PUMST, BI 874, p. 7. Two other gravel pits existed in 1940; one beside the camp abattoir, the other adjacent to the penal block.

14. Pilecki, [Raport 1945], PUMST, BI 874, p. 7; Piekarski, *Escaping*, p. 143.

15. Dwork, van Pelt, *Auschwitz*, pp. 177–81.

16. Pilecki, *The Auschwitz*, loc. 814; Pilecki, [Raport 1945], PUMST, BI 874, p. 7.

17. Pilecki, [Raport 1945], PUMST, BI 874, pp. 7–8.

18. Pilecki, *The Auschwitz*, loc. 833; Pilecki, [Raport 1945], PUMST, BI 874, p. 8.

19. Pilecki, *The Auschwitz*, loc. 866; Pilecki, [Raport 1945], PUMST, BI 874, p. 8.

20. Pilecki, [Raport 1945], PUMST, BI 874, p. 8.

21. Pilecki, [Raport 1945], PUMST, BI 874, p. 8.

22. Pilecki, [Raport 1945], PUMST, BI 874, p. 8.

23. Pilecki, *The Auschwitz*, loc. 7794; Pilecki, [Raport 1945], PUMST, BI 874, p. 9.

24. Pilecki, [Raport 1945], PUMST, BI 874, p. 6, p. 27; Kielar, *Anus Mundi*, p. 34; Kłodziński, "Rola," pp. 113–26; Ciesielski, [Raport 1943], AAN, 202/XVIII/1, p. 3; Pilecki, [Zamiast], Materiały, vol. 223c, APMA-B, p. 1.

25. Pilecki, [Zamiast], Materiały, vol. 223c, APMA-B, p. 2–3.

26. Pilecki, [Raport 1945], PUMST, BI 874, p. 9; Ciesielski, [Raport 1943], AAN, 202/XVIII/1, p. 5; Redzej, [Raport 1943], AAN, 202/XVIII/1, p. 36; Radlicki, *Kapo*, p. 87; Dobrowolska, *The Auschwitz*, loc. 1687; Albin, *List*, p. 53; Urbanek, Oświadczenia, vol. 44, APMA-B, p. 3; Wolny, Oświadczenia, vol. 33, APMA-B, p. 17; Białas, Oświadczenia, vol. 94, APMA-B, vol. 94, p. 24; Kowalski, *Niezapomniana*, pp. 245–47. Most prisoners claim that there was only one giant roller, but there were also a few smaller ones.

27. Gutheil, *Einer*, pp. 79–92; Albin, *List*, p. 49; Bernacka, "Otto," pp. 8–9; Pilecki, [Raport 1945], PUMST, BI 874, p. 10.

28. Pilecki, *The Auschwitz*, loc. 929; Pilecki, [Raport 1945], PUMST, BI 874, p. 10.

29. Pilecki, *The Auschwitz*, loc. 929; Pilecki, [Raport 1945], PUMST, BI 874, p. 10.

30. Pilecki, [Raport 1945], PUMST, BI 874, p. 10.

31. Lasik et al., *Auschwitz*, vol. I, pp. 70–71.

32. Filip, *Żydzi*, p. 51, pp. 139–43; Steinbacher, *Auschwitz*, p. 9; Dwork, van Pelt, *Auschwitz*, p. 205.

33. Pilecki, [Raport 1945], PUMST, BI 874, pp. 10–11.

34. Pilecki, [Raport 1945], PUMST, BI 874, p. 11.

35. Pilecki, [Raport 1945], PUMST, BI 874, pp. 10–11.

Chapter 5: Resistance

1. Pilecki, [Raport 1945], PUMST, BI 874, p. 11.

2. Höss, *The Commandant*, loc. 200; Pilecki, [Raport 1945], PUMST, BI 874, p. 12; Dwork, van Pelt, *Auschwitz*, p. 188.

3. Pilecki, [Raport 1945], PUMST, BI 874, p. 11.

4. Pilecki, [Raport 1945], PUMST, BI 874, p. 13.

5. Pilecki, [Raport 1945], PUMST, BI 874, p. 13.

6. Siedlecki, *Beyond*, p. 151.

7. Pilecki, *The Auschwitz*, loc. 2418; Pilecki, [Raport 1945], PUMST, BI 874, p. 12.

8. Świętorzecki, Interview, February 14, 1970; Pilecki, [Raport 1945], PUMST, BI 874, p. 6; Radlicki, *Kapo*, pp. 68–71, p. 87.

9. Świętorzecki, Interview, February 14, 1970; Pilecki, [Raport 1945], PUMST, BI 874, p. 6.

10. Pilecki, [Raport 1945], PUMST, BI 874, p. 8. There was an additional member named Roman Zagner, about whom little is known. Kielar, *Anus Mundi*, p. 44;

Kowalski, Wspomnienia, vol. 96, APMA-B, p. 242; Pilecki, [Klucz], Wspomnienia, vol. 183, APMA-B, p. 79; Cyra, *Rotmistrz*, p. 50.

11. Iwaszko et al., *Auschwitz*, vol. II, p. 69.

12. Fejkiel, *Medycyna*, in Bidakowski, Wójcik, *Pamiętniki*, p, 472; Iwaszko et al., *Auschwitz*, vol. II, p. 61; Dobrowolska, *The Auschwitz*, loc. 3310, loc. 3356, loc. 3363; Ziółkowski, *Byłem*, pp. 45–46; Smoleń, "Czarna," p. 4. A camp shop was also in operation that sold cigarettes and stationery. Prisoners were permitted to receive a small allowance from their families.

13. Nowacki, Wspomnienia, vol. 151, APMA-B, p. 139; Piekarski, *Escaping*, p. 46.

14. Piekarski, *Escaping*, p. 45.

15. Piekarski, *Escaping*, p. 45.

16. Piekarski claimed that Witold told him Auschwitz was to become "a very large extermination camp to house Polish freedom fighters," but it's likely he was applying the camp's later function to his memory of his conversation with Witold. Piekarski, *Escaping*, p. 44.

17. Siedlecki, *Beyond*, p. 154; Pilecki, *The Auschwitz*, loc. 1011; Pilecki, [Raport 1945], PUMST, BI 874, p. 11.

18. Stupka, Oświadczenia, vol. 68, APMA-B, p. 124, p. 127; Stupka, Interview, September 21, 2016; Pilecki, [Raport 1945], PUMST, BI 874, p. 29; Kajtoch, Wspomnienia, vol. 27, APMA-B, pp. 6–7; Plaskura, Oświadczenia, vol. 105, APMA-B, p. 42.

19. Iwaszko et al., *Auschwitz*, vol. II, pp. 419–26; Ostrowska, [Wspomnienia 1], p. 5; Pilecki, [Raport 1945], PUMST, BI 874, p. 29; Wysocki, *Rotmistrz*, p. 47.

20. Czech, *Auschwitz*, pp. 29–39; Kowalczyk, *Barbed*, p. 35; Langbein, *People*, p. 70.

21. Fejkiel, *Więźniarski*, p. 120; Pilecki, Interview, May 17 and 19, 2016; Pilecka–Optułowicz, Interview, February 1, 2016; Szpakowski, Interview, January 31, 2017.

22. Pilecki, [Raport 1945], PUMST, BI 874, p. 13.

23. Iwaszko et al., *Auschwitz*, vol. II, pp. 429–33.

24. Pilecki, [Raport 1945], PUMST, BI 874, p. 36; Iwaszko et al., *Auschwitz*, vol. II, p. 430; Wielopolski, Interview, May 18, 2017; Rostkowski, *Świat*, p. 57; Rowecki, [Wytyczne do działań sabotażowo-dywersyjnych], March 19, 1940, in Czarnocka et al., *Armia*, vol. I, p. 313, Sosnkowski, [List], November 28, 1940, no. 162 [no. 94], in Iranek-Osmecki et al., *Armia*, vol. II, p. 649; Wachsmann, *KL*, p. 483. Although the SS had ordered that prisoners should not

normally be released during wartime, Auschwitz had a looser policy in its early months. Cyra, *Rotmistrz*, p. 42; Garliński, *Fighting*, p. 276; Dębski, *Oficerowie*, s.v. Aleksander Wielopolski.

25. Pilecki, [Raport 1945], PUMST, BI 874, p. 19; Dębski, *Oficerowie*, s.v. Aleksander Wielopolski; Pilecki, [Raport 1945], PUMST, BI 874, p. 35; Setkiewicz, "Pierwsi," p. 16. The roll figures for October 1940 have not been preserved, and it's not clear if Witold had access to them. One of the reports sent to London partly based on information that Pilecki gathered estimates that around 20 to 25 percent of some 6,500 Polish prisoners had died by November 1940. This is in line with the camp figures we have for the end of the year, when Commandant Höss agreed to a request by the Archbishop of Poland, Adam Sapieha, to send parcels to each prisoner. In December 31, the number of prisoners stood at 7,879, but Höss requested that only 6,000 parcels be sent. The camp in Auschwitz-Obóz w Oświęcimiu November 1940—part published as The German Occupation of Poland May 1941; Carter, [Report], NARS, 800.20211/924, RG 59.

26. Dembiński, [Raport], PUMST, A. 680, p. 593; Hastings, *Bomber*, loc. 1543; Westermann, "The Royal," p. 197.

27. Lasik et al., *Auschwitz*, vol. I, p. 266; Dembiński, [Raport], PUMST, A. 680, p. 593.

28. Pilecki, [Raport 1945], PUMST, BI 874, p. 36; Czech, *Auschwitz*, p. 32.

29. Nowacki, Wspomnienia, vol. 151, APMA-B, p. 145; Kozłowiecki, *Ucisk*, p. 205.

30. Dering, cited in Garliński, *Fighting*, p. 25.

31. Kielar, *Anus Mundi*, p. 40.

32. Garliński, *Fighting*, p. 25; Kielar, *Anus Mundi*, p. 40; Czech, *Auschwitz*, p. 32; Setkiewicz, *Zaopatrzenie*, p. 57.

33. Pilecki, [Raport 1945], PUMST, BI 874, p. 14.

34. Pilecki, [Raport 1945], PUMST, BI 874, p. 14.

35. Pilecki, *The Auschwitz*, loc. 1028; Pilecki, [Raport 1945], PUMST, BI 874, p. 14.

36. Paczuła, Oświadczenia, vol. 108, APMA-B, p. 72; Setkiewicz, *Voices*, vol. 6, p. 6.

37. Pilecki, [Raport 1945], PUMST, BI 874, p. 13; Ciesielski, [Raport 1943], AAN, 202/XVIII/1, p. 4.

38. Piekarski, *Escaping*, p. 51.

39. Piekarski, *Escaping*, p. 53.

40. Piekarski, *Escaping*, p. 54.

41. Iwaszko et al., *Auschwitz*, vol. II, pp. 81–82.
42. Fejkiel, *Więźniarski*, p. 23; Collingham, *The Taste*, loc. 235; Russell, *Hunger*, loc. 234, loc. 1245, loc. 1374; Butterly, Shepherd, *Hunger*, p. 158.
43. Pilecki, *The Auschwitz*, loc. 1161; Pilecki, [Raport 1945], PUMST, BI 874, p. 15.
44. Pilecki, [Raport 1945], PUMST, BI 874, p. 24; Piekarski, *Escaping*, p. 70; Kowalski, Wspomnienia, vol. 96, APMA-B, p. 190.
45. Pilecki, *The Auschwitz*, loc. 1178; Pilecki, [Raport 1945], PUMST, BI 874, p. 16.
46. Dering, [Wspomnienia], p. 17; Iwaszko et al., *Auschwitz*, vol. II, p. 300.
47. Pilecki, *The Auschwitz*, loc. 1174; Piekarski, *Escaping*, p. 75.
48. Pilecki, [Raport 1945], PUMST, BI 874, p. 16.
49. Pilecki, [Raport 1945], PUMST, BI 874, p. 16.
50. Kowalski, *Niezapomniana*, p. 201; Ringleblum, *Notes*, loc. 1777.
51. Czech, *Auschwitz*, p. 40.
52. Czech, *Auschwitz*, p. 40; Świętorzecki, Oświadczenia, vol. 76, APMA-B, pp. 101–2; Dobrowolska, *The Auschwitz*, loc. 3017; Bartoszewski, *Mój*, pp. 53–54.
53. Świętorzecki, Wspomnienia, vol. 86, APMA-B, p. 233; Dobrowolska, *The Auschwitz*, loc. 3017.
54. Strzelecka, *Voices*, vol. 3, p. 8, p. 21; Redzej, [Raport 1943], AAN, 202/XVIII/1, p. 38; Tomaszewski, Wspomnienia, vol. 66, APMA-B, p. 108; Ławski, Wspomnienia, vol. 154/154a, APMA-B, p. 69.
55. Pilecki, [Raport 1945], PUMST, BI 874, p. 23.
56. Rablin, Oświadczenia, vol. 29, APMA-B, p. 80; Piper, *Auschwitz*, vol. III, p. 198; Dwork, van Pelt, *Auschwitz*, pp. 219–22. The almond smell was added by Zyklon B's manufacturers to allow the gas to be detected.
57. Strzelecka, *Voices*, vol. 3, p. 29; Pilecki, [Raport 1945], PUMST, BI 874, pp. 23–24; Redzej, [Raport 1943], AAN, 202/XVIII/1, p. 37a.
58. Pilecki, [Raport 1945], PUMST, BI 874, p. 25.
59. Pilecki, [Raport 1945], PUMST, BI 874, p. 25.
60. Pilecki, [Raport 1945], PUMST, BI 874, p. 25.

Chapter 6: Bomber Command

1. Wielopolski, Interview, May 18, 2017.
2. Allen, *The Fantastic*, loc. 1819; Matusak, *Wywiad*, p. 32, p. 35.
3. Mulley, *The Spy*, p. 61; Leski, *Życie*, pp. 68–71; Olson, *Last*, loc. 2625.

4. Aleksander's oral message was not the only source of news about the camp that autumn—it seems some scattered postcards and smuggled letters had reached Warsaw. There had also been other released prisoners and a few escapes. For the status of Polish political prisoners and the Hague and Geneva conventions, see Lasik et al., *Auschwitz*, vol. I, pp. 43–44; Gross, Renz, *Der Frankfurter*, vol. 1, p. 598; Reisman, Antoniou, *Laws*, pp. 38–42, pp. 47–56.

5. Dembiński, [Raport], PUMST, A. 680, p. 593.

6. Fleming, *Auschwitz*, p. 24; Dembiński, [Raport], PUMST, A. 680, p. 592; Rowecki included Wielopolski's report in his later "Report on the internal situation until January 30th 1941," which reached London in March 1941 via Stockholm; the "Part III. The camp in Oświęcim" described the camp's conditions and suffering of prisoners (PUMST, A. 441, p. 10).

7. Dembiński, [Raport], PUMST, A. 680, p. 592.

8. Dembiński, [Raport], PUMST, A. 680, p. 588, pp. 591–92; Westermann, "The Royal," p. 197.

9. Walker, *Poland*, loc. 649; McGilvray, *A Military*, loc. 649; Olson, Cloud, *For Your*, pp. 96–97.

10. Olson, *Island*, loc. 1497.

11. McGilvray, *A Military*, loc. 1957; Olson, *Last*, loc. 1532–59.

12. Iwaszko et al., *Auschwitz*, vol. II, pp. 419–26; Kochavi, *Prelude*, pp. 7–9; van Pelt, *The Case*, pp. 129–32.

13. Gardiner, *The Blitz*, p. 43.

14. Gardiner, *The Blitz*, pp. 89–90.

15. Manchester, Reid, *The Last*, loc. 3606; Roberts, *Churchill*, pp. 607–8.

16. Milton, *Ministry*, loc. 1640.

17. Dalton, *Diary*, pp. 132–33; McGilvray, *A Military*, loc. 1863.

18. Westermann, "The Royal," p. 197; Gardiner, *Blitz*, p. 141, pp. 230–41.

19. Overy, *The Bombing*, p. 261; Hastings, *Bomber*, loc. 1543.

20. Hastings, *Bomber*, loc. 1543.

21. Westermann, "The Royal," p. 201; Hastings, *Bomber*, loc. 1814; Westermann, "The Royal," p. 197; Bines, *The Polish*, p. 111.

22. Hastings, *Bomber*, loc. 1732; [Sprawozdanie, notatki informacyjne, raporty z okupacji sowieckiej, przesłuchanie kurierów i przybyszów z Polski, XII 1939–IV 1942], PUMST, SK.39.08.

23. Westermann, "The Royal," p. 202.

24. Westermann, "The Royal," p. 204.

25. Bines, *The Polish*, pp. 31–32; Wilkson, *Gubbins*, loc. 1728.

26. Garliński, *Fighting*, p. 75; Walker, *Poland*, loc. 1031; Zabielski, *First*, p. 10.

27. Zabielski, *First*, pp. 9–10; Bines, *The Polish*, p. 40.

28. Zabielski, *First*, pp. 11–12.

Chapter 7: Radio

1. Pilecki, [Raport 1945], PUMST, BI 874, pp. 24–25; Król, Oświadczenia, vol. 76, APMA-B, p. 204.

2. Pilecki, [Raport 1945], PUMST, BI 874, p. 26; Lifton, *The Nazi*, pp. 30–35, pp. 129–33.

3. Siedlecki, *Beyond*, p. 170.

4. Langbein, *People*, p. 393; Lifton, *The Nazi*, p. 266; Dering, [Wspomnienia], pp. 193–94.

5. Pilecki, [Raport 1945], PUMST, BI 874, p. 22; Siedlecki, *Beyond*, p. 170; Schwarz, [Raport], March 17, 1942, APMA–B, D–AuI–3a; Strzelecka, *Voices*, vol. 3, p. 15, p. 21.

6. Bartoszewski, *Mój*, pp. 50–51; Piekarski, *Escaping*, p. 79.

7. Piekarski, *Escaping*, p. 79.

8. Piekarski, *Escaping*, p. 79.

9. Piekarski, *Escaping*, pp. 77–78.

10. Dering, [Wspomnienia], p. 83.

11. Hahn, Interview, April 24, 2018.

12. Fleming, *Auschwitz*, p. 59; Stargardt, *The German*, p. 66, p. 119. By the end of 1941, German officials estimated more than a million Germans were listening to BBC German-language broadcasts. Breitman, *Official*, p. 156.

13. Olson, *Last*, loc. 2335.

14. Świętorzecki, Interview, February 14, 1972; Taul, Wspomnienia, vol. 62, APMA-B, p. 36.

15. Gutheil, *Einer*, pp. 79–92; Ptakowski, *Oświęcim*, p. 97; Gliński, Oświadczenia, vol. 95, APMA-B, p. 6; Drzazga, Oświadczenia, vol. 33, APMA-B, p. 51; Pilecki, [Raport 1945], PUMST, BI 874, p. 35.

16. Pilecki, [Raport 1945], PUMST, BI 874, p. 26.

17. Świętorzecki, Oświadczenia, vol. 76, APMA-B, p. 97; Pilecki, [Raport 1945], PUMST, BI 874, p. 32.

18. Świętorzecki, Interview, February 14, 1972; Wachsmann, *KL*, p. 207; Setkiewicz, *Z dziejów*, p. 55; Dwork, van Pelt, *Auschwitz*, p. 207.

19. Frączek, Wspomnienia, vol. 66, APMA-B, p. 162.

20. Pilecki, [Raport 1945], PUMST, BI 874, p. 30; Kowalski, *Niezapomniana*, pp. 240–65; Kowalczyk, *Barbed*, vol. II, p. 10.

21. Piekarski, *Escaping*, p. 83; Höss, *Commandant*, p. 121.

22. Piekarski, *Escaping*, p. 83; Pilecki, [Raport W], AAN, 202/XVIII/1, p. 74.

23. Pilecki, *Report W*, pp. 40–41; Pilecki, [Raport W], AAN, 202/XVIII/1, p. 74.

24. Pilecki, *Report W*, pp. 40–41; Pilecki, [Raport W], AAN, 202/XVIII/1, p. 74.

25. Iwaszko et al., *Auschwitz*, vol. II, p. 83; Pilecki, [Raport 1945], PUMST, BI 874, p. 27; Porębski, Oświadczenia, vol. 102, APMA-B, p. 28. The mortality rate among the prisoners stood at around 50 percent. Bartoszewski, *Mój*, p. 23; Porębski, Oświadczenia, vol. 102, APMA-B, pp. 27–28; Dobrowolska, *The Auschwitz*, loc. 1092, loc. 1143.

26. Pilecki, [Raport 1945], PUMST, BI 874, p. 27.

27. Pilecki, [Raport 1945], PUMST, BI 874, p. 27.

28. Pilecki, *The Auschwitz*, loc. 1725; Pilecki, [Raport 1945], PUMST, BI 874, p. 28.

29. Pilecki, [Raport 1945], PUMST, BI 874, p. 29.

30. Pilecki, [Raport 1945], PUMST, BI 874, p. 28.

31. Pilecki, [Raport 1945], PUMST, BI 874, pp. 28–29.

32. Pietrzykowski, Oświadczenia, vol. 88, APMA-B, p. 10.

33. Pietrzykowski, Oświadczenia, vol. 88, APMA-B, pp. 9–10; Rablin, Oświadczenia, vol. 29, APMA-B, p. 97.

34. Pietrzykowski, Oświadczenia, vol. 88, APMA-B, p. 10; Albin, *List*, pp. 89–90.

35. Pietrzykowski, Oświadczenia, vol. 88, APMA-B, p. 10; Pilecki, [Raport 1945], PUMST, BI 874, p. 6, p. 27.

36. Pietrzykowski, Oświadczenia, vol. 88, APMA-B, p. 11.

37. Pietrzykowski, Oświadczenia, vol. 88, APMA-B, p. 11.

38. Pietrzykowski, Oświadczenia, vol. 88, APMA-B, p. 11.

39. Piekarski, *Escaping*, p. 99; Lasik et al., *Auschwitz*, vol. I, p. 19; Gawron, *Ochotnik*, pp. 23–26.

40. Świętorzecki, Oświadczenia, vol. 76, APMA-B, pp. 104–5; 202/III-8, p. 21, in Marczewska, Ważniewski et al., *Zeszyty* (1968), p. 6. In the report about the camp that appeared in the underground press that summer the prison population was put at 12,500, possibly using data from an earlier release. Świętorzecki, Oświadczenia, vol. 76, APMA-B, p. 101; Gawron, *Ochotnik*, pp. 26–28; Kowalczyk, *Barbed*, vol. II, p. 14, p. 36; Kowalski, *Niezapomniana*, p. 218, p. 223; Setkiewicz, *Zapomniany*, pp. 61–65; Cyra, *Jeszcze raz*, no

pages given; Kowalski, *Niezapomniana*, p. 228. Batko was not the only prisoner who sacrificed his life for another prisoner. Monk Maksymilian Kolbe did the same on July 29, 1941. Pilecki, [Raport 1945], PUMST, BI 874, p. 37; Redzej, [Raport 1943], AAN, 202/XVIII/1, p. 40a.

41. Cywiński, Lachendro, Setkiewicz, *Auschwitz*, p. 196; Pilecki, [Raport 1945], PUMST, BI 874, p. 6. No record of Warsaw's response to Karol's report has been preserved.

42. Świętorzecki, Oświadczenia, vol. 76, APMA-B, p. 106; Gawron, *Ochotnik*, p. 203.

43. Świętorzecki, Oświadczenia, vol. 76, APMA-B, p. 105.

44. Pietrzykowski, Oświadczenia, vol. 88, APMA-B, pp. 19–20.

Chapter 8: Experiments

1. Ciesielski, *Wspomnienia*, pp. 45–47; Höss, *Commandant*, p. 157.

2. Redzej, [Raport 1943], AAN, 202/XVIII/1, p. 39; Kłodziński, "Dur," p. 47.

3. Allen, *The Fantastic*, loc. 319; Diem, Wspomnienia, vol. 172, APMA-B, p. 9.

4. Wachsmann, *KL*, p. 246.

5. Iwaszko et al., *Auschwitz*, vol. II, p. 296, p. 322; Diem, Wspomnienia, vol. 172, APMA-B, p. 120; Pilecki, [Raport 1945], PUMST, BI 874, p. 54.

6. Hill, Williams, *Auschwitz*, p. 63; Jaworski, *Wspomnienia*, p. 183.

7. In 1947, the Polish government charged Dering with war crimes relating to his role as a surgeon during Nazi experiments on the sex organs of mostly Jewish male and female prisoners. Dering, who was in London at the time, was arrested and investigated by British authorities. Dering insisted that he was one of several prisoners ordered by the Germans to perform the operations and that as a prisoner he had no choice but to obey. After a nineteen–month investigation he was released and allowed to remain in the United Kingdom. IPN, GK_174_183_pda, BU_2188_14, BU_2188_15, GK_164_27_t1.

8. Garliński, *Fighting*, p. 71; Stargardt, *The German*, p. 158; Snyder, *Black*, loc. 475; Wachsmann, *KL*, pp. 259–60; Dwork, van Pelt, *Auschwitz*, pp. 258–62. On June 23, Höss ordered the Jews in the penal company to be beaten to death, likely as a symbolic contribution to the war effort. Hałgas, Oświadczenia, vol. 89, APMA-B, p. 165; Setkiewicz, "Pierwsi," p. 26; Kobrzyński, Wspomnienia, vol. 129, APMA-B, p. 28.

9. Rawicz, [Pobyt], p. 21.

10. Dwork, van Pelt, *Auschwitz*, p. 262; Wachsmann, *KL*, pp. 259–60, p. 279; Czech, *Auschwitz*, p. 74.

11. Ciesielski, [Raport 1943], AAN, 202/XVIII/1, p. 8; Pilecki, [Raport 1945], PUMST, BI 874, p. 39; Redzej, [Raport 1943], AAN, 202/XVIII/1, p. 41a; Porębski, Oświadczenia, vol. 22, APMA-B, p. 59; Wolny, Oświadczenia, vol. 33, APMA-B, p. 19; Redzej, [Raport 1943], AAN, 202/XVIII/1, p. 41a; Lasik et al., *Auschwitz*, vol. I, p. 67.

12. Ciesielski, *Wspomnienia*, p. 69.

13. Ciesielski, *Wspomnienia*, p. 69.

14. Gawron, *Ochotnik*, pp. 72–99.

15. Kowalski, *Niezapomniana*, p. 231.

16. Kłodziński, "Pierwsza," p. 43; Cyra, "Dr Władysław," p. 75.

17. Czech, *Auschwitz*, p. 75; Strzelecka, *Voices*, vol. 3, p. 12; Ławski, Wspomnienia, vol. 154/154a, APMA-B, p. 21; Hałgas, "Oddział," p. 53.

18. Kłodziński, "Pierwsza," p. 43; Czech, *Kalendarz*, p. 75.

19. Dering, [Wspomnienia], p. 81; Wachsmann, *KL*, pp. 243–52.

20. Wachsmann, *KL*, pp. 243–52. The T4 program was named after its headquarters' address at Tiergartenstrasse 4 in Berlin.

21. Dering, [Wspomnienia], p. 81.

22. Kłodziński, "Pierwsza," pp. 39–40; Rawicz, [Pobyt], p. 20; Lasik et al., *Auschwitz*, vol. I, p. 86; Czech, *Kalendarz*, p. 75; Stapf, Oświadczenia, vol. 148, APMA-B, p. 101; Dobrowolska, *The Auschwitz*, loc. 3922; Gawron, Wspomnienia, vol. 48, APMA-B, p. 77. According to some accounts both Krankemann and Siegruth were hung by prisoners during the journey: Pilecki, [Raport 1945], PUMST, BI 874, p. 50.

23. Dering, [Wspomnienia], p. 28; Kowalski, Wspomnienia, vol. 96, APMA-B, p. 203.

24. Dering, [Wspomnienia], p. 81.

25. Kłodziński, "Pierwsze," pp. 83–84.

26. Kielar, *Anus Mundi*, p. 61; Pilecki, [Raport 1945], PUMST, BI 874, p. 50; Wachsmann, *KL*, p. 267.

27. Wachsmann, *KL*, p. 267; Dering, [Wspomnienia], p. 80.

28. Czech, *Auschwitz*, p. 85; Kłodziński, "Pierwsze," p. 84.

29. Kłodziński, "Pierwsze," p. 84.

30. Kłodziński, "Pierwsze," p. 84.

31. Kielar, *Anus Mundi*, p. 60; Kłodziński, "Pierwsze," p. 87; Czech, *Auschwitz*, p. 86; Piper, *Auschwitz*, vol. III, p. 57, p. 117.

32. Kłodziński, "Pierwsze," p. 88.

33. Czech, *Auschwitz*, pp. 86–87; Diem, Wspomnienia, vol. 172, APMA-B, p. 131. "[I saw] for the first time a whole pile of gassed dead bodies," Höss recalled for a Polish magistrate later. "I felt uncomfortable and shuddered, though I had imagined death by gassing as worse." Langbein, *People*, p. 303.

34. Pilecki, [Raport 1945], PUMST, BI 874, p. 39.

35. Diem, Wspomnienia, vol. 172, APMA-B, p. 131; Kielar, *Anus Mundi*, p. 64.

36. Pilecki, [Raport 1945], PUMST, BI 874, p. 39.

37. Kłodziński, "Pierwsze," p. 89; Kielar, *Anus Mundi*, p. 66.

38. Pilecki, [Raport 1945], PUMST, BI 874, p. 40. In Witold's W Report, he records his name in a short list of prisoners released from the camp, along with Aleksander Wielopolski and Czesław Wąsowicz (see below). In a second list he records prisoners released from the camp who carried reports for the organization, in which neither Dipont, Wielopolski, nor Wąsowicz is mentioned. It seems that Witold may have been drawing a distinction between his recruits who carried messages and those outside the organization. In any event, Dipont was a witness to the Soviet gassing to Warsaw. Pilecki, *Report W*, p. 6.

39. Pilecki, [Raport 1945], PUMST, BI 874, p. 39; Rablin, Oświadczenia, vol. 29, p. 81; Wachsmann, *KL*, pp. 268–69; Höss, *Commandant*, p. 147.

40. Nowacki, Wspomnienia, vol. 151, p. 107; Pilecki, [Raport 1945], PUMST, BI 874, p. 40.

41. Czech, *Auschwitz*, pp. 93–102; Gawron, *Ochotnik*, p. 145; Wachsmann, *KL*, p. 280; Nowacki, Wspomnienia, vol. 151, APMA-B, pp. 107–9.

42. Gawron, *Ochotnik*, p. 148.

43. Gawron, *Ochotnik*, p. 148.

44. Rawicz, [List], September 25, 1957. Rawicz letters courtesy of Andrzej Kunert unless stated otherwise. See earlier note for the likely role of Wąsowski.

45. Dwork, van Pelt, *Auschwitz*, pp. 263–68. The new crematorium was initially to be built at the main camp, but the location was subsequently moved to Birkenau.

46. Setkiewicz, *Zaopatrzenie*, p. 58.

47. Schulte, *London*, in Hackmann, Süß, *Hitler's*, p. 211; Olszowski, "Więźniarska," pp. 182–87; Höss, *The Commandant*, p. 137; for example of memorizing reports see Rawicz, [Raport], date unknown.

48. Rawicz, [List], 1957.

49. Rawicz, Interview, March 5, 2017; Rawicz, Oświadczenia, vol. 27, APMA-B, p. 38; Pilecki, [Raport 1945], PUMST, BI 874, p. 55.

50. Gawron, *Ochotnik*, p. 103, p. 131.

51. Gawron, *Ochotnik*, p. 131.

52. Gawron, *Ochotnik*, p. 131.

53. Witold's recruit among the tanners was Stanisław Kazuba. Piekarski, *Escaping*, p. 149; Pilecki, *The Auschwitz*, loc. 2294; Pilecki, [Raport 1945], PUMST, BI 874, p. 42.

54. Czech, *Auschwitz*, p. 105; Banach, Proces Załogi Esesmańskiej, vol. 55, APMA-B, pp. 102–3; Taul, Oświadczenia, vol. 9, APMA-B, p. 1267; Pilecki, [Raport 1945], PUMST, BI 874, p. 37.

55. Gawron, *Ochotnik*, p. 167.

56. Gawron, *Ochotnik*, p. 167.

57. Gawron, *Ochotnik*, p. 167.

58. Rawicz, Oświadczenia, vol. 27, APMA-B, p. 39; Rawicz, [List], 1957.

59. Gawron, *Ochotnik*, pp. 173–74.

60. Gawron, *Ochotnik*, pp. 173–74.

Chapter 9: Shifts

1. Szarota, *Okupowanej*, p. 267; Bartoszewski, *1859*, p. 291; Bernstein, Rutkowski, "Liczba," p. 84; Ringelblum, *Notes*, loc. 3484; Zimmerman, *The Polish*, p. 95.

2. A couple of stories appeared that October in *Informacja bieżąca*, the underground newspaper, with sparse descriptions of the killings in a special bunker in the camp. One of the articles concluded that the gas was being tested for use on the eastern front. *Informacja bieżąca* 21, 202/III-7, p. 12, in Marczewska, Ważniewski et al., *Zeszyty* (1968), p. 14; 202/III-28, p. 447, in Marczewska, Ważniewski et al., *Zeszyty* (1968), p. 11.

3. Lewandowski, *Swedish*, pp. 45–49; Thorsell, *Warszawasvenskarna*, p. 167; Gistedt, *Od operetki*, pp. 88–102.

4. Wyczański, *Mikrofilm*, p. 25.

5. Korboński, *Fighting*, p. 157; Thorsell, *Warszawasvenskarna*, p. 134; Lewandowski, *Swedish*, p. 62; Thugutt, [List], November 19, 1941, PISM, A.9.III.4/14; Siudak, [List], December 29, 1941, PISM, A.9.III.4/14; Garliński, *Fighting*, p. 58.

6. Roberts, *Churchill*, p. 651.

7. Roberts, *Churchill*, p. 652; Breitman, *Official*, pp. 89–92.

8. Terry, "Conflicting," p. 364.

9. Breitman, *Official*, pp. 92–93; Roberts, *Churchill*, p. 651.

10. Roberts, *Churchill*, p. 678; Laqueur, *The Terrible*, p. 91; Breitman, *Official*, pp. 92–93. Himmler still appears to have guessed that Churchill was receiving German intercepts. Shortly afterward, he told police units to stop sending figures over the radio and to change their codes, with the result that intelligence from the eastern front largely dried up. Gilbert, *Churchill*, loc. 58. Churchill's career to date suggested a sensitivity to Jewish matters that was not always shared by his colleagues. "Even Winston had a fault," one parliamentarian noted. "He was too fond of Jews."

11. Kochavi, *Prelude*, p. 15.

12. Breitman, *Official*, p. 101; Laqueur, Breitman, *Breaking*, p. 124; Laqueur, *The Terrible*, p. 100.

13. Kochavi, *Prelude*, p. 7; Westermann, "The Royal," p. 199; Fleming, *Auschwitz*, p. 58; Polish Ministry of Information, *Polish Fortnightly Review*, July 1, 1942 [Press Bulletin]; Breitman, *Official*, p. 102; Ziegler, *London*, p. 175. The first newspaper to mention Auschwitz was the *Scotsman* in 1942. Fleming, *Auschwitz*, p. 131.

14. Breitman, *FDR*, loc. 3772.

15. Kochavi, *Prelude*, pp. 14–15.

16. Puławski, *W obliczu*, p. 180. The section on Auschwitz in the *Black Book* drew upon "Report on the internal situation until January 30th 1941," which reached London in March 1941 via Stockholm and was partly based on Witold's report (PUMST, A. 441, p. 10).

17. Kochavi, *Prelude*, pp. 14–15; Breitman, Lichtman, *FDR*, loc. 3775.

18. Puławski, *W obliczu*, pp. 170–89; Widfeldt, Wegmann, *Making*, pp. 22–25.

19. Stafford, *Britain*, pp. 65–69; Wilkinson, *Foreign*, loc. 1730; see Dziennik Polski, June 11, 1942, cited in Engel, *In the Shadow*, p. 181, p. 209; Fleming, *Auschwitz*, p. 96.

Chapter 10: Paradise

1. Pilecki, [Raport 1945], PUMST, BI 874, p. 71, p. 47.

2. Syzdek, "W 45," p. 5; Kobrzyński, Wspomnienia, vol. 129, APMA-B, p. 6; Świebocki, *Auschwitz*, vol. IV, pp. 74–77.

3. Syzdek, "W 45," p. 5; Pilecki, [Raport 1945], PUMST, BI 874, p. 45; Stransky, Oświadczenia, vol. 84, AMPA-B, p. 46; Rawicz, [List], August 22, 1957. Rawicz mistakenly identifies Frankiewicz as Frankowski.

4. Rawicz, Oświadczenia, vol. 27, APMA-B, p. 37; Gawron, Wspomnienia,

vol. 48, APMA-B, p. 96, p. 98, p. 100; Pilecki, [Raport 1945], PUMST, BI 874, p. 45; Pilecki, *The Auschwitz*, loc. 2262; Pilecki, [Raport 1945], PUMST, BI 874, p. 41.

5. Gawron, *Ochotnik*, p. 185.

6. Lasik et al., *Auschwitz*, vol. I, p. 181; Rawicz, Oświadczenia, vol. 27, APMA-B, p. 37; Rawicz, [List], August 31, 1957.

7. 202/I-32, p. 71, in Marczewska, Ważniewski et al., *Zeszyty* (1968), p. 54. In fact the number of surviving Soviet POWs that spring was around 150. Schulte, *London*, in Hackmann, Süß, *Hitler's*, pp. 222–23.

8. Urbańczyk, Wspomnienia, vol. 54, APMA-B, p. 35; Diem, "Ś.P. Kazimierz," pp. 45–47; Stupka, Oświadczenia, vol. 68, APMA-B, p. 124.

9. Stupka, Interview, September 24, 2016.

10. Breitman, *Official*, pp. 110–16; Schulte, *London*, in Hackmann, Süß, *Hitler's*, pp. 222–23.

11. Lasik et al., *Auschwitz*, vol. I, pp. 166–67; Breitman, *Official*, pp. 112–14; Pilecki, [Raport 1945], PUMST, BI 874, p. 51; Piekarski, *Escaping*, p. 108.

12. Hahn, Interview, May 5, 2018; Pilecki, [Raport 1945], PUMST, BI 874, p. 51.

13. Pilecki, [Raport 1945], PUMST, BI 874, p. 51; Piekarski, *Escaping*, p. 122.

14. Piekarski, *Escaping*, p. 123.

15. Piekarski, *Escaping*, p. 108.

16. Piekarski, *Escaping*, p. 108.

17. Piekarski, *Escaping*, p. 109.

18. Dwork, van Pelt, *Auschwitz*, pp. 263–65, pp. 295–301; Lasik et al., *Auschwitz*, vol. I, pp. 80–81; Wachsmann, *KL*, pp. 294–96; Hilberg, *The Destruction*, p. 138.

19. Dwork, van Pelt, *Auschwitz*, p. 126, p. 294.

20. Wachsmann, *KL*, p. 294.

21. Molenda, "Władysław," p. 53; Nosal, Oświadczenia, vol. 106, APMA-B, p. 51.

22. Piekarski, *Escaping*, p. 109.

23. Piekarski, *Escaping*, p. 109.

24. Piekarski, *Escaping*, p. 114.

25. Piekarski, *Escaping*, p. 114.

26. Piekarski, *Escaping*, p. 114.

27. Piekarski, *Escaping*, p. 115.

28. Piekarski, *Escaping*, p. 115.

29. Piekarski, *Escaping*, p. 116.

30. Piekarski, *Escaping*, p. 116.

31. Piekarski, *Escaping*, p. 116; Pilecki, [Raport 1945], PUMST, BI 874, p. 51.

32. Pilecki, [Raport 1945], PUMST, BI 874, p. 35; Redzej, [Raport 1943], AAN, 202/XVIII/1, p. 42. The new camp was at one stage intended for an area near the village of Rajsko. *Raj* in Polish means paradise, which may have been another reason for the new camp's nickname.

33. Gawron, *Ochotnik*, p. 224.

34. Czech, *Auschwitz*, p. 145; Gawron, Wspomnienia, vol. 48, APMA-B, p. 13.

35. Gawron, *Ochotnik*, p. 227; Gawron, Wspomnienia, vol. 48, APMA-B, p. 13.

36. Gawron, *Ochotnik*, p. 227.

37. Gawron, Wspomnienia, vol. 48, APMA-B, p. 13; Pilecki, [Raport 1945], PUMST, BI 874, p. 53.

38. Gawron, *Ochotnik*, p. 227.

39. Gawron, *Ochotnik*, p. 227.

40. Czech, *Auschwitz*, p. 148; Gawron, *Ochotnik*, p. 247.

41. Pilecki, [Raport 1945], PUMST, BI 874, p. 53.

42. Wolny, Oświadczenia, vol. 33, APMA-B, p. 19; Porębski, Oświadczenia, vol. 22, APMA-B, pp. 59–60; Dwork, van Pelt, *Auschwitz*, p. 301; Czech, *Auschwitz*, p. 151. Porębski doesn't specifically refer to the arrival of Slovak transports in his postwar memoir, but he is the most likely source of the information reaching the main camp that spring given his underground connection.

43. Czech, *Auschwitz*, p. 151; Pilecki, [Raport 1945], PUMST, BI 874, p. 47, p. 57; Redzej, [Raport 1943], AAN, 202/XVIII/1, p. 41.

44. Pilecki, [Raport 1945], PUMST, BI 874, p. 57. In later describing the scene Witold used the derogatory term *Żydek* or "little Jew" to describe the victims. Witold used both *Żydzi* and the pejorative diminutive *Żydki* in his 1945 report. He used the latter seven times (out of a total of thirty-seven specific references to Jews). In prewar Polish, *Żydki* could be used in an anti-Semitic context. Witold appears to deploy the term to emphasize the helplessness and weakness of Jews, as in this scene, where he contrasts the plight of the victim with the murderous Jewish kapo.

45. Pilecki, [Raport 1945], PUMST, BI 874, p. 48. No such SS document has come to light.

46. Lasik et al., *Auschwitz*, vol. I, p. 233.

47. Lasik et al., *Auschwitz*, vol. I, pp. 104–6; Pilecki, [Raport 1945], PUMST, BI 874, p. 50.

48. Rawicz, Oświadczenia, vol. 27, APMA-B, p. 40; Rawicz, [List], September 23, 1957; Piekarski, *Escaping*, p. 132.

49. Rawicz, [List], September 25, 1957; Pilecki, [Raport 1945], PUMST, BI 874, p. 50.

50. Ostańkowicz, *Ziemia*, p. 180. Twelve hundred Soviet POWs and patients from the main camp died in the Isolation Station in March when the SS restricted their rations to a single cup of soup a day and forced them to stand outside day and night. Czech, *Auschwitz*, p. 157.

51. Wachsmann, *KL*, p. 301; Pietrzykowski, Oświadczenia, vol. 88, APMA-B, p. 18. Teddy does not date his witnessing of the gassing, but it's likely he recorded the first such incident he saw in the camp. His description also shares elements with Müller, Broad, and Paczyński. Müller, *Eyewitness*, p. 19.

52. Broad, [Testimony], cited in Smoleń et al., *KL Auschwitz*, p. 129; Langbein, *People*, p. 69.

53. Müller, *Eyewitness*, p. 11.

54. Paczyński, Oświadczenia, vol. 100, APMA-B, p. 102.

55. Müller, *Eyewitness*, pp. 13–15.

56. Wachsmann, *KL*, pp. 291–94; Gawron, *Ochotnik*, p. 248.

57. Czech, *Auschwitz*, pp. 167–68; Müller, *Eyewitness*, p. 18.

58. Czech, *Auschwitz*, pp. 167–68; Wachsmann, *KL*, pp. 301–2; Pilecki, [Raport 1945], PUMST, BI 874, p. 52; Wolny, Oświadczenia, vol. 33, APMA-B, p. 19; Porębski, Oświadczenia, vol. 22, APMA-B, p. 59. Henryk says he began actively collaborating with the Sonderkommando in June, but he appears to have understood what was happening to the Jews from the start of the gassings. His likely source was a member of the Sonderkommando. The unit was transferred to Birkenau from the main camp on May 9, 1942. Czech, *Auschwitz*, p. 164; Bartosik, Martyniak, Setkiewicz, *Wstęp*, in idem, *Początki*, p. 15.

59. Piper, *Auschwitz*, vol. III, pp. 181–82; Wolny, Oświadczenia, vol. 33, APMA-B, p. 19; Porębski, Oświadczenia, vol. 21, APMA-B, pp. 11–31. For an example of the type of information Sonderkommando members shared, see Pogozhev, *Escape*, loc. 1950; Wachsmann, *KL*, pp. 307–14; Rees, *Auschwitz*, loc. 2153.

60. Gawron, *Ochotnik*, p. 223.

61. Gawron, *Ochotnik*, p. 234.

62. Gawron, Wspomnienia, vol. 48, APMA-B, p. 122.

63. Gawron, *Ochotnik*, p. 248; Gawron, in Pawlicki (dir.), *Witold*. The extent of Witold's knowledge about the mass murder of Jews in Birkenau is unclear. By his own account he sent at least one report about the "mass gassing" prior to November 1942. Pilecki, *Report W*, p. 25. Wincenty Gawron attests to his role

in carrying one oral report from the camp in May 1942 just as the Little Red House in Birkenau was becoming operational. Wincenty's memoir contains some factual errors but is accurate in many key features and offers an explanation of why the Jews were being targeted that echoes Witold's own in his subsequent writings. A second report was carried by Stanisław Jaster, a written record of which is preserved from July 1942. It clearly describes the actions of the Sonderkommando, although references to their Jewish identity have been removed. This almost certainly happened as a result of editing in Warsaw. See later endnote. By his own account, Witold sent at least one report about the "mass gassing" prior to November 1942. Pilecki, *Report W*, p. 25.

64. The SS looting of Jews arriving in the camp was meticulously planned, but the total wealth extracted is unlikely to have been more than several hundred million Reichsmarks. Wachsmann, *KL*, p. 379.

65. Wincenty mentions that Jews were coming to the camp from "Holland and Belgium"; this must be a misremembering, as no Jewish transports arrived from those countries until July. It's possible that he was confused by the fact that the first transport from France contained a large proportion of foreign (non-French) and stateless Jews.

66. Gawron, *Ochotnik*, p. 250.

67. Gawron, *Ochotnik*, p. 254.

68. Gawron, *Ochotnik*, p. 254.

69. Gawron, *Ochotnik*, p. 255.

70. Gawron, *Ochotnik*, p. 247.

71. Gawron, *Ochotnik*, p. 255.

72. Gawron, *Ochotnik*, p. 257.

73. Gawron, *Ochotnik*, p. 258.

74. Gawron, *Ochotnik*, p. 259.

75. Gawron, *Ochotnik*, p. 259.

76. Gawron, *Ochotnik*, p. 259.

77. Gawron, *Ochotnik*, p. 260.

Chapter 11: Napoleon

1. Gawron, *Ochotnik*, p. 260.

2. Gawron, *Ochotnik*, p. 272.

3. Wood, *Karski*, loc. 1957; Bartoszewski, *1859*, p. 315; Segieda, [Raport], PISM, A.9.III.2a t.3. In fact, the number was around one million Jewish dead.

4. Zimmerman, *Polish*, p. 146; Ringelblum, *Notes*, loc. 4337; Wood, *Karski*, loc. 2341.

5. Breitman, *FDR*, loc. 3826.

6. Zimmerman, *The Polish*, p. 130, p. 137; Breitman, *FDR*, loc. 3826; Fleming, *Auschwitz*, pp. 97–103.

7. By contrast, Churchill had reacted to news of the Nazis' destruction of the Czech village of Lidice with immediate calls for retaliatory destruction of three German villages. Churchill was subsequently advised against the plan. Roberts, *Churchill*, p. 736; Wood, *Karski*, loc. 2404; Gilbert, *Auschwitz*, pp. 74–80; Wyman, *Abandonment*, pp. 124–26.

8. Breitman, *FDR*, loc. 3828; Stola, "Early," p. 8.

9. British and American officials had yet to focus on the role of the camp. In July, the Polish exile government had once again featured Auschwitz in their main English-language publication, including an account of the gas experiments against Soviet POWs the year before. The article's description of the IG Farben factory under construction near the camp drew some interest as a potential target for bombing. Fleming, *Auschwitz*, pp. 132–33; Rice, *Bombing*, cited in Neufeld, *Bombing*, p. 160.

10. Grabowski, *Kurierzy*, p. 188; Segieda, [Raport], PISM, A.9.III.2a t.3.

11. Segieda, [Raport], HIA, box 28, folder 7; Bleja, Interview, September 21, 2016; Mastalerz, Interview, September 20, 2016; Frazik, "Wojenne," p. 410.

12. Iranek-Osmecki, *Powołanie*, p. 110; Milton, *Churchill's*, loc. 2227; Tucholski, *Cichociemni*, pp. 68–70.

13. Segieda, [Raport], PISM, A.9.III.2a t.3. It's possible he played a role in bringing Stasiek's June 1 report to Warsaw in the first place, but with the absence of records it's not possible to establish what Napoleon knew of the emerging Holocaust in the camp before his mission there.

14. Segieda, [Raport], PISM, A.9.III.2a t.3; Lewandowski, *Swedish*, pp. 71–77. The arrest of the Swedes might have been in response to the publicity surrounding the Bund report; the Polish deputy defense minister in London, Izydor Modelski, warned about the risks of publicizing material brought by couriers a few weeks later. Fleming, *Auschwitz*, p. 95.

15. Jekiełek, *W pobliżu*, pp. 27–28, p. 92; Kożusznik, *Oświadczenia*, vol. 12, APMA-B, p. 8; Czech, *Auschwitz*, p. 164.

16. Klęczar, Interview, March 4, 2017; Jekiełek, *W pobliżu*, p. 62; Paczyńska, *Grypsy*, pp. xlv–xlvi.

17. Jekiełek, Interview, March 4, 2017; Klęczar, Interview, March 4, 2017; Czech, *Auschwitz*, p. 198.

18. Segieda, [Raport], PISM, A.9.III.2a t.3; 202/I-32, p. 71, in Marczewska, Ważniewski et al., *Zeszyty* (1968), p. 54. The figures in Stasiek's report are not entirely straightforward. He stated the number of male and female Jews registered in the camp, and that those not registered were gassed. To ascertain the actual number gassed the Warsaw underground had to add up the total number of arrivals and subtract the total number of registered prisoners (it seems Stasiek likely replicated the figures the SS themselves used). For likely authorship of June and July reports from the camp, see Rawicz, [List], September 23, 1957.

19. 202/I-31, pp. 214–29, in Marczewska, Ważniewski et al., *Zeszyty* (1968), p. 70; Segieda, [Raport], PISM, A.9.III.2a t.3.

20. Jekiełek, *W pobliżu*, pp. 27–28, p. 92; Kożusznik, Oświadczenia, vol. 12, APMA-B, p. 8; Czech, *Auschwitz*, p. 164; Kożusznik family, Interview, October 20, 2017; Rybak, Interview, March 8, 2017; Segieda, [Raport], PISM, A.9.III.2a t.3. Napoleon's description of some of the letters he read allows for the source material to be identified in the reports the Warsaw underground sent to London.

Chapter 12: Deadline

1. Höss, *Commandant*, p. 120; Pilecki, [Raport 1945], PUMST, BI 874, p. 48; Taul, Wspomnienia, vol. 62, APMA-B, p. 27.

2. Piekarski, *Escaping*, p. 85.

3. Pilecki, [Raport 1945], PUMST, BI 874, p. 56; Langbein, *People*, p. 29; Redzej, [Raport 1943], AAN, 202/XVIII/1, p. 45; Ciesielski, [Raport 1943], AAN, 202/XVIII, 1, p. 58.

4. Piekarski, *Escaping*, p. 85. The plan almost fell apart when the spy was transferred to the SS hospital outside the camp, but he died two days later from the injection.

5. Czech, *Auschwitz*, p. 165, p. 167.

6. Rawicz, [List], August 8, 1956; Rawicz, Oświadczenia, vol. 27, APMA-B; Rawicz, [Raport], date unknown.

7. Rawicz, [List], August 8, 1956; Rawicz, Oświadczenia, vol. 27, APMA-B; Rawicz, [Raport], date unknown.

8. Pilecki, [Raport 1945], PUMST, BI 874, p. 69, p. 71, p. 111; Rawicz, [List], August 8, 1956; Lasik et al., *Auschwitz*, vol. I, p. 299. It's worth noting that the uprising plan was formulated before the start of the Holocaust in the camp.

9. Pilecki, [Raport 1945], PUMST, BI 874, p. 54; Langbein, *People*, p. 29; Redzej, [Raport 1943], AAN, 202/XVIII/1, p. 45; Ciesielski, [Raport 1943], AAN, 202/XVIII/1, p. 58.

10. Dering, [Wspomnienia], p. 89; Allen, *The Fantastic*, loc. 550; Gawron, *Ochotnik*, p. 222; Pilecki, [Raport 1945], PUMST, BI 874, p. 48; Motz, [Testimony], August 28, 1971; Allen, *The Fantastic*, loc. 550. The use of lice to infect Germans with typhus is attested to elsewhere in other prisons and on trains. See Siedlecki, *Beyond*, p. 167. Several microbiologists were sent to Auschwitz around 1942 for plotting to poison German officers by putting typhoid germs in their food. Allen, *The Fantastic*, loc. 1633.

11. Piekarski, *Escaping*, p. 126.

12. Pietrzykowski, Wspomnienia, vol. 161, APMA-B, p. 141; Langbein, *People*, p. 240.

13. Dering, [Wspomnienia], p. 86, p. 141; Langbein, *People*, p. 240.

14. Dering, [Wspomnienia], p. 86.

15. Dering, [Wspomnienia], p. 86.

16. Czech, *Auschwitz*, p. 165; Kielar, *Anus Mundi*, p. 128; Dering, [Wspomnienia], p. 90.

17. Pilecki, *Report W*, p. 31; Czech, *Auschwitz*, p. 171; Piekarski, *Escaping*, p. 138.

18. Pilecki, [Raport 1945], PUMST, BI 874, p. 69; Pilecki, [Raport W], AAN, 202/XVIII/1, p. 31; Rawicz, [List], September 23, 1957; Bartosiewicz, [Wywiad], Ossolineum, 87/00; Bartosiewicz, Oświadczenia, vol. 84, APMA-B, p. 127; Rawicz, [List], September 23, 1957.

19. Chrościcki, Oświadczenia, vol. 11, APMA-B, pp. 4–5; Czech, *Auschwitz*, p. 174.

20. Pilecki, *The Auschwitz*, loc. 3083; Pilecki, [Raport 1945], PUMST, BI 874, p. 62.

21. Rawicz, [List], August 31, 1957.

22. Szmaglewska, *Dymy*, p. 14.

23. Kowalczyk, *Barbed*, vol. II, p. 155. August was not part of decision-making, but he recalled the order to proceed with the escape.

24. Chrościcki, Oświadczenia, vol. 11, APMA-B, pp. 4–5.

25. Kowalczyk, *Barbed*, vol. I, pp. 159–64.

26. Ostańkowicz, *Ziemia*, p. 187; Czech, *Auschwitz*, p. 178; Dering, [Wspomnienia], p. 77.

27. Czech, *Auschwitz*, pp. 180–81; Sobolewicz, *But I*, p. 131; Chrościcki, Oświadczenia, vol. 11, APMA-B, pp. 5–6; Langbein, *People*, p. 67.

28. Sobański, *Ucieczki*, pp. 47–48; Piechowski, Interview, October 14, 2016.

29. [Raport], no. 6/42, PISM, A.9.III.2a.55.2a.55. In the version of Witold's message that made it to London, references to the Holocaust in the report were edited out. See later endnote.

30. Piechowski, *Byłem*, p. 70

31. Piechowski, *Byłem*, pp. 74–75.

32. Piechowski, *Byłem*, p. 79.

33. Piechowski, *Byłem*, p. 79; Sobański, *Ucieczki*, pp. 44–50; Pilecki, [Raport 1945], PUMST, BI 874, p. 59; Pawłowski, Wałczek (dir.), *Jaśer.*

34. Pilecki, *The Auschwitz*, loc. 2976; Pilecki, [Raport 1945], PUMST, BI 874, p. 59.

35. Pilecki, [Raport—Nowy Wiśnicz], Wspomnienia, vol. 130, APMA-B, p. 111.

36. Dwork, van Pelt, *Auschwitz*, pp. 300–302; Wachsmann, *KL*, pp. 302–3.

37. Wachsmann, *KL*, p. 304; Dwork, van Pelt, *Auschwitz*, pp. 302–5; Redzej, [Raport 1943], AAN, 202/XVIII/1, p. 43.

38. Dwork, van Pelt, *Auschwitz*, pp. 302–5; Czech, *Auschwitz*, p. 179; Sobolewicz, *But I*, pp. 134–38; 202/I-31, pp. 95–97, in Marczewska, Ważniewski et al., *Zeszyty* (1968), p. 47.

39. Pilecki, *The Auschwitz*, loc. 2890; Pilecki, [Raport 1945], PUMST, BI 874, p. 57.

40. Pilecki, *The Auschwitz*, loc. 2890; Pilecki, [Raport 1945], PUMST, BI 874, p. 57.

41. Paczyńska, *Grypsy*, p. XXXIII. Witold doesn't acknowledge Napoleon's mission in his later writings, but Stanisław Kłodziński was a member of his organization and a close confidant of Stasiek. 202/I-31, pp. 214–29, in Marczewska, Ważniewski et al., *Zeszyty* (1968), p. 70.

42. 202/I-31, pp. 95–97, in Marczewska, Ważniewski et al., *Zeszyty* (1968), p. 47.

43. Vrba, *I Cannot*, p. 9.

44. Höss, *Death*, p. 286.

45. Höss, *Death*, p. 286.

Chapter 13: Paperwork

1. Paczyńska, *Grypys*, pp. XLV–XLVI; Segieda, [Raport], PISM, A.9.III.2a t.3.

2. Segieda, [Raport], PISM, A.9.III.2a t.3; 202/I-32, p. 71, in Marczewska, Ważniewski et al., *Zeszyty* (1968), p. 54; Taul, Oświadczenia, vol. 9, APMA-B, p. 1267.

3. Napoleon also carried a small bag of Kok-Saghyz seeds that had been smuggled out of the Nazis' secretive plant-breeding center in the village of Rajsko outside the camp. Himmler had acquired the seeds following the invasion of the Soviet Union and made the development of the rubber-rich plant a top priority at Rajsko, believing it might alleviate Germany's chronic rubber shortage. Stealing the seeds was a clever piece of industrial espionage. Segieda, [Raport], PISM, A.9.III.2a t.3; Zimmerman, *The Polish*, p. 151.

4. Jekiełek, [Konspiracja], AZHRL, R-VI-2/547, p. 130; Molin, Interview, September 23, 2017.

5. Urynowicz, *Czerniaków*, pp. 322–33.

6. Zimmerman, *The Polish*, p. 152; Stola, "Early," p. 9.

7. Engel, *In the Shadow*, p. 300; Segieda, [Raport], PISM, A.9.III.2a t.3. These were, of course, the same rumors that had circulated about German atrocities in World War I, which was duly noted by British officials when they learned of them.

8. Wood, *Karski*, loc. 2687; Rohleder, [Bundesanschaftschaftsakten], BA, E 4320 (B) 1990/133, Bd. 67, C.12.4440, cited in database to Kamber, *Geheime*.

9. Segieda, [Raport], PISM, A.9.III.2a t.3; 202/I-32, p. 71, in Marczewska, Ważniewski et al., *Zeszyty* (1968), p. 54.

10. Segieda, [Raport], PISM, A.9.III.2a t.3; Jekiełek, [Konspiracja], AZHRL, R-VI-2/547, p. 130; Nowak, *Courier*, p. 77.

11. Wanner, "Flüchtlinge," pp. 227–71; Bergier et al., *Final Report*, pp. 22–23. Switzerland expelled 24,398 people during the war years, and 19,495 of them were Jewish. Many more were likely turned away at the border. Juliusz Kühl suggests there were around 7,000 Polish Jewish refugees in the country. Kühl, [Memoir], USHMM, RG-27.001*08, p. 31.

12. Hastings, *The Secret*, loc. 6446.

13. Breitman, *Official*, pp. 138–41. Schulte's information was sent via telegram by Gerhart Riegner, who worked for the World Jewish Congress in Geneva. Until the pioneering research of Richard Breitman and Walter Laqueur, the identity of Schulte was unknown, and attention focused on Riegner's act of sending the

information rather than Schulte's of supplying it. I generally refer to "Schulte's information" in the following pages.

14. Kühl, [Memoir], USHMM, RG-27.001*08, p. 32.

15. Napoleon left no record of the meeting, so the only account of it comes from Kühl, who wrote it with care to hide the identity of the courier who accompanied him. But given the subsequent conversation about the liquidation of the Warsaw Ghetto, it seems likely to have been Napoleon. Kühl, [Report], USHMM, RG-27.001*05, microfiche 1, p. 1.

16. Rambert, *Bex*, pp. 62–81; Nahlik, *Przesiane*, p. 240; Kühl, [Memoir], USHMM, RG-27.001*08, p. 31; Haska, "Proszę," pp. 299–309; Kranzler, *Brother's*, pp. 200–202.

17. Kühl, [Memoir], USHMM, RG-27.001*05, microfiche 1, p. 1; Zieliński, "List," p. 159.

18. Kühl, [Memoir], USHMM, RG-27.001*05, microfiche 1; Segieda, [Raport], PISM, A.9.III.2a t.3.

19. Kamber, *Geheime*, p. 577. Kühl's report had a wide impact. It was sent to New York via the Polish legation's secret radio transmitter, and information from it was subsequently sent to FDR at the White House (it's unlikely he read it) and was discussed in senior British and American circles. This suggests that if Napoleon had revealed what he knew of Auschwitz at that juncture, he would have forced the West to confront the mass murder in the camp almost two years before they in fact did.

20. Segieda, [Raport], PISM, A.9.III.2a t.3; Fleming, *Auschwitz*, p. 111, p. 207.

21. Gilbert, *Auschwitz*, p. 54, p. 61.

22. [Depesza nr 38], PISM, A.9.III.4; [Depesza nr 40], PISM, A.9.III.4.

23. [Depesza nr 38], PISM, A.9.III.4.

Chapter 14: Fever

1. Czech, *Auschwitz*, pp. 208–11; Wachsmann, *KL*, p. 304.

2. Pilecki, [Raport 1945], PUMST, BI 874, p. 68; Pilecki, [Raport 1943], AAN, 202/XVIII/1, p. 73; Iwaszko et al., *Auschwitz*, vol. II, p. 164.

3. Pilecki, [Raport 1945], PUMST, BI 874, p. 58, p. 68; Piekarski, *Escaping*, p. 148.

4. Langbein, *People*, p. 298; Pilecki, *The Auschwitz*, loc. 4098; Pilecki, [Raport 1945], PUMST, BI 874, pp. 87–88.

5. Kielar, *Anus Mundi*, p. 147; Langbein, *People*, p. 140; Setkiewicz, *The Private*, p. 121.

6. Pilecki, *The Auschwitz*, loc. 3346, loc. 3748; Pilecki, [Raport 1945], PUMST, BI 874, p. 68, p. 79.

7. Pilecki, [Raport—Nowy Wiśnicz], Wspomnienia, vol. 130, APMA-B, p. 111.

8. Kobrzyński, Wspomnienia, vol. 129, APMA-B, p. 45; Smoczyński, "Ostatnie," no pages given.

9. Olszowski, "Więźniarska," p. 186.

10. Smoczyński, "Ostatnie," no pages given; Kobrzyński, Wspomnienia, vol. 129, APMA-B, p. 46. It appears that the SS was already aware of Stasiek's identity from his earlier interrogation in Warsaw. The parcel may have served as a reminder to Grabner of Stasiek's presence and coincided with an SS cull of prisoners with resistance records.

11. Pilecki, [Raport 1945], PUMST, BI 874, p. 51; Piekarski, *Escaping*, p. 117; Ciesielski, *Wspomnienia*, p. 68. The existence of a camp radio is based on testimonies of Witold, Edek, and Kon. Another testimony describes finding the radio equipment, partially destroyed, in the attic of block 17. Taul, Oświadczenia, vol. 9, APMA-B, pp. 1264–71. After the war, Kazimierz Rawicz dismissed the idea of a radio station. "Everything is correct, everything is all right, and only that unfortunate radio-station is a serious mistake in that account. I don't know what on earth made him fantasise and add such a detail, which did not happen and under which I couldn't sign [WP's account] under any circumstances." Rawicz, [List do L. Serafińskiej], August 4, 1958; Materiały, vol. 220, APMA-B, p. 25. Rawicz, however, left the camp before the radio was operational.

12. Biernacki, [List], Materiały Ruchu Oporu, vols. 1–2, APMA-B, p. 10; Kłodziński, [List do W. Jekiełka i T. Lasockiej], November 24, 1942, cited in Paczyńska, *Grypsy*, p. 676: "In Krankenbau [hospital] there is about two thousand people. Mortality rate about thirty people per day, year ago was about eighty people. Thirty-sixty people (among them four to six Poles) dying every day from phenol injections." Pilecki, [Raport 1945], PUMST, BI 874, p. 63.

13. Dering, [Wspomnienia], p. 29, p. 103, pp. 139–42.

14. Dering, [Wspomnienia], p. 139; Wierusz, Oświadczenia, vol. 77, APMA-B, p. 21.

15. Diem, Wspomnienia, vol. 172, APMA-B, p. 141; Kielar, *Anus Mundi*, p. 128; Dering, [Wspomnienia], p. 104; Wierusz, Oświadczenia, vol. 77, APMA-B, p. 21; Radlicki, *Kapo*, pp. 104–6.

16. Pietrzykowski, Oświadczenia, vol. 88, APMA-B, p. 22.

17. Taubenschlag, *To Be*, p. 76.

18. Dering, [Wspomnienia], p. 105.

19. Dering, [Wspomnienia], p. 105.

20. Dering, [Wspomnienia], p. 105.

21. Dering, [Wspomnienia], p. 105.

22. Kielar, *Anus Mundi*, p. 105.

23. Kielar, *Anus Mundi*, p. 105.

24. Kielar, *Anus Mundi*, p. 108.

25. Kielar, *Anus Mundi*, p. 108.

26. Czech, *Auschwitz*, p. 229; Pilecki, *Report W*, p. 22. Witold says Dering also saved twenty prisoners by providing them with orderly uniforms.

27. 202/I-31, pp. 214–29, in Marczewska, Ważniewski et al., *Zeszyty* (1968), p. 70. Info came from a letter sent from the camp by Edward Biernacki to Wojciech Jekiełek (see Jekiełek, *W pobliżu*, pp. 116–17).

28. Pilecki, [Raport 1945], PUMST, BI 874, pp. 63–64; Strzelecka, *Voices*, vol. 3, p. 18.

29. Pilecki, [Raport 1945], PUMST, BI 874, pp. 63–64.

30. Pilecki, [Raport 1945], PUMST, BI 874, p. 64.

31. Pilecki, [Raport 1945], PUMST, BI 874, p. 66. Witold describes a bombing raid on the night he entered the hospital suffering from typhus. There is no evidence that such a raid took place, but it might well have formed part of Witold's fevered dreams during his illness.

32. Pilecki, [Raport 1945], PUMST, BI 874, p. 66.

33. Pilecki, *The Auschwitz*, loc. 3275; Pilecki, [Raport 1945], PUMST, BI 874, p. 66.

34. Pilecki, [Raport 1945], PUMST, BI 874, p. 67.

35. Setkiewicz, *Zaopatrzenie*, p. 60; Redzej, [Raport 1943], AAN, 202/XVIII/1, p. 46.

36. Czech, *Auschwitz*, p. 164; Pogozhev, *Escape*, loc. 1950.

37. It has not been possible to identify Steinberg's first name. Laurence, *Auschwitz*, loc. 2122; Pogozhev, *Escape*, loc. 1950.

38. Laurence, *Auschwitz*, p. 2122; Pilecki, *Report W*, p. 34; Pogozhev, *Escape*, loc. 2052.

39. Ostańkowicz, *Ziemia*, p. 232.

40. Ostańkowicz, *Ziemia*, p. 232.

41. Ostańkowicz, *Ziemia*, p. 233.

42. Steinberg's unit never made a breakout attempt. It appears they were betrayed by the kapo of the second Sonderkommando unit, Adolph Weiss, who pre-

sumably feared that any action by Steinberg's unit would result in the death of his men. Both units were gassed in December 1942. Wetzler, Oświadczenia, vol. 40, APMA-B, p. 28.

43. Pilecki, *Report W*, pp. 22–24; Ciesielski, [Raport 1943], AAN, 202/XVIII/1, p. 10; Langbein, *People*, p. 88; Iwaszko, Kłodziński, "Bunt," pp. 119–22.

Chapter 15: Declaration

1. Friedenson, Kranzler, *Heroine*, p. 91.
2. Gilbert, *Auschwitz*, pp. 67–68. British intelligence analysts had picked up the role of Auschwitz as a collecting point for Jews via intercepted radio messages, but the data referred only to those prisoners registered in the camp as workers and not those gassed. Schulte, *London*, p. 211, cited in Hackmann, Süß, *Hitler's*, p. 211; Breitman, Laqueur, *Breaking*, p. 125; Breitman, *Official*, p. 143. The British knew far more than the Americans as to German persecution of Jews, via decoded radio messages, which they had yet to share with their U.S. counterparts.
3. Breitman, Laqueur, *Breaking*, p. 124; Laqueur, *The Terrible*, p. 100; Breitman, Lichtman, *FDR*, loc. 3440; Lipstadt, *Beyond*, p. 321.
4. Rowecki, [Depesza nr 803], October 3, 1942, in Iranek-Osmecki et al., *Armia*, vol. VI, p. 261; Pilecki, [Raport 1945], PUMST, BI 874, p. 59; 202/I-31, pp. 214–29, in Marczewska, Ważniewski et al., *Zeszyty* (1968), p. 70. There is further evidence of the underground's tampering with Auschwitz material. Jaster's report clearly describes the action of the Sonderkommando in Birkenau. But the fact that they were Jewish and tasked with killing Jews is missing. Meanwhile the underground journalist Natalia Zarembina was writing a book about Auschwitz for mass circulation that drew from Stasiek's reports but painted it as an exclusively Polish concentration camp. Fleming, *Auschwitz*, p. 360.
5. Rowecki, [Depesza no 803], October 3, 1942, in Iranek-Osmecki et al., *Armia*, vol. VI, p. 261; Zimmerman, *Polish*, p. 103; Engel, *In the Shadow*, p. 202. Rowecki did send one report in September that briefly mentioned that Jews were being gassed in Auschwitz; it was based on Stasiek's first reporting. The reference formed a small part of a longer discussion of Nazi and Soviet occupation policies, and appears to have drawn little attention. The report was translated and included in a longer summary that was sent to the Polish legation in New York toward the end of November, but it appears to have gone no further. Fleming, *Auschwitz*, pp. 135–45.

6. Gilbert, *Auschwitz*, pp. 88–92; Fleming, *Auschwitz*, pp. 157–62.

7. Gilbert, *Auschwitz*, p. 86; Wyman, *The Abandonment*, pp. 73–74; Breitman, Lichtman, *FDR*, loc. 3993. The Polish government released its own report on the same day as the Jewish Agency's, which listed the death camps of Bełżec, Sobibór, and Treblinka but made no mention of Auschwitz. The State Department refrained from publishing the findings of its own investigation.

8. Leff, *Buried*, pp. 155–56; Wyman, *The Abandonment*, pp. 73–74.

9. Breitman, Lichtman, *FDR*, loc. 4012.

10. Raczyński, *In Allied*, p. 126; Breitman, *Official*, p. 151.

11. Wasserstein, *Britain*, p. 34; Fleming, *Auschwitz*, p. 96; Breitman, *Official*, p. 145. The arrival of the courier Jan Karski in London in November 1942 helped to galvanize the Polish exile government's response.

12. Republic of Poland, *The Mass*, December 1942, NA, FCO 371/30924, C12313; Breitman, *Official*, pp. 228–29; Manchester, Reid, *The Last*, loc. 3676.

13. Breitman, *Official*, p. 153; Czech, *Auschwitz*, p. 276; Bruland, *Holocaust*, pp. 668–71.

14. Gilbert, *Auschwitz*, pp. 96–98.

15. Breitman, *Official*, p. 157; Gilbert, *Auschwitz*, p. 99.

16. Cohen, *Eleanor*, p. 181; Breitman, *Official*, p. 170; Gilbert, *Auschwitz*, p. 109.

17. Rowecki, [Depesza nr 803], October 3, 1942, in Iranek-Osmecki et al., *Armia*, vol. VI, p. 261; Rowecki, [Depesza], December 23, 1942, in Iranek-Osmecki et al., *Armia*, vol. II, pp. 393–94; Rowecki, [Planowanie powstania powszechnego 1940–1944], December 23, 1942, PUMST, A.379, p. 43; Piper, *Voices*, vol. 8, p. 37.

18. Westermann, "The Royal," p. 204; Biddle, *Allied*, in Neufeld, Berenbaum, *The Bombing*, pp. 38–39. The discussion about bombing Auschwitz usually focuses on the Allied debate in the summer of 1944. However, as the impact of Witold's first report from the camp shows, the proposal to bomb the camp was already under discussion by the RAF in January 1941. Scholars are divided as to how effective an Allied attempt to bomb the camp would have been. Rowecki, [Depesza nr 803], October 3, 1942, in Iranek-Osmecki et al., *Armia*, vol. VI, p. 261; Gilbert, *Auschwitz*, p. 107; Breitman, *Official*, p. 169.

19. Breitman, *Official*, p. 169; Gilbert, *Auschwitz*, p. 107.

20. Gilbert, *Auschwitz*, p. 119; Breitman, *Official*, p. 175. The Swiss lawyers Richard Lichtheim and Gerhard Riegner had been sending reports through the American legation in Bern for several months. On February 10, 1943, State officials drafted a telegram to the ambassador discouraging him from granting them

further access to the legation's transmitter. The message was couched in general terms so as to avoid any charge of impropriety. But the American embassy took the hint. The next time Riegner appeared with news of a Nazi attempt to deport fifteen thousand Jewish spouses of German nationals to Auschwitz, he was instructed to send his message via the public telegraph office.

Chapter 16: Breakdown

1. Pilecki, *Report W*, p. 19.
2. Iwaszko et al., *Auschwitz*, vol. II, p. 409; Pilecki, *Report W*, p. 19.
3. Pilecki, [Raport 1945], PUMST, BI 874, p. 3; Pilecki, [Raport W], AAN, 202/XVIII/1, p. 69.
4. Pilecki, [Raport 1945], PUMST, BI 874, p. 3; Pilecki, [Raport W], AAN, 202/XVIII/1, p. 69.
5. Piekarski, *Escaping*, p. 23.
6. Piekarski, *Escaping*, p. 23.
7. Piekarski, *Escaping*, p. 23.
8. Pilecki, [Klucz], Wspomnienia, vol. 183, APMA-B, p. 79; Sowul, Oświadczenia, vol. 72, APMA-B, p. 16.
9. Pilecki, [Raport 1945], PUMST, BI 874, p. 73; Sowul, Oświadczenia, vol. 72, APMA-B, p. 19; Iwaszko et al., *Auschwitz*, vol. II, p. 390.
10. Piekarski, *Escaping*, p. 148. Fred was shot upon recovery on March 3, 1943. Czech, *Auschwitz*, p. 342.
11. Wierusz, Oświadczenia, vol. 77, APMA-B, p. 21; Langbein, *People*, pp. 221–22; Dering, [Wspomnienia], p. 7; Diem, Wspomnienia, vol. 172, AMPA-B, p. 9; Iwaszko et al., *Auschwitz*, vol. II, p. 367; Wachsmann, *KL*, p. 341; Iwaszko et al., *Auschwitz*, vol. II, pp. 361–65.
12. Piekarski, *Escaping*, p. 77; Pilecki, [Raport teren S], AAN, 202/XVIII/1, p. 88.
13. Piper, *Auschwitz*, vol. III, p. 159; Dwork, van Pelt, *Auschwitz*, pp. 324–25; Pilecki, [Raport 1945], PUMST, BI 874, p. 74; 202/II-35, p. 84, in Marczewska, Ważniewski et al., *Zeszyty* (1968), pp. 79–80. It seems that Witold and other members of the underground thought that the bodies would be disposed of in electric incinerators (and not the coke-fired ovens actually used).
14. Frączek, Wspomnienia, vol. 66, APMA-B, pp. 163–64; Pilecki, *Report W*, p. 27; Piekarski, *Escaping*, pp. 144–45; Komski, Oświadczenia, vol. 71, APMA-B, p. 64; Ławski, Wspomnienia, vol. 154/154a, APMA-B, p. 147, p. 148; Harat, [Działalność], no pages given; Kajtoch, Wspomnienia, vol. 27,

APMA-B, pp. 1–149; Kuczbara, [Grypsy], Materiały Ruchu Oporu, vol. X, APMA-B, p. 6, p. 9, p. 11; Dwork, van Pelt, *Auschwitz*, pp. 324–25. The escape was conceived of by the camp dentist, Bolesław Kuczbara.

15. Pilecki, *Report W*, p. 27; Piekarski, *Escaping*, pp. 144–45; Komski, Oświadcze-nia, vol. 71, APMA-B, p. 64; Ławski, Wspomnienia, vol. 154/154a, APMA-B, p. 147, p. 148; Harat, [Działalność], no pages given; Kajtoch, Wspomnienia, vol. 27, APMA-B, pp. 1–149. The Harats sheltered the men in their home in Libiąż. Mieczysław, Jan, and Otto were subsequently recaptured, the former hanging himself in the transport returning him to Auschwitz. Bolesław was apprehended in Warsaw and appears to have died in police custody. Jan and Otto survived the war.

16. Pilecki, [Raport 1945], PUMST, BI 874, p. 74; Ostańkowicz, *Ziemia*, p. 266; Czech, *Auschwitz*, p. 313.

17. Pilecki, [Raport 1945], PUMST, BI 874, p. 75.

18. Pilecki, [Raport 1945], PUMST, BI 874, p. 75; Pilecki, *Report W*, p. 35; Pilecki, [Raport W], AAN, 202/XVIII/1, p. 72.

19. Pilecki, [Raport 1945], PUMST, BI 874, p. 86. By 1943, a third of the prison-ers were employed servicing the camp: Iwaszko et al., *Auschwitz*, vol. II, p. 89. Selections in the hospital were also curtailed, and Polish inmates were no longer sent to be gassed as some had prior to December 1942. Wachsmann, *KL*, p. 347.

20. Pilecki, [Raport 1945], PUMST, BI 874, pp. 79–80.

21. Pilecki, [Raport 1945], PUMST, BI 874, p. 69.

22. Pilecki, [Raport 1945], PUMST, BI 874, p. 69; Ciesielski, [Raport 1943], AAN, 202/XVIII/1, p. 12; Redzej, [Raport 1943], AAN, 202/XVIII/1, p. 45a; Głowa, Wspomnienia, vol. 94, APMA-B, pp. 138–39.

23. Głowa, Oświadczenia, vol. 36, APMA-B, p. 6; Dering, [Wspomnienia], p. 50; Głowa, Oświadczenia, vol. 94, APMA-B, p. 140.

24. Pilecki, *Report W*, p. 115. Witold says two hundred children were murdered, but the total figure was less than one hundred.

25. Iwaszko et al., *Auschwitz*, vol. II, p. 156; Pilecki, *Report W*, p. 44; Pilecki, [Raport W], AAN, 202/XVIII/1, pp. 75–76; Ciesielski, [Raport 1943], AAN, 202/XVIII/1, p. 7.

26. Czech, *Auschwitz*, p. 367; Pilecki, *Report W*, p. 44; Piekarski, *Escaping*, p. 157.

27. Pilecki, *Report W*, p. 116; Ciesielski, *Wspomnienia*, pp. 101–2.

28. Pilecki, [Raport 1945], PUMST, BI 874, p. 83; Piekarski, *Escaping*, p. 157.

29. Czech, *Auschwitz*; Pilecki, *Report W*, p. 117; Redzej, [Raport 1943], AAN, 202/XVIII/1, p. 43.

30. Czech, *Kalendarz*, p. 362, p. 370; Iwaszko et al., *Auschwitz*, vol. II, pp. 349–58; Wachsmann, *KL*, p. 316; Diem, Wspomnienia, vol. 172, APMA-B, pp. 134–35; Dering, [Wspomnienia], pp. 116–17; Ławski, Wspomnienia, vol. 154/154a, APMA-B, p. 94.

31. Zabawski, Wspomnienia, vol. 98, APMA-B, p. 83.

32. Pilecki, [Raport 1945], PUMST, BI 874, p. 85.

33. Pilecki, [Raport 1945], PUMST, BI 874, p. 85.

34. Pilecki, [Raport 1945], PUMST, BI 874, p. 85.

35. Pilecki, *The Auschwitz*, loc. 4049; Pilecki, [Raport 1945], PUMST, BI 874, p. 86.

36. Zabawski, Wspomnienia, vol. 98, APMA-B, p. 90; Ostrowska, [Wspomnienia 1], p. 5.

37. Pilecki, [Raport 1945], PUMST, BI 874, p. 85.

Chapter 17: Impact

1. Segieda, [Raport], PISM, A.9.III.2a t.3.

2. Segieda, [Raport], PISM, A.9.III.2a t.3.

3. Segieda, [Raport], PISM, A.9.III.2a t.3; Frazik, "Wojenne," p. 413; Avni, *Spain*, p. 106.

4. Siudak, [List], February 9, 1943, PUMST, A.9.E. t.107.

5. Segieda, [Raport], PISM, A.9.III.2a t.3.

6. Wood, *Karski*, loc. 2780; Fleming, *Auschwitz*, p. 129.

7. O'Reilly, [Memo], February 26, 1943, NA, HS 9/1337/7.

8. Napoleon does not place his investigation of Nazi brutality in Auschwitz at the top of his report. In fact, it comes toward the end, after discussions about the relations of various Polish political parties. This likely reflects the concerns of his interlocutors at the Polish Ministry of Interior. Fleming, *Auschwitz*, pp. 168–73. Napoleon's first mention of Auschwitz concerns his theft of the Kok-Saghyz seeds. The seeds were swiftly sent for testing, but the resulting plants were revealed to be of low rubber content. Orkan, [Depesza], November 15, 1943, London, HIA, box 52, folder 18.

9. Zimmerman, *The Polish*, p. 191. The number was three hundred thousand, according to Nazi figures. Wachsmann, *KL*, p. 293.

10. Zimmerman, *The Polish*, p. 191.

11. Gilbert, *Allies*, p. 119, pp. 126–27; Breitman, *Official*, pp. 178–79; Zimmerman, *The Polish*, p. 191.

12. Fleming, *Auschwitz*, pp. 173–75. It's not clear if Savery was given the camp's death toll of 502,000, but he already knew from the State Department investigation that two million Jews had been murdered. The figure from Auschwitz corresponded to what might be expected from a Europe-wide program of extermination. The Polish government was well aware that the limited broadcast distribution meant public response would be likewise curtailed. See Fleming, *Auschwitz*, p. 123.

13. Olson, *Last*, loc. 2085.

14. Fleming, *Auschwitz*, p. 174.

15. Napoleon briefed the Polish Jewish politician Ignacy Schwarzbart on or before April 18, 1943. In a subsequent write-up of the meeting, Schwarzbart noted that Napoleon had visited him on his own initiative, although it seems likely that Napoleon had received careful coaching from the Polish interior ministry on what to say. Schwarzbart arranged for the notes of Napoleon's interview to be written up the same day for distribution to Berl Locker, chairman of the Jewish Agency in London, and Rabbi Irving Miller, a leading American Zionist who was visiting London. "How to publish it we shall consider jointly," Schwarzbart wrote in a cover letter to the two men (YVA M2. 261). At the end of April, Schwarzbart sent copies of his conversation to the British Section of the World Jewish Congress's offices in London and New York and the Jewish Agency in Palestine. As a result of its dispatch to the U.S., the British and American censors also picked up a copy. It was widely distributed among officials but did not attract further debate. The Polish government returned to the idea of bombing Auschwitz in August 1943, without success. Schwarzbart, [Archives], IPN, BU_2835_15, p. 37.

16. Laqueur, *The Terrible*, p. 96.

17. Zimmerman, *The Polish*, p. 218.

18. Sehn, *Obóz*, p. 135.

19. Siudak, [List], June 22, 1943, HIA, box 52, folder 15.

Chapter 18: Flight

1. Pilecki, [Raport 1945], PUMST, BI 874, p. 91.

2. Pilecki, [Raport 1945], PUMST, BI 874, p. 88.

3. Pilecki, *The Auschwitz*, loc. 3969; Pilecki, [Raport 1945], PUMST, BI 874, p. 84.

4. Pilecki, *The Auschwitz*, loc. 3969; Pilecki, [Raport 1945], PUMST, BI 874, p. 84.

5. Pilecki, [Raport 1945], PUMST, BI 874, p. 88; Langbein, *People*, p. 75; Der-

ing, [Wspomnienia], p. 23; Szarbel, [Zeznanie], IPN, BU_2188_14, pp. 110–13; Garliński, *Fighting*, p. 175.

6. Langbein, *People*, p. 75; Pilecki, [Raport 1945], PUMST, BI 874, p. 88.
7. Pilecki, *The Auschwitz*, loc. 4140; Pilecki, [Raport 1945], PUMST, BI 874, p. 89.
8. Pilecki, *Report W*, p. 61; Pilecki, [Raport 1945], PUMST, BI 874, p. 89; Pilecki, [Raport W], AAN, 202/XVIII/1, p. 81.
9. Pilecki, *The Auschwitz*, loc. 4146; Pilecki, [Raport 1945], PUMST, BI 874, p. 89.
10. Pilecki, *The Auschwitz*, loc. 4152; Pilecki, [Raport 1945], PUMST, BI 874, p. 89; Fejkiel, *Więźniarski*, pp. 108–9.
11. Fejkiel, *Medycyna*, in Bidakowski, Wójcik, *Pamiętniki*, p. 507; Pilecki, [Raport 1945], PUMST, BI 874, p. 89, p. 90.
12. Diem, Wspomnienia, vol. 172, APMA-B, p. 151; Pilecki, *The Auschwitz*, loc. 4241; Pilecki, [Raport 1945], PUMST, BI 874, p. 90.
13. Pilecki, *The Auschwitz*, loc. 4200; Pilecki, [Raport 1945], PUMST, BI 874, p. 90.
14. Pilecki, [Raport 1945], PUMST, BI 874, p. 91.
15. Czech, *Auschwitz*, p. 33.
16. Pilecki, *The Auschwitz*, loc. 4241; Pilecki, [Raport 1945], PUMST, BI 874, p. 92.
17. Pilecki, *The Auschwitz*, loc. 4241; Pilecki, [Raport 1945], PUMST, BI 874, p. 92.
18. Pilecki, [Raport 1945], PUMST, BI 874, p. 92.
19. Pilecki, [Raport 1945], PUMST, BI 874, p. 93.
20. Ciesielski, *Wspomnienia*, pp. 115–16.
21. Ciesielski, *Wspomnienia*, pp. 115–16.
22. Ciesielski, *Wspomnienia*, p. 118.
23. Ciesielski, *Wspomnienia*, pp. 121–22.
24. Pilecki, [Raport 1945], PUMST, BI 874, p. 94.
25. Pilecki, *The Auschwitz*, loc. 4344; Pilecki, [Raport 1945], PUMST, BI 874, p. 94.
26. Pilecki, *The Auschwitz*, loc. 4364; Pilecki, [Raport 1945], PUMST, BI 874, p. 94.
27. Pilecki, *The Auschwitz*, loc. 4364; Pilecki, [Raport 1945], PUMST, BI 874, p. 94.
28. Pilecki, [Raport 1945], PUMST, BI 874, p. 95.

29. Pilecki, [Raport 1945], PUMST, BI 874, p. 95.

30. Ciesielski, *Wspomnienia*, p. 128; Pilecki, [Raport 1945], PUMST, BI 874, p. 95.

31. Ciesielski, *Wspomnienia*, p. 128; Pilecki, [Raport 1945], PUMST, BI 874, p. 95.

32. Pilecki, [Raport 1945], PUMST, BI 874, p. 96.

33. Ciesielski, *Wspomnienia*, p. 128.

34. Pilecki, *The Auschwitz*, loc. 4420; Pilecki, [Raport 1945], PUMST, BI 874, p. 96.

35. Pilecki, [Raport 1945], PUMST, BI 874, p. 96.

36. Pilecki, [Raport 1945], PUMST, BI 874, p. 96.

37. Pilecki, *The Auschwitz*, loc. 4461; Pilecki, [Raport 1945], PUMST, BI 874, p. 97.

38. Pilecki, *The Auschwitz*, loc. 4461; Pilecki, [Raport 1945], PUMST, BI 874, p. 97.

39. Pilecki, *The Auschwitz*, loc. 4482; Pilecki, [Raport 1945], PUMST, BI 874, p. 97.

40. Ciesielski, *Wspomnienia*, p. 128.

41. Pilecki, [Raport 1945], PUMST, BI 874, p. 98.

42. Pilecki, [Raport 1945], PUMST, BI 874, p. 99.

43. Ciesielski, *Wspomnienia*, pp. 139–43.

44. Ciesielski, *Wspomnienia*, pp. 139–43.

45. Pilecki, *The Auschwitz*, loc. 4565; Pilecki, [Raport 1945], PUMST, BI 874, p. 100.

46. Pilecki, *The Auschwitz*, loc. 4565; Pilecki, [Raport 1945], PUMST, BI 874, p. 100.

47. Pilecki, *The Auschwitz*, loc. 4575; Pilecki, [Raport 1945], PUMST, BI 874, p. 100.

48. Pilecki, [Raport 1945], PUMST, BI 874, p. 100.

49. Pilecki, [Raport 1945], PUMST, BI 874, p. 100.

50. Pilecki, [Raport 1945], PUMST, BI 874, p. 101.

51. Pilecki, *The Auschwitz*, loc. 4622; Pilecki, [Raport 1945], PUMST, BI 874, p. 101.

52. Pilecki, *The Auschwitz*, loc. 4622; Pilecki, [Raport 1945], PUMST, BI 874, p. 101.

53. Serafiński, [Ucieczka], p. 2.

54. Pilecki, *The Auschwitz*, loc. 4630; Pilecki, [Raport 1945], PUMST, BI 874, p. 102.

55. Pilecki, *The Auschwitz*, loc. 4637; Pilecki, [Raport 1945], PUMST, BI 874, p. 102.

56. Serafiński, [Ucieczka], p. 3.

57. Pilecki, [Raport—Nowy Wiśnicz], Wspomnienia, vol. 130, APMA-B, pp. 110–13.

58. Pilecki, [Raport 1945], PUMST, BI 874, p. 102.

59. Redzej, Wspomnienia, vol. 178, APMA-B, p. 110.

60. Serafiński, [Ucieczka], p. 3.

61. Pilecki, [Raport W], AAN, 202/XVIII/1, p. 84.

62. Pilecki, [Raport 1945], PUMST, BI 874, p. 102.

63. Fejkiel, *Medycyna*, in Bidakowski, Wójcik, *Pamiętniki*, pp. 507–9; Pilecki, [Raport 1945], PUMST, BI 874, p. 102.

64. Możdżeń, Oświadczenia, vol. 3, APMA-B, p. 101.

65. Zabawski, Wspomnienia, vol. 98, APMA-B, p. 95.

66. Zabawski, Wspomnienia, vol. 98, APMA-B, p. 95.

67. Pilecki, [Raport 1945], PUMST, BI 874, p. 102.

Chapter 19: Alone

1. Gistedt, *Od operetki*, p. 108.

2. Ostrowski, Interview, March 9, 2016, p. 247; Bartoszewski, *1859*, p. 564.

3. Ostrowski, Interview, March 9, 2016; Pilecki, Akta sprawy, Protokół przesłuchania Witolda Pileckiego, Materiały, vol. 223, APMA-B, p. 85.

4. Czarnecka, *Największa*, pp. 109–201; Pawłowski, Walczak (dir.), *Jaster*; Paulsson, *Secret*, p. 21.

5. Paulsson, *Secret*, p. 21; 202/II-35, p. 84, in Marczewska, Ważniewski et al., *Zeszyty* (1968), pp. 79–80.

6. Pilecka-Optułowicz, Interview, May 17, 2016; Ostrowski, Interview, March 9, 2016; Pilecki, Akta sprawy, Protokół przesłuchania Witolda Pileckiego, Materiały, vol. 223, APMA-B, p. 85.

7. Pilecki, [List], October 19, 1943, IPN.

8. Pilecki, [List], October 19, 1943, IPN.

9. Bartoszewski, *1859*, p. 656.

10. Pilecki, [Raport 1945], PUMST, BI 874, p. 103.

11. Pilecki, *The Auschwitz*, loc. 4698; Pilecki, [Raport 1945], PUMST, BI 874, p. 103; Pilecki, [Raport W], AAN, 202/XVIII/1, p. 23.

12. Pilecki, *Report W*, p. 79; Pilecki, [Raport W], AAN, 202/XVIII/1, p. 33.

13. Walter-Janke, *W Armii*, p. 260.

14. Pilecki, [Raport 1945], PUMST, BI 874, p. 103; Albin, *List*, p. 198; Machnowski, "Sprawa," p. 127. Edward Ciesielski arrived in Warsaw in December 1943 and likely brought news of his latest exchanges with the camp.

15. Pilecki, [Zamiast], Materiały, vol. 223c, APMA-B, p. 1.

16. Szpakowski, Interview, January 31, 2017; Pilecki, Akta sprawy, Protokół przesłuchania Tadeusza Sztrum de Sztrema, Materiały, vol. 223a, APMA-B, p. 398.

17. Abramow-Newerly, Interview, October 2, 2017.

18. Pilecki, [Zamiast], Materiały, vol. 223c, APMA-B, pp. 3–4.

19. Pilecki, [Zamiast], Materiały, vol. 223c, APMA-B, p. 1.

20. Pilecki, [Raport 1945], PUMST, BI 874, p. 103.

21. Abramow-Newerly, Interview, October 2, 2017.

22. Abramow-Newerly, *Lwy*, pp. 153–56.

23. Marrus, *The Nazi*, Part 5: "Public Opinion and Relations to Jews"; Abramow-Newerly, Interview, October 2, 2017.

24. Pilecki, Interview, July 11, 2016.

25. Pilecki, Interview, July 11, 2016.

26. Klukowski, *Diary*, p. 257.

27. Pilecki, [Raport 1945], PUMST, BI 874, p. 102.

28. Bartoszewski, *1859*, p. 656; "War and Internationa [*sic*] Situation," February 22, 1944, Hansard, U.K. Parliament.

29. Bartoszewski, *1859*, p. 656.

30. Fieldorf, Zachuta, *Generał*, p. 277; Kuciński, *August*, p. 77.

31. Pilecka-Optułowicz, Interview, May 17, 2016.

Chapter 20: Uprising

1. The figure of ten reports includes Witold's oral and written accounts described in this book. The number may have been higher taking into account other members of his organization who left the camp bearing his instructions.

2. Gilbert, *Allies*; Breitman, *Official*, p. 211.

3. On June 12, 1944, Emanuel Scherer and Anzelm Reiss went to the Polish minister of the interior requesting that the underground attack Auschwitz and other camps. In July, John Pehle of the War Rescue Board dismissed the idea of a land attack on the basis that "the apparently deep-rooted anti-Semitism" of Poles would prevent the attack from occurring in "good faith." It's not clear whether

he was responding to the debate in Allied capitals or had drawn his own conclusions. Fleming, *Auschwitz*, p. 255. Komorowski didn't entirely dismiss the proposal of a ground operation. It made sense to have a force ready in the worst-case scenario that the Nazis decided to liquidate the camp and kill everyone in it, but he remained skeptical that a force could be moved into position.

4. Pilecki, [Raport W], AAN, p. 79. At the end of July, Komorowski dispatched a courier to Auschwitz to contact what was left of the camp resistance to develop a plan, which included blowing up the crematoria and gas chambers in Birkenau. The courier was shot and captured in September and subsequently interned in Auschwitz.

5. Richie, *Warsaw*, p. 164.

6. Davies, *Rising '44*, loc. 8673.

7. Bartoszewski, *1859*, p. 696; Korboński, *Fighting*, p. 345.

8. Korboński, *Fighting*, p. 345.

9. Richie, *Warsaw*, p. 133.

10. Richie, *Warsaw*, p. 133; Davies, *Rising '44*, loc. 2598.

11. Pilecki, Akta sprawy, Protokół przesłuchania Witolda Pileckiego, Materiały, vol. 223, APMA-B, p. 73.

12. Richie, *Warsaw*, p. 136.

13. Davies, *Rising '44*, loc. 2598; Richie, *Warsaw*, p. 136.

14. Richie, *Warsaw*, p. 179.

15. Iranek-Osmecki, *Powołanie*, p. 427.

16. Nowak, *Courier*, p. 240; Walasek, Interview, May 19, 2016.

17. Forczyk, *Warsaw 1944*, p. 38, cited in Richie, *Warsaw*, p. 193; Nowak, *Courier*, p. 240; Walasek, Interview, May 19, 2016.

18. Walasek, Interview, May 19, 2016; Hałko, *Kotwica*, p. 22.

19. Walasek, Interview, May 19, 2016; Sierchuła, Utracka, "Historia," pp. 216–17.

20. Nowak, *Courier*, p. 240; Davies, *Powstanie '44*, p. 329.

21. Richie, *Warsaw*, p. 244.

22. Zimmerman, *The Polish*, p. 385; Richie, *Warsaw*, p. 216.

23. Sierchuła, Utracka, "Historia," pp. 216–17; Richie, *Warsaw*, p. 242.

24. Remlein, [Wspomnienia].

25. Sierchuła, Utracka, "Historia," pp. 216–17.

26. Sierchuła, Utracka, "Historia," pp. 216–17.

27. Sierchuła, Utracka, "Historia," pp. 216–17; Zalewski, Interview, October 17, 2016; Richie, *Warsaw*, p. 425.

28. Sierchuła, Utracka, "Historia," p. 6; Richie, *Warsaw*, p. 222.

29. Sierchuła, Utracka, "Historia," p. 218.

30. Sierchuła, Utracka, "Historia," p. 218.

31. Sierchuła, Utracka, "Historia," p. 7; Pilecki, [Raport 1945], PUMST, BI 874, p. 104.

32. Sierchuła, Utracka, "Historia," pp. 216–17; Remlein, [Wspomnienia]; Korboński, *Fighting*, p. 370.

33. Richie, *Warsaw*, p. 269.

34. Nowak, *Courier*, p. 358. Komorowski had been frantically radioing for air support since the start of the uprising, but little was available. The logistical difficulties of airdropping supplies six hundred miles over the Alps and past enemy air patrols were considerable. The British and Americans had asked the Soviets to use their air bases nearby in Ukraine for refueling but had received no response, a clear message that Stalin already considered Poland within the Soviet Union's sphere of influence.

35. Zalewski, Interview, October 17, 2016.

36. Richie, *Warsaw*, p. 269.

37. Walasek, Interview, May 19, 2016.

38. Sierchuła, Utracka, "Historia," p. 218; Walasek, Interview, May 19, 2016. The Germans had also deployed a unit recruited from Russian nationalists opposed to Communism known as Russkaya Osvoboditelnaya Narodnaya Armiya, or RONA for short.

39. Sierchuła, Utracka, "Historia," p. 222; Walasek, Interview, May 19, 2016.

40. Walendzik, Interview, October 12, 2016.

41. Bartoszewski, *1859*, p. 772, p. 787; Osęka, "Zabawa," p. 64.

42. Richie, *Warsaw*, p. 572. For a list of victims of the shelter attack, see Cichy, "Polacy," p. 15. Henryk Bursztyn and an unnamed teenager survived. Abram Bursztyn, Henryk Herszbajn, and Josek Tenenbaum witnessed events outside the shelter. Some of their testimony was gathered in the subsequent underground investigation (see AAN, 203/X-32, pp. 64–65). Postwar interviews also feature in Willenberg, *Revolt*, p. 186. The commander Wacław Stykowski claimed the murders were carried out by German infiltrators (see AAN, 203/X-32, pp. 62–63). Wacław Zagórski, who addressed the incident with Stykowski, made a similar claim in his own initial account of the incident (see AAN, 203/X-32, pp. 58–59). Zagórski subsequently implied that Stykowski's men were involved in the murders. Stykowski denied the allegation. (WIH, III/43/4, p. 76; Stykowski, *Kapitan*, p. 322; Stykowski, Interview, September 12, 2018.) Walasek, Interview, May 20, 2016.

43. Davies, *Powstanie '44*, pp. 515–17.
44. Zagórski, *Seventy*, p. 205.
45. Walasek, Interview, May 20, 2016.
46. Gawron, [Opowiadania], p. 1.
47. Gawron, [Opowiadania], p. 1.
48. Richie, *Warsaw*, p. 578.
49. The exact figure of the dead is unknown but lies somewhere between 130,000 and 150,000 civilians and 17,000 uprisers. Heydecker, *Mója*, pp. 230–38.
50. Zagórski, *Seventy*, p. 205.

Chapter 21: Return

1. Ostrowska, [Wspomnienia 1], p. 9.
2. Ostrowska, [Wspomnienia 1], p. 9; Ostrowska, [Wspomnienia 2], pp. 5–6; Zalewski, Interview, October 17, 2016; Bednorz, *Lamsdorf*, p. 24.
3. Kisielewicz, *Oflag*, p. 57, p. 111, p. 109; Wołosiuk, "Znałem," p. 1.
4. Applebaum, *Iron*, p. 104.
5. Kisielewicz, *Oflag*, p. 54, p. 170; Ollier, email, August 16, 2001.
6. Kisielewicz, *Oflag*, p. 54, p. 170; Ollier, email, August 16, 2001.
7. Pilecki, Akta sprawy, Protokół rozprawy głównej, Spis adresów, Materiały, vol. 223b, APMA-B, p. 659, p. 642.
8. Pilecki, Akta sprawy, Protokół rozprawy głównej, Spis adresów, Materiały, vol. 223b, APMA-B, p. 659, p. 642.
9. Mierzanowski, Wspomnienia, vol. 203, APMA-B, p. 85; Pilecki, Akta sprawy, Protokół rozprawy głównej, Spis adresów, Materiały, vol. 223b, APMA-B, p. 642; Mierzanowski, Wspomnienia, vol. 203, APMA-B, p. 85; Radomska et al., *Nasza*, p. 153.
10. Pilecki, *The Auschwitz*, loc. 2468; Pilecki, [Raport 1945], PUMST, BI 874, p. 47; Pilecki, Akta sprawy, [Meldunek nr 2], Materiały, vol. 223b, APMA-B, p. 555; Pilecki, Akta sprawy, Protokół rozprawy głównej, Materiały, vol. 223b, APMA-B, p. 676.
11. Pilecki, Akta sprawy, [Meldunek nr 2], Materiały, vol. 223b, APMA-B, p. 555; Pilecki, Akta sprawy, Protokół rozprawy głównej, Materiały, vol. 223b, APMA-B, p. 676.
12. Pilecki, Akta sprawy, [Meldunek nr 5], Materiały, vol. 223b, APMA-B, p. 556.
13. Lowe, *Savage*, pp. 233–47.

14. Pilecki, Akta sprawy, Protokół przesłuchania Witolda Pileckiego, Materiały, vol. 223, APMA-B, p. 131.

15. Zaremba, *Wielka*, p. 340; Ostrowska, Zaremba, "Kobieca," pp. 64–69.

16. Orłowska, Interview, November 13, 2018.

17. Applebaum, *Iron*, p. 248.

18. Pilecki, Akta sprawy, Protokół przesłuchania Witolda Pileckiego, Materiały, vol. 223, APMA-B, pp. 14–18; Pilecki, Akta sprawy, Protokół przesłuchania Makarego Sieradzkiego, Materiały, vol. 223a, APMA-B, p. 363, p. 372.

19. Pilecki, Akta sprawy, Protokół przesłuchania Marii Szelągowskiej, Materiały, vol. 223, APMA-B, p. 190; Pilecki, Akta sprawy, Protokół przesłuchania Makarego Sieradzkiego, Materiały, vol. 223a, APMA-B, p. 363, p. 372.

20. Pilecki, Akta sprawy, [Meldunek nr 2], Materiały, vol. 223a, APMA-B, p. 555.

21. Pilecki, Interviews, February 5, 2016, and March 11, 2016.

22. Pilecki, Akta sprawy, Protokół przesłuchania Witolda Pileckiego, Materiały, vol. 223, APMA-B, p. 78; Heuener, *Auschwitz*, p. 69.

23. Heuener, *Auschwitz*, pp. 66–69.

24. Pilecki, Akta sprawy, Protokół rozprawy głównej, Materiały, vol. 223b, APMA-B, p. 651.

25. Cyra, *Rotmistrz*, p. 158.

26. Pilecki, Akta sprawy, [Tragedia kielecka], Materiały, vol. 223a, APMA-B, pp. 542–43. Witold speculated inaccurately in his report that the attack against Kielce's Jews was a deliberate Communist provocation.

27. Applebaum, *Iron*, p. 217. Pilecki, Witold, Akta sprawy przeciwko Witoldowi Pileckiemu/innym Tragedia Kielecka, Materiały, vol. 223a, APMA–8, pp. 542–43.

28. Pilecki, Akta sprawy, Protokół przesłuchania Wacława Alchimowicza, Materiały, vol. 223a, APMA-B, pp. 403–7; Pilecki, Akta sprawy, Protokół przesłuchania Witolda Pileckiego, Materiały, vol. 223a, APMA-B, p. 117.

29. Pilecki, [Zamiast], Materiały, vol. 223c, APMA-B, p. 5.

30. Pawlicki (dir.), *Witold*; Baliszewski, Uziębło (dir.), *Rewizja*.

31. Leśniewski, "Czy przygotowano," p. 2.

32. Pilecki, [Wiersz], May 14, 1947, UOP, 1768/III/9, p. 267.

33. Szejnert, *Śród żywych*, p. 132; Pilecki, Akta procesowe, ASS MON, vol. 5, p. 33.

34. Ostrowska, [Wspomnienia 1], p. 12.

35. Pilecki, Akta sprawy, Protokół rozprawy głównej, vol. 5, ASS MON, pp. 25–26.

36. Ostrowska, Wspomnienia, vol. 179, APMA-B, pp. 155–56; Pilecki, Interview, July 20, 2018.

37. Pilecki, Akta sprawy, vol. 5, ASS MON, pp. 107–17; Pilecki, Akta sprawy, Protokół rozprawy głównej, Materiały, vol. 223b, APMA-B, p. 691.

38. The Serafiński family also begged Cyrankiewicz to intervene and bring to the court's attention Witold's work in the camp. Cyrankiewicz replied that the matter was in Bierut's hands.

39. Pilecka, [List do Bolesława Bieruta], date unknown, ASS MON, vol. 5, p. 194, in Cyra, *Rotmistrz*, pp. 190–91.

40. Stępień, Wspomnienia, vol. 179, APMA-B, pp. 176–77; Płużański, *Obława*, p. 181.

Epilogue

1. Poleszak, Wnuk, *Zarys*, in Wnuk et al., *Atlas*, p. 22. In subsequent testimony Eleonora Ostrowska accused Cyrankiewicz of deliberately conspiring to have Witold murdered. According to Eleonora, Witold had written to Cyrankiewicz in 1947 unhappy with his co-opting of the story of the camp resistance and threatening to expose Cyrankiewicz's collaboration with the Germans in the camp. No record of the letter has been found, although Witold did allude to it once under interrogation, and twice spoke of a speech Cyrankiewicz was due to give about the underground. There is no evidence that Cyrankiewicz was an SS agent in the camp. See Pilecki, Akta sprawy, [List Aliny Bieleckiej], Materiały, vol. 223b, APMA-B, p. 831. The new exhibition crudely conformed to Soviet ideology at the start of the Cold War. Its first exhibit, entitled "The Sources of Genocide," compared the Nazis' genocidal policies to British and American imperialism. Heuener, *Auschwitz*, p. 102.

2. Incredibly, the state prosecutor who'd sought the death penalty against Witold, Czesław Łapiński, still worked as a military lawyer and briefly tried to block access.

3. Edek Ciesielski published the first memoir about Witold and the early camp underground in 1966. (Edek sadly died of a stroke at the age of forty in 1962.) Over the course of his research Edek had reached out to Kazimierz Rawicz, leading to a fascinating exchange of letters between the men. It appears they made a research trip together to Auschwitz, where they were able to access a copy of Witold's W report. Ciesielski, [List], July 6, 1958. Ciesielski's letters were accessed courtesy of Marek Popiel. Cyra deciphered Witold's Report W in 1991 and published it, with a biography of Witold (*Biuletyn TOnO*, 1991/12).

SELECT BIBLIOGRAPHY

List of Abbreviations
AAN—Archiwum Akt Nowych
AN—Archiwum Narodowe w Krakowie
APMA–B—Archiwum Państwowego Muzeum Auschwitz–Birkenau
ASS MON—Archiwum Służby Sprawiedliwości Ministerstwa Obrony
Narodowej
AZHRL—Archiwum Zakładu Historii Ruchu Ludowego
BA—Bundesarchiv
CAW—Centralne Archiwum Wojskowe
DGFP—Deutsche Gesellschaft für Personalführung
FBI—Fritz Bauer Institut
HHStAW—Hessisches Staatsarchiv Wiesbaden
HIA—Hoover Institution Archives
IP—Instytut Pileckiego
IPN—Instytut Pamięci Narodowej
LHCMA—Liddell Hart Centre for Military Archives, King's College London
NA—The National Archives in London
NARS—National Archives and Records Service
NRW—Archive in Nordrhein-Westfalen
PAN—Polska Akademia Nauk
PISM—The Polish Institute and Sikorski Museum
PUMST—The Polish Underground Movement Study Trust
SPP—Studium Polski Podziemnej
TOnO—Towarzystwo Opieki nad Oświęcimiem
UOP—Urząd Ochrony Państwa
USHMM—United States Holocaust Memorial Museum
WFD—Wytwórnia Filmów Dokumentalnych
WIH—Wojskowy Instytut Historyczny

YVA—Yad Vashem Archives
ŻIH—Żydowski Instytut Historyczny

Abramow–Newerly, Jarosław. Interview, October 2, 2017.

Abramow–Newerly, Jarosław. *Lwy mojego podwórka*. Warszawa: Rosner & Wspólnicy, 2002.

Albin, Kazimierz. Interview, May 21, 2016.

Albin, Kazimierz. *List gończy. Historia mojej ucieczki z Oświęcimia i działalności w konspiracji*. Warszawa: PMA–B. Książka i Wiedza, 1996.

Allen, Arthur. *The Fantastic Laboratory of Dr. Weigl: How Two Brave Scientists Battled Typhus and Sabotaged the Nazis*. New York: W. W. Norton & Company, 2014. Kindle.

Anders, Władysław. *Bez ostatniego rozdziału. Wspomnienia z lat 1939–1946*. Lublin test, 1995.

Apel Rady Narodowej do Parlamentów Wolnych Państw w sprawie zbrodni niemieckich w Polsce. *Dziennik Polski*, June 11, 1942, cited in Engel, *In the Shadow*, p. 181, p. 209.

Applebaum, Anne. *Iron Curtain: The Crushing of Eastern Europe, 1944–1956*. London: Penguin Books, 2017.

Avni, Haim. *Spain, the Jews, and Franco*. Philadelphia: Jewish Publication Society, 1982.

Bagiński, Henryk. *Zbiór drożni na terytorium Rzeczypospolitej polskiej. Dodatek statystyczny*. Cz. 3. *Obszar północno–wschodni*. Warszawa: Ministerstwo Spraw Wojskowych, 1924.

Baliszewski, Dariusz; Uziębło, Ewa (dir.). *Rewizja nadzwyczajna—Witold Pilecki*. 1998. TV Edukacyjna.

Banach, Ludwik. [Testimony], Proces Załogi esesmańskiej, vol. 55, APMA–B, pp. 102–3.

Bartosiewicz, Henryk. [Wywiad], September 14, 1970, Stagenhoe. Ossolineum. 87/00, Archive of Józef Garliński.

Bartosiewicz, Henryk. Oświadczenia, vol. 84, APMA–B, pp. 117–38.

Bartosik, Igor; Martyniak, Łukasz; Setkiewicz, Piotr. *Początki obozu Birkenau w świetle materiałów źródłowych*. Oświęcim: PMA–B, 2017.

Bartosik, Igor; Martyniak, Łukasz; Setkiewicz, Piotr. *Wstęp*, in idem. *Początki obozu Birkenau w świetle materiałów źródłowych*. Oświęcim: PMA–B, 2017.

Bartoszewski, Władysław. *1859 dni Warszawy.* Kraków: Znak, 2008.

Bartoszewski, Władysław. *Mój Auschwitz: rozmowę przeprowadzili Piotr M. A. Cywiński i Marek Zając.* Kraków: Znak, 2010.

Bartoszewski, Władysław; Komar, Michał. *Wywiad rzeka.* Warszawa: Świat Książki, 2006.

Bartys, Czesław. Oświadczenia, vol. 63, APMA–B, pp. 132–38.

Bauer, Yehuda. *Could the US Government Have Rescued European Jewry?* Jerusalem: Yad Vashem Publications, 2018.

Bednorz, Róża. *Lamsdorf Łambinowice. Zbrodnie cierpienia pamięć.* Katowice: Muzeum Martyrologii i Walki Jeńców Wojennych w Łambinowicach, 1981.

Bergier, Jean–François; Bartoszewski, Wladyslaw; Friedländer, Saul; James, Harold; Junz, Helen B.; Kreis, Georg; Milton, Sybil; Picard, Jacques; Tanner, Jakob; Thürer, Daniel; Voyame, Joseph (eds.). *Final Report. Independent Commission of Experts Switzerland—Second World War: Switzerland, National Socialism, and the Second World War.* Zurich: Pendo Editions, 2002.

Bernacka, Monika. "Otto Küsel. Green Triangle. On the 100th Anniversary of his Birth." *Oś,* 2009/5, pp. 8–9.

Bernstein, Tatiana; Rutkowski, Adam. "Liczba ludności żydowskiej i obszar przez nią zamieszkiwany w Warszawie w latach okupacji hitlerowskiej." *Biuletyn ŻIH* 26, 1958/2, pp. 73–114.

Białas, Stanisław. Oświadczenia, vol. 94, APMA–B, vol. 94, pp. 23–26.

Bidakowski, Kazimierz; Wójcik, Tadeusz (eds.). *Pamiętniki lekarzy.* Warszawa: Czytelnik, 1964.

Biddle, Tami Davis. *Allied Airpower: Objective and Capabilities,* in Neufeld, Berenbaum (ed.), *The Bombing,* pp. 35–51.

Bielecki, Jerzy. *Kto ratuje jedno życie . . . Opowieść o miłości i ucieczce z Obozu Zagłady.* Oświęcim: Chrześcijańskie Stowarzyszenie Rodzin Oświęcimskich, 1999.

Biernacki, Edward. [List], Materiały Ruchu Oporu, vols. 1–2, APMA–B, p. 10.

Bikont, Anna. *The Crime and the Silence: Confronting the Massacre of Jews in Wartime Jedwabne.* Trans. Alissa Valles. New York: Farrar, Straus & Giroux, 2015.

Bines, Jeffrey. *The Polish Country Section of the Special Operations Executive 1940–1946: A British Perspective.* [Dissertation.] Scotland: University of Stirling, 2008.

Bishop, Patrick. *Air Force Blue: The RAF in World War Two—Spearhead of Victory.* London: William Collins, 2017.

Bleja, Henryk. Interview, September 21, 2016.

Blum, Aleksander. *O broń i orły narodowe.* Pruszków: Ajaks, 1997.

Bogacka, Marta. *Bokser z Auschwitz: losy Tadeusza Pietrzykowskiego.* Warszawa: Demart, 2012.

Bogusz, Jerzy. Interview, December 19, 2015.

Breitman, Richard. *Official Secrets: What the Nazis Planned, What the British and Americans Knew.* London: Allen Lane, 1998.

Breitman, Richard; Laqueur, Walter. *Breaking the Silence.* New York: Simon & Schuster, 1987.

Breitman, Richard; Lichtman, Allan J. *FDR and the Jews.* Cambridge: Harvard University Press, 2014.

Brewda, Alina. *I Shall Fear No Evil.* London: Corgi, 1966.

Broad, Pery. [Testimony], cited in Smoleń, *KL Auschwitz,* pp. 103–49.

Brochowicz–Lewiński, Zbigniew. [Raport.] CAW, I.302.4. 466.

Brown, Kate. *A Biography of No Place: From Ethnic Borderland to Soviet Heartland.* Cambridge: Harvard University Press, 2009. Kindle.

Bruland, Bjarte. *Holocaust in Norway. Registration. Deportation. Extermination.* Oslo: Dreyers forlag, 2017.

Bryan, Julien. *Warsaw: 1939 Siege.* New York: International Film Foundation, 1959.

Brzoza, Czesław; Sowa, Andrzej Leon. *Historia Polski 1918–1945.* Kraków: Wydawnictwo Literackie, 2009.

Budarkiewicz, Włodzimierz. "Wspomnienia o rtm. Witoldzie Pileckim." *Przegląd kawalerii i broni pancernej,* 1987/127, pp. 57–61.

Bujniewicz, Ireneusz (ed.). *Kolejnictwo w polskich przygotowaniach obronnych i kampanii wrześniowej.* Cz. 1: *Opracowania i dokumenty.* Warszawa: Tetragon, 2011.

Butterly, John R.; Shepherd, Jack. *Hunger: The Biology and Politics of Starvation.* Hanover: Dartmouth College Press, 2010.

Carter, John Franklin. [Report on Poland and Lithuania.] NARS, RG 59, 800.20211/924.

Celt, Marek. *Raport z podziemia 1942.* Wrocław–Warszawa–Kraków: Ossolineum, 1992.

Chlebowski, Cezary. *Pozdrówcie góry Świętokrzyskie.* Warszawa: Czytelnik, 1985.

Chróścicki, Tadeusz Lucjan. Oświadczenia, vol. 11, APMA-B, pp. 1–11.

Chrzanowski, Wiesław. *Więźniowie polityczni w Polsce 1945–1956.* Dębogóra: Wydawnictwo Dębogóra, 2015.

Cichy, Michał. "Polacy—Żydzi: czarne karty powstania." *Gazeta Wyborcza,* January 23, 1994.

Ciesielski, Edward. [Raport 1943.] AAN, 202/XVIII/1, pp. 1–91.

Ciesielski, Edward. *Wspomnienia oświęcimskie*. Kraków: Wydawnictwo Literackie, 1968.

Cohen, Susan. *Rescue the Perishing: Eleanor Rathbone and the Refugees*. Elstree: Vallentine Mitchell, 2010.

Collingham, Lizzie. *The Taste of Empire: How Britain's Quest for Food Shaped the Modern World*. Rochester: Vintage Digital, 2017. Kindle.

Cuber-Strutyńska, Ewa. "Witold Pilecki. Konfrontacja z legendą o 'ochotniku do Auschwitz.'" *Zagłada Żydów. Studia i Materiały*, 2014/10, pp. 474–94.

Cyra, Adam. "Dr Władysław Dering—pobyt w Auschwitz i więzieniu brytyjskim." *Biuletyn informacyjny AK*, 2015/2, pp. 73–79.

Cyra, Adam. *Jeszcze raz o prof. Marianie Batce*: http://cyra.wblogu.pl/tag/batko [May 16, 2018].

Cyra, Adam. *Rotmistrz Pilecki. Ochotnik do Auschwitz*. Warszawa: RM, 2014.

Cywiński, Piotr; Lachendro, Jacek; Setkiewicz, Piotr. *Auschwitz od A do Z. Ilustrowana historia obozu*. Oświęcim: PMA-B, 2013.

Czarnecka, Daria. *Największa zagadka Polskiego Państwa Podziemnego. Stanisław Gustaw Jaster—człowiek, który zniknął*. Warszawa: Wydawnictwo Naukowe PWN, 2016.

Czarnocka, Halina; Suchcitz, Andrzej (eds.). *Armia Krajowa w dokumentach 1939–1945*. Vol. I. CZ. 1–2. Warszawa: IPN, SPP, PISM, 2015.

Czech, Danuta. *Auschwitz Chronicle, 1939–1945*. New York: Henry Holt, 1997.

Czech, Danuta. *Kalendarz wydarzeń w KL Auschwitz*. Oświęcim: PMA–B, 1992.

Czech, Danuta; Kłodziński, Stanisław; Lasik, Aleksander; Strzelecki, Andrzej (eds.). *Auschwitz 1940–1945. Central Issues in the History of the Camp*. Vol. V: *Epilogue*. Trans. William Brandt. Oświęcim: PMA–B, 2000.

Dalton, Hugh; (Ben Pimlott [ed.]). *The Second World War Diary of Hugh Dalton, 1940–45*. London: Cape, 1986.

Davies, Norman. *Powstanie '44*. Kraków: Znak, 2004.

Davies, Norman. *Rising '44: The Battle for Warsaw*. London: Pan Books, 2007.

Dębski, Jerzy. *Oficerowie Wojska Polskiego w obozie koncentracyjnym Auschwitz 1940–1945. Słownik biograficzny*. Oświęcim: PMA–B, 2016.

Dekel, Mikhal. [Browar Near Skater's Pond]. Material courtesy of the author.

Dembiński, Stanisław. [Raport], December 28, 1940. Dokumentacja Oddziału VI Sztabu Naczelnego Wodza, 1940. PUMST, A. 680.

Dering, Władysław. [Wspomnienia], pp. 1–200. Material courtesy of Adam Cyra.

Diem, Rudolf, "Ś.P. Kazimierz Jarzębowski." *Przegląd geodezyjny*, 1947/2, pp. 45–47.

Diem, Rudolf. Wspomnienia, vol. 172. APMA–B. pp. 1–235.

Dmytruk, Nykanor. "Z novogo pobutu." *Ethnografichnyi visnyk*, 1926/2, pp. 31–37.

Dobrowolska, Anna. *The Auschwitz Photographer*. Warsaw: Anna Dobrowolska, 2015.

Drzazga, Alojzy. Oświadczenia, vol. 33, APMA–B, pp. 45–56.

Duraczyński, Eugeniusz. *Rząd polski na uchodźstwie 1939–1945: organizacja, personalia, polityka*. Warszawa: Książka i Wiedza, 1993.

Dwork, Debórah; van Pelt, Robert Jan. *Auschwitz*. New York: W. W. Norton & Company, 2002.

Dziubek, Marcin. *Niezłomni z oddziału "Sosienki."* *Armia Krajowa wokół KL Auschwitz*. Oświęcim: Stowarzyszenie Auschwitz Memento; Kraków: Wydawnictwo Rudy Kot, 2016.

Engel, David. *In the Shadow of Auschwitz: The Polish Government-in-exile and the Jews, 1939–1942*. Chapel Hill: University of North Carolina Press, 2012.

Engelking, Barbara; Libionka Dariusz. *Żydzi w powstańczej Warszawie*. Warszawa: Stowarzyszenie Centrum Badań nad Zagładą Żydów, 2009.

Faliński, Stanisław Sławomir. "Ideologia Konfederacji Narodu." *Przegląd Historyczny*, 1985/76 (1), pp. 57–76.

Favez, Jean-Claude. *The Red Cross and the Holocaust*. Trans. J. Fletcher, B. Fletcher. Cambridge: Cambridge University Press, 1999.

Fejkiel, Władysław. *Medycyna za drutami*, in Bidakowski, Wójcik, *Pamiętniki*, pp. 404–546.

Fejkiel, Władysław. *Więźniarski szpital w KL Auschwitz*. Oświęcim: PMA–B, 1994.

Fieldorf, Maria; Zachuta, Leszek. *Generał Fieldorf "Nil." Fakty, dokumenty, relacje*. Warszawa: Oficyna Wydawnicza RYTM, 1993.

Filar, Alfons. *Śladami kurierów tatrzańskich 1939–1944*. Warszawa: Agencja Wydawnicza CB, 2008.

Filip, Lucyna. *Żydzi w Oświęcimiu*. Oświęcim: Scientia, 2003.

Fleming, Michael. *Auschwitz, the Allies, and Censorship of the Holocaust*. Cambridge: Cambridge University Press, 2014.

Foot, Michael. *Six Faces of Courage*. Yorkshire: Leo Cooper, 2003. Kindle.

Forczyk, Robert. *Warsaw 1944. Poland's Bid for Freedom*. London: Bloomsbury Publishing, 2009.

Frączek, Seweryn. Wspomnienia, vol. 66, APMA–B, pp. 162–65.

Frank, Hans. *Extracts from Hans Frank's Diary*. Thomas J. Dodd Papers, Storrs: University of Connecticut, November 10, 1939.

Frazik, Wojciech. "Wojenne losy Napoleona Segiedy, kuriera Rządu RP do kraju." *Studia Historyczne*, 1998/3 (162), pp. 407–15.

Friedenson, Joseph; Kranzler, David. *Heroine of Rescue: The Incredible Story of Recha Sternbuch, Who Saved Thousands from the Holocaust*. New York: Mesorah Publications Ltd., 1984.

Ganusovitch, Itzchak; Manor, Alexander; Lando, Aba (eds.). *Book of Lida*. Tel Aviv: Irgun yotse Lida be–Yiśra'el u–Va'ad ha–'ezrah li–Yehude Lida ba–Artsot ha–Berit, 1970.

Gardiner, Juliet. *The Blitz: The British Under Attack*. New York: HarperPress, 2010.

Garlicka, Aleksandra (ed.). *Zarzewie 1909–1920: wspomnienia i materiały*. Warszawa: Pax, 1973.

Garliński, Józef. *Fighting Auschwitz: The Resistance Movement in the Concentration Camp*. Trans. Józef Garliński. London: Julian Friedmann Publishers Ltd., 1975.

Gawron, Wincenty. [Opowiadania.] Material courtesy of Ewa Biały and Adam Wojtasiak. No pages given.

Gawron, Wincenty. *Ochotnik do Oświęcimia*. Oświęcim: Wydawnictwo Calvarianum, Wydawnictwo PMA–B, 1992.

Gawron, Wincenty. Wspomnienia, vol. 48, APMA–B, pp. 1–331.

Gelman, Abraham. *Economic Life of Jewish Lida before World War II*, in Ganusovitch, Manor, Lando, *Book*, pp. 83–85.

Gilbert, Martin. *Auschwitz and the Allies*. London: Vintage UK, 2001.

Gilbert, Martin. *Churchill: A Life*. New York: Holt Paperbacks, 1992.

Gistedt, Elna. *Od operetki do tragedii. Ze wspomnień szwedzkiej gwiazdy operetki warszawskiej*. Trans. M. Olszańska. Warszawa: Czytelnik, 1982.

Gliński, Bogdan. Oświadczenia, vol. 95, APMA–B, pp. 63–90.

Głowa, Stanisław. Oświadczenia, vol. 36, APMA–B, pp. 13–17.

Głowa, Stanisław. Oświadczenia, vol. 36, APMA–B, pp. p. 1–7.

Głowa, Stanisław. Oświadczenia, vol. 36, APMA–B, pp. 8–12.

Głowa, Stanisław. Oświadczenia, vol. 70, APMA–B, pp. 100–102.

Głowa, Stanisław. Oświadczenia, vol. 108, APMA–B, pp. 77–103.

Głowa, Stanisław. Wspomnienia, vol. 181, APMA–B, pp. 1–176.

Głowa, Stanisław. Wspomnienia, vol. 94, APMA–B, pp. 138–39.

Gnatowski, Leon. [Raport.] CAW, I.302.4.466. Material courtesy of Wojciech Markert.

Goebbels, Joseph. *The Goebbels Diaries, 1942–1943*. Trans. Louis P. Lochner. London: Penguin Books, 1984.

Gombrowicz, Witold. *Polish Memories*. Trans. Bill Johnson. New Haven: Yale University Press, 2011.

Gorzkowski, Kazimierz. *Kroniki Andrzeja. Zapiski z podziemia 1939–1941.* Warszawa: Wydawnictwo Naukowe PWN, 1989.

Grabowski, Waldemar. *Kurierzy cywilni (kociaki) na spadochronach. Zarys problematyki*, in Majzner, *Si vis Pacem*, pp. 175–202.

Gross, Jan T. *Polish Society Under German Occupation: The Generalgouvernement 1939–1944.* Princeton and Guilford: Princeton University Press, 1979.

Gutheil, Jorn-Erik. *Einer, muss überleben: Gespräche mit Auschwitzhäftlingen 40 Jahre danach.* Düsseldorf: Der Kleine Verlag, 1984.

Gutman, Israel; Krakowski, Shmuel. *Unequal Victims: Poles and Jews During World War Two.* New York: Holocaust Library, 1986.

Hackmann, Rüdiger; Süß, Winfried (eds.). *Hitler's Kommissare. Sondergewalten in der nationalsozialistischen Diktatur.* Göttingen: Wallstein Verlag, 2006.

Hahn, Stefan L. Interview, April 24, 2018.

Hałgas, Kazimierz. "Oddział chirurgiczny szpitala obozowego w Oświęcimiu w latach 1940–1941." *Przegląd Lekarski*, 1971/1, pp. 48–54.

Hałgas, Kazimierz. Oświadczenia, vol. 89, APMA–B, pp. 161–88.

Hałgas, Kazimierz. Oświadczenia, vol. 95, PMA–B, pp. 231–47.

Hałko, Lech. *Kotwica herbem wybranym.* Warszawa: Askon, 1999.

Hančka, Great. *Bogumił Šwjela*, in Šołta, Kunze, Šěn, *Nowy.*

Harat, Andrzej; (Dęsoł–Gut, Ewa; Kowalska, Ewa [eds.]). *Działalność Armii Krajowej w Okręgu Śląskim we wspomnieniach porucznika Andrzeja Harata: działalność AK na terenie Libiąża.* Libiąż: Urząd Miejski, 2016.

Haska, Agnieszka. "'Proszę Pana Ministra o energiczną interwencję'. Aleksander Ładoś (1891–1963) i ratowanie Żydów przez Poselstwo RP w Bernie." *Zagłada Żydów. Studia i Materiały*, 2015/11, pp. 299–309.

Häsler, Alfred A. *The Lifeboat Is Full.* Trans. Charles Lam Markmann. New York: Funk & Wagnalls, 1969.

Hastings, Max. *Bomber Command.* London: Zenith Press, 2013. Kindle.

Hastings, Max. *The Secret War: Spies, Codes and Guerrillas 1939–1945.* New York: Harper, 2016. Kindle.

Herbert, Ulrich. *Hitler's Foreign Workers: Enforced Foreign Labor in Germany Under the Third Reich.* Cambridge: Cambridge University Press, 1997.

Heuener, Jonathan. *Auschwitz, Poland, and the Politics of Commemoration, 1945–1979.* Athens: Ohio University Press, 2003.

Heydecker, Joe J. *Moja wojna. Zapiski i zdjęcia z sześciu lat w hitlerowskim Wermachcie.* Trans. B. Ostrowska. Warszawa: Świat Książki, 2009.

Hilberg, Raul. *The Destruction of the European Jews*. New Haven: Yale University Press, 1961.

Hill, Mavis Millicent; Williams, Leon Norman. *Auschwitz in England*. London: Panther, 1966.

Hodubski, Franciszek. [Protokół przesłuchania świadka]. Ostrów Mazowiecka, August 5, 1947, IPN, Bl 407/63. K. 296/47, GK 264/63, SOŁ 63, pp. 0343–0344.

Hołuj, Tadeusz; Friedman, Philip. *Oświęcim*. Warszawa: Spółdzielnia Wydawnicza "Książka," 1946.

Höss, Rudolf. *Commandant of Auschwitz: The Autobiography of Rudolf Höss*. Trans. Constantine FitzGibbon. London: Phoenix, 2000. Kindle.

Höss, Rudolf. *Death Dealer: The Memoirs of the SS Kommandant at Auschwitz*. Trans. Andrew Pollinger. Cambridge: Da Capo Press, 1996.

Iranek-Osmecki, Kazimierz; Bokiewicz, Zbigniew; Czarnocka, Halina; Garliński, Józef; Jastrzębski, Leonard; Jordanowa, Wanda; Olszewska, Jadwiga; Otocki, Włodzimierz; Pełczyński, Tadeusz; Suchcitz, Andrzej; Zawadzki-Żenczykowski, Tadeusz (eds.). *Armia Krajowa w dokumentach 1939–1945*. Vols. I–VI. Wrocław–Warszawa–Kraków: Ossolineum, 1990–1991.

Iranek-Osmecki, Kazimierz. *Powołanie i przeznaczenie: wspomnienia oficera Komendy Głównej AK 1940–1944*. Warszawa: Państwowy Instytut Wydawniczy, 1998.

Iwaszko, Tadeusz. "Ucieczki więźniów obozu koncentracyjnego Oświęcim." *Zeszyty oświęcimskie 7*. Oświęcim: PMA–B, 1963, pp. 3–53.

Iwaszko, Tadeusz; Kłodziński, Stanisław. "Bunt skazańców 28 października 1942 r. w oświęcimskim bloku nr 11." *Przegląd Lekarski*, 1977/1, pp. 119–22.

Iwaszko, Tadeusz; Kubica, Helena; Piper, Franciszek; Strzelecka, Irena; Strzelecki, Andrzej (eds.). *Auschwitz 1940–1945. Central Issues in the History of the Camp*. Vol. II: *The Prisoners—Their Life and Work*. Trans. William Brandt. Oświęcim: PMA–B, 2000.

Jagoda, Zenon; Kłodziński, Stanisław; Masłowski, Jan. "Sny więźniów obozu oświęcimskiego." *Przegląd Lekarski*, 1977/34, pp. 28–66.

Jaworski, Czesław Wincenty. *Wspomnienia oświęcimskie*. Warszawa: Instytut Wydawniczy PAX, 1962.

Jaźwiec, Jan. *Pomnik dowódcy*. Warszawa: Ludowa Spółdzielnia Wydawnicza, 1971.

Jekiełek, Jan. Interview, March 4, 2017.

Jekiełek, Wojciech. [Konspiracja chłopska w okresie II wojny światowej w powiecie bialskim]. AZHRL, R–VI–2/547, pp. 1–172.

Jekiełek, Wojciech. *W pobliżu Oświęcimia*. Warszawa: Ludowa Spółdzielnia Wydawnicza, 1963.

Jezierski, Alfons Sylwester. [Wspomnienia.] CAW, I.302.4.466.

Jud, Ursina. *Liechtenstein und die Flüchtlinge zur Zeit des Nationalsozialismus*. Vaduz/Zurich: Chronos, 2005.

Kajtoch, Janina. Wspomnienia, vol. 27, APMA–B, pp. 1–149.

Kamber, Peter. *Geheime Agentin, Roman*. Berlin: Basis Druck Verlag, 2010.

Kantyka, Jan; Kantyka, Sławomir. *Oddani sprawie. Szkice biograficzne więźniów politycznych KL Auschwitz–Birkenau*. Vols. I–II. Katowice: Fundacja dla Wspierania Śląskiej Humanistyki. Zarząd Wojewódzki TOnO, 1999.

Kantyka, Jan; Kantyka, Sławomir. *Władysław Dering—nr 1723*, in idem, *Oddani*, vol. II, pp. 259–92.

Karski, Jan. *Story of a Secret State: My Report to the World*. Washington, D.C.: Georgetown University Press, 2014.

Karski, Jan. *The Tragedy of Szmul Zygielbojm*. Warsaw: Warsaw, 1967.

Karwowska–Lamparska, Alina. "Rozwój, radiofonii i telewizji." *Telekomunikacja i techniki informacyjne*, 2003/3–4, pp. 20–47.

Kawecka–Starmachowa, Bolesława. *Sto potraw z ziemniaków*. Kraków: Wydawnictwo Obywatelskiego Komitetu Pomocy, 1940.

Kielar, Wiesław. *Anus Mundi: Five Years in Auschwitz*. Trans. from the German by Susanne Flatauer. Harmondsworth: Penguin, 1982.

Kisielewicz, Danuta. *Oflag VIIA Murnau*. Opole: Centralne Muzeum Jeńców Wojennych w Łambinowicach–Opolu, 1990.

Klęczar, Krystyna. Interview, March 4, 2017.

Klukowski, Zygmunt. *Diary from the Years of Occupation 1939–44*. Champaign: University of Illinois Press, 1993.

Kłodziński, Stanisław. "Dur wysypkowy w obozie Oświęcim I." *Przegląd Lekarski*, 1965/1, pp. 46–76.

Kłodziński, Stanisław. "Pierwsza oświęcimska selekcja do gazu. Transport do 'sanatorium Dresden.'" *Przegląd Lekarski*, 1970/1, pp. 39–50.

Kłodziński, Stanisław. "Pierwsze zagazowanie więźniów i jeńców radzieckich w obozie oświęcimskim." *Przegląd Lekarski*, 1972/1, pp. 80–94.

Kłodziński, Stanisław. "Rola kryminalistów niemieckich w początkach obozu oświęcimskiego." *Przegląd Lekarski*, 1974/1, p. 113–26.

Kobrzyński, Stefan. Wspomnienia, vol. 129, APMA–B, pp. 1–49.

Kochanski, Halik. *The Eagle Unbowed: Poland and the Poles in the Second World War*. Cambridge: Harvard University Press, 2014.

Kochavi, Arieh J. *Prelude to Nuremberg: Allied War Crimes Policy and the Question of Punishment*. Chapel Hill: University of North Carolina Press, 2005.

Komisja Historyczna. *Polskie siły zbrojne w drugiej wojnie światowej*. Londyn: Instytut Historyczny im. gen. Sikorskiego, 1952, vol. 1, part 1.

Komorowski, Tadeusz. *The Secret Army: The Memoirs of General Bór–Komorowski*. Barnsley, South Yorkshire: Frontline Books, 2011.

Komski, Jan. Oświadczenia, vol. 71, APMA–B, pp. 57–78.

Korboński, Stefan, *Fighting Warsaw: The Story of the Polish Underground State, 1939–1945*. New York: Hippocrene Books, 2004.

Kotowicz, Stanisław. *Jak Napoleon Segieda szedł do Wojska Polskiego?* Buenos Aires: Buenos Aires, 1941.

Kowalczyk, August. *A Barbed Wire Refrain: An Adventure in the Shadow of the World*. Trans. Witold Zbirohowski–Kościa. Oświęcim: PMA–B, 2011.

Kowalski, Edward. Wspomnienia, vol. 96, APMA–B, pp. 158–265.

Kowalski, Stanisław, *Niezapomniana przeszłość. Haftling 4410 opowiada*. Oświęcim: PMA–B, 2001.

Kozłowiecki, Adam. *Ucisk i strapienie*. Vols. I–II. Kraków: WAM, 1995.

Kożusznik family, Interview, October 20, 2017.

Kożusznik, Władysława. Oświadczenia, vol. 12, APMA–B, pp. 7–23.

Kranzler, David. *Brother's Blood: The Orthodox Jewish Response During the Holocaust*. New York: Mesorah Publications, 1987.

Król, Henryk. Oświadczenia, vol. 76, APMA–B, pp. 191–210.

Kuciński, Dominik. *August Fieldorf "Nil."* Warszawa: Bollinari Publishing House, 2016.

Kuczbara, Janusz. [*Grypsy*]., Materiały Ruchu Oporu, vol. X, APMA–B. p. 6, p. 9, p. 11.

Kühl, Juliusz. [Memoir], USHMM, RG–27.001*08, p. 31.

Kühl, Juliusz. [Report], USHMM, RG–27.001*05, Miscellaneous reports, microfiche 1, p. 1.

Kunert, Andrzej Krzysztof. *Słownik biograficzny konspiracji Warszawskiej*, 1939–1944. Vols. I–II. Warszawa: Instytut Wydawniczy Pax, 1987.

Lachendro, Jacek. "Orkiestry w KL Auschwitz." Trans. William Brand. *Auschwitz Studies 27*. Oświęcim: PMA–B, 2015, pp. 7–148.

Lachendro, Jacek. *Zburzyć i zaorać . . . ? Idea założenia Państwowego Muzeum Auschwitz–Birkenau w świetle prasy polskiej w latach 1945–1948*. Oświęcim: PMA–B, 2007.

Lacki, Stanisław. "Burza nad Nowogródczyzną. (Kronika)." *Ziemia Lidzka—*

Miesięcznik krajoznawczo–regionalny, 1939/IV (7–8), pp. 229–30: http://pawet .net/files/zl_1939_7_8.pdf [January 20, 2019.]

Landau, Ludwik. *Kronika lat wojny i okupacji.* Vols. I–III. Warszawa: PWN, 1962–1963.

Langbein, Herman. *People in Auschwitz.* Trans. Harry Zohn. London: University of North Carolina Press, 2004.

Łapian family, Interview, May 15, 2017.

Laqueur, Walter. *The Terrible Secret: Suppression of the Truth about Hitler's "Final Solution."* London: Penguin Books, 1982.

Lasik, Aleksander; Piper, Franciszek; Setkiewicz, Piotr; Strzelecka, Irena (eds.). *Auschwitz 1940–1945. Central Issues in the History of the Camp.* Vol. I: *The Establishment and Organization of the Camp.* Trans. William Brandt. Oświęcim: PMA–B, 2000.

Ławski, Zenon. Wspomnienia, vol. 154/154a, APMA–B, pp. 1–393.

Leff, Laurel. *Buried by the Times: The Holocaust and America's Most Important Newspaper.* Boston: Northeastern University Press, 2005.

Leski, Kazimierz. *Życie niewłaściwie urozmaicone. Wspomnienia oficera wywiadu i kontrwywiadu AK.* Warszawa: Wydawnictwo Naukowe PWN, 1989.

Leśniewski, Andrzej. "Czy przygotowano proces Mikołajczyka?" *Przegląd Katolicki.* 19.02.1989/8, p. 2.

Lewandowski, Jozef. *Swedish Contribution to the Polish Resistance Movement During World War Two, 1939–42.* Trans. T. Szafar. Uppsala: Acta Universitatis Upsaliensis, 1979.

Lewitt, Chana. *When the Germans Arrived in Ostrów,* in Margolis, *Memorial,* pp. 442–43.

Lifton, Robert Jay. *The Nazi Doctors: Medical Killing and the Psychology of Genocide.* New York: Basic Books, 1988.

Lipstadt, Deborah E. *Beyond Belief: The American Press and the Coming of the Holocaust, 1933–1945.* New York: Touchstone, 1993.

Lowe, Keith. *Savage Continent: Europe in the Aftermath of World War II.* New York: St. Martin's Press, 2012.

Lukas, Richard C. *Forgotten Holocaust: The Poles Under German Occupation, 1939–1944.* New York: Hippocrene Books, 2012. Kindle.

Machnowski, Jan. "Sprawa ppłk. Gilewicza." *Kultura.* Paryż, 1963/4, pp. 125–30.

Majzner, Robert (ed.). *Si Vis Pacem, Para Bellum. Bezpieczeństwo i Polityka Polski.* Częstochowa, Włocławek: Wydawnictwo Akademii im. Jana Długosza, 2013.

Malinowski, Kazimierz. *Tajna Armia Polska, Znak, Konfederacja Zbrojna: zarys genezy, organizacji i działalności.* Warszawa: Instytut Wydawniczy PAX, 1986.

Manchester, William; Reid, Paul. *The Last Lion: Winston Spencer Churchill: Defender of the Realm, 1940–1965.* Boston: Little, Brown & Company, 2012. Kindle.

Marczewska, Krystyna; Ważniewski, Władysław (eds.). *Zeszyty Oświęcimskie: numer specjalny (I) opracowany przez Zakład Historii Partii przy KC PZPR przy współpracy Państwowego Muzeum w Oświęcimiu.* Oświęcim: PMA–B, 1968.

Margolis, Arye (ed.). *Memorial Book of the Community of Ostrow–Mazowiecka.* Tel Aviv: Association of Former Residents of Ostrow–Mazowiecka, 1960.

Markert, Wojciech. *77. Pułk Strzelców Kowieńskich w latach 1918–1939.* Pruszków: Ajaks, 2003.

Marrus, Michael (ed.). *The Nazi Holocaust.* Part 5: "Public Opinion and Relations to Jews." Berlin: De Gruyter, 1989.

Mastalerz, Mieczysław. Interview, September 21, 2016.

Matusak, *Wywiad,* p. 32, p. 35.

McGilvray, Evan. *A Military Government in Exile: The Polish Government in Exile, 1939–1945: A Study of Discontent.* Warwick: Helion & Company, 2013. Kindle.

Mierzanowski, Jan. Wspomnienia, vol. 203, APMA–B, pp. 82–104.

Mikusz, Józef. Oświadczenia, vol. 68, APMA–B, pp. 21–36.

Mikusz, Józef. Oświadczenia, vol. 99, APMA–B, pp. 156–59.

Milton, Giles. *Churchill's Ministry of Ungentlemanly Warfare: The Mavericks Who Plotted Hitler's Defeat.* London: Picador, 2017. Kindle.

Minkiewicz, Władysław. *Mokotów. Wronki. Rawicz. Wspomnienia 1939–1954.* Warszawa: Instytut Prasy i Wydawnictw "Novum," 1990.

Mitkiewicz, Leon. *W Najwyższym Sztabie Zachodnich Aliantów 1943–1945.* Londyn: Katolicki Ośrodek Wydawniczy Veritas, 1971.

Mitkiewicz, Leon. *Z Gen. Sikorskim na Obczyźnie.* Paryż: Instytut Literacki, 1968.

Moczarski, Kazimierz. *Conversations with an Executioner.* Trans. Mariana Fitzpatrick. Englewood Cliffs: Prentice–Hall, 1981.

Molenda, Antoni. *Władysław Plaskura (1905–1987).* Katowice: TOnO, 1995.

Molin, Andrzej. Interview, September 23, 2017.

Motz, Eugeniusz. [Testimony.] An appendix to the letter from Eugeniusz Motz to Józef Garliński, August 28, 1971, Warszawa.

Możdżeń, Andrzej. Oświadczenia, vol. 3, APMA–B, pp. 371–76.

Müller, Filip. *Eyewitness Auschwitz: Three Years in the Gas Chambers.* Chicago: Ivan R. Dee, 1999.

Mulley, Clare. *The Spy Who Loved: The Secrets and Lives of Christine Granville*. New York: St. Martin's Griffin, 2014.

Münch, Hans. *Analyse von Nahrungsmittelproben (1947)*, Materiały, vol. 35, APMA–B, pp. 5–47.

Nahlik, Stanisław Edward. *Przesiane przez pamięć*. Kraków: Zakamycze, 2002.

Naruszewicz, Władysław. *Wspomnienia Lidzianina*. Warszawa: Bellona, 2001.

Nejmark, Helena. *The Destruction of Jewish Ostrów*, in Margolis, *Memorial*, pp. 445–46.

Neufeld, Michael J.; Berenbaum, Michael (eds.). *The Bombing of Auschwitz: Should the Allies Have Attempted It?* New York: St. Martin's Press, 2000.

Nosal, Eugeniusz. Oświadczenia, vol. 106, APMA–B, pp. 29–30.

Nosal, Eugeniusz. Oświadczenia, vol. 132, APMA–B, pp. 164–91.

Nowacki, Zygmunt. Wspomnienia, vol. 151, APMA–B, pp. 65–163.

Nowak, Jan. *Courier from Warsaw*. Detroit: Wayne State University Press, 1983.

Nowak, Jan. *Kurier z Warszawy*. Warszawa–Kraków: ResPublica, 1989.

O'Connor, Gary. *The Butcher of Poland: Hitler's Lawyer Hans Frank*. Staplehurst: Spellmount Publishers, 2014. Kindle.

Ollier, Michael. Email, August 16, 2001.

Olson, Lynne. *Last Hope Island*. New York: Random House, 2017, Kindle edition.

Olson, Lynne; Cloud, Stanley. *For Your Freedom and Ours: The Kosciuszko Squadron— Forgotten Heroes of World War II*. Estbourne: Gardners Books, 2004.

Olszowski, Jan. "Więźniarska kancelaria w obozie oświęcimskim." *Przegląd Lekarski*, 1982/1–2, pp. 182–87.

Olszowski, Jan. Wspomnienia, vol. 127, APMA–B, pp. 54–88.

Orłowska, Marta. Interview, November 13, 2018.

Osęka, Piotr. "Zabawa pod barykadą." *Przekrój*, 2004/8.

Ostańkowicz, Czesław. *Ziemia parująca cyklonem*. Łódź: Wydawnictwo Łódzkie, 1967.

Ostrowska, Eleonora. [Wspomnienia 1.] Warszawa: 1981/82. Material courtesy of Andrzej Ostrowski.

Ostrowska, Eleonora. [Wspomnienia 2: Upadek powstania na Starym Mieście i okres popowstaniowy.] Warszawa: 1993, pp. 1–12. Material courtesy of Andrzej Ostrowski.

Ostrowska, Eleonora. Wspomnienia, vol. 179, APMA–B, pp. 143–58.

Ostrowska, Joanna; Zaremba, Marcin. "Kobieca gehenna." *Polityka*, 2009/10, pp. 64–66.

Ostrowski, Marek. Interviews, March 9, 2016; May 1, 2016; October 10, 2017.

Overy, Richard. *The Bombing War*. London: Allen Lane, 2009.

Paczkowski, Andrzej. *Aparat bezpieczeństwa w latach 1944–1956. Taktyka, strategia, metody.* Vol. I. Warszawa: Instytut Studiów Politycznych PAN, 1994.

Paczuła, Tadeusz. Oświadczenia, vol. 108, APMA–B, pp. 70–72.

Paczyńska, Irena (ed.). *Grypsy z Konzentrationslager Auschwitz Józefa Cyrankiewicza i Stanisława Kłodzińskiego.* Kraków: Wydawnictwo Uniwersytetu Jagiellońskiego, 2013.

Paczyński, Józef. Oświadczenia, vol. 100, APMA–B, pp. 92–122.

Paulsson, Gunnar S. *Secret City: The Hidden Jews of Warsaw, 1940–1945.* New Haven: Yale University Press, 2013.

Pawlicki, Tadeusz (dir.). *Witold.* 1990. Studio A. Munka.

Pawłowski, Marek T.; Walczak, Małgorzata (dir.). *Jaster. Tajemnica Hela.* 2014. Polski Instytut Sztuki Filmowej.

Pęziński, Andrzej Franciszek. [Ostrów Mazowiecka z dystansu.] Material courtesy of Michał Dekiel.

Piątkowska, Antonina. Wspomnienia, vol. 66, APMA–B, pp. 116–19.

Picard, Jacques. *Die Schweiz und die Juden 1933–1945: Schweizerischer Antisemitismus, jüdische Abwehr und internationale Migrations–und Flüchtlingspolitik.* Zurich: Chronos, 1994.

Piechowski, Kazimierz. *Byłem numerem . . . : historie z Auschwitz.* Warszawa: Wydawnictwo Sióstr Loretanek, 2003.

Piechowski, Kazimierz. Interview, October 14, 2016.

Piekarski, Konstanty. *Escaping Hell: The Story of a Polish Underground Officer in Auschwitz and Buchenwald.* Toronto: Dundum Press, 2009.

Pieńkowska, Janina. [Wspomnienia 1.] AAN, 2/2505/0/–/194—Fundacja Archiwum Polski Podziemnej 1939–1945. Foundation of the Polish Undergroud Archives, 1939–1945.

Pietrzykowski, Tadeusz. Oświadczenia, vol. 88, APMA–B, p. 1–38.

Pietrzykowski, Tadeusz. Wspomnienia, vol. 161, APMA–B, pp. 140–5.

Pilecka, Maria. [Dzieje rodu Pileckich. Saga]. Materiały, vol. 223c, APMA–B, pp. 1–116.

Pilecka, Maria. [List do Bolesława Bieruta], data unknown. ASS MON. vol. 5, p. 194, in Cyra, *Rotmistrz.*

Pilecka-Optułowicz, Zofia. Interviews, February 1, 2016; May 17, 2016; July 14, 2016.

Pilecki, Andrzej. Interviews, February 1, 2016; February 2, 2016; February 5, 2016; March 11, 2016; May 16, 2016; May 17, 2016; May 19, 2016; May 21, 2016; July 11, 2016; October 10, 2017; July 20, 2018.

476 · SELECT BIBLIOGRAPHY

Pilecki, Andrzej; Krzyszkowski, Mirosław; Wasztyl, Bogdan. *Pilecki. Śladami mojego taty.* Kraków: Znak, 2015.

Pilecki, Witold. *The Auschwitz Volunteer: Beyond Bravery.* Trans. Jarek Garliński. Los Angeles: Aquila Polonica, 2014. Kindle.

Pilecki, Witold. [Klucz do raportu W z 1943 roku]. Wspomnienia, vol. 183, APMA–B, p. 79.

Pilecki, Witold. [List do córki], October 18, 1943, IPN: https://pilecki.ipn.gov.pl/rp /pilecki–nieznany/listy/7108,List–do–corki–Zosi.html [January 20, 2019].

Pilecki, Witold. [List do Generała Pełczyńskiego], October 19, 1945, PUMST, BI 6991, pp. 1–2.

Pilecki, Witold. [Pod Lidą]. Materiały, vol. 223c, APMA–B, pp. 26–54.

Pilecki, Witold. [Raport—Nowy Wiśnicz], Wspomnienia, vol. 130, APMA–B, pp. 110–20.

Pilecki, Witold. [Raport 1945]. PUMST, BI.874, pp. 1–104.

Pilecki, Witold. [Raport teren S]. AAN, 202/XVIII/1, p. 88.

Pilecki, Witold. [Raport W]. AAN, 202/XVIII/1, pp. 64–87.

Pilecki, Witold. *Report W KL Auschwitz 1940–1943 by Captain Witold Pilecki.* Trans. Adam J. Koch. Melbourne: Andrzej Nowak with the Polish Association of Political Prisoners in Australia, 2013.

Pilecki, Witold. [W jaki sposób znalazłem się w Oświęcimiu]. PUMST, BI 6991.

Pilecki, Witold. [Wiersz do pułkownika Różańskiego]. May 14, 1947. UOP, 1768/ III/9, p. 267.

Pilecki, Witold. [Zamiast wstępu—słów kilka do przyjaciół moich tych, którzy byli stale na ziemi]. Materiały, vol. 223c, APMA–B, pp. 1–5.

Pilecki, Witold. [Życiorys]. Materiały, vol. 223c, APMA–B. No pages given.

Pilecki, Witold. Akta procesowe Witolda Pileckiego. ASS MON, vol. 5, p. 33, cited in Cyra, *Rotmistrz.*

Pilecki, Witold. Akta sprawy przeciwko Witoldowi Pileckiemu i innym. [List Aliny Bieleckiej], Materiały, vol. 223b, APMA-B, p. 831.

Pilecki, Witold. Akta sprawy przeciwko Witoldowi Pileckiemu i innym. [List do Prezydenta Polski], May 7, 1948, Materiały, vol. 223b, pp. 773–5.

Pilecki, Witold. Akta sprawy przeciwko Witoldowi Pileckiemu i innym. [Meldunek nr 2], Materiały, vol. 223b, APMA-B, p. 555.

Pilecki, Witold. Akta sprawy przeciwko Witoldowi Pileckiemu i innym. Protokół przesłuchania Makarego Sieradzkiego, Materiały, vol. 223a, APMA–B, pp. 361–67.

Pilecki, Witold. Akta sprawy przeciwko Witoldowi Pileckiemu i innym. Protokół przesłuchania Marii Szelągowskiej, Materiały, vol. 223, APMA–B, pp. 150–65.

Pilecki, Witold. Akta sprawy przeciwko Witoldowi Pileckiemu i innym Protokół przesłuchania podejrzanego Tadeusza Płużańskiego, Materiały, vol. 223, APMA–B, pp. 184–223.

Pilecki, Witold. Akta sprawy przeciwko Witoldowi Pileckiemu i innym. Protokół przesłuchania Tadeusza Sztrum de Sztrema, Materiały, vol. 223a, APMA–B, pp. 397–402.

Pilecki, Witold. Akta sprawy przeciwko Witoldowi Pileckiemu i innym. Protokół przesłuchania Witolda Pileckiego, Materiały, vol. 223, APMA–B, pp. 10–317.

Pilecki, Witold. Akta sprawy przeciwko Witoldowi Pileckiemu i innym. Protokół rozprawy głównej, Materiały, vol. 223b, APMA–B, pp. 639–93.

Pilecki, Witold. Akta sprawy przeciwko Witoldowi Pileckiemu i innym. Protokół przesłuchania Wacława Alchimowicza, Materiały, vol. 223a, APMA–B, pp. 403–10.

Pilecki, Witold. Akta sprawy przeciwko Witoldowi Pileckiemu i innym. Protokół przesłuchania Witolda Pileckiego, Materiały, vol. 223a, APMA–B, pp. 117–21.

Pilecki, Witold. Akta sprawy przeciwko Witoldowi Pileckiemu i innym. [Meldunek nr 5], Materiały, vol. 223b, APMA–B, p. 556.

Pilecki, Witold. Akta sprawy przeciwko Witoldowi Pileckiemu i innym. [Tragedia kielecka], Materiały, vol. 223a, APMA-B, pp. 542–3.

Pilecki, Witold. Akta sprawy przeciwko Witoldowi Pileckiemu i innym. Protokół rozprawy głównej. Spis adresów, Materiały, vol. 223b, APMA–B, pp. 639–42.

Pilecki, Witold. Akta sprawy przeciwko Witoldowi Pileckiemu i innym. Protokół przesłuchania Witolda Pileckiego przez oficera śledczego MBP Stefana Alaborskiego z 10 czerwca 1947 roku, Materiały, vol. 223, APMA–B, pp. 81–93.

Pilecki, Witold. Akta sprawy przeciwko Witoldowi Pileckiemu i innym. Protokół przesłuchania Witolda Pileckiego przez oficera śledczego MBP ppor. Eugeniusza Chimczaka z 8 maja 1947 roku, Materiały, vol. 223, APMA–B, pp. 73–76.

Pilecki, Witold. Akta sprawy Witolda Pileckiego. Protokół rozprawy głównej, vol. 5, ASS MON, pp. 25–26, cited in Cyra, *Rotmistrz*.

Pilecki, Witold. Akta sprawy Witolda Pileckiego. vol. 5, ASS MON, pp. 107–17, cited in Cyra, *Rotmistrz*.

Pilecki, Witold. Akta sprawy Witolda Pileckiego. Zeznanie w śledztwie Witolda Pileckiego, ASS MON, vol. 1, p. 74, cited in Cyra, *Rotmistrz*.

Piper, Franciszek (ed.). *Auschwitz 1940–1945: Central Issues in the History of the*

Camp. Vol. III: *Mass Murder.* Trans. William Brandt. Oświęcim: PMA–B, 2000.

Piper, Franciszek. *Auschwitz: How Many Perished Jews, Poles, Gypsies.* Kraków: Poligrafia ITS, 1992.

Piper, Franciszek. *Ilu ludzi zginęło w KL Auschwitz? Liczba ofiar w świetle źródeł i badań 1945–1990.* Oświęcim: PMA–B, 1992.

Piper, Franciszek. *Voices of Memory 8: Poles in Auschwitz.* Oświęcim: PMA–B, 2011.

Piper, Franciszek; Strzelecka, Irena (eds). *Księga Pamięci. Transporty Polaków z Warszawy do KL Auschwitz 1940–1944.* Oświęcim: PMA–B, 2000.

Plaskura, Władysław. Oświadczenia, vol. 82, APMA–B, pp. 50–69.

Plaskura, Władysław. Oświadczenia, vol. 105, APMA–B, pp. 38–45a.

Plaskura, Władysław. Oświadczenia, vol. 115, APMA–B, pp. 131–47.

Pluta, Wacław. Oświadczenia, vol. 129, APMA–B, pp. 187–92.

Pluta-Czachowski, Kazimierz. *".. . gdy przychodzi czas—trzeba odejść."* Ze wspomnień o gen. Stefanie Roweckim, in Garlicka, Zarzewie.

Płużański, Tadeusz M. *Obława na wyklętych. Polowanie bezpieki na Żołnierzy Wyklętych.* Zakrzewo: Replika, 2017.

Pogozhev, Andrey. *Escape from Auschwitz.* Barnsley: Pen & Sword Military, 2007 Kindle edition.

Poleszak, Sławomir; Wnuk, Rafał. *Zarys dziejów polskiego podziemia niepodległościowego 1944–1956,* in Wnuk et al., *Atlas,* pp. xxii–xxxiv.

Polish Ministry of Information. *The Black Book of Poland.* New York: G. P. Putnam's Sons, 1942.

Polonsky, Antony. *My Brother's Keeper: Recent Polish Debates on the Holocaust.* London: Routledge, 1990.

Porębski, Henryk. Oświadczenia, vol. 21, APMA–B, pp. 11–31.

Porębski, Henryk. Oświadczenia, vol. 22, APMA–B, pp. 59–60.

Porębski, Henryk. Oświadczenia, vol. 102, APMA–B, pp. 27–28.

Pozimski, Jerzy. Wspomnienia, vol. 52, APMA–B, pp. 109–77.

Pszenicki, Krzysztof. *Tu mówi Londyn. Historia Sekcji Polskiej BBC.* Warszawa: Rosner and Wspólnicy, 2009.

Ptakowski, Jerzy. *Oświęcim bez cenzury i bez legend.* London: Myśl Polska, 1985.

Puławski, Adam. "Kwestia sowieckich jeńców wojennych w polityce Polskiego Państwa Podziemnego." *Rocznik Chełmski,* 2014/18, pp. 231–94.

Puławski, Adam. *Wobec niespotykanego w dziejach mordu.* Chełm: Stowarzyszenie Rocznik Chełmski, 2018.

Puławski, Adam. *W obliczu zagłady. Rząd RP na uchodźstwie, Delegatura Rządy RP na Kraj, ZWZ–AK wobec deportacji Żydów do obozów zagłady (1941–1942).* Lublin IPN, 2009.

Rablin, Andrzej. Oświadczenia, vol. 29, APMA–B, pp. 78–85.

Raczyński, Edward. *In Allied London.* London: Weidenfeld & Nicolson, 1962.

Radlicki, Ignacy. *Kapo odpowiedział—Auschwitz. Wspomnienia adwokata z obozu koncentracyjnego.* Warszawa: Redakcja "Palestry," 2008.

Radomska, Maria et al. (eds.). *Nasza niezwykła szkoła. Porto San Giorgio—Foxley 1945–1948.* Londyn: Koło Szkoły Porto San Giorgio—Foxley, 1985.

Rambert, Eugene. *Bex Et Ses Environs (1871).* Whitefish: Kessinger Publishing, 2010.

Rawicz (Popiel), Barbara. Interview, March 5, 2017.

Rawicz, Jerzy. *Kariera szambelana.* Warszawa: Czytelnik, 1971.

Rawicz, Kazimierz. [List do L. Serafińskiej]. August 4, 1958. Materiały, vol. 220, APMA–B, pp. 167–68.

Rawicz, Kazimierz. [List], August 8, 1956; [List], 1957; [List], August 8, 1957; [List], August 22, 1957; August 31, 1957; [List], September 23, 1957; [List], 1957; [Raport], date unknown. Material courtesy of Andrzej Kunert.

Rawicz, Kazimierz. Oświaczenia, vol. 27, APMA–B, pp. 33–41, pp. 41a–41h.

Rawicz–Heilman, Kazimierz. [Pobyt w obozie w Oświęcimiu], pp. 1–64. Manuscript in the possession of Marek Popiel.

Redzej, Jan. [Raport 1943.] AAN, 202/XVIII/1, pp. 33–47a.

Rees, Laurence. *Auschwitz: A New History.* New York: PublicAffairs, 2015. Kindle.

Reisman, Michael; Antoniou, Chris T. *The Laws of War: A Comprehensive Collection of Primary Documents on International Laws Governing Armed Conflict.* New York: Vintage, 1994.

Remlein, Janusz. [Wspomnienia]. https://www.1944.pl/archiwum–historii–mo wionej/janusz–remlein,1137.html [December 27, 2018].

Republic of Poland, Ministry of Foreign Affairs. *The Mass Extermination of Jews in German Occupied Poland.* December 1942. NA, FCO 371/30924, C12313.

Richie, Alexandra. *Warsaw 1944: Hitler, Himmler, and the Warsaw Uprising.* New York: Farrar, Straus & Giroux, 2013.

Ringelblum, Emmanuel. *Notes from the Warsaw Ghetto.* San Francisco: Pickle Partners Publishing, 2015. Kindle.

Ringelblum, Emmnuel. *Polish–Jewish Relations During the Second World War.* Evanston: Northwestern University Press, 1992.

Roberts, Andrew. *Churchill: Walking with Destiny.* New York: Viking, 2018.

Rohleder, Joachim. [Bundesanschaftschaftsakten]. Schweizerisches B4, E 4320 (B) 1990/133, Bd. 67.

Romanowicz, Jerzy. "Czy W. Pilecki zostanie zrehabilitowany?" *Głos Pomorza*, 09–10.12.1989.

Romanowicz, Jerzy. "Zgrupowanie 'Chrobry II' w Powstaniu Warszawskim." *Słupskie Studia Historyczne*, 2003/10, pp. 293–303.

Romanowski, Andrzej. "Tajemnica Witolda Pileckiego." *Polityka*, 2013/20.

Rostkowski, Jerzy. *Świat Muszkieterów. Zapomnij albo zgiń*. Warszawa: Rebis, 2016.

Roth, Markus. *The Murder of the Jews in Ostrów Mazowiecka in November 1939*, in Zalc, Bruttman, *Microhistories*, pp. 227–41.

Rowecka–Mielczarska, Irena. *Father: Reminiscences About Major General Stefan "Grot" Rowecki*. Trans. Elżbieta Puławska. Warszawa: Presspol, 1983.

Rowiński, Aleksander. *Zygielbojma śmierć i życie*. Warszawa: Rój, 2000.

Russell, Sharman Apt. *Hunger: An Unnatural History*. New York: Basic Books, 2008.

Rutkowski, Tadeusz Paweł. *Stanisław Kot 1885–1975. Biografia polityczna*. Warszawa: Dig, 2000.

Rybak, Krystyna. Interview, March 8, 2017.

Sawicki, Jan (dir.). *Rotmistrz Witold Pilecki*. 1991. TVP Edukacyjna 1991.

Schulte, Jan E. *London war informiert. KZ–Expansion und Judenverfolgung. Entschlüsselte KZ–Stärkemeldungen vom Januar 1942 bis zum Januar 1943 in den britischen National Archives in Kew*, in Hackmann, Süß (eds.), *Hitler's*, pp. 183–207.

Schwarzbart, Ignacy. [Archives 1943–45.] IPN. BU_2835_15.

Segieda, Napoleon. HIA. Stanislaw Mikolajczyk Papers. Box 28, Folder 7.

Segieda, Napoleon. [Raport.] PISM, A.9.III.2a t.3.

Sehn, Jan. *Obóz koncentracyjny Oświęcim-Brzezinka Auschwitz-Birkenau*. Warszawa: Wydawnictwo Prawnicze, 1964.

Serafińska, Zofia. *Ziemniaki na pierwsze . . . , na drugie . . . , na trzecie*. Warszawa: Gebethner i Wolff, 1940.

Serafiński, Tomasz. [Ucieczka skazanych.] Nowy Wiśnicz: 1965. Document in the possession of Maria Serafińska–Domańska.

Setkiewicz, Piotr. *Głosy Pamięci 13: Załoga SS w KL Auschwitz*. Oświęcim: PMA–B, 2017.

Setkiewicz, Piotr. "Pierwsi Żydzi w KL Auschwitz." *Zeszyty Oświęcimskie 19*. Oświęcim: PMA–B, 2016, pp. 7–46.

Setkiewicz, Piotr (ed.). *The Private Lives of the Auschwitz SS*. Trans. William Brand. Oświęcim: PMA–B, 2014.

Setkiewicz, Piotr (ed.). *Studia nad dziejami obozów koncentracyjnych w okupowanej Polsce*. Oświęcim: PMA–B, 2011.

Setkiewicz, Piotr. *Voices of Memory 6: The Auschwitz Crematoria and Gas Chambers.* Oświęcim: PMA–B, 2011.

Setkiewicz, Piotr. *Z dziejów obozów IG Farben Werk Auschwitz 1941–1945.* Oświęcim: PMA–B, 2006.

Setkiewicz, Piotr. *Zaopatrzenie materiałowe krematoriów i komór gazowych Auschwitz: koks, drewno, cyklon,* in Setkiewicz, *Studia,* pp. 46–74.

Setkiewicz, Piotr. "Zapomniany czyn Mariana Batko." *Pro Memoria,* 06.2002–01.2003/17–18, pp. 61–64.

Siciński, Antoni. "Z psychopatologii więźniów funkcyjnych. Ernst Krankemann." *Przegląd Lekarski,* 1974/1, pp. 126–30.

Siedlecki, Janusz Nel. *Beyond Lost Dreams.* Lancaster: Carnegie Publishing, 1994.

Sierchuła, Rafał; Utracka, Katarzyna. "Historia oddziału WIG—rtm. Witolda Pileckiego." *Grot. Zeszyty Historyczne poświęcone historii wojska i walk o niepodległość,* 2015/39–40, pp. 213–23.

Słuchoński, Artur. [Wspomnienia.] Chronicles of Terror. IP, 019 Sluchonski_Artur _2_skan_AK: www.chroniclesofterror.pl.

Smoczyński, Juliusz. "Ostatnie dni Stanisława Dubois." *Kurier Polski,* 03.02.1980/25. No pages given.

Smoleń, Kazimierz. "'Czarna giełda' w obozie." *Wolni ludzie,* 1948/3, p. 4.

Smoleń, Kazimierz; Czech, Danuta; Iwaszko, Tadeusz; Jarosz, Barbara; Piper, Franciszek; Polska, Irena; Świebocka, Teresa (eds.). *KL Auschwitz Seen by SS.* Trans. Constantine FitzGibbon, Krystyna Michalik. Oświęcim: PMA–B, 2005.

Snyder, Timothy. *Black Earth: The Holocaust as History and Warning.* New York: Tim Duggan Books, 2016.

Snyder, Timothy. *Bloodlands: Europe Between Hitler and Stalin.* New York: Basic Books, 2012.

Snyder, Timothy. *The Reconstruction of Nations: Poland, Ukraine, Lithuania, Belarus, 1956–1999.* New Haven: Yale University Press, 2003.

Sobański, Tomasz. *Ucieczki oświęcimskie.* Warszawa: Wydawnictwo MON, 1987.

Sobolewicz, Tadeusz. *But I Survived.* Oświęcim: PMA–B, 1998.

Šolta, Jan; Kunze, Pětr; Šěn, Franc (eds.). *Nowy biografiski słownik k stawiznam a kulturje Serbow.* Budyšin Ludowe nakładnistwo Domowina, 1984.

Sowa, Andrzej Leon. *Kto wydał wyrok na miasto? Plany operacyjne ZWZ–AK (1940–1944) i sposoby ich realizacji.* Kraków: Wydawnictwo Literackie, 2016.

Sowul, Czesław. Oświadczenia, vol. 72, APMA–B, pp. 160–81.

Stafford, David. *Britain and European Resistance: 1940–1945: A Survey of the Special Operations Executive, with Documents.* London: Thistle Publishing, 2013.

Stapf, Adam. Oświadczenia, vol. 29, APMA–B, pp. 86–94.

Stapf, Adam. Oświadczenia, vol. 55, APMA–B, pp. 1–6.

Stapf, Adam. Wspomnienia, vol. 110, APMA–B, pp. 75–105.

Stapf, Adam. Oświadczenia, vol. 148, APMA–B, pp. 96–138.

Stargardt, Nicholas. *The German War: A Nation Under Arms, 1939–1945. Citizens and Soldiers.* New York: Basic Books, 2015.

Steinbacher, Sybille. *Auschwitz: A History.* Trans. Shaun Whiteside. London: Harper Perennial, 2006. Kindle.

Stępień, Jan. Wspomnienia, vol. 179, APMA–B, pp. 176–7.

Stola, Dariusz. "Early News of the Holocaust from Poland." *Holocaust and Genocide Studies,* 1997/11, pp. 1–27.

Stola, Dariusz. *Nadzieja i zagłada: Ignacy Schwarzbart—żydowski przedstawiciel w Radzie Narodowej RP (1940–1945).* Warszawa: Oficyna Naukowa, 1995.

Stoves, Rolf O. G. *Die 1. Panzer–Division 1935–1945.* Dornheim: Podzun–Verlag, 1976.

Stranský, Karl. Oświadczenia, vol. 84, APMA–B, pp. 44–58.

Strzelecka, Irena. *Voices of Memory 2: Medical Crimes: The Experiments in Auschwitz.* Oświęcim: PMA–B, 2011.

Strzelecka, Irena. *Voices of Memory 3: Medical Crimes. The Hospitals in Auschwitz.* Oświęcim: PMA–B, 2008.

Stupka family. Interviews, September 21, 2016; September 24, 2016.

Stupka, Helena. Oświadczenia, vol. 68, APMA–B, pp. 124–32.

Stykowski, Jacek. Interview, September 12, 2018.

Stykowski, Jacek. *Kapitan "Hal." Kulisy fałszowania prawdy o Powstaniu Warszawskim '44.* Warszawa: Capital, 2017.

Syzdek, Włodzimierz. "W 45 rocznicę śmierci Stanisława Dubois. Był człowiekiem działania." *Za wolność i lud,* 22.08.1987/34, p. 5.

Szarota, Tomasz. *Okupowanej Warszawy dzień powszedni. Studium Historyczne.* Warszawa: Czytelnik, 2010.

Szarota, Tomasz. *Stefan Rowecki "Grot."* Warszawa: PWN, 1985.

Szczepański, Marian. Video recollection [July 14, 1995], APMA–B, V–246.

Szejnert, Małgorzata. *Śród żywych duchów.* Kraków: Znak, 2012.

Szmaglewska, Seweryna. *Dymy nad Birkenau.* Warszawa: Czytelnik, 1971.

Szmaglewska, Seweryna. *Smoke over Birkenau.* Trans. Jadwiga Rynas. Warszawa: Książka i Wiedza; Oświęcim: PMA–B, 2008.

Szpakowski, Ludomir. Interview, January 31, 2017.

Szpilman, Władysław. *The Pianist: The Extraordinary True Story of One Man's Survival in Warsaw, 1939–1945.* Trans. Anthea Bell. New York: Picador, 2000.

Szwajkowski, Kazimierz. [Zeznania.] IPN, Oddziałowa Komisja Ścigania Zbrodni Przeciwko Narodowi Polskiemu, S/139/12/Zn, pp. 137–42.

Świebocki, Henryk. *London Has Been Informed . . . : Reports by Auschwitz Escapees.* Oświęcim: PMA–B, 2002.

Świebocki, Henryk. "Przyobozowy ruch oporu w akcji niesienia pomocy więźniom KL Auschwitz." *Zeszyty Oświęcimskie 19.* Oświęcim: PMA–B, 1988.

Świebocki, Henryk (ed.). *Auschwitz, 1940–1945: Central Issues in the History of the Camp.* Vol. IV: *The Resistance Movement.* Trans. William Brandt. Oświęcim: PMA–B, 2000.

Świętorzecki, Karol. Interviews, February 14, 1970; February 14, 1972, http://www .infopol.com/ms/070531all_restored.wav [January 20, 2019].

Świętorzecki, Karol. Oświadczenia, vol. 76, APMA–B, pp. 88–110.

Świętorzecki, Karol. Wspomnienia, vol. 86, APMA–B, pp. 232–7.

Tabeau, Jerzy. [Sprawozdanie], in *Zeszyty oświęcimskie. Raporty uciekinierów z KL Auschwitz.* Oświęcim: PMA–B, 1991, pp. 77–130.

Targosz, Franciszek. Oświadczenia, vol. 144, APMA–B, pp. 193–200, pp. 209–17.

Taubenschlag, Stanisław. *To Be a Jew in Occupied Poland: Cracow–Auschwitz–Buchenwald.* Trans. from the French by David Herman. Oświęcim: Frap—Books, 1998.

Taul, Roman. Oświadczenia, vol. 9, APMA–B, pp. 1264–71, pp. 1273–85.

Taul, Roman. Wspomnienia, vol. 62, APMA-B, pp. 26–59.

Tereszczenko, Jan. Interview, November 1, 2016.

Tereszczenko, Jan B. *Wspomnienia warszawiaka egocentrysty. "JA."* Warszawa: Muzeum Historyczne m. st. Warszawy, 2012.

Terry, Nicholas. "Conflicting Signals: British Intelligence on the 'Final Solution' Through Radio Intercepts and Other Sources." *Yad Vashem Studies,* 2004/32, pp. 351–96.

Thomas, *German,* p. 8.

Thompson, Mark Christian. *Anti–Music: Jazz and Racial Blackness in German Thought Between the Wars.* New York: State University of New York Press, 2008.

Thorsell, Staffan. *Warszawasvenskarna: De som lät världen veta.* Stockholm: Albert Bonniers förlag, 2014. Kindle.

Thugutt, Mieczysław. [List], November 19, 1941. PISM, A.9.III.4/14.

Tomaszewski, Aleksander. Wspomnienia, vol. 66, APMA–B, pp. 107–14.

Tomicki, Jan. *Stanisław Dubois.* Warszawa: Iskry, 1980.

Tooze, Adam. *The Wages of Destruction: The Making and Breaking of the Nazi Economy.* London: Penguin, 2008. Kindle.

Tracki, Krzysztof. *Młodość Witolda Pileckiego*. Warszawa: Wydawnictwo Sic!, 2014.

Tucholski, Jędrzej. *Cichociemni*. Warszawa: Instytut Wydawniczy PAX, 1984.

Tumielewicz, Józef. [Kronika.] Material courtesy of Stanisław Tumielewicz.

Tymowski, Stanisław Janusz. *Zarys historii organizacji społecznych geodetów polskich*. Warszawa: Państwowe Przedsiębiorstwo Wydawnictw Kartograficznych, 1970.

Unknown author. [Zasady konspiracji.] AAN, 2/2505/0/–/194—Fundacja Archiwum Polski Podziemnej 1939–1945. Foundation of the Polish Underground Archives, 1939–1945.

Urbanek, Jerzy. Oświadczenia, vol. 44, APMA–B, pp. 1–13.

Urbańczyk, Zygmunt. Wspomnienia, vol. 54, APMA–B, pp. 11–50.

Urynowicz, Marcin. *Adam Czerniaków 1880–1942. Prezes getta warszawskiego*. Warszawa: IPN, 2009.

van Pelt, Robert. *The Case for Auschwitz: Evidence from the Irving Trial*. Bloomington: Indiana University Press, 2016.

Vrba, Rudolf. *I Cannot Forgive*. Vancouver: Regent College Publishing, 1997.

Wachsmann, Nikolas. *KL: A History of the Nazi Concentration Camps*. New York: Farrar, Straus & Giroux, 2016.

Walasek, Bohdan. Interview, May 19, 2016.

Walasek, Bohdan. [Wspomnienia], Muzeum Powstania Warszawskiego: https:// www.1944.pl/archiwum–historii–mowionej/bohdan–zbigniew–walasek,2545 .html [January 16, 2019.]

Walendzik, Janusz. Interview, October 12, 2016.

Walker, Jonathan. *Poland Alone: Britain, SOE and the Collapse of the Polish Resistance, 1944*. Stroud: The History Press, 2011. Kindle.

Walter-Janke, Zygmunt. *W Armii Krajowej na Śląsku*. Katowice: Wydawnictwo Śląsk, 1986.

Wanat, Leon. *Apel więźniów Pawiaka*. Warszawa: Książka i Wiedza, 1976.

Wanat, Leon. *Za murami Pawiaka*. Warszawa: Książka i Wiedza, 1985.

Wanner, Gerhard. "Flüchtlinge und Grenzverhältnisse in Vorarlberg 1938–1944. Einreise–und Transitland Schweiz." *Rheticus Vierteljahresschrift der Rheticus–Gesellschaft*. 1998/3–4, pp. 227–71.

War and Internationa [sic] Situation. February 22, 1944. Hansard. U.K. Parliament: https://api.parliament.uk/historic-hansard/commons/1944/feb/22/war-and-in ternationa-situation [January 22, 2019].

Wasserstein, Bernard. *Britain and the Jews of Europe, 1939–1945*. London: Leicester University Press, 1999.

Westermann, Edward B. "The Royal Air Force and the Bombing of Auschwitz:

First Deliberations, January 1941." *Holocaust and Genocide Studies*, 2001/15, pp. 70–85.

Whaley, W. Gordon; Bowen, John S. *Russian Dandelion (Kok–Saghyz): An Emergency Source of Natural Rubber*. US Dept. of Agriculture, 1947.

Widelec, Jakob. *A Diary of Four Weeks with the Nazis in Ostrów*, in Margolis, *Memorial*, pp. 421–8.

Widfeldt, Bo; Wegman, Rolph. *Making for Sweden*. Walton-on-Thames: Air Research Publications, 1999.

Wielopolski, Piotr. Interview, May 18, 2017.

Wierusz, Witold. Oświadczenia, vol. 77, APMA–B, pp. 13–37.

Wierzbicka, Agnieszka. "Żyd, Żydzi, Żydy, Żydki—Stereotypes and Judgments Ingrained in the Polish Language." *Acta Universitis Lodzensis. Folia Linguistica*, 2015/49, pp. 57–67.

Wilkinson, Peter. *Foreign Fields: The Story of an SOE Operative*. Staplehurst: Spellmount Publishers, 2013. Kindle.

Willenberg, Samuel. *Revolt in Treblinka*. Warszawa: ŻIH, 1992.

Winstone, Martin. *The Dark Heart of Hitler's Europe: Nazi Rule in Poland Under the General Government*. London: I. B. Tauris, 2014. Kindle.

Wiśnicka, Maria (dir.). *Sprawa szpiega Pileckiego*. 1991. WFD Warszawa Zespół Filmowy WIR.

Witowiecki, Tadeusz. *Tu mówi "Żelazo."* Łódź: Wydawnictwo Łódzkie, 1966.

Wnuk, Rafał; Poleszak, Sławomir; Jaczyńska, Agnieszka; Śladecka, Magdalena (eds.). *Atlas Polskiego Podziemia Niepodległościowego 1944–1956*. Warszawa-Lublin: IPN, 2007.

Wolny, Edward. Oświadczenia, vol. 33, APMA–B, pp. 25–6.

Wołosiuk, Bruno. "Znałem rotmistrza Pileckiego." *Słowo Powszechne*, 1980/49, pp. 19–26.

Wood, E. Thomas. *Karski: How One Man Tried to Stop the Holocaust*. Lubbock: Gihon River Press and Texas Tech University Press, 2014.

Wortmán, Marek (dir.). *Ucieczka z Oświęcimia*. 1998. TVP.

Wróbel, Janusz. *Na rozdrożu historii. Repatriacja obywateli polskich z Zachodu w latach 1945–1949*. Łódź: IPN, 2009.

Wyczański, Andrzej. *Mikrofilm. Nowa postać książki*. Wrocław: Ossolineum, 1972.

Wyman, David. *The Abandonment of the Jews: America and the Holocaust 1941–1945*. New York: New Press, 2007.

Wysocki, Wiesław Jan. *Rotmistrz Witold Pilecki 1901–1948*. Warszawa: Rytm, 2009.

Zabawski, Edmund. Wspomnienia, vol. 98, APMA–B, pp. 83–103.

Zabielski, Józef. *First to Return*. London: Garby Publications, 1976.

Zaborowski, Leszek (ed.). *Chronicles of Terror. German Atrocities in Warsaw-Wola, August 1944*. Vol. II. Warszawa: Witold Pilecki Center for Totalitarian Studies [IP], 2018.

Zagórski, Wacław. *Seventy Days*. Trans. John Welsh. London: Panther Books, 1959.

Zagórski, Wacław. *Wicher wolności. Dziennik powstańca*. Warszawa: Czytelnik, 1990.

Zalc, Claire; Bruttman, Tal (eds.). *Microhistories of the Holocaust*. New York: Berghahn Books, 2016.

Zalewski, Jerzy. Interview, October 17, 2016.

Zaremba, Marcin. *Wielka trwoga. Polska 1944–1947*. Kraków: Znak, 2012.

Zaremba, Zygmunt. *Wojna i konspiracja*. Kraków: Wydawnictwo Literackie, 1991.

Zawadzki, Antoni. [Zeznania.] IPN, Oddziałowa Komisja Ścigania Zbrodni Przeciwko Narodowi Polskiemu, S/139/12/Zn, pp. 124–8.

Ziegler, Philip. *London at War: 1939–1945*. New York: Sinclair-Stevenson Ltd., 1995.

Zieliński, Jan. "List posła Ładosia i doktora Kühla." *Zeszyty Literackie*, 2000/4, pp. 157–67.

Zimmerman, Joshua D. *The Polish Underground and the Jews, 1939–1945*. Cambridge: Cambridge University Press, 2015.

Ziółkowski, Michał. *Byłem od początku w Auschwitz*. Gdańsk: Marpress, 2007.

Znak. [Deklaracja ideowa grupy "ZNAK."] AAN, 2/2505/0/–/194.

Zwerin, Mike. *Swing Under Nazis: Jazz as a Metaphor for Freedom*. New York: Cooper Square Press, 2000.

Лаўрэш, Леанід Лявонцьевіч. "Яўрэі Ліды." *Маладосць*, 2016/4, pp. 141–54.

Лаўрэш, Леанід Лявонцьевіч. "Лідчына ў 1936–1939 гг. у люстэрку прэсы". *Лідскі летапісец*. 2014/66 (2), pp. 25–93.

Лаўрэш, Леанід Лявонцьевіч. "13 траўня 1901 г. нарадзіўся Вітольд Пілецкі." *Лідскі Летапісец*, 2016/2 (74), pp. 15–9.

Лаўрэш, Леанід Лявонцьевіч. "Лідчына ў 1924–1929 гг. у люстэрку прэсы." *Ліоскі летапісец*, 2015/69 (1), pp. 25–94.

Ярмонт, Евгения. *В тени замка Гедимина Лида. Воспоминания детства*. Grodno: КЛФ «Сталкер», 1995, pp. 93–4, cited in Лаўрэш, "Лідчына," p. 76.

INDEX